Michel Christian, Sandrine Kott, Ondřej Matějka (Eds.)
Planning in Cold War Europe

Rethinking the Cold War

―――

Edited by Kirsten Bönker and Jane Curry

Volume 2

Planning in Cold War Europe

Competition, Cooperation, Circulations (1950s–1970s)

Edited by
Michel Christian, Sandrine Kott, Ondřej Matějka

DE GRUYTER
OLDENBOURG

Published with the support of the Swiss National Science Foundation.

ISBN 978-3-11-070796-0
e-ISBN (PDF) 978-3-11-053469-6
e-ISBN (EPUB) 978-3-11-053240-1

https://doi.org/10.1515/9783110534696

This work is licensed under the Creative Commons Attribution-NonCommercial-NoDerivs 4.0 International License. For details go to http://creativecommons.org/licenses/by-nc-nd/4.0/.

Library of Congress Control Number: 2018948744

Bibliographic information published by the Deutsche Nationalbibliothek
The Deutsche Nationalbibliothek lists this publication in the Deutsche Nationalbibliografie; detailed bibliographic data are available on the Internet at http://dnb.dnb.de.

© 2020 Walter de Gruyter GmbH, Berlin/Boston
This volume is text- and page-identical with the hardback published in 2018.
Cover image: right: Picture on a Slovak box of matches from the 1950s – author unkonwn
left: Stamp printed in 1984. Ninth plan 1984–1989: to modernize France. drawn by Rémy Peignot, © la poste
Typesetting: 3w+p GmbH, Rimpar
Printing: CPI books GmbH, Leck

www.degruyter.com

Acknowledgements

This book grew out of a research project funded by the Swiss National Fund "Competing Modernities, Shared Modernities, Europe between East and West (1920s-1970s)." The contributions published in this volume were discussed during a workshop that was made possible thanks to the generous support of the University of Geneva and the Swiss National Fund.

The transformation of the stimulating debates that took place during the conference into a collective volume was greatly assisted by an important number of our colleagues, to whom we would like to express our gratitude.

First of all, during the workshop, we greatly benefited from insightful and inspiring remarks by Alexander Nützenadel (Humboldt Universität Berlin), Lorenzo Mechi (University of Padova), Michel Alacevich (University of Bologna), Sara Lorenzini (University of Trento), Corinna Unger (EUI, Florence), Malgorzata Mazurek (Columbia University), Michal Pullmann (Charles University) and Pál Germuska (EUI, Florence).

We wish to thank the authors of the contributions to this book for their timely cooperation and their openness to our comments, which allowed for the efficient preparation of a coherent collective volume.

Two anonymous reviewers provided us with encouraging, as well as very constructive remarks, which helped us to substantially improve the first version of the manuscript. We are very grateful for the time and energy they both invested in their careful review of our texts.

Ian Copestake played a substantial role in the transformation of our nationally-coloured versions of the English language into a more consistent ensemble from a linguistic point of view.

Last but not least, we want to express our gratitude to Kirsten Bönker, who accepted this project with great enthusiasm, and to editors Elise Wintz and Rabea Rittgerodt as well, who, with friendly insistence, kept encouraging us to navigate the writing and revision process smoothly and rapidly.

Michel Christian, Sandrine Kott, Ondřej Matějka

Table of Contents

Michel Christian, Sandrine Kott, Ondřej Matějka
Planning in Cold War Europe: Introduction —— 1

Part 1: Planning a New World after the War

Francine McKenzie
Peace, Prosperity and Planning Postwar Trade, 1942–1948 —— 21

Daniel Stinsky
A Bridge between East and West? Gunnar Myrdal and the UN Economic Commission for Europe, 1947–1957 —— 45

Part 2: High Modernism Planning

Isabelle Gouarné
Mandatory Planning versus Indicative Planning? The Eastern Itinerary of French Planners (1960s-1970s) —— 71

Katja Naumann
International Research Planning across the Iron Curtain: East-Central European Social Scientists in the ISSC and Vienna Centre —— 97

Sandrine Kott
The Social Engineering Project. Exportation of Capitalist Management Culture to Eastern Europe (1950–1980) —— 123

Sari Autio-Sarasmo
Transferring Western Knowledge to a centrally planned Economy: Finland and the Scientific-Technical Cooperation with the Soviet Union —— 143

Ondřej Matějka
Social Engineering and Alienation between East and West: Czech Christian-Marxist Dialogue in the 1960s from the National Level to the Global Arena —— 165

Simon Godard
The Council for Mutual Economic Assistance and the failed Coordination of Planning in the Socialist Bloc in the 1960s —— 187

Part 3: **Alternatives to Planning**

Benedetto Zaccaria
Learning from Yugoslavia? Western Europe and the Myth of Self-Management (1968–1975) —— 213

Vítězslav Sommer
Managing Socialist Industrialism: Czechoslovak Management Studies in the 1960s and 1970s —— 237

Michael Hutter
Ecosystems Research and Policy Planning: Revisiting the Budworm Project (1972–1980) at the IIASA —— 261

Michel Christian
"It is not a Question of rigidly Planning Trade" UNCTAD and the Regulation of the International Trade in the 1970s —— 285

Jenny Andersson
Planning the Future of World Markets: the OECD's Interfuturs Project —— 315

Works Cited —— 345

Michel Christian, Sandrine Kott, Ondřej Matějka
Planning in Cold War Europe: Introduction[1]

> There exists no alternative to economic planning. There is, therefore, no case to be made for or against economic planning, for or against free enterprise or free trade. Ever more State intervention and economic planning is part of the historical trends. . . . In reality, it was never, and is certainly not now, a choice. It is a destiny.[2] (Gunnar Myrdal)

The conclusion of Gunnar Myrdal's Ludwig Mond lecture in Manchester in 1950 makes clear that the concept of economic planning was firmly impressed on the mental maps of an influential segment of the European intellectual elite in the early postwar years. The charismatic economist (a Nobel Prize laureate in 1974), sociologist, politician and international civil servant was part of a transnational milieu of publicly engaged academicians, mainly from Europe. As faithful followers of the Enlightenment ethos, they believed in (social) science as the key tool for the improvement of society. Myrdal and his wife Alva appropriated the post-World War Two infrastructure of international organizations, considering it to be an excellent springboard for bringing their reformist ambitions closer to reality. The husband and wife team became transnational symbols of this conviction and were portrayed as the "most popular Swedes, downright charged by the United Nations with the task of saving the world."[3] The principle of rational planning was a cornerstone of their thought and action.

Recent, and widely acclaimed, historical works have confirmed the extent of the influence that leaders like the Myrdals (and their ideas on planning) had on the continental and global level. Tony Judt described it in eloquent terms in his magisterial *Postwar: A History of Europe since 1945* where he labelled economic planning as the "political religion" of European elites after 1945.[4] Similarly, Marc Mazower, in his *Dark Continent* (with reference to Karl Mannheim), elaborated on the "striking fact" of the broad consensus among postwar European political elites for whom "there [was] no longer any choice between planning and lais-

---

[1] This entire volume has been made possible by a generous grant from the the Swiss National Fund and is part of a four-year project entitled "*Shared modernities or competing modernities? Europe between West and East (1920s-1970s)*". We are also grateful for the support of the PRVOUK research funding scheme (Charles University, Prague).
[2] Gunnar Myrdal, "The Trend toward Economic Planning," *The Manchester School of Economic and Social Studies* 19 (1951): 40.
[3] Thomas Etzemüller, *Die Romantik der Rationalität. Alva & Gunnar Myrdal. Social Engineering in Schweden* (Bielefeld: Transcript, 2010), 43.
[4] Tony Judt, *Postwar: A History of Europe Since 1945* (London: Vintage, 2010), 67.

sez-faire, but only between good planning and bad."⁵ Eric Hobsbawm in his *Age of Extremes* explored how plans and planning became "buzzwords" in European politics in the interwar period. Economic planning was embraced by "the politicians, officials and even many of the businessmen of the postwar West, who were convinced that the return of laissez-faire and the unrestricted free market was out of the question."⁶ More recently, David Engerman, in his contribution to *The Cambridge History of the Second World War*, emphasized the rise of "planning euphoria" and "planning phobia," two sides of a postwar "planning boom."⁷ Engerman, however, convincingly argued that both its opponents and proponents overestimated "the power of planning."⁸

These works confirm the centrality of planning thought in the postwar period. However, the widespread appeal of faith in planning must not hide the fact that there were many conceptions of planning and that the notion was and still is both ambiguous and malleable. Planning had a long history and contained many layers. Its earliest use dates to the eighteenth century and the building of cities and roads. It expanded to bureaucratic settings, and the coordination or control of individuals' actions. "Planning authorities", "planning committees" and "planning consultants" became everyday expressions at the turn of the twentieth century.⁹ Their emergence reflected a range of new practices, actors and social relations, all subject to planning. Historians have now begun to analyze the many manifestations of planning, in studies of "social planning" and various forms of "scientific" social engineering. For example, historians and social scientists have examined how, starting in the mid-nineteenth century, state officials and experts, searched for instruments of social improvement in order to prevent or contain social conflict. Researchers subsequently showed that because social planning depended on knowledge about how specific societies functioned, this led to the professionalization of the production of such applicable knowledge. Within a wider process known as the "scientification of the social,"¹⁰ social planning became the ultimate goal of the social sciences. Planning

---

5 Mark Mazower, *Dark Continent: Europe's Twentieth Century* (New York: Vintage, 2000), 203–204.
6 Eric Hobsbawm, *Age of Extremes: The Short Twentieth Century: 1914–1991* (London: Abacus, 1995), 96, 272.
7 David C. Engerman, "The Rise and Fall of Central Planning," in *The Cambridge History of the Second World War. Volume III: Total War: Economy, Society and Culture*, ed. Michael Geyer (Cambridge: Cambridge University Press, 2015), 575, 576, 593.
8 Engerman, "The Rise and Fall," 598.
9 See "planning" in the *Oxford English Dictionary*, www.oed.com
10 Raphael Lutz, "Embedding the Human and Social Sciences in Western Societies, 1880–1980: Reflections on Trends and Methods of Current Research," in *Engineering Society: The Role of the*

emerged as a way of dealing with changing political situations. Its intellectual aspirations have usually included a desire to "contribute to making the social world predictable in the face of modern uncertainties, or in the stronger version, to reshape it according to a master plan for improvement."[11] By the mid-1980s, critical thinkers already saw planning as an endeavor aimed at controlling and dominating individuals in society. They argued that the various forms of planning that blossomed in the twentieth century originated in a nineteenth century matrix for which urban, industrialized Europe was the experimental ground.[12] In recent years, the production of histories of social scientific knowledge (including planning) from a European or trans-European perspective has gained momentum.[13] The focus has expanded to urban planning[14] and to colonial and post-colonial fields of study.[15]

Economic planning represents a particularly important sub-field of this type of research. It was in the 1930s when "planning" began to be widely used in relation to national economic activity. By the early 1960s, the rise of economic planning thought and practice in the economic field had been identified by economists such as Myrdal and Jan Tinbergen as a secular trend, which had originated at the end of the nineteenth century and which was reinforced by specific historical circumstances like wars, crises, and revolutions.[16] Economic planning brought new technical meanings to the initial notion of planning. It

---

Human and Social Sciences in Modern Societies, 1880–1980, ed. Kerstin Brückweh, Dirk Schumann, Richard F. Wetzell and Benjamin Ziemann (Basingstoke: Palgrave, 2012), 41–58. See also Stefan Couperus, Liesbeth van de Grift, and Vincent Lagendijk, "Experimental Spaces – Planning in High Modernity," *Journal of Modern European History* 13 (2015): special issue, no. 4.
11 Peter Wagner, "Social Science and Social Planning during the Twentieth Century," in *Cambridge History of Science, vol. 7: The Modern Social Sciences*, ed. Theodore M. Porter and Dorothy Ross (Cambridge: Cambridge University Press, 2003), 591.
12 Arturo Escobar, "Planning" in *The Development Dictionary. A Guide to Knowledge as Power*, ed. Wolfgang Sachs (London and New York: Zed Books, 2007), 132–145.
13 See for example Brückweh, *Engineering Society*; Christiane Reinecke and Thomas Mergel, *Das Soziale ordnen: Sozialwissenschaften und gesellschaftliche Ungleichheit im 20. Jahrhundert* (Frankfurt am Main: Campus, 2012); Kiran Klaus Patel and Sven Reichardt, "The Dark Sides of Transnationalism: Social Engineering and Nazism, 1930s–1940s," *Journal of Contemporary History*, 51 (2016): 3–21; Thomas Etzemüller, *Die Ordnung der Moderne: Social Engineering im 20. Jahrhundert* (Bielefeld: Transcript, 2009).
14 Stefan Couperus and Harm Kaal, "In Search of the Social: Languages of Neighborhood and Community in Urban Planning in Europe and Beyond, 1920–1960," special section in the *Journal of Urban History* 42 (2016): 978–91.
15 Valeska Huber, "Introduction: Global Histories of Social Planning," *Journal of Contemporary History* 52 (2017): 3–15.
16 Jan Tinbergen, *Central Planning* (New Haven: Yale University Press, 1964), 5.

introduced distinctions between "planning" as a stage in policy process, as an accounting and budgetary tool, and as a reflection on intended and unintended consequences of the management of various decisions. In the latter case, it had a feedback effect on social planning which mimicked a large range of practices elaborated by economic planning.

Since the end of the Cold War, historians have interpreted the period stretching from the 1890s to the late 1970s as a distinct era in global history, characterized by a shared belief in the benefits of planned modernity and development. Ulrich Herbert and the historians inspired by his insights into Europe in the age of "High Modernity"[17] started a debate that has continued ever since, particularly in the area of economic development.[18] Nevertheless, the rise of various historical forms of economic planning, as well as the making and circulation of planning models, has not yet been the target of systematic research. From state intervention during the World Wars One and Two, through *Gosplan*, the New Deal and Nazi *Zentralplanung*, the different models of economic planning have all been studied separately.

In our volume, we seek to do justice to the plasticity of the notion of planning. In order to historicize planning, our definition is necessarily broad. The contributions to this work highlight and explain the economic, social, and intellectual aspects of planning and approaches to planning and how these have played out across time and space. Of course, this diversity of emphasis is the outcome of the variety of geographical and chronological contexts in which ideas about planning were formulated and implemented. Throughout the twentieth century, times of crisis have been fertile moments for planning and there is a well developed historiography on planning in moments of economic crisis and global conflicts. The policy of the New Deal in the United States, implemented in the 1930s, has been well-researched as a case study of planning used to overcome a deep economic and social depression.[19] Likewise, it was an economic crisis that ended the New Economic Policy (NEP) in the Soviet Union and led to a shift to central economic planning and to the idea of "building socialism in one

---

[17] Ulrich Herbert, "Europe in High Modernity: Reflections on a Theory of the Twentieth Century," *Journal of Modern European History* 5 (2007): 5–21.
[18] Mark Frey and Sönke Kunkel, "Writing the History of Development: A Review of the Recent Literature," *Contemporary European History* 20 (2011): 215–232; Corinna R. Unger, "Histories of Development and Modernization: Findings, Reflections, Future Research," *H-Soz-Kult* 9.12.2010, http://hsozkult.geschichte.hu-berlin.de/forum/2010–12–001 (accessed 9 February 2018).
[19] Kiran K. Patel, *The New Deal. A Global History* (Princeton: Princeton University Press, 2016); David Ekbladh, *The Great American Mission: Modernization and the Construction of an American World Order* (Princeton: Princeton University Press, 2010).

country."[20] The two world wars offered multiple occasions to think about planning and its implementation. During World War One and its aftermath, all the states at war took on new, unprecedented economic prerogatives, especially in industry, despite the prevailing laissez-faire ideology of this era.[21] World War Two sparked the development of large-scale "war economies" in the Soviet Union, Nazi Germany, and the United States. International-level planning between the Allies took place in a Combined Production and Resources Board and in the United Nation Relief and Rehabilitation Administration (UNRRA). UNRRA, a gigantic logistical system linked to US and British troops, functioned from 1943 to 1949 and was deployed in various places in the world from Europe to China in order to meet basic, immediate postwar economic needs for health care, food, clothing and housing.[22]

The aim of our volume is to show that the Cold War was also a time of active planning at national and international levels. So far historians have studied Cold War planning mainly as a manifestation of "technical internationalism," which was embodied in the international organizations established by the United Nations after 1945.[23] Despite the fact that several historians have pointed out the structural similarities between Marxist-inspired thought and Western theories of modernization,[24] much of the scholarship on the development of planning ideas and practices between 1945 and 1989 has concerned itself with only one side or the other of the Iron Curtain.[25]

Our collection will show that these two models and practices of planning should be studied together. While competing against each other, the two blocs shared many ideas about planning, a fact that did not go unnoticed even while the Cold War was under way, and several scholars compared the plans

---

20 As analyzed by Karl Polanyi as early as 1944 in *Great Transformation: The Political and Economic Origins of Our Time* (Boston: Beacon Press, 2001).
21 Engerman, "The Rise and Fall," 578 on.
22 Craig N. Murphy, *The United Nations Development Programme: A Better Way?* (Cambridge: Cambridge University Press, 2006), 34–40. There are a few more recent studies on UNRRA, including Jessica Rheinisch, Ben Shephard and Rana Mitter.
23 Daniel Speich-Chassé, "Technical Internationalism and Economic Development at the Founding Moment of the UN System," in *International Organizations and Development, 1945–1990*, ed. Marc Frey, Sönke Kunkel, and Corina Unger (Basingstoke: Palgrave Macmillan, 2014), 23–45.
24 For a systematic comparison, see Gilbert Rist, *Le développement: histoire d'une croyance occidentale* (Paris: Presses de la Fondation nationale des sciences politiques, 2007), 180–186.
25 Michael J. Ellman, *Socialist Planning* (New York: Cambridge University Press, 2014).

and systems of the West[26] and the East,[27] usually focusing on UN international organizations.[28] Those works gave rise to the "theory of convergence," introduced at the beginning of the 1960s by sociologists and economists, who argued that industrial societies shared common economic and social characteristics.[29] Their interpretations underlined the fact that socialist and capitalist systems borrowed solutions to similar problems from each other,[30] so that they were "converging" toward an increasingly similar socio-economical model of developed society. As we now know, instead of a "convergence," one of the two competing systems collapsed spectacularly. "Convergence" could never eliminate the political, economic and social competition between the two blocs. However, that should not prevent scholars from examining genuine circulations or exchanges of knowledge or practices. Many of their recent studies have done this in the technical,[31] scientific,[32] cultural[33] and economic fields,[34] particularly as regards the role of specific actors.[35]

With that in mind, our book has two objectives. On the one hand, in line with the research trends outlined above, this volume will study planning as

---

[26] Alexander Eckstein, *Comparison of Economic Systems: Theoretical and Methodological Approaches* (Berkeley: University of California Press, 1973); Morris Bornstein, *Plan and Market: Economic Reform in Eastern Europe* (New Haven: Yale University Press, 1973); Morris Bornstein, *Economic Planning, East and West* (Cambridge: Ballinger PubCo, 1975).

[27] Tigran Sergeevich Khachaturov, *Methods of Long-Term Planning and Forecasting: Proceedings of a Conference Held by the International Economic Association at Moscow* (London: Macmillan, 1976).

[28] U Thant, *Planning for Economic Development: report of the secretary-general transmitting the study of a group of experts* (New York: United Nations, 1963–1965, 3 volumes).

[29] Raymond Aron, *Sociologie des sociétés industrielles. Esquisse d'une théorie des régimes politiques* (Paris: Centre de documentation universitaire, 1961); Talcott Parsons, *Structure and Process in Modern Societies* (Glencoe: Free Press, 1960).

[30] John K. Galbraith, *The New Industrial State* (Boston: Houghton Mifflin, 1967); Tinbergen, *Central Planning*.

[31] Sari Autio-Sarasmo and Katalin Miklóssy, *Reassessing Cold War Europe* (New York: Routledge, 2011).

[32] Ludovic Tournès, *Sciences de l'homme et politique: les fondations philanthropiques américaines en France au XXe siècle* (Paris: Classiques Garnier, 2011).

[33] Patrick Major and Rana Mitter, *Across the Blocs: Cold War Cultural and Social History* (London: Frank Cass, 2004); Ioana Popa, "La circulation transnationale du livre: un instrument de la guerre froide culturelle," *Histoire@Politique* 15 (2011): 25–41.

[34] Vincent Lagendijk, *Electrifying Europe: The Power of Europe in the Construction of Electricity Networks* (Amsterdam: Aksant, 2008).

[35] Martin Kohlrausch, Katrin Steffen and Stefan Wiederkehr, eds., *Expert Cultures in Central Eastern Europe. The Internationalization of Knowledge and the Transformation of Nation States since World War I.* (Osnabrück: Fibre Verlag, 2010).

an expression of a widespread belief in modernity on both sides of the East-West divide. On the other, ideas and practices of planning will be an entry point to question the very notion of the "Cold War." Such an approach is fully in tune with new studies of the Cold War, which have recently emphasized the porosity of the Iron Curtain and stressed convergence between the two blocs.[36] The contributions in this volume will bring to light the shared inspirations and circulations of models of planning in the context of the bipolar structure of Europe after 1945. The ideas and discussions surrounding planning reflected the East-West competition between two models of economic and social organization, but they also revealed specific commonalities and complementarities. This paradox, which has been largely overlooked by the historiography of the Cold War and planning alike, is at the core of this book. The volume brings together well-documented contributions based on new empirical research that approach the story of planning from a variety of angles. They deal not only with traditional areas of interest in economic and social planning, but also open the doors to lesser-known (or simply unknown) fields in the planning of scientific research and environmental management.

They also take into account various levels of planning. The national level has long been a research focus for the historiography of planning, (re)examining aspects of national histories, including the relationship between planning and politics in postwar Britain[37] and the peculiar form taken by statism in France.[38] Sev-

---

[36] Among a rich and growing historiography in this field, see in particular Alexander Badenoch and Andreas Fickers, *Materializing Europe Transnational Infrastructures and the Project of Europe* (Basingstoke: Palgrave Macmillan, 2010); Jeremi Suri, "Conflict and Co-operation in the Cold War: New Directions in Contemporary Historical Research," *Journal of Contemporary History* 46 (2011): 5–9; Peter Romijn, Giles Scott-Smith, and Joes Segal, eds., *Divided Dreamworlds? The Cultural Cold War in East and West* (Amsterdam: Amsterdam University Press, 2012); Autio-Sarasmo and Miklóssy, *Reassessing*; Frederico Romero and Angela Romano, eds., "European Socialist Regimes Facing Globalisation and European Co-operation: Dilemmas and Responses," *European Review of History* 21 (2014), special issue; Egle Rindzeviciute, *The Power of Systems. How Policy Sciences Opened Up the Cold War* (Cornell: Cornell University Press, 2017); Matthieu Gillabert and Tiphaine Robert, *Zuflucht suchen. Phasen des Exils aus Osteuropa im Kalten Krieg / Chercher refuge. Les phases d'exil d'Europe centrale pendant la Guerre froide* (Basel: Schwabe, 2017).

[37] Glen O'Hara, *From Dreams to Disillusionment* (Palgrave Macmillan, Basingstoke, 2007); Daniel Ritschel, *The Politics of Planning: The Debate on Economic Planning in Britain in the 1930s* (Oxford: Clarendon Press, 1997); Richard Toye, *The Labour Party and the Planned Economy 1931–1951* (Rochester: Boydell, 2003).

[38] Richard F. Kuisel, *Capitalism and State in Modern France: Renovation and Economic Management in the 20. Century* (Cambridge: Cambridge University Press, 1983); Philippe Mioche, *Le Plan Monnet, genèse et élaboration, 1941–1947* (Paris: Publ. de la Sorbonne, 1987); Michel Margairaz,

eral contributions in this book deal with national planning and the circulation of various planning models originating in countries such as France (Isabelle Gouarné), Finland and the Soviet Union (Sari Autio-Sarasmo), Czechoslovakia (Vítězslav Sommer), and Yugoslavia (Zaccharia Benedetto). However, other contributors examine planning at the regional (Bloc) level, including the Council of Economic Mutual Assistance (CMEA) (Simon Godard) and the Organization for Economic Co-operation and Development (OECD) (Jenny Andersson). Attention is paid to the Pan-European level (Daniel Stinsky, Katja Naumann, Sandrine Kott) and even to the global scale, as reflected in the careful analyzes of the activities of international organizations with a global reach (Francine McKenzie, Michel Christian, Ondřej Matějka).

The analysis of East-West circulations, conflicts, and competition lie at the heart of each contribution. Taken as a whole, they document three fundamental aspects of the transnational history of planning in postwar Europe: actors, spaces and temporalities.

The actors of planning

Who were the people who formulated, preached, sustained and proselytized the "religion" of planning in both the East and West? In what domains were they principally engaged? Is it possible to identify common traits in their career trajectories?

These questions are implicit in all the contributions. In several of them, we encounter some of the "usual suspects," well known from previous works on planning: experts in various fields (most often relating to economic matters) who were socialized at different stages of their lives within various international organizations, and who, in some cases, held executive positions in the secretariats of those international organizations. Daniel Stinsky (inspired by Wolfram Kaiser and Johan Schot) links these actors' trajectories to the emergence of "technocratic internationalism," mainly in UN agencies. Gunnar Myrdal is the classic example of this phenomenon.

The focus on East-West exchanges in our volume allows us to identify lesser known, yet not less important, actors in the history of planning. People whose careers were linked to the rise of cybernetics and computer science emerge as

---

"La faute à 68? Le Plan et les institutions de la régulation économique et financière: une libéralisation contrariée ou différée?," in *Mai 68 entre libération et libéralisation. La grande bifurcation*, ed. Michel Margairaz and Danielle Tartakowsky (Rennes, PUR, 2010), 41–62. See also the contributon of Isabelle Gouarné in this volume.

a particularly interesting group. Since the mid-1960s at least, computers and computer specialists have been key proponents of planning increasingly complex approaches in the field of the environment and elsewhere. This is shown in detail by Michael Hutter, who describes the case of the budworm pest and the corresponding research project carried out at the International Institute for Applied Studies Analysis (IIASA). It is also true of the contribution by Sandrine Kott in relation to management strategies promoted by the International Labor Organization (ILO). Due to an important East-West technological imbalance in the field of informatics, computers and computer analysts played a role in connecting the East and the West, with repercussions that extended beyond the sphere of planning. In fact, as Kott hypothesizes, one of the reasons that Eastern countries enrolled in Western-led management training programs through the ILO was that they gained access to otherwise almost unattainable computer technology. The interest was reciprocal. Western firms profited from trade openings in the Eastern bloc linked to the transfer of high-tech goods. The case of Nokia, examined here by Sari Autio-Sarasmo, offers an interesting example in this regard.

Ondřej Matějka's chapter further elucidates the importance of computer expertise and technology. He shows that anxieties about cybernetics constituted common ground for Western and Eastern Marxist philosophers and Christian theologians. In the mid-1960s, they entered into an improbable but intense dialogue in which they denounced the "dehumanizing effects" of ever more "technicized" planning and management strategies executed with computerized tools. Hence, even in the theological sphere, seemingly distant from the new technologies being applied to planning and management, computers represented an important, connective East-West issue. The challenge of such technology was one of the constitutive components of a particular Christian-Marxist "channel," which functioned without regard to the Iron Curtain.

Furthermore, attention to unexpected circulations through, across, under and beyond the political divide on the European continent draws attention to important and so far little-explored features in the profiles of transnationally active planners. First of all, several of our contributions reveal a certain marginality of those actors on the national level: Katja Naumann introduces the Polish philosopher Adam Schaff, who embarked on an international career at the Vienna Center of the International Social Sciences Council after he suffered the consequences of an anti-Semitic wave inside Polish academia. Daniel Stinsky argues that Myrdal himself opted for the United Nations Economic Commission for Europe (UNECE) after he became the "target of popular dissatisfaction" in Sweden due to his participation in the negotiation of ambitious trade deals with the Soviet Union. Isabelle Gouarné highlights the domestic political marginality of French leftists – often from Jewish or Protestant backgrounds – but who were the key figures in establishing a channel to economic planners in Hungary and, to some extent, the Soviet Union. These French state economists (such as Étienne Hirsch, Claude Gruson, and Jean Saint-Geours) were able to reconcile their leftist preferences with the opportunities offered by De Gaulle statism.

The leftist leanings of postwar planners come as no surprise, but our East-West analyzes offer enough material to highlight the importance of *"reformisme"* and the social democratic international networks in which these ideas circulated. Both Myrdals, in the initial phase of this story, found a safe haven in Stockholm to plan the future of Europe. They were surrounded by members of the *Internationale Gruppe Demokratischer Sozialisten,* which brought together socialist emigrés from all corners of wartime Europe (including Bruno Kreisky and Willy Brandt). The solidity of these networks was confirmed after the Iron Curtain divided the continent. Benedetto Zaccaria makes an essential contribution to this largely unknown story when he persuasively describes how Western social democrats, from the 1960s on, were fascinated with the Yugoslav model of self-management. Zaccaria introduces personalities like Sicco Mansholt, a member of the Dutch Labour Party who, as the President of the European Commission, praised Yugoslav successes; the German Social Democrat leader Herbert Wehner, who pointed to the achievements made by Yugoslav self-management in the Bundestag; and the philosopher Alexander Marc, who called the attention of his French followers to the Balkan country that had succeeded, according to him, in "replacing the Soviet model of the almighty State with that of Society."

In her analysis of the transfer of management ideas and practices between West and East, Sandrine Kott confirms the existence of this stable social democratic internationalism. She underlines the continuous connections between Czech social democrats in the ILO who had been exiled to the West and those who had remained in Prague. The impact of these exchanges on the national and local level would be a rich future research project. Kott points in this direction when she refers to thousands of local *cadres* in Romania, Bulgaria, Poland, and Czechoslovakia who underwent training organized by the ILO. Western (often British) experts in management led this training. Kott identifies the existence and influence of such a "transnationally minded technocratic milieu" which played an important role not only during the Cold War but also in the years of the post-1989 transition out of communism.

The spaces of planning

The second thematic cluster addressed by this volume concerns the spatiality of planning. What were the spaces and the levels where planning was a subject for debate and an important social practice? Which spaces produced and inspired planners from both East and West?

The domains of planning introduced by our contributors are expansive. These domains existed on the national, continental and the global level. Only within such a wide perspective can one conclude that the European continent was central to the history of planning. As Daniel Stinsky explains in his contribution, Myrdal believed that the rebuilding of postwar Europe should be based on international planning. He also contended that national economies should be coordinated across the growing East-West divide, and stressed the importance of planning issues in UNECE. Isabelle Gouarné also emphasizes Europe's centrality and importance in her study of the exchanges between French planners and their Eastern counterparts. She identifies a genuine "European pole" which developed from the lively interactions between economic experts from both sides of the Iron Curtain, and which produced a plethora of ideas and models for managing national economies. The most visible evidence of those interactions was the convergence in the socio-economic debates inside the European space in the 1960s and 1970s, which in the 1980s were overshadowed by the rapid rise of neoliberal thought connected to American hegemony. Katja Naumann makes a similar case when she analyzes the activities of the Vienna Center, where East and West European social scientists attempted to plan and to carry out large scale research projects together. Among other things, those research projects aimed to "Europeanize" comparative social research and overcome North American "data imperialism".

Not every corner of the Old Continent was equally welcoming to planners or produced the remarkably lively planning thought and practices found elsewhere. Our volume brings substantial nuance to the geography of planning initiatives inside the "European pole." In fact, several contributions in this book agree on the particular importance of the European periphery and border zones as seedbeds for the cultivation of planners, sites of lively intellectual debate on planning, spaces for implementation of planning practices, and experimental laboratories for planners coming from various backgrounds and places.

It is useful to distinguish the different scales of planning with nuanced observation and reflection. On the micro level, we can identify peripheral spaces that proved to be especially welcoming for planning debates and research. Besides the well-known internationalist center in Geneva (home to the UNECE, the United Nations Conference on Trade and Development (UNCTAD), the World Council of Churches (WCC) and the GATT), Vienna seemed to play host as a site of frequent encounters between planners. Vienna's position on the borderline between the Western and Eastern blocs made it attractive as another center for the headquarters of international organizations, including the International Atomic Energy Agency (IAEA) and the United Nations Industrial Development Organization (UNIDO). The city's prestige grew during the Cold War because of its hospitality to East-West joint ventures of all kinds. Chapters on the Vienna Center and the IIASA provide concrete details about this pragmatic dimension of the city's international community.

Geneva and Vienna are central spaces in our story mainly for reasons related to organization and infrastructure: they were an accessible and convenient locale for East-West encounters. Countries on the periphery of Europe played a more complex role at the meso-level of interaction. Two examples in our volume – Yugoslavia and Finland – reveal a multi-layered phenomenon. Benedetto Zaccaria unpacks the reasons and conditions for the development of a genuine Western fascination with Yugoslav self-management, which reached its apex in the mid-1970s. In fact, Western observers' attraction to Yugoslavia was only partly attributable to the inspirational theories on economic management introduced by its experts. Westerners were also enchanted by Yugoslavia's promotion of itself as a "laboratory" for evaluating in real time the pros and cons of its planning system, halfway between the highly centralized Soviet model and looser Western planning measures. Similarly, Hungarian economists (as related in Isabelle Gouarné's chapter) and Czech philosophers and theologians (in Ondřej Matějka's account) understood that presenting their countries as "testing grounds" for various contemporary theories of economic models and socio-theological hypotheses substantially improved their chances of attracting the attention of their counterparts from capitalist countries. Yugoslavia's special appeal in this regard produced concrete results in terms of advantageous business deals with the West, in particular Yugoslavia's 1970 trade agreement with the European Economic Community (EEC), which was the first to be signed between the EEC and a socialist country.

Sari Autio-Sarasmo's account of the benefits accruing to Finland from its position on the Eastern periphery of Western Europe, closely linked to the Soviet Union, further enriches our understanding of the mutual instrumentalizations related to planning. In fact, Finnish enterprises progressively learned to adjust to the functioning of the centrally planned economy next door. They played the role of privileged trade partner with the Soviet Union, in part because they were forced to do so by the postwar constellation of power in Europe. In the long run, the predictable rhythm of Soviet five-year plans, stable demand from Moscow for high-tech goods, and persistent Soviet difficulties in implementing innovative procedures domestically (as they sought to achieve self-sufficiency in communications, for instance) all proved to be water of life for Finnish companies such as Nokia. Nokia's success in the capitalist world is undeniably related to this exceptionally well-protected business environment. It existed on a sort of lee side that allowed it to invest extensively in modernization projects and thus acquire a particularly advantageous position in the global arena.

If we mount one step higher on the scale of observation, Eastern Europe after 1945 emerges as a special regional case in terms of both economic and social planning. The socialist regimes in power there established state-planned economies and launched an in-depth transformation of their societies based on the Soviet model. However, as Simon Godard stresses in his contribution, the Eastern European model of economic planning was never monolithic. Not only did the Eastern bloc's internal diversity in this area increase as it implemented a range of economic reforms beginning in the 1950s, but its member countries failed to coordinate their national plans. Simon Godard argues that this failure to coordinate did not result from economic inefficiency but from political processes emphasizing national identities. According to this interpretation, Eastern European countries used the Council of Mutual Economic Assistance (CMEA) to shift the balance of power within the Eastern bloc.

Nor was the Eastern bloc itself a self-contained monolith, as official discourses suggested. Before Eastern and Central European countries formed a "bloc", they constituted a "European first periphery," as seen from the perspective of the Western "center" in the interwar years – as Sandrine Kott reminds us. In her contribution, she argues that this perception of a peripheral position was not completely abandoned after 1945. The Eastern part of the continent became a site for testing new management strategies exported from Anglo-Saxon countries through international organizations. Interest in opportunities for experimentation increased from the early 1960s against the background (or sometimes, the specter) of a rapidly rising Third World, which became omnipresent in every approach to planning and development. Consequently, in certain fields the European Eastern periphery was considered (at least in theory) to be a potential bridge to the underdeveloped South, be it in management, in theological dialogue or in trade agreements like those encouraged by UNCTAD.[39]

Temporalities of planning

Interest in bridging the West-East-South divides, which was widespread in the late 1960s and early 1970s, was overshadowed in the sphere of planning by a

---

39 This aspect is further developed in Michel Christian, Sandrine Kott, Ondřej Matějka, "International Organizations in the Cold War: the Circulation of Experts beyond the East-West Divide," *Acta Universitatis Carolinae. Studia Territorialia* 1 (2017): 35–60.

more defensive type of thought aimed at preventing the demise of Western global dominance, or at least slowing it down. This is one of the key points of Jenny Andersson's contribution to our volume. Her analysis substantially enriches understanding of the chronological milestones in the history of planning between East and West, which is the third thematic cluster addressed by most of the chapters in this volume. The importance of this chronology justifies our decision to organize this volume along a time-line of the rise and fall of the influence of the "political religion" of planning in East-West relations.

The early days of planning are relatively well covered, for example in the studies of Judt or Engerman, who emphasized how the world wars accelerated intellectuals' enthusiasm for all kinds of non-conformist ideas that had been popular in the interwar years.[40] Two contributions in our volume adopt an international perspective and deal with the first dreams of large-scale planning. Besides an inescapable homage to Gunnar Myrdal and UNECE, we find it important to remember one story of a planning failure on the macro level: the rise and fall of the International Trade Organization (ITO), the most ambitious postwar project aimed at regulating global trade movements, as detailed by Francine McKenzie. Although the ITO grew out of the experiences and hopes of the interwar and war periods, it could not survive the mounting pressure of early Cold War realities and the retreat of planning thought in the United States in the late 1940s.

References to pre-1945 planning initiatives and thought are certainly not limited to the two contributions that form the first part of our book. Our volume in fact demonstrates the importance of the interwar roots of postwar developments in East-West planning. Katja Naumann insists on that point when she explains the genesis of Central European social scientists' connections to the West. Similarly, the influence of Czech actors inside the ILO and other management-oriented assistance activities stemmed from networks first forged in the 1920s, as Sandrine Kott explains in her chapter.

The "classical planners" who grew up in, and were formed directly or indirectly by the self-confident, goal-oriented ethos of European High Modernity, lived their (last) moments of glory in the 1960s, as the, correspondingly extensive Part Two of this volume illustrates. That European ethos was shaped by the conviction that people and societies could be improved through rationally planned action. After Charles de Gaulle returned to power in France, planners held key positions inside the institutional architecture of the state-run parts of the French economy (see the contribution by Gouarné), social scientists from all corners of Europe launched ambitious comparative research schemes through the Interna-

---

40 Judt, *Postwar*, 67on.

tional Social Science Council (Naumann), numerous Western modernizers became hypnotized by Yugoslav self-management practices (Zaccaria), the ILO financed impressive management development centers (Kott) and the founding of UNCTAD in 1964 restored the regulation of world trade atop the international agenda (Christian). The oil shock of the 1970s and the end of the Bretton Woods system in 1973 did not automatically call into question the ability of planners to master an economic crisis. As Jenny Andersson makes clear, the early 1970s was characterized by the blossoming of "worldwide" analyzes and planning proposals in the spheres of trade, finance, industrialization and development. It was only later in the decade that the planning approaches began to lose ground to neoliberal ideas.

Michel Christian's chapter on UNCTAD offers an interesting perspective on the transitional years between the planning euphoria and the planning phobia that became palpable in the 1970s and 1980s. Founded as a response to the earlier failure of the ITO after the Havana Conference in 1948, UNCTAD raised the profile of planning in relation to international trade and espoused new trade regulations more favorable to developing countries. UNCTAD's strength was based on the presumed legitimacy of state intervention and economic planning in the economic field. The intellectual framework that supported the European postwar consensus allowed a reconciliation of Keynesian economic regulation and socialist state planning. But as Christian also explains, the progressive marginalization of UNCTAD owed much to the rise of neoliberal ideology after the late 1970s and its global impact.

Several other contributions (assembled in the third part of this volume) further explain the turn away from planning in the 1970s.[41] Jenny Andersson uncovers the anxieties of influential elites, mainly in North America, who reacted to the challenge of global interdependence by trying to find tools that would preserve Western dominance of the world economy. Her analysis describes significant shifts on the conceptual level. "Planning," which was narrowly linked to the progressively outdated modernizing ethos of the postwar decades, gave way to "scenarios" and "models" that better fit the worldviews of new managers of an increasingly ungovernable global arena. Michael Hutter points in the same direction when he presents the goals formulated by IIASA experts in the 1970s. There were no more ambitious large-scale development projects. Instead, the catchword of the moment was to "control and stabilize" through "modules"

---

[41] The 1970s are undoubtedly one of the main areas of current historiographical research, for recent developments in this field see, among many other works, Elke Seefried, "Politics and Time from the 1960s to the 1980s," *The Journal of Modern European History* 13 (2015), special issue 3.

and "packages of techniques." In that particular field, experts ceased to promote change and began to focus on stopping, or at least limiting, some of the disastrous consequences of previous large-scale "modern" projects such as the extensive use of DDT. Both Hutter and Christian justifiably link their reflections on the debates of the 1970s and 1980s to present-day discussions of climate change and the continuing problematic effects of global imbalances in trade. In that way our volume lends historical consciousness to the issues burning in our contemporary public space.

Conclusion

Dealing with planning models and their circulation in international thought and practices offers new insight into the European dimension of the Cold War. First, it calls into question the master narrative of the clash between two superpowers. The history of the Cold War in Europe, as seen from the planning angle, does not focus on the Berlin blockade, the smashing of the Prague Spring, and the Euromissiles crisis. Instead it reveals that even though the European continent was divided into two blocs, in buffer states such as Finland, Austria and, in its own way, Yugoslavia there were numerous and varied contacts above, below, beyond and through the Iron Curtain. The contributions to this volume also show that social-democratic parties and organizations have remained a stable part of political life in Europe, in sharp contrast to the United States. This social-democratic milieu was instrumental in creating bridges between West and East, especially in fields like planning. Our collective volume also underlines the deep history of contacts between the two halves of Europe (dating back to before World War Two), which stretched from trade and industry to culture and education. Because of those past ties, the Cold War could not be waged in Europe simply as a confrontation between two superpowers. Last but not least, from French *planism* to Hungarian market-based reforms of its centrally managed economy, planning thought and practices highlighted the internal diversity of the two blocs, which was in many ways the result of the circulation of planning models between East and West. Dealing with planning in this way raises substantial questions about contacts, exchanges, and circulations, which can and should be more widely taken into account in new histories of the Cold War.

Second, this transnational history of the Cold War leads to a reevaluation of the role of Eastern Europe in the conventional narrative of European history, which has all too often been reduced to the history of the Western part of the continent. The contributions in this volume show that Eastern Europe was more than an extension of the West in the interwar years or a lost or kidnapped part of it during the Cold War. Already in the interwar years in most of these countries, political elites, both conservative and social democratic, developed state-led economic and social projects to overcome what they saw as structural underdevelopment. Many of the postwar international planners came from Eastern Europe. Communist politicians built on prewar know-how; meanwhile central planning became one of the main tools to enforce the socialist development project. Up to the 1970s, Eastern European countries thus constituted genuine laboratories for planning; in that sense they remained a source of inspiration for some planners in Western Europe. Moreover, their own history of relative underdevelopment, made these countries suitable exporters of planning expertise to newly decolonized countries, putting them in a central mediating position between West and South.[42]

Finally, the various contributions highlight the fluidity of the notion of planning. As seen at the beginning of this Introduction "planning" as an analytical category has been used in various intellectual contexts: economy, political science, sociology, history, yet always in connection with modernity. Most of the contributions in this volume use the term in relation to those various analytical dimensions. There is more to be done in producing a micro-history of planning in a pan-European context, to confront those analytical categories that we as scholars are using with the language of the above-mentioned actors on the ground. Did they know or claim that they were "planning"? How did the use of the term change and evolve over time? Which kinds of practical tools did the various actors use to "plan"? We hope that this volume will provide a useful analytical framework for future research in this direction.

---

[42] For more on this aspect, see Christian, Kott, Matějka, "International Organizations", 53–58.

Part 1: **Planning a New World after the War**

Francine McKenzie
Peace, Prosperity and Planning Postwar Trade, 1942–1948

Most histories of the Second World War focus on key battles, strategy and leadership, the management of resources, and the workings of alliances. While these are all essential aspects of the Second World War, they leave out a crucial element: planning for peace. No one believed that the end of the Second World War would automatically restore peace. As John Winant, the US ambassador to London explained: "Planning for peace is an essential part of the job of winning the war."[1] Long before the outcome of the war could be predicted, officials from the countries that made up the Grand Alliance developed social, economic, and diplomatic plans that would address long-standing and recent challenges to improve living conditions, modernize economies, and prevent another war. While American and British officials were in the forefront of planning efforts, small countries, governments in exile, world leaders including Pope Pius, public intellectuals, and everyday citizens prepared plans to combat malnutrition, contain nationalism, and promote human rights, amongst many other problems associated with war, hardship and injustice. This was part of the "planning euphoria" of the Second World War and people explained their ideas about a future peace in blueprints and treatises, drafts and designs, some well-developed and some piecemeal.[2]

Planning also applied to efforts to reconstruct the global economy. There was widespread belief that a peaceful world must also be prosperous. Three international organizations – the International Monetary Fund (IMF), the International Bank for Reconstruction and Development (IBRD), and the International Trade Organization (ITO) – were seen as the main pillars of a postwar global economy that would be stable and growing. But if there was far-reaching support for planning a postwar global economy, there were many ideas about its nature, workings and priorities. Despite the association of planning with Soviet economic management in the 1930s, the World War Two variant of economic planning

---

[1] Draft of a speech for Mr. Winant on Carrying out the Atlantic Charter, n.d., Cox papers, box 100, postwar –foreign, Franklin D. Roosevelt Library [FDRL].
[2] David C. Engerman, "The rise and fall of central planning" in *The Cambridge History of the Second World War. Volume 3, Total War: Economy, Society and Culture*, ed. Michael Geyer and Adam Tooze (Cambridge: Cambridge University Press, 2015), 575–576. Planning for the peace shared some of the characteristics of wartime planning, including a conceptual "fuzziness", a wide range of applications, and a confidence that plans were rational solutions to problems.

https://doi.org/10.1515/9783110534696-003

was more procedural and pragmatic than ideological. There were some fundamental points associated with plans for postwar trade, but above all planning meant advance preparations, deep study, and a multilateral process. This approach conformed to Gunnar Myrdal's belief that international civil servants should be "post-ideological, rational and problem-oriented planners", as Daniel Stinsky explains in his chapter.[3] This methodological conception of planning was evident in the construction of a new global trade system. American and British officials led the way with early designs for the ITO upon which they put a liberal impress. As discussions widened to include more members of the wartime alliance, it became clear that there were numerous priorities at play. Between 1942 and 1948, the original Anglo-American draft which had focused on lowering tariffs was revised and expanded to include interventionist practices, regional economic arrangements, and the promotion of development. The result was a significantly different vision of global trade than the one that had emerged in wartime. Three insights emerge from a study of planning and negotiations of the ITO: first, the priorities associated with trade reflected diverse national goals, including development, reconstruction, modernization, and regional trade blocs; second, real efforts were made to accommodate different national economic goals and practices within the trade system[4]; third, trade priorities were fundamentally politicized, in that they were seen as the way to achieve objectives associated with authority, status, leadership, security and sovereignty.

This chapter begins by examining wartime enthusiasm for planning in general and for trade specifically. It makes the case that planning had a few substantive implications for the workings of the global trade system, in particular about the management of trade by government and the importance of international institutions to oversee and uphold an internationalist conception of trade. The chapter then discusses plans and negotiations, starting in 1942 with British and American designs and meetings, and ending in 1948 at the Havana conference at which 56 countries participated. Despite drastic revisions to the ITO char-

---

3 Daniel Stinsky, "Western European or All-European Cooperation? The OEEC, the European Recovery Program, and the United Nations Economic Commission for Europe (ECE), 1947–1961," in *Warden of the West? The OECD and the Global Political Economy, 1948 to Present*, ed. Mathieu Leimgruber and Matthias Schmelzer. Transnational History Series (New York: Palgrave Macmillan, forthcoming).
4 This is similar to the conclusion reached by Eric Helleiner. As he explained, "efforts to reconcile liberal multilateralism with the state-led developmental goals of poorer countries were in fact at the centre of the politics that created the postwar international financial order." Eric Helleiner, *Forgotten Foundations of Bretton Woods: International Development and the Making of the Postwar Order* (Ithaca: Cornell University Press, 2014), 3.

ter, participating nations were by and large satisfied with the result, confirming the belief that there were many routes to a liberal global trade order.

The planning Zeitgeist in the Second World War: Managed trade and international organizations

Making peace was a daunting challenge. But in wartime, it seemed urgent and unavoidable. Planning seemed to be the only way to come to grips with such a complex undertaking. Moreover, officials believed that planning could effect change which was clearly needed in the global community.[5] The Beveridge and Morgenthau Plans were two of the best known examples of wartime planning and they conveyed the ambition, urgency, and necessity of planning to ensure that large scale challenges could be addressed to achieve justice, progress, and security. There were critics of planning. Some people claimed that planning was a panacea, assumed to have transformative powers based on misunderstanding the issues at hand. Others feared it encroached on freedoms or was elitist and undemocratic.[6] But the critics' voices were drowned out by the advocates of planning which included people who could not be dismissed as delusional utopians, as so many advocates of peace had been in the past.[7] For instance, US President Roosevelt endorsed planning: he foretold a future of destruction following the war "unless we plan now for the better world we mean to build." Richard Law, the minister of state in the British Foreign Office, conveyed the sense of obligation to servicemen to ensure a better future that informed planning efforts: "He felt that these young men and the sacrifices they were called upon to make on the battlefields were a challenge to all who were respon-

---

5 G.L. Schwartz, 'Why Planning?' (London: A Signpost Special, 1944), 3. World War II Subject Collection, Box 26, Hoover Institution.
6 G.L. Schwartz.
7 See for example Carr's dismissal of the views of Norman Angell who believed that economic interdependence would strengthen global peace. Although Angell was awarded the Nobel Peace Prize in 1933, he was dismissed by Carr as a utopian whose ideas were aspirational and unrealistic. Interestingly, Carr did endorse state planning of the economy as well as plans for postwar Europe. Norman Angell, *The Great Illusion: a study of the relation of military power to national advantage* (London: Heinemann, 1912), vii, ix, 30–1. Jeremy Weiss, "E. H. Carr, Norman Angell, and Reassessing the Realist-Utopian Debate", *The International History Review* 35, no. 5 (2013): 1160–1161.

sible for planning the future."[8] Although there was persistent scepticism about whether or not future wars could be prevented,[9] planning imbued the quest for peace with legitimacy because plans were seen as realistic rather than quixotic, informed by diplomatic and technical expertize rather than romantic dreams, and were the product of careful deliberation and the benefit of past experience.

The circumstances of war legitimized the necessity of planning at the international level. In the interwar years, planning was developed in relation to national economic strategies. As Joanne Pemberton has explained in the cases of Britain and Australia, some people called for its international application, lest the development of national plans spark conflict amongst states. But in general the idea of international planning between the wars was not favored because it constrained a state's ability to implement economic policies. She argues that by the end of the 1930s planning had become parochial, associated with national and imperial spaces.[10] But during the war, unchecked state power was identified as one of the principal causes of the conflict and people were prepared to accept international plans which restricted the authority of states. As Law said during Anglo-American discussions of postwar trade in 1943, "[p]eople were capable, at this moment, of sacrificing immediate advantage for the long-term gain, but when the moment of danger was removed they would be in a different mood."[11] Ernest Bevin, Britain's minister of labour, agreed that in wartime people accepted "control, regulation and discipline" because it was necessary to survive. This was now also seen as essential to security in peacetime. Hence Bevin urged statesmen to "stand together resolutely and hold on to some form of controls while the foundations of peace, stability and orderly development are being worked out."[12] The circumstances of war created the opportunity to think differently about the peace, placing collective well-being above national interests and accepting that international regulation required some constraints on

---

[8] Informal Economic Discussions, Plenary, 1rst meeting, 20 Sept. 1943, CAB78/14, The National Archives (TNA).
[9] "Post-war Planning Must Show that Men Can Prevent Wars If They Take the Necessary Steps." Presenting Postwar Planning to the Public, Confidential Report from the Office of Public Opinion Research, Princeton University, Winant Papers, FDRL. Note that 58% of those asked said there would be future wars.
[10] Joanne Pemberton, "The Middle Way: The Discourse of Planning in Britain, Australia and at the League of Nations in the Interwar Years," *Australian Journal of Politics and History* 52, no. 1 (2006): 49, 51, 58.
[11] Informal Economic Discussions, Plenary, 20 Sept. 1943.
[12] Bevin's Address, International Labour Office, Emergency Committee of the Governing Body, Draft Minutes of the Fifth Session, 20–24 April 1942, CAB117/100, TNA.

national sovereignty. But the emphasis on international planning and coordination never meant that national interests were secondary. A liberal trade order was linked to national priorities of recovery and full employment, about which there was apprehension as states transitioned from a wartime to a peacetime economy.

A reconstructed economy that promoted stable growth, sustained full employment, and distributed benefits across classes and countries was a priority in government planning efforts. The importance of economic growth to future peace was influenced by the experience of the Great Depression, which in countries like the US, Britain and Canada centred on the problem of mass unemployment, and the Second World War, two catastrophes which many believed were causally linked. Although laissez-faire liberalism had been discredited in the 1930s, a liberal spirit informed the postwar trade system based on the internationalist logic that interdependence and prosperity were essential to peace.[13] Furthermore, cooperative trade relations between states, even if still competitive, were seen as essential to preserving peace. As Harry Hawkins, one of the leading economic planners in the US State Department, put it in 1944: "Nations which are economic enemies are not likely to remain political friends for long."[14]

In wartime and postwar discussions, many used the term free trade or freer trade to describe the liberal trade system, but what they were talking about was a system of managed freer trade. The planned trade approach was not restricted to those involved with the ITO. As Daniel Stinky has shown, Gunnar Myrdal was also a "free-trading planner."[15] Although officials wanted states to remain the central actors in the postwar international order,[16] they envisaged a liberal trade regime that depended on state support while also restraining state authority.[17] The creation of an international organization would establish a forum and define rules and obligations that would facilitate international cooperation and limit the nationalistic options of its members. Rules and obligations left room for flexibility about specific trade practices, in contrast to the exacting details and

---

[13] Katherine Barbieri and Gerald Schneider, "Globalization and Peace: Assessing New Directions in the Study of Trade & Conflict," *Journal of Peace Research* 36, no. 4 (1999): 389.
[14] Quoted in John H. Jackson, *World Trade and The Law of GATT* (Indianapolis: Bobbs-Merrill, 1969), 38.
[15] Stinsky, "A Bridge between East and West".
[16] Letter to Cadogan, 31 May 1942, FO371/31538, TNA. The author not only wanted nations to be the basic unit of international society but he wanted Britain to remain the 'Top Nation.'
[17] G. John Ikenberry makes a similar point about the essential compromise that defined Bretton Woods such that it appealed to people with diametrically opposed ideas, from laissez faire to planners. "A World Economy Restored: Expert Consensus and the Anglo-American Post-War Settlement," *International Organization* 46, no. 1 (Winter 1992): 307–308, 315–316, 318.

state imposed targets that defined some socialist planning models. Nonetheless, there was tension about the role of the state, at once constrained by rules and obligations and enhanced by actively managing national and international trade. Tony Judt has explained that "faith in the state" defined the planning ethos of the interwar years.[18] But during the war, mistrust of nationalism offset that faith. Postwar trade plans reflected this tension, simultaneously depending on and curbing state sovereignty and market forces.

Planning a liberal trade order in wartime

In the United States, a poll from January 1943 found that 65% of Americans believed planning should begin right away.[19] In fact, by 1943 American plans for postwar trade were well underway. The State Department was at the centre of American trade policy because of the influence of Cordell Hull, the Secretary of State from 1933–1944. During the First World War, Hull had come to the conclusion that global peace depended on freer trade. He was not alone in this belief. The corollary – that economic conditions could be a cause of conflict – reinforced the appeal of liberalization. The US had defined a liberal trade policy in the 1930s as a way to combat the Depression and defuse geopolitical antagonism. The principles that had informed the Reciprocal Trade Agreements Act of 1934 (RTAA) were internationalism, reciprocity, the Most Favoured Nation (MFN) principle, and liberalization through lower tariffs. The start of the war did not dent the confidence of Hull or the State Department that liberalization and internationalism were the key ingredients of a successful postwar trade order that would engender peace and prosperity. As a result, the principles of the RTAA continued to guide American planners during and after the war.[20] The apparent tension between the traditional role of the market as the main arbiter of global trade and government action that kept markets open and upheld liberal trade practices was easily reconciled.

---

18 Tony Judt, *Postwar: A History of Europe Since 1945* (New York: Penguin Books, 2010), 69.
19 "Presenting Postwar Planning to the Public," Confidential Report from the Office of Public Opinion Research, Princeton University, Winant Papers, Box 217, Reconstruction: Presenting Post-war Planning to the People, FDRL.
20 Irwin, Mavroidis and Sykes have concluded from this that the GATT "represented a continuation and expansion of U.S. efforts during the 1930s." Douglas A. Irwin, Petros C. Mavroidis, Alan O. Sykes, *The Genesis of the GATT* (Cambridge: Cambridge University Press, 2008), 12. I think this view overstates American authorship.

American officials assumed that other governments would resist a liberal international trade order. To pin down support for trade liberalization, the US attached a consideration to the Lend-Lease agreement of 1941 by which they loaned or leased vital war materials to Britain, the Soviet Union and other countries fighting the Axis powers. The consideration called for support for an open economy after the war. At this stage, American efforts focused on securing promises to support liberal trade after the war. They did not lay out concrete ideas in a blueprint or a detailed plan.

Instead, the first trade plan was developed in Britain by James Meade, a future Nobel Laureate but then a young economist in the Economic Section of the War Cabinet Offices. In 1940, he had returned from the Economic and Financial Organization (EFO) of the League of Nations where his internationalist perspective had been reinforced. The EFO brought together economists from all over the world who were intent on restoring "stability and growth" to the world economy and who believed that international organizations facilitated cooperation as well as curbed the narrow self-interest and inconsistent policies of national governments.[21] Meade endorsed liberal trade not only because it was consistent with his intellectual leanings, but also because he believed that economic practices and conditions were root causes of geopolitical conflicts. As he wrote in his 1940 book *The Economic Basis on a Durable Peace:* "to a certain extent, the causes of international conflict are economic in character".[22]

In 1942, he drafted a blueprint for a reconstructed global trade organization. His plan – called the International Commercial Union – put his international and liberal ideas front and centre. Meade believed that the best trade system for Britain was one in which freer trade prevailed. This would give Britain access to as many markets as possible which was in turn the key to maintaining high levels of employment for people working in all forms of export producing industries. He acknowledged that Britain would face many challenges after the war – including lost markets and a shortage of convertible currency – but he believed that in the long run freer trade was the best policy for Britain: "If ever there was a community which had an interest in the general removal of restrictions to trade, it is the United Kingdom." Hence his plan banned quantitative restrictions and excessive export subsidies, removed restrictions on currency exchange and eliminated preferential prices. To work, his plan required regulation of the global liberal trade system; he did not leave all to the free hand of the market.

---

[21] Patricia Clavin, *Securing the World Economy: the Reinvention of the League of Nations, 1920– 1946* (Oxford: Oxford University Press, 2013), 5, 6.
[22] Irwin, Mavroidis and Sykes, *Genesis*, 25. Also see 25–30 for their description of Meade's draft.

Meade's plan also made some allowance for historical and political factors that influenced trade policies and patterns. For example, where a special and recognizable geopolitical or political relationship existed, nations could exchange moderate preferential tariffs; he set the rate at 10% *ad valorem*. This had particular relevance to Britain as there was significant support for retaining the preferential tariff system of the British Empire and Commonwealth.[23]

Meade's plan was criticized by leading Treasury officials who feared that freer trade would exacerbate Britain's balance of payments problems after the war.[24] John Maynard Keynes, whose ideas about Britain's postwar economy were based on dire forecasts and the need for mechanisms to stave off external forces that could destabilize the British economy, was outspoken in his opposition to Meade's plan. Meade described Keynes' views on postwar trade as more extreme than those of Schacht.[25] Keynes was not the only critic of Meade's plan. Others called for bilateral trade agreements and increased trade within the sterling area. British policymakers looked to the past – the Depression – and the future – unknown but ominous even if Britain emerged victorious in the war – and decided to support Meade's liberalizing plan, with a few safeguards, such as the use of quantitative restrictions to offset balance of payments problems. Meade's plan for postwar trade combined long-standing ideas about British trade, in particular freer trade, along with more recent shifts in favour of intervention and protection. Joanne Pemberton has suggested this represented an organic evolution of British trade policy, rather than an abrupt departure, and that it was also a hybrid policy "between unregulated laissez faire and dictatorship."[26]

When British and American trade experts met in secret in Washington in 1943, they were pleasantly surprised to learn that their ideas were largely compatible, emphasizing liberalization and multilateralism. There was disagreement. They understood the workings of international trade differently. The British stressed high rates of employment as a precondition to the growth of world trade whereas the Americans believed that higher employment would follow the removal of barriers to trade. Some disagreements became heated, such as over the fate of imperial preferences. Although imperial preference was a constant source of conflict between the US and Britain,[27] it should not obscure the extent

---

[23] Francine McKenzie, *Redefining the Bonds of Commonwealth, 1939–1948: The Politics of Preference* (Basingstoke: Palgrave Macmillan 2002), 40.
[24] Irwin, Mavroidis and Sykes, *Genesis*, 30–37.
[25] Author interview with Meade, 24 May 1993.
[26] Pemberton, "The Middle Way": 59.
[27] For an in-depth account, see McKenzie, *Redefining the Bonds of Commonwealth*, 102–106, 134–137, 138–155, 199–220.

to which their respective approaches to the postwar trade order aligned. In fact, British officials had decided before the meeting that if there was substantial agreement they would share Meade's plans with the Americans. Meade's plan was distributed. Harry Hawkins described the "remarkable progress" that had been made and observed that differences were on questions of means, not on substantive policies.[28]

Anglo-American discussions about trade had been held in secret, but their ideas were widely known because British officials met with representatives of the Commonwealth (Canada, Australia, New Zealand, and South Africa) and India to discuss postwar trade in advance of Anglo-American meetings in 1943 and 1944. James Meade recalled that the purpose of these meetings was to remove those aspects that were most obnoxious to members of the Commonwealth. He did not remember any significant change arising from them. In his words, the postwar trade plan remained an Anglo-American product.[29] Nonetheless, Dominion officials did not hold back their criticisms of the British trade plan. While Canada found itself broadly in agreement with British and American ideas, reflecting the importance of these two markets to Canadian exports, Australia's representative – Nugget Coombs – objected to the emphasis on tariff reduction. He insisted that conditions of full employment, income and rising standards of living were essential to an expanding economy and these "positive measures" were needed in addition to "negative measures", meaning lowering tariffs, to create demand which would stimulate growth in global trade.[30] Coombs repeated his argument in favor of a positive approach in 1944, making clear that there had to be multiple paths leading to a liberal trade order if all states were to benefit. That meant developing countries should be able to use protective tariffs and other discriminatory or restrictive practices to encourage industrial development and diversification. Officials from New Zealand and South Africa backed up this approach because industrial development and diversification were high priorities in their national postwar economic plans. While Australia, New Zealand and South Africa do not always leap to mind when thinking about developing countries of the 1940s, their dependence on one market (Britain) as well as a handful of primary commodities as exports were characteristics of developing economies. By arguing for positive measures and the use of protective practices to promote industrial development, they made development a

---

[28] Thomas W. Zeiler, *Free Trade Free World* (Chapel Hill: University of North Carolina Press, 1999), 36.
[29] Author interview with Meade.
[30] Post-War Commercial Policy Discussions, UK, India and the Dominions, 1rst meeting, 15 June 1943, T230/129, TNA.

priority of the postwar trade order and revealed their understanding that trade could help or hinder this aim.[31]

European governments in exile were also aware that postwar planning had begun, although according to Meade they were not consulted.[32] But exclusion did not mean that officials from the governments in exile were inactive. For example, Belgium established a Commission d' Etude des Problèmes d'Après-Guerre (CEPAG) to consider postwar issues and put Paul van Zeeland, former prime minister, in charge. CEPAG argued that smaller European nations should be involved in postwar planning, in the hope they could "avoid the postwar agenda being dictated by the Americans and the British."[33] Thierry Grosbois has also pointed out the politico-diplomatic reasons behind the creation of the Benelux customs union in 1944: to bolster their standing so that the great powers would take their point of view into consideration.[34]

CEPAG produced several reports during the war, the first of which acknowledged the economic causes of war and peace and advised against a return to the "lawless competition" that had existed before the war. Its recommendations emphasized the need for regional economic arrangements for Europe.[35] CEPAG's fifth report from 1943 made a forceful case for regional solutions to international problems.[36] This idea played out in other European groups. For example, in a 1944 discussion sponsored by the Association France-Grande Bretagne-États-Unis on the organization of peace, one of the lead speakers – Bordaz – identified the need for a trade plan for Western Europe.[37] Bordaz subsequently noted that the challenge was to find functional groups – he thought France, Belgium, the Netherlands was one workable option – which would allow them to "overcome selfish nationalism", all in the service of universal peace.[38]

---

[31] The inclusion of development in these discussions reinforces Eric Helleiner's argument about the centrality of development in the establishment of the IMF and World Bank. See Eric Helleiner, *Forgotten Foundations of Bretton Woods*, 3.
[32] Author interview with Meade.
[33] Jean F. Crombois, *Camille Gutt and Postwar International Finance* (London: Pickering & Chatto, 2011), 63–65.
[34] Thierry Grosbois, "La Belgique et le Benelux: de l'universalisme au régionalisme, " in *La Belgique, les petits États et la construction européenne*, ed. Michel Dumoulin, Geneviève Duchenne, and Arthe Van Laer (Bern: Peter Lang, 2004), 60.
[35] CEPAG First Report, July 1941 in *Documents on the History of European Integration*, vol. 4, ed. W. Lipgens (Berlin, New York: De Gruyter, 1985), 420–421.
[36] CEPAG Fifth Report, Aug 1943, in Lipgens, *Documents*, 441–443.
[37] "Pierre Cot and … Bordaz: Post-war International Organization," 25 Feb. 1944, in Lipgens, *Documents*, 314.
[38] "Bordaz: Postwar Economic Organization," 28 April 1944, in Lipgens, *Documents*, 326–327.

The reports of CEPAG, as well as the ideas and plans articulated by Europeans in exile and members of the resistance, cohered around the need for a regional economic arrangement after the war. Europe was a distinct space that had to confront particular challenges, or what Jean Monnet called "the European problem."[39] A regional economic bloc also seemed the best way to confront the challenge of postwar reconstruction. As Lucia Coppolaro has explained, European officials conceived of trade liberalization along regional lines in order to bring about recovery from the war. "The liberalization of Western European trade started on a regional basis" that "bypass[ed] Bretton woods multilateralism."[40] But a regional arrangement did not necessarily clash with the universalism of postwar organizations. Grosbois agreed that the creation of the Benelux customs union had a universalist spirit; it was a regional arrangement meant to support and benefit from the global liberal trade order.[41] Along similar lines, Diane de Bellefroide contends that the representatives on CEPAG imagined "a three tiered international society", with the regional level of primary relevance after the war, but comfortably sitting between the national and world levels.[42] However, regional arrangements for postwar Europe ended up being pushed aside in the plans of Britain and the United States. Early in the war, British and American groups working on the postwar order had considered regional organization as building blocks of a global system, but that approach was supplanted by American proposals in favour of a global order carved into spheres led by regional hegemons: the United States, Britain, China and the Soviet Union.[43]

International trade meetings after the war

The next stage of planning postwar trade involved wider consultation with the goal of eliciting broad support for the ITO. The representatives of 17 countries[44] gathered at Church House in London in the autumn of 1946. Committees were

---

39 Jean Monnet, "Imagining Peace" in Lipgens, *Documents*, 303.
40 Lucia Coppolaro, *The Making of a World Trading Power: The European Economic Community (EEC) in the GATT Kennedy Round Negotiations (1963–67)* (Farnham: Ashgate, 2013), 17.
41 Grosbois, " La Belgique et le Benelux, " 91
42 Diane de Bellefroide, "The Commission pour l'Etude des Problèmes d'Après-Guerre (CEPAG), 1941–1944," in *Europe in Exile: European Exile Communities in Britain, 1940–45*, ed. Martin Conway and José Gotovitch (New York and Oxford: Berghan Books, 2001), 130.
43 Lipgens, *Documents*, 5–18.
44 Australia, Belgium, Brazil, Britain, Canada, Chile, China, Cuba, Czechoslovakia, France, India, New Zealand, South Africa, the Netherlands, Norway, Poland and the United States.

established to review all aspects of what was now called a Suggested Charter for World Trade, including employment policy, commercial policy, restrictive practices, commodity policy and the organization and structure of the ITO. At Church House, people drew attention to the fact that the draft served the interests of developed countries. For example, India's representative called for an industrial development policy and lambasted the trade charter because it would permit industrialized countries – the US, Britain and Canada were singled out – to "force their goods on markets abroad." Indian officials insisted that they have recourse to the same kinds of protective tariffs behind which these nations had first developed their industrial potential.[45] Coombs repeated the argument about the need for full employment and positive measures to stimulate economic growth and demand. American accounts singled out Australia and India for making the most substantive criticisms of the charter on the grounds that it favoured countries that were already industrialized at the expense of developing countries. In other words, industrialized countries would profit "by keeping the backward countries in a position of economic dependence."[46] Their concerns were shared by representatives from China, Chile, and Brazil, or what one US official called the "underdeveloped areas bloc".[47] The recognition that trade could help or hinder economic development was acknowledged at this early stage and resulted in significant modifications, crucially permitting the use of quantitative restrictions for the purpose of development.[48]

American reports expressed surprise at the "unexpected vigor" of support for the trade proposals from western European participants, especially Belgium, France, the Netherlands and Norway. Clair Wilcox, the director of the Office of Trade Agreements, concluded that they were "motivated by a strong desire to follow the U.S. line on trade policy" and suggested that the reason for the general backing of the Suggested Draft was "confidence in our fairness and objectivity

---

[45] Note of a meeting in High Commissioner's office, 2 Nov. 1946, RG25/3844/9100-A-40 pt. 1, Library and Archives Canada [LAC].

[46] The Director of the Office of International Trade Policy (Wilcox) to the Secretary of State, Confidential Report To the Secretary of State from the Chairman of the United States Delegation To the First Meeting of the Preparatory Committee for an International Conference on Trade and Employment, 27 Dec. 1946, FRUS 1946, Vol. 1, document 704. See also, Irwin, Mavroidis and Sykes, *Genesis*, 78.

[47] Report of Treasury Participation in London Meeting of the United Nations Preparatory Committee of the International Conference on Trade and Employment, 4 Dec. 1946, Papers of John W. Snyder, Truman Library [TL].

[48] Irwin, Mavroidis and Sykes, *Genesis*, 79.

and is a tribute that could scarcely have been paid to any other power."⁴⁹ But other accounts revealed that western European nations were concerned above all with the length of the transition period. France and Czechoslovakia pressed for as long a transition period as possible (the Czechs apparently suggested it should last 30–50 years) because during this period they would be allowed to use quantitative restrictions to limit imports. The European representatives also insisted that they should be classed along with developing countries – then referred to as underdeveloped countries – which would mean they would benefit from exceptions to the rules of the trade charter.⁵⁰ The main point to take away is not of unexpected support for trade liberalization, but the search for ways to navigate within this emerging trade order to exempt themselves from rules and obligations, at least in the short term when recovery would be an all-consuming challenge.

The Soviet Union was absent from Church House, claiming a shortage of personnel rather than a lack of interest.⁵¹ While American officials doubted that the Soviet Union had much interest in negotiations to reduce tariffs, the acting Secretary of State Dean Acheson did not want anything done to preclude their eventual participation: "We should always be in position to say we have kept door wide open to Russian participation and not give slightest basis for propaganda charge that US unilaterally precluded such participation."⁵² American records indicate a desire to maintain working relations with the Soviet Union. Canadian accounts were more pessimistic. They anticipated "an all-out attack" on the ITO by communist parties around the world alleging that it was an instrument of Wall Street and big business. The Canadians feared that such an attack would undermine support amongst those on the political left, such as in trade unions and socialist countries. They suggested revising some of the wording to dilute "the strong flavour of the philosophy of private capitalism and laissez-faire" and to make the case that the ITO was the means to combat "economic chauvinism" and create " 'one world', or to go as far in that direction as proves possible." In particular, they could show the compatibility of the trade liberali-

---

49 The Director of the Office of International Trade Policy (Wilcox) to the Secretary of State, Confidential Report.
50 Note of a meeting in High Commissioner's office.
51 American Ambassador in Soviet Union (Smith) to the Secretary of State, 23 Nov. 1946, FRUS 1946, Vol. 1, document 701. The American ambassador doubted these claims and believed the Soviet Union had no wish to join the ITO. Available at: https://history.state.gov/historicaldocuments/ebooks.
52 The Acting Secretary of State to the Ambassador in Soviet Union (Smith), 7 Nov. 1946, FRUS 1946, Vol. I, document 700.

zation approach of the ITO and "progressive methods of economic planning."[53] American officials shared Canadian concerns about the polarizing effect of the ITO. Echoing Winston Churchill's May 1946 warning of an iron curtain descending in Europe, Paul Nitze, the director of the Office of International Trade Policy, warned that if the ITO was exclusively associated with a liberal ideology, the result might be to "draw an economic line farther to the west than would otherwise be necessary."[54]

American officials were satisfied with the outcome of the Church House meeting. Over three quarters of their provisions were unchanged, an outcome they described as a "tremendous victory." Wilcox explained that accommodation rather than intransigence had allowed the US to retain control of the process and the substance of the trade proposals.[55] Moreover, in Nitze's opinion, the amendments had improved the trade charter, making it "better balanced and more complete" as well as "a truly international document to which all delegates at the conference have contributed" without detracting from "the essential principles of the American position."[56] Despite the changes there was still a strong sense of American authorship, as Clair Wilcox explained to Will Clayton, the Assistant Secretary of State for economic affairs.

> The United States has set the program. It has written the document. It has planned the organization. It has outlined the procedure. The rest of the world is now moving in step with us, in confidence that we are acting in good faith and that we shall do those things that we have urged them to do, and that we ourselves have promised to do.[57]

Other senior officials concluded that American leadership had unprecedented credibility but that it could only be sustained if the US is "prepared to practice what it preached."[58] This conclusion reveals much about how American officials

---

[53] International Trade Organization Project, Some General Observations on the U.S. Draft Charter, n.d., RG25/F-6/1035/8-H, LAC.

[54] The Director of the Office of International Trade Policy (Wilcox) to the Secretary of State, 27 Dec. 1946, FRUS 1946, Vol. 1, document 704. He added that the ITO could survive without the Soviet Union as a member, but the situation would be more difficult if the Soviet Union actively opposed the ITO.

[55] Wilcox to Clayton, 16 Nov. 1946, RG43, Box 111, National Archives Records Administration [NARA].

[56] Memorandum by the deputy director of the office of international trade policy (Nitze) to the undersecretary of state for economic affairs (Clayton), 5 Dec. 1946, Annex 2: Results of the London Conference, FRUS 1946, Vol. 1, document 703.

[57] Wilcox to Clayton, 26 Oct. 1946, RG43, Box 111, NARA.

[58] The Director of the Office of International Trade Policy (Nitze) to the Secretary of State, 27 Dec. 1946, FRUS 1946, Vol. 1, document 704.

perceived their own leadership rather than accurately conveys the views of other countries, many of which were wary of American economic domination. The American insights also reveal a particular understanding of multilateralism. Although Canadian officials described multilateralism as "a positive internationalist principle" which stemmed from a logic of benevolent interdependence,[59] and others viewed multilateralism as an inclusive process that resulted in decisions arrived at through give and take, in American eyes it also meant endorsement of their own ideas and policies. And yet, their belief in the universal relevance of liberal trade did not translate into rigid insistence on compliance, but rather was reconciled with a variety of practices and policies that would all ultimately lead to a liberal trade order.

Trade liberalization: The Geneva Conference and tariff negotiations, April-October 1947

The circle widened at the Geneva conference at which 23 states participated. Most of the time was dedicated to bilateral tariff negotiations (123 pairings in all) which would then be bundled together and extended to all participants through the application of the Most Favoured Nation rule. The effect would be to extend the reduction of tariffs far beyond the two countries negotiating a new tariff rate. Despite many public statements about the widespread benefits of lower tariffs, once negotiations began concessions were grudging and were contingent on adequate compensation. Negotiations between Britain and the United States were particularly acrimonious as American expectations that imperial preferences would be dismantled clashed with British insistence on retaining them for their economic and geopolitical advantages as well as their symbolic meaning. After months of frustrating negotiations, in which it was clear that Britain would make few concessions affecting imperial preferences, Will Clayton, leader of the US delegation in Geneva, returned to Washington and advised President Truman and Secretary of State Marshall to quit the conference.

But the onset of the Cold War changed the stakes at the Geneva conference. The participants were no longer establishing a trade order to uphold peace; they were affirming a global capitalist order that was essential to their survival. Truman and Marshall understood that the Anglo-American dispute encouraged exploitative interpretations of American leadership in the communist world. For example, Soviet accounts explained American insistence on concessions affecting

---

59 International Trade Organization Project.

imperial preference as a way to break up the economic links that connected Commonwealth members. While the Americans might write off such a view as propaganda, the British ambassador believed that the Soviet interpretation was largely accurate.[60] American officials were also well aware that the dispute with the UK would be seen as an example of American heavy-handedness, of "taking advantage of the one that was down and out."[61] Britain was a vital Cold War ally and so the negotiations in Geneva would have to succeed to communicate their common cause. The strength of allies and the cultivation of a western alliance offset American insistence on the elimination of imperial preferences, even though imperial preferences contradicted the basic tenets of a liberal and multilateral trade order and offended American democratic convictions.

The focus on tariff negotiations in Geneva left little time for discussion of the principles that defined the trade charter. Their work consisted mostly of clarification.[62] The charter would be the focus of the next major gathering in Havana with 56 participating nations. In the meantime, the chapter dealing with trade was hived off and packaged with the results of tariff negotiations as the General Agreement on Tariffs and Trade. The idea was for participating states to abide by its terms, in the expectation that it would shortly be superceded by the ITO. Starting in January 1948, eight participating states ratified the GATT.

Competing priorities: Liberalization, regional trade, and development at the Havana Conference, 1947–1948

Since the publication of the Proposals for Expansion of World Trade and Employment in 1945, the text had been revised through international discussions, taking into account the concerns and priorities of other states, including reconstruction, modernization, industrialization, full employment, protection and development. The focus, however, was still on trade liberalization, although it was repositioned as a long term goal to work toward rather that a policy to enforce right away. After several rounds of consultation, and many modifications as a

---

60 Tel 2089 from Moscow to Foreign Office, 17 Sept. 1947, FO371/62317, TNA.
61 McKenzie, *Redefining the Bonds of Commonwealth*, 216.
62 Irwin, Mavroidis, and Sykes, *Genesis*, 116.

result, many assumed that the work was near completion and that "the Charter needed little more than polishing."[63]

Instead of polishing, the charter was overhauled at Havana. Over 800 amendments were proposed and the final purpose and scope of the ITO charter was substantially revised. Developing nations constituted the majority at Havana and their representatives were quick to denounce the draft charter. For example, the representative of Mexico objected to the emphasis on the removal of barriers to trade that could wipe out the rudimentary core of industrialization that developing nations had built up; he insisted that the charter should have focused on global economic inequality and proposed positive measures by which to promote "the economic development of all nations and the international co-operation required to expedite it."[64]

Wilcox, a senior member of the American delegation, recalled that developing countries portrayed the ITO as "one-sided," serving the interests of the great industrial powers, and irrelevant to developing countries.[65] American officials took this criticism seriously because of its Cold War implications. The Soviet Union continued to portray the Trade and Employment proceedings as an attempt by the strongest powers to enrich themselves at the expense of poorer nations. An article in *TRUD*, the official publication of the Soviet Trade Unions, characterized American conduct at Havana as imperialist, with the aim of opening the world's markets to American monopolies, thereby establishing American global dominance by "enslav[ing] not only Europe, but the whole world."[66] Internal American reflections on the Cold War concluded that the ITO must succeed because the Soviet Union would make "heavy propaganda use of the Habana failure". Failure would also be a blow to American credibility and prestige, a "decisive set-back" to capitalism and liberalism, would unleash trade discrimination, and weaken the emerging Western alliance because the "non-Russian world . . . would be without a rudder in the international economic sea." The Americans concluded that a weak version of the ITO was better than nothing.

---

[63] Michael Hart, *Also Present at the Creation: Dana Wilgress and the United Nations Conference on Trade and Employment at Havana* (Ottawa: Centre for Trade Policy and Law, 1995), 44.
[64] Address by Ramón Betata, President, the Mexican Delegation, United Nations Conference on Trade and Employment, 26 Nov. 1947, ITO/32, http://gatt.stanford.edu/page/home, GATT Digital Library [GDL], (accessed 29 April 2015).
[65] Wilcox, 1949, cited in Irwin, Mavroidis and Sykes, *Genesis*, 95.
[66] "Blackmail at Havana," translation, *TRUD*, 28 Dec. 1947 in RG43: Records of International Conferences, Commissions and Expositions, subject file 1947–48, Habana Conference – General to Interim Commission – ITO Post Habana, NARA.

Moreover, they continued to see the ITO, even with its many modifications as "the very embodiment of economic liberalism in the international realm."[67]

Situating the ITO in a polarized, zero-sum geopolitical framework made it easy for American officials to agree to substantial revisions to the trade charter, although a spirit of accommodation had been evident throughout the negotiations. The most significant change was to elevate development as the main objective of the postwar trade system. The Havana charter defined development as "the productive use of the world's human and material resources," with an eye to promoting "industrial and general economic development of all countries." Development was at the nexus of interlocking economic goals including full employment, productivity of labour, rising demand, economic stability, higher income levels, and expanding international trade.[68]

But development was not the only element that was reopened. Western European representatives also proposed revisions to the charter to permit regional economic organization and cooperation. By the time the Havana conference began in late 1947, their governments were working on reconstruction and, in part with the Marshall Plan in mind, economic organization along regional lines was at the forefront of their plans for recovery. This spilled over into the Havana conference in relation to the creation of customs unions. Jean Royer, a French delegate, made a case that European "economic integration" should be viewed as a positive contribution to the goals of the ITO.[69] Even though the US had rejected a regional approach to trade during the war, in a Cold War context they came to see European integration as a way to resist communist advances.[70] The Cold War imparted a new meaning to trade liberalization, emphasizing security rather than peace and stability. The main effect on the ITO charter was to permit customs unions and free trade areas (Article 42). The article included some criteria to ensure that such agreements would genuinely benefit the expansion of world trade and stipulated that the organization would have oversight authority "to avoid abuse and to guarantee that such arrangements do not deteriorate into new discriminatory preferential regimes."[71]

Although some American officials feared that accommodation would weaken the ITO, they professed to be satisfied with the extensive revisions made to the

---

[67] Memo, Brown and Coppock to Wilcox, 30 Dec. 1947, Papers of Clayton-Thorp, TL.
[68] Article 8, UN Conference on Trade and Employment, Final Act and Related Documents, 1948.
[69] Third Committee: Commercial Policy. Summary Record of the Forty-Fourth Meeting, Havana, Cuba, 11 March 1948, E/Conf.2/C.3/SR.44, 13 March 1948, GDL.
[70] Grosbois, "La Belgique et le Benelux," 71.
[71] Report of the Canadian Delegation to the UN Conference on Trade and Employment at Havana, in Hart, *Also Present at the Creation*, 118.

charter. Will Clayton, leader of the US delegation, praised the results of their deliberations. He believed that the Havana charter would still establish a liberal, multilateral, and prosperous global trade order. "This may well prove to be the greatest step in history toward order and justice in economic relations among the members of the world community and toward a great expansion in the production, distribution and consumption of goods throughout the world."[72]

The speeches of Western European officials also praised the revised charter which now allowed regional economic organization. They insisted that this change was consistent with the trade creating and liberalizing mandate of the ITO. As Speekenbring of the Netherlands put it, regional economic units would make a "very valuable contribution to the expansion of world trade."[73] French officials had been particularly conscious of American authorship of earlier drafts which predisposed them to doubt that such an initiative could also serve French interests effectively. Grousset of France described the previous iteration as an American draft, whereas the "profoundly modified" ITO charter was more genuinely representative and inclusive. In a salve to American sensitivity, he added that these changes had left the "original idea of the draft Charter . . . intact."[74]

Interestingly, the representatives of states which had successfully pressed for development to be made a priority professed the greatest disappointment with the Havana charter. Chilean and Colombian officials lamented the premise that nations at different stages of economic development should nonetheless behave according to the same standards and expectations.[75] One size did not fit all, but the one size approach had largely prevailed. Many developing countries also believed that economically advanced states bore a special responsibility to encourage economic development. As the Chilean official put it, there was a "need for the economically stronger countries to co-operate altruistically in the work of speedily improving the standards of living of the weak countries."[76] This post-colonial view made justice the driving force behind trade policy as op-

---

[72] Statement by Clayton, Chairman, Delegation of the United States of America, 23 March 1948, ITO/194, GDL (accessed 14 July 2012).
[73] Speech by Mr. A. B. Speekenbring, President of the Netherlands Delegation before Final Plenary Session, ITO/210, GDL. (accessed 28 January 2017).
[74] Speech delivered by Mr. P. Grousset, Minister of France, Head of the French Delegation, at the Final Plenary Session, 22 March 1948, ITO/211, GDL (accessed 29 January 2017).
[75] Statement by Muller, President of the Delegation of Chile, 21 March 1948, ITO/188, GDL; Speech at the 17th Plenary Meeting on Behalf of the Delegation of Colombia by H.E. Dr. Fulgencio Lequerica Veles, Minister of Colombia, 20 March 1948, ITO/187, GDL (accessed 17 March 2012).
[76] Statement by Muller, 21 March 1948.

posed to efficiency, competition, and comparative advantage that had informed British and American conceptions of the postwar trade order. Nugget Coombs, the Australian representative who had been one of the first to point out the need for positive measures to support development, praised the charter for balancing two competing ideas of economic freedom: one revolved around the removal of barriers to trade, the other focused on opportunities. As he explained:

> To many of us, mere absence of restraint, while an important element in freedom, is, taken by itself, a negative and empty thing. . . . [I]f economic freedom is to be a real and living thing, it must mean economic opportunity. . . . [P]ositive opportunity does not automatically come to the under-developed, the under-privileged, the unemployed, and to the poverty-stricken.[77]

Despite Clayton's confidence that the Havana charter would be implemented, in the end the United States government did not ratify the ITO. The Havana charter was submitted to Congress in 1949, but did not move toward ratification. Although people expected it would be reintroduced in 1950, it was not. Thomas Zeiler has explained the American failure to ratify the ITO as a result of the Cold War which recast compromises such that managed trade became "a threat to the foundations of capitalism".[78] Richard Toye similarly argues that the many compromises turned off potential backers, a situation made more serious when some of the key officials involved in negotiating the ITO resigned.[79] Restricting state authority with respect to trade policy was also a factor as many American politicians clamoured for unfettered sovereignty to combat Cold War threats.

That left the GATT – a series of bilateral trade agreements to lower tariffs bundled with the commercial policy chapter of the ITO charter – to oversee the expansion and regulation of global trade for the next 50 years. The General Agreement was the result of Anglo-American collaboration with some wider consultation in 1946 and 1947. Some modifications had been made to take into account the priorities of other participants, but the GATT's focus was to promote trade liberalization by lowering tariffs. It belonged to an earlier and more exclusive stage of planning and throughout its history its claims to universalism would be challenged by those who described it as a rich man's club and an Anglo-American sphere of influence. As a result, GATT members restored development as a fundamental goal and permitted regional customs unions. But frus-

---

[77] Speech by Coombs, Head of the Australian Delegation Before Final Plenary Session, 22 March 1948, ITO/212, GDL (accessed 18 March 2012).
[78] Zeiler, *Free Trade, Free World*, 150.
[79] Richard Toye, "Developing Multilateralism: the Havana Charter and the Fight for the International Trade Organisation, 1947–1948", *The International History Review*, 25, no. 2 (2003): 303.

trations linked to development and the oversight of regional trade blocs meant these members turned to alternatives, including UNCTAD and the EEC, both of which were seen as threats to the GATT.[80] The perceived shortcomings of the GATT however did not discredit the planning approach, particularly in relation to development as Michel Christian's chapter shows. In UNCTAD, officials believed that planning was needed to establish the New International Economic Order. However, like the planners behind the ITO, their objectives were not fulfilled. Their failure can partly be explained by the limited ability of planners to change the dynamics and norms of international relations.

Conclusions

The global trade system began as a plan, first drafted by James Meade, revised in collaboration with the United States, and further modified through ever wider international negotiations that allowed countries at different stages of economic development and with different national economic priorities to put their mark on it. Even with the failure of the ITO, the GATT had also been revised to take into account the priorities and preferences of other states, such that it included provisions that promoted industrial development and permitted regional trade. Planning postwar trade never required doctrinaire adherence to liberal trade ideas. There was acceptance that the global trade order involved departures from key tenets of liberal economic theory, in particular about the role of governments and international authority to enforce rules and obligations. In addition, liberal trade could not be implemented if it caused domestic economic hardship.[81] Rather, a liberal trade order was widely seen as the best long term option for all peoples and countries, but countries would move toward that goal at different speeds and by a variety of routes that did not sabotage domestic postwar plans linked to modernization, reconstruction, employment, and social welfare.

---

80 I discuss these challenges to the GATT elsewhere. See Francine McKenzie, "Free Trade and Freedom to Trade: The Development Challenge to GATT" in, *International Organizations and Development, 1945–1990*, ed. Marc Frey, Sönke Konkel, and Corinna R. Unger (Basingstoke: Palgrave Macmillan, 2014),150–170 and Francine McKenzie, "The GATT-EEC Collision: The Challenge of Regional Trade Blocs to the General Agreement on Tariffs and Trade, 1950–1967", *The International History Review*, 32, no. 2 (2010): 229–252.
81 See John G. Ruggie, "International regimes, transactions, and change: embedded liberalism in the postwar economic order", in *International Regimes*, ed. S. Krasner (Ithaca: Cornell University Press, 1983), 195–232.

The plans and negotiations that led to the GATT/ITO were also never only about economic principles and ideas. In individual plans, as well as in international negotiations, political priorities were attached to trade, especially political interests linked to power, sovereignty, and influence. For example, the British wanted to preserve imperial preference as a way of maintaining a tie with other members of the Empire and Commonwealth, an association that many believed was essential to keeping Britain in the top tier of states after the war. Western European governments pushed for regional trade arrangements which they saw as a way to address causes of conflict, recover from the devastation of war, and resume their standing as an international leader. American ideas about trade were originally conceived as a way to make the community of states more democratic, but as the Cold War emerged, the liberal trade order became a way to defend capitalism and democracy. Many years later, Michael Smith, deputy United States Trade Representative, likened the GATT and the Marshall Plan to "an arrow in the Western world's quiver."[82] Finally, poorer countries made the case for development because it would also enhance their standing, independence and influence in world affairs. Political aims stuck to trade plans and policies. Focusing only on the soundness of various ideas and theories about trade does not fully explain the commitment to particular trade priorities and practices.

Some readers might be surprised that this account of the ITO is not an American story, or even an Anglo-American story. Although many authors claim that the GATT was an American creation and that it was sustained by American hegemony, the postwar trade order was planned and negotiated through a multilateral process. The General Agreement of 1947 more strongly reflected Anglo-American ideas and interests than the ITO, but it too had been revised to broaden its relevance and legitimacy. Planning facilitated multilateral cooperation and American participation in the planning process demonstrated that it valued compromises and consensus, so long as it could still recognize its ideas and interests in the final product. Although the US is often portrayed as a hegemon and leader, it is important to recognize its commitment to multilateralism.[83]

The association of the ITO with planning and multilateralism contributed to its demise as it revealed that the organization was not made only in America's likeness, nor was it an exclusive instrument for American global interests. Even though less was heard about planning global trade after the war, many national and international civil servants and experts continued to have confidence

---

[82] Alfred E. Eckes, *Revisiting U.S. Trade Policy: Decisions in Perspective* (Athens: Ohio University Press, 2000), 22.
[83] Toye makes a similar point. See "Developing Multilateralism," 284.

in planning as a way to realize ambitious and often transformative objectives, as the other chapters in this volume reveal. Planning did not always work as expected. Indeed, there have been many cases of planning backfiring, creating new problems. But it was still widely viewed as a way to tackle complex global economic and social challenges, particularly in relation to development. Planning therefore persisted as a method to bring about what were seen as desirable changes even though many different ideas and ideologies shaped international plans. Perhaps what made planning so durable was its post-ideological potential, as Stinsky has suggested. Even though the ITO failed, the GATT showed over its 50 year existence that it was possible to reconcile seemingly incompatible views about state-directed and free market economic systems.

Daniel Stinsky
A Bridge between East and West? Gunnar Myrdal and the UN Economic Commission for Europe, 1947–1957

This chapter explores the impact of an archetypical social planner, the Nobel prize-winning Swedish economist Gunnar Myrdal, on both the national and international level. As a public intellectual and politician, Myrdal shaped the "Swedish Model" of an interventionist, full-employment welfare state. In 1947, Myrdal became Executive Secretary of the newly founded UN Economic Commission for Europe (ECE). During his formative tenure between 1947 and 1957, Myrdal shaped the Secretariat and the policy outlook of this international organization (IO). ECE started as the first permanent IO dedicated specifically to economic cooperation in Europe, and as a potential gateway to the integration of European economies, but the advent of the East-West conflict frustrated its pan-European ambitions. As a UN organization, ECE included both the United States and the USSR, together with their respective European allies, and neutral countries. The Commission, formally ECE's central decision-making organ, became paralyzed by international tension. Nonetheless, ECE remained a space where East and West continued to meet on economic issues. "ECE gained support from the European reaction against . . . the cold war which gave it an importance above and beyond its practical achievements" a British scholar wrote in 1957; "it seemed to be one of the few remaining bridges between east and west."[1]

Myrdal used the allegory of ECE being a "bridge between East and West" frequently. He was convinced that such a bridge "must be built, even if no-one crosses it for the time being."[2] How did ECE seek to reestablish East-West cooperation, and in how far did it succeed? Was it possible for Myrdal to transfer his ideas about planning and international economic cooperation from the Swedish context to ECE? In this chapter, I argue that ECE's insistence on saving East-West cooperation was crucially linked to its Executive Secretary, and Myrdal's previous experience in Sweden. The obstinacy on the Secretariat's part was a risky course, but it achieved its goal of maintaining a bridge that could be crossed

---

[1] David Wightman, "East-West Cooperation and the United Nations Economic Commission for Europe," *International Organization* 11, no. 1 (1957): 2.
[2] Quoted in Anika de la Grandville to Václav Kostelecký, 28 April 1980. Arbetarrörelsens arkiv och bibliotek (ARBARK), Václav Kosteleckýs arkiv, 3332/4/3/5 Övriga handlingar rörande ECE.

in the future. Myrdal and ECE did not break the Cold War deadlock; but the organization managed to survive the height of the tensions during the Korean War, and stood ready for increased cooperation immediately after the death of Stalin.

The key area in which Myrdal and the ECE Secretariat sought to facilitate East-West cooperation was trade. As Swedish minister of commerce 1945–47, Myrdal concluded a series of bilateral trade agreements with countries in East and West. At ECE, Myrdal sought to revive all-European trade in a multilateral environment, but this agenda had little success initially.[3] ECE survived its first years due to its entrenchment in various other intergovernmental functions, e. g. coal allocation, the secretariat's scientific work, and inland transport. Its efforts to facilitate trade were frustrated by economic bloc formation on both sides of the descending Iron Curtain. Nonetheless, the Secretariat's continued exertion to revive trade connections provides a strong example of an international bureaucracy acting as an independent policy agent. The ECE Secretariat "regularly went against the grain of the consensus of the regional blocks and more powerful states," as Vincent Lagendijk has argued.[4] Myrdal "was instrumental in shaping the set of cultural values of the organization": he established ECE as a practical economic research institute and a meeting place for East and West, ostensibly disinterested in political quarrels, with the Secretariat maintaining considerable sway over the agenda and process at ECE.[5] Due to its focus on technical cooperation, ECE embodied, as Wolfram Kaiser and Johan Schot put it, "the technocratic internationalist approach during the Cold War."[6]

The technocratic internationalism characterizing the ECE Secretariat shared several features with the benevolent, post-political social planners Myrdal imagined as the driving force in modernizing Swedish society in the 1930s. Myrdal's career, oscillating between academia, national politics and international bureaucracy, raises questions about the role of social science in administration. The Swedish experience is linked to ECE by the "promises of economic expertise" Daniel Speich-Chassé has emphasized. After 1945, economists gained a new importance in the shaping of political processes. Economics transformed from "just one of several 'arm-chair' sciences within the family of the social sci-

---

[3] On other institutional contexts for trade policy in postwar Europe, see Francine McKenzie's contribution in this volume.
[4] Vincent Lagendijk, "The Structure of Power: The UNECE and East-West Electricity Connections, 1947–1975," Comparativ 24, no. 1 (2014): 55.
[5] Ibid.
[6] Wolfram Kaiser and Johan Schot, *Writing the Rules for Europe. Experts, Cartels and International Organisations* (Basingstoke / New York: Palgrave Macmillan, 2014), 77.

ences" to "a crucial source in global political discourse, second only to legal practice and international law."⁷ Swedish economists during the interwar period were pioneers in this transnational development. Myrdal's assistant at ECE, Melvin Fagen, wrote retrospectively that "the emphasis given by Myrdal to economic analyzes of high professional quality reflected essentially his views as a social scientist on the importance of research as a basis for action."⁸ Myrdal's ambition as a scholar was "to understand society as a dynamic entity, conceived to operate like a machine, an image in the techno-spirit of Enlightenment reason and rationalism," as Sven Eliæson puts it.⁹ If society could be understood as a machine, it could not only be analyzed, but also optimized. The relationship between society and the social scientist Myrdal conceived of was thus similar to that between the engine and the engineer: Social scientists were not only in the business of understanding society, but also in the business of maintaining and improving it.¹⁰ This technocratic ideal, with its radical implications, had a considerable impact in Sweden, but economic and social planning in one country had its limitations. "We have constructed the 'Swedish model' as if we lacked history and as if we were alone in the world," Myrdal wrote in a rare moment of self-reproach.¹¹

Planning on a national scale required international coordination. While Myrdal and his wife Alva developed their ideal of social science as a driving force for rational change in the national context, they transferred it to the international level from the 1940s onwards. The Myrdals are the only married couple to receive Nobel Prizes in different fields. As a diplomat and UN official herself, Alva Myrdal was awarded the Nobel Peace Prize. Their biographer Thomas Etzemüller writes that the Myrdals became national icons, portrayed in Swedish media as the "most popular Swedes, downright charged by the UN with the task of saving the world."¹² When measured against such expectations, Gunnar Myrdal's suc-

---

7 Daniel Speich Chassé, "Towards a Global History of the Marshall Plan. European Post-War Reconstruction and the Rise of Development Economic Expertise," in *Industrial Policy in Europe after 1945. Wealth, Power and Economic Development in the Cold War*, ed. Christian Grabas and Alexander Nützenadel (New York: Palgrave Macmillan, 2014), 189.
8 Melvin M. Fagen, "Gunnar Myrdal and the Shaping of the United Nations Economic Commission for Europe," *Coexistence* 25 (1988): 427–435.
9 Sven Eliæson, "Gunnar Myrdal: A Theorist of Modernity," *Acta Sociologica* 43, no. 4 (2000): 331–341.
10 Thomas Etzemüller, ed. *Die Ordnung Der Moderne: Social Engineering Im 20. Jahrhundert* (Bielefeld: transcript, 2009).
11 Quoted in Eliæson, "Gunnar Myrdal: A Theorist of Modernity," 339.
12 Thomas Etzemüller, *Die Romantik der Rationalität. Alva & Gunnar Myrdal. Social Engineering in Schweden* (Bielefeld: transcript, 2010), 43.

cess at ECE was limited at best. But what the ECE Secretariat's persistence to facilitate East-West cooperation against the odds (and the superpowers' resistance) does showcase instead is the ability of IOs to maintain an independent policy agenda, and to adapt to external circumstances, allowing them to carve out niches to justify their continued existence.

The chapter proceeds in two steps. The first section sketches in broad strokes Myrdal's engagement as a public intellectual and politician in Sweden during the 1930s and 40s. It explores Myrdal's views on post-political social planning and his influence on the Swedish Labor Party SAP. I argue that Myrdal's contacts in the US and with continental social democrats in exile during World War Two shaped his opinion on pan-European economic cooperation, and informed his actions as minister of commerce. In the second section, I explore the international coordination of reconstruction plans at ECE and trail the Secretariat's efforts to facilitate East-West cooperation, especially on trade. I argue that while Myrdal's dedication to revive East-West trade risked the goodwill of Western governments, particularly in the US, his efforts were ultimately successful in establishing a space for limited cooperation on the technical level.

Myrdal as a public intellectual

Myrdal's experience as a public intellectual and politician in Sweden during the 1930s and 40s deeply influenced the strategic goals he set for ECE during his formative tenure as Executive Secretary. ECE's self-declared aim of providing a bridge between East and West was rooted in Myrdal's inclusive trade policy toward the USSR as minister of commerce 1945–1947, and his wartime involvement with continental social democrats in exile. Myrdal's theoretical and practical participation in social and economic planning goes back even further, and is deeply entangled with the development of the Swedish welfare state. Myrdal is regularly credited as a key architect of the "Swedish Model."[13] He has even been called a "Swedish Roosevelt," and although this characterization overstates his influence, it hints at Myrdal's involvement in Sweden's political, social, and economic reconfiguration during the 1930s.[14]

Planning and proto-Keynesian macroeconomic policies were central to Sweden's coping with unemployment and economic crisis. Sweden's progressive

---

[13] Ibid.; William Barber, *Gunnar Myrdal: An Intellectual Biography*, Great Thinkers in Economics (Basingstoke: Pelgrave Macmillan, 2008).
[14] Örjan Appelqvist, "Gunnar Myrdal i svensk politik 1943–1947: En svensk Roosevelt och hans vantolkade nederlag," *NORDEUROPAforum* 9, no. 1 (1999): 33–55.

leadership used deficit spending to provide emergency relief, but also to create jobs on public works projects and to enhance popular social security. Experts and planners, especially social scientists, were key actors in the discourses and politics of mid-century Sweden.[15] One British scholar was impressed with the "great respect" being "paid to the professional economist," and found it curious that although Swedish economists "often take part in the hurly-burly of politics, the authority attaching to their pronouncements is not thereby weakened."[16] Preexisting institutions cemented the strong standing the comparatively young social sciences enjoyed. Swedish society changed fundamentally in the early twentieth century, from an agrarian, bureaucratic monarchy into an industrial, parliamentary democracy. Despite the introduction of universal suffrage and a parliamentary government, public policy-making did not devolve into parliamentary bargaining. Instead, leaders of political parties and interest groups were absorbed into modernized versions of Sweden's deeply rooted system of state-centered, consultative policy-making. Investigatory commissions and parliamentary committees, once tools of the monarchical bureaucracy, carried on in the new democratic polity. Such bodies mobilized the expertise of the modern social sciences through the direct participation of researchers in their investigations.[17]

Particularly influential on both the political and the theoretical level was the *arbetslöshetsutredning*, a committee of inquiry on unemployment appointed in 1926.[18] Myrdal joined in 1931, after returning from a visiting professorship in Geneva. The later UN Secretary-General Dag Hammarskjöld, then a graduate student in his mid-20s, was the committee's secretary.[19] Two other members of the committee would later occupy important positions at ECE: Karin Kock became Swedish head delegate and long-serving chairwoman of the Commission, and Ingvar Svennilson was the author of a major study on European recovery for the ECE

---

15 Margaret Weit and Theda Skocpol, "The State Structures and the Possibilities for 'Keynesian' Responses to the Great Depression in Sweden, Britain, and the United States," in *Bringing the State Back In*, ed. Peter B. Evans, Dietrich Rueschemeyer, and Theda Skocpol (Cambridge: Cambridge University Press, 1985), 107–108.
16 Brinley Thomas, *Monetary Policy and Crises: A Study of Swedish Experience* (London: Routledge, 1936), xviii.
17 Weit and Skocpol, "The State Structures and the Possibilities for 'Keynesian' Responses to the Great Depression in Sweden, Britain, and the United States," 130.
18 Eskil Wadensjö, "The Committee on Unemployment and the Stockholm School," in *The Stockholm School of Economics Revisited*, ed. Lars Jonung (Cambridge, MA: Cambridge University Press, 1991).
19 Örjan Appelqvist, "Civil Servant or Politician? Dag Hammarskjöld's Role in Swedish Government Policy in the Forties," *Sveriges Riksbank Economic Review*, no. 3 (2005): 83.

Research Division.[20] Following the election of an SAP government in 1932, countercyclical spending as suggested by the *arbetslöshetsutredning* became government policy, and helped to mitigate the effects of the global economic crisis in Sweden. Besides its political impact, the committee was the intellectual nucleus for a Swedish brand of proto-Keynesian economics labeled the "Stockholm School." Reacting to the publication of Keynes' *General Theory* in 1936, Bertil Ohlin argued that the Swedish unemployment committee had published similar ideas already four years earlier.[21] The policy recommendations issued by the committee and their theoretical work were indeed a form of Keynesianism *avant la lettre*. Myrdal's was the most radical voice in propagating countercyclical, debt-financed spending to achieve full employment. Ohlin and Hammarskjöld favored a less interventionist approach of "framework planning" through monetary instruments and infrastructure investments.[22] It is, however, hardly convincing to call the committee members a "school," since their collaboration remained temporary and did not constitute a coherent economic theory.[23]

For Myrdal, the 1930s were a time of rapid career advances. For the academic year 1929/30, he and Alva had received Rockefeller Foundation grants that brought them to the United States, just in time to witness the 1929 stock market crash and the unfolding Great Depression first hand. After this experience, Alva and Gunnar Myrdal came to see "politics, interference in society as a purpose in life."[24] In 1933, Gunnar became a full professor in Stockholm and a member of the Swedish parliament's Upper House. The Rockefeller Foundation noted with content in its files that Myrdal was "rapidly becoming the driving force in intellectual circles in Stockholm," and that the Foundation had "placed its money on a winning horse."[25]

While Myrdal's political aspirations stalled after being sidelined in parliament, he continued to pursue an intellectual agenda of radical societal change, executed by experts and planners. In the progressive magazine *Spektrum*, Myrdal

---

[20] Ingvar Svennilson, *Growth and Stagnation in the European Economy* (Geneva: United Nations, 1954).
[21] Bertil Ohlin, "Some Notes on the Stockholm Theory of Savings and Investment," *Economic Journal* 47(1937).
[22] Assar Lindbeck, "Dag Hammarskjöld as Economist and Government Official," *Sveriges Riksbank Economic Review*, no. 3 (2005): 9–10.
[23] Etzemüller, *Die Romantik der Rationalität. Alva & Gunnar Myrdal. Social Engineering in Schweden*, 60.
[24] James Angresano, *The Political Economy of Gunnar Myrdal: An Institutional Basis for the Transformation Problem* (Cheltenham, UK and Lyme, NH: Edward Elgar, 1997), 46.
[25] Rockefeller Foundation Records, Projects, RG 1.1 (FA386). Series 800: Sweden; Subseries 800.S: Sweden – Social Sciences. Folder: Myrdal, Karl Gunnar, 1932–35, Box 10, Folder 101.

outlined an ambitious social policy program.²⁶ He built his argument on an assumed consensus on equality and rising prosperity as the key social values in the industrialized world: "We have come to accept certain moral standards . . . '[T]echnically' everyone has the right to live equally well. . . . Is the egalitarianism of enlightenment philosophy beginning to penetrate all our assumptions?"²⁷ By basing his argument on an assumed consensus on enlightenment values, Myrdal created a quasi-democratic legitimation for his proposals. Based on this assumed *volonté générale*, social policy needed to be problem-oriented, not embedded in political doctrine. Myrdal proclaimed that a new "social policy ideology" would leave the hitherto dominant ideologies of bourgeois Liberalism and revolutionary Marxism behind. This post-ideological ideology sought to achieve radical change through the means of cool, technical reasoning:

> This new social policy ideology carries radical and in some ways revolutionary possibilities. It is intellectual, cool, and rational, while the old, still ruling ideologies were decisively sentimental. [The new ideology] is free from liberal roadblocks to innovation. It is far too technical, on the other hand, to get lost in overly general and quixotic ideal constructions. . . . Its romanticism is the engineer's.²⁸

Myrdal considered shifting power to experts and planners – social engineers – to be the strategic solution to all kinds of problems.²⁹ He thus postulated a rational, scientific approach to social questions as a basis for political power. The social sciences were particularly well positioned to facilitate social change. With *Kris i befolkningsfrågan* [Crisis in the population question, 1934], Alva and Gunnar Myrdal published a bestselling book that developed this technocratic ideal further.³⁰ Based on an analysis of population trends in Sweden, the Myrdals predicted a deep social and economic crisis that served them as legitimization for far-reaching reforms. To combat falling birthrates, the Myrdals suggested a radical re-distribution of capital to improve living standards. Childcare, wages, dwellings, education, physical and mental health care – all of this had to be improved, rationalized, and made accessible to everyone. *Kris i befolkningsfrågan* picked up

---

26 Gunnar Myrdal, "Socialpolitikens dilemma," *Spektrum* 3 (1932); Johan Svedjedal, *Spektrum 1931–1935: Den svenska drömmen. Tidskrift och förlag i 1930-talets kultur* (Stockholm: Wahlström & Widstrand, 2011).
27 Quoted in Göran B. Nilsson, "Den sociala ingenjörskonstens problematik. En orättfärdigt dissektion av den unge Gunnar Myrdal " in *Den svenska modellen*, ed. Per Thullberg and Kjell Östberg (Lund: Studentlitteratur, 1998), 167.
28 Quoted in ibid.
29 Etzemüller, *Die Ordnung der Moderne: Social Engineering Im 20. Jahrhundert.*
30 Alva Myrdal and Gunnar Myrdal, *Kris i befolkningsfrågan* (Stockholm: Bonniers, 1934).

on several debates of the 1930s; next to progressive ideas like public nursery schools and improved working conditions for women, the Myrdals discussed race biology and eugenics as potential solutions to the perceived population crisis. While they dismissed race biology as unscientific, they considered forced sterilization of disabled people a viable option. The book was a major influence on the SAP around party leader Per Albin Hansson. Still in 1981, Myrdal said that "the welfare program we laid out . . . was fully in line with Per Albin's dream of the good People's Home".[31]

Myrdal did not limit his claim that social engineering should constitute the driving force for social change to Sweden. In 1938, he returned to the United States, to head a large-scale research project on race relations and democracy for the Carnegie Corporation of New York. The concluding book, *An American Dilemma: The Negro Problem and Modern Democracy* (1944) combined a detailed sociological analysis with a clear-cut political message: If America could overcome racial segregation and fulfill its own democratic promise at home, it would rightfully assume world leadership in a postwar democratic order. The book's closing words predicted a crucial role for social science and social engineering:

> [S]ocial engineering will increasingly be demanded. . . . We are entering an era where fact-finding and scientific theories of causal relations will be seen as instrumental in planning controlled social change. The American social scientist, because of the New Deal and the War, is already acquiring familiarity with planning and practical action. . . . [T]his never-ending reconstruction of society is the supreme task of social science. . . . [W]e have today in social science a greater trust in the improvability of man and society than we have ever had since the Enlightenment.[32]

An American Dilemma became a sociological classic, with a lasting impact on the American Civil Rights Movement in the 1950s and 60s.[33] It established Myrdal's international reputation as a researcher, and it also laid the groundwork for his subsequent political career. During his time in America, Myrdal met Polish economist and fellow Rockefeller stipendiary Oskar Lange, who was then at the University of Chicago. At the Yalta Conference, Lange served as a go-between for

---

31 Ola Sigurdson, *Den lyckliga filofosin: Etik och politik hos Hägerström, Tingsten, makarna Myrdal och Hedenius* (Stockholm: Brutus Östlings bokförlag 2000), 126.
32 Gunnar Myrdal, Richard Sterner, and Arnold Marshall Rose, *An American Dilemma: The Negro Problem and Modern Democracy* (New York; London: Harper and brothers publ., 1944), 1022–1024.
33 Maribel Morey, "A Reconsideration of an American Dilemma," *Reviews in American History* 40, no. 4 (2012): 686–692.

Roosevelt and Stalin, and later became the Polish communist regime's first ambassador to Washington, DC. As such, Lange had a crucial role in the formation of ECE, and as Polish diplomat would sometimes participate in ECE Commission sessions.

Back in wartime Stockholm, Gunnar and Alva Myrdal participated in the meetings of the *Internationale Gruppe Demokratischer Sozialisten* [International Group of Democratic Socialists], a remarkable gathering of social democrats in exile from Germany and German-occupied territories. Unlike other social democrat groupings that were at the forefront of anti-communism, the *Internationale Gruppe* advocated continental social democracy as a mediator between Western liberal democracy and Soviet communism.[34] Among the 14 nationalities represented in the group were many Scandinavians and Germans, but also Czechoslovaks, Poles, and Hungarians. The group was dissolved at the end of the war, and its participants maintained only loose contact. Many had remarkable careers in IOs and national governments. Wladek Malinowski, a Polish economist, came to Stockholm as a refugee with the help of a Swedish committee including the Myrdals. Malinowski later joined the UN secretariat in New York and became chief of the Regional Commissions Section, the body coordinating ECE and the other regional commissions at UNHQ.[35] David Owen, the later UN Assistant Secretary-General for Economic Affairs, was a liaison officer for the British Royal Air Force in Sweden and participated in some of the group's meetings.[36] Owen would later propose Myrdal for the post of Executive Secretary at ECE to UN Secretary-General Trygve Lie, a Norwegian social democrat who knew Myrdal through his own contacts in the group. Other regular participants included later chancellors of West Germany and Austria, Willy Brandt and Bruno Kreisky.[37] While the group remained a loose association of World War Two exiles rather than a network centered around a set of core political beliefs, its deliberations on reconciliation between the West and the USSR would echo in Myrdal's East-West trade policy at ECE as well as in Brandt's *Ostpolitik*.

---

34 On factional struggles within social democracy, see Scott H. Krause, "Neue Westpolitik: The Clandestine Campaign to Westernize the SPD in Cold War Berlin, 1948–1958," *Central European History* 48 (2015).
35 See footnote 20 in Václav Kostelecký, *The United Nations Economic Commission for Europe: The Beginning of a History* (Gothenburg: Graphic Systems, 1989), 45.
36 Örjan Appelqvist, "Rediscovering Uncertainty: Early Attempts at a Pan-European Post-War Recovery," *Cold War History* 8, no. 3 (2008): 341.
37 Scott H. Krause and Daniel Stinsky, "For Europe, Democracy and Peace: Social Democratic Blueprints for Postwar Europe in Willy Brandt and Gunnar Myrdal's Correspondence," *Themenportal Europäische Geschichte* (2015), www.europa.clio-online.de/essay/id/artikel-3799; Klaus Misgeld, "Politik för Österrike. Bruno Kreisky och Sverige," *Arbetarhistoria* 125, no. 1 (2008).

On May 1, 1943, the group published a manifesto called the *Peace Goals of the International Group of Democratic Socialists*. Brandt, Kreisky, and Myrdal were among its principal authors.[38] The manifesto proposed a system of organized international cooperation in the economic and social area, to replace conflicts between nation states and the anarchy of capitalist economies. At the center of the group's ideas was a loosely federal European system, embedded in the global organization of a new League of Nations. The manifesto's authors emphasized that regional cooperation should never be directed against certain other countries, especially the USSR. Instead, they wanted to positively engage others through economic cooperation. Continental Europe should act as an arbitrator between the Anglo-American democracies and the USSR. An alliance of neutral countries in Europe's center, including a de-nazified Germany and stretching from Scandinavia to Italy, should counterbalance the great powers.[39] While no party or government adopted the *Peace Goals*, the work on the manifesto influenced the later political practice of its authors. Myrdal himself provides the best example.

Already in the fall of 1943, Myrdal returned to the US, to negotiate about reestablishing trade contacts on behalf of the Swedish government. Neutral Sweden profited from exporting iron ore, pulp, and machinery to Nazi Germany, but relations to the Allied countries suffered. Myrdal's good reputation and contacts after *An American Dilemma* made him the ideal candidate to try and fix commercial relations with America. After three months, however, Myrdal did not return with a trade agreement, but with a new political manifesto. In *Varning för fredsoptimismen* [Warning of peace optimism], he warned that the alliance between the US, UK, and the Soviet Union would break very soon after the war.[40] As Republicans gained momentum in Congress, the book predicted that America would return to isolationism. A new economic crisis comparable to or worse than the Great Depression would follow. Myrdal doubted, therefore, that America could simply replace Germany as Sweden's most important trading partner. Echoing the *Peace Goals*, Myrdal argued instead that in an upcoming conflict between the Western democracies and the USSR, Sweden must pursue active, "in-

---

38 *Die "Internationale Gruppe Demokratischer Sozialisten" in Stockholm, 1942–1945: Zur sozialistischen Friedensdiskussion während des Zweiten Weltkrieges* (Uppsala: Almquist & Wicksell, 1976).
39 Gunnar Myrdal to Václav Kostelecký, cited in Örjan Appelqvist, "Gunnar Myrdal i svensk politik 1943–1947: En svensk Roosevelt och hans vantolkade nederlag," *NORDEUROPAforum* 9, no. 1 (1999). n.p.
40 Gunnar Myrdal, *Varning för fredsoptimismen* (Stockholm: Bonnier, 1944).

ternationalist neutrality," and engage in trade with both sides.⁴¹ While the predicted crisis in America never came, Myrdal stayed true to the ideal of reconciliation, both as a government minister and at ECE.

In the SAP government formed in 1945, Myrdal became minister of commerce, succeeding the Liberal Party leader and fellow "Stockholm School" economist Ohlin. The *Internationale Gruppe*'s deliberations about positively engaging the USSR in economic relations, together with Myrdal's own prediction of economic crisis in America, guided his decisions as minister. Myrdal advocated "organized free trade" as part of a system of international planning.⁴² Against the experience of the Great Depression, complete free trade seemed neither possible nor desirable. At the same time, European reconstruction plans depended on lower trade barriers, and the ability to buy and sell abroad. For small and export-dependent Sweden, trade was particularly vital. To compensate for the loss of the German market, Myrdal thus concluded no less than 20 bilateral trade agreements in rapid sequence. Personal contacts from the *Internationale Gruppe* and to Oskar Lange in Poland proved useful for several of these agreements. In 1946, parliament ratified Myrdal's biggest and most controversial project: a five-year trade and credit agreement with the USSR. Russia was, then, still perceived as Sweden's hereditary enemy, and the Red Army's invasion of Finland had stirred up anti-Soviet feelings only recently. The trade agreement with its generous loan to Stalin was therefore highly unpopular. When Myrdal announced a return to rationing in the winter of 1946/47, newspapers blamed the shortages of imported goods like coffee on the Russian loan. Myrdal personally became the target of popular dissatisfaction, and was increasingly isolated in government. When asked to head the newly founded ECE as Executive Secretary in this heated atmosphere, Myrdal did not hesitate to give up his cabinet post.

East-West cooperation at ECE

At ECE, Myrdal became the head of an organization that was quite similar to the inclusive European order built on economic cooperation envisioned by the *Internationale Gruppe*: It was a European organization embedded in the global UN system, and offered the possibility to engage both the US and the USSR. Instead of having to rely on a series of short-term, bilateral trade agreements, ECE offered

---

41 Quoted in Appelqvist, "Gunnar Myrdal i Svensk Politik 1943–1947: En svensk Roosevelt och hans vantolkade nederlag."
42 Ibid. On planning and trade, see also Francine McKenzie's and Michel Christian's contributions in this volume.

the chance to conclude multilateral deals. Likewise, Myrdal's ideas on post-political planning, developed in interwar Sweden, were elevated to an all-European scale. It soon emerged that reconstruction plans projected on a national level ran into considerable obstacles if they were not coordinated internationally. The challenges of reconstruction, encapsulated in the so-called bottleneck problems of transport and resource distribution, seemed to call for the rational judgment of the planner.

Despite the trend toward bloc formation that dominated Europe in the late 1940s, ECE tried to maintain East-West cooperation. Myrdal called East-West trade ECE's "responsibility *par préférence*."[43] The preference for a recovery of East-West trade over a full *Westintegration* that guided Myrdal's actions as minister of commerce now became a leitmotif for ECE. Without a resurgence of East-West trade, he feared that economic recovery would be deterred. An exclusive consolidation of Western Europe as a viable economic area seemed impossible not only to Myrdal. A study by the Marshall Plan organization OEEC assumed in 1948 that without a continued influx of US dollars, Western Europe could only become sustainable if the volume of intra-European trade tripled from its 1947 value.[44] In practice, however, the volume of East-West trade declined sharply each year between 1946 and the summer of 1953, when it began to recover by 15–25% annually.[45] Despite this trend, Myrdal and the secretariat sought to establish ECE as the champion of East-West cooperation, a strategy with little initial success that risked the goodwill of Western governments.

Prior to his appointment at ECE, Myrdal was skeptical about the politics of the new UN System, but praised the technocratic potential of IOs. When the UN Economic and Social Council (ECOSOC) and other bodies in its orbit were first projected, Myrdal doubted that "the lively thinking about organizational planning in the international economic and social area" would lead to any results as long as economic IOs were dependent on the UN's political organs.[46] At the

---

[43] Gunnar Myrdal, Two Notes on ERP and East-West Trade, December 1949. UNOG Archives ARR 14/1360, Box 71.

[44] Gunther Mai, "Osthandel und Westintegration 1947–1957. Europa, die USA und die Entstehung einer hegemonialen Partnerschaft," in *Vom Marshallplan zur EWG. Die Eingliederung der Bundesrepublik Deutschland in die westliche Welt*, ed. Ludolf Herbst, Werner Bührer, and Hanno Sowade (Munich: R. Oldenbourg Verlag, 1990), 204.

[45] Melvin M. Fagen, "The Work of the Committee on the Development of Trade, 1949–1957," in *The Economic Commission for Europe. A General Appraisal*, ed. UNECE (Geneva: United Nations, 1957), VII–1.

[46] Gunnar Myrdal, "Speciella organ på det ekonomiska och sociala området," in *Fred och säkerhet efter andra världskriget. Ett svenskt diskussionsinlägg*, ed. Utrikespolitiska Institutet (Uppsala: Almquist & Wicksells, 1945), 170.

same time, however, Myrdal expressed some admiration for the League of Nations. While the League "made a fiasco as a political organ for international peace and security," it "carried out a great deal of useful, technical work in the economic, social and humanitarian field through its secretariat, various specialized commissions and expert committees."[47] Technocratic coordination, as detached as possible from the politics of IOs and executed by expert committees and secretariats, not unlike the Swedish committees of inquiry, became the ideal ECE pursued under Myrdal's leadership.

Among the European IOs that mushroomed during the late 1940s and the 1950s, ECE stood for "all-European economic co-operation," as Myrdal called it in a lecture before Soviet economists in Moscow.[48] ECE was "all-European" in the sense that it was open to every country geographically located on the European continent, with the addition of the United States as an occupying power and as Europe's most important trading partner. Franco-Spain and Germany were initially excluded, but allowed to join later on. Countries that were not full UN members from the beginning, like Switzerland or Hungary, were nonetheless invited to participate. ECE did not have access to funds that could be distributed to member states, like the European Recovery Program (ERP) did, and it did not have legislative competences like today's European Union (EU). It was thus about "economic co-operation" in the sense that it did not seek to supersede or replace, but to coordinate national economic policies.

ECE's creators at the UN anticipated the international coordination of reconstruction plans to be a key activity for the new organization. With state planning on the rise across Europe, reconstruction plans were often at conflict with each other. "Most of them contemplate a substantial increase in exports, increase which in aggregate and if uncoordinated could clearly not be achieved," as Eric Wyndham White summarized the problem.[49] Wyndham White was the secretary of ECE's predecessor, the Emergency Economic Committee for Europe (EECE), and in 1947 became Secretary-General of the General Agreement on Tar-

---

47 Ibid.
48 Gunnar Myrdal, The United Nations Economic Commission for Europe as an Organ of All-European Economic Co-Operation. Lecture given under the auspices of the Institute of Economics of the Academy of Sciences of the USSR, 9 March 1956. United Nations Offices in Geneva (UNOG) Archives ARR 14/1360, Box 1, Folder 'Gunnar Myrdal Important.'
49 Eric Wyndham White: Draft Note for the Secretariat of the United Nations on the Economic Commission for Europe, 9th January 1947. The National Archives (TNA): FO 371/62382: Establishment of an Economic Commission for Europe.

iffs and Trade (GATT).⁵⁰ A lack of international coordination for reconstruction, he argued, would lead to painful waste and delay: "Skill, labour and capital so urgently needed for the economic recovery of Europe would have been misapplied and this at the most critical time."⁵¹ ECE was founded to provide such coordination. It inherited a focus on technical cooperation from its predecessors, the UN Relief and Rehabilitation Administration (UNRRA) and the three emergency or "e-organizations."⁵² These were Wyndham White's EECE, the European Coal Organization (ECO), and the European Central Inland Transport Organization (ECITO).⁵³ The e-organizations suffered from coordination difficulties and an inconsistent membership. To solve this problem, Walt Whitman Rostow, a young economist in the US State Department, proposed to merge the emergency organizations into one permanent, all-European organization with consistent membership.⁵⁴ This idea was particularly attractive to Poland and other war-devastated countries facing a prospective gap in foreign aid after the termination of UNRRA. ECE also offered the possibility of a long-term settlement of common economic interests. To Rostow, "ECE appeared as a possible realistic first step along the slow path towards a democratically negotiated, economic unity in Europe."⁵⁵

ECE belonged to a type of postwar IOs developed to tackle the immediate needs of reconstruction. These IOs, like UNRRA, the e-organizations, and the Western European OEEC, were intergovernmental and technocratic. Governments retained the right to take decisions and to implement them at home, and were formally voting on equal footing. Because most issues dealt with at ECE were highly specialized, governments often sent technical experts rather than diplomats. International bureaucracies gained an important role as providers of statistical data and reports on which technical committees based their decisions, effectively turning secretariats into agenda-setters.

ECE's pratical achievements during its first years were, for the most part, relevant to problems of reconstruction and infrastructure development and to re-

---

50 Rogério de Souza Farias, "Mr GATT: Eric Wyndham White and the Quest for Trade Liberalization," *World Trade Review* 12, no. 03 (2013).
51 Eric Wyndham White: Draft Note for the Secretariat of the United Nations on the Economic Commission for Europe, 9 January 1947. TNA: FO 371/62382: Establishment of an Economic Commission for Europe.
52 Jessica Reinisch, "Internationalism in Relief: The Birth (and Death) of UNRRA," *Past and Present* Supplement 6 (2011): 258–289.
53 "Relief and Reconstruction Organizations," *International Organization* 1, no. 2 (1947).
54 Walt W. Rostow, "The Economic Commission for Europe," 3 (1949): 254–256.
55 Ibid.

source distribution. Between 1947 and 1950, ECE organized the international allocation of coal. Most of the coking coal that many reconstruction plans depended on came from the Ruhr: "We effectively allocated German coal in the ECE" UK delegate Lord Derek Ezra remembered, "with all the countries there, East and West."⁵⁶ In the transport sector, ECE began to develop several international projects already during the 1950s that continue today to shape road mobility in Europe and beyond, e.g. standardized road signs and traffic rules, the *Transports Internationeaux Routiers* (TIR) system, and the European highway network of e-roads.⁵⁷

The Secretariat had an important part in all of these accomplishments. The influence planners in international bureaucracies could wield on policy, however, was much more subtle than Myrdal's influence on the SAP and the Swedish state as a public intellectual, not least due to the advent of the Cold War.

As the Cold War began in earnest by the end of 1947, bloc formation on both sides became the defining feature of politics in ECE. Myrdal suspected that the creation of ECE in 1946/47 happened at "the last moment when such a decision could have been taken."⁵⁸ Two major problems dominated ECE during its first five years, as Myrdal summarized in 1952: "One was relations with the OEEC and the second, the apparent boycott by eastern European countries of the work of the technical committees."⁵⁹ In the West, OEEC emerged as a competing IO with a similar portfolio and overlapping membership.⁶⁰ Western governments disagreed over how to use the two IOs: While the US wanted to retain them both,

---

56 Lord Derek Ezra interviewed by F. Duchêne, London, January and April 1989. Historical Archives of the European Union (HAEU): EUI Oral History Collections, http://archives.eui.eu/oral_history/INT497 (accessed 20 July 2016).
57 Frank Schipper, "All Roads Lead to Europe: The E-Road Network 1950–1970," in *T2M Conference, working document* (Paris: Transnational Infrastructures of Europe, 2006); *Driving Europe: Building Europe on Roads in the Twentieth Century* (Amsterdam: Amsterdam University Press, 2008); Kiran Klaus Patel and Johan Schot, "Twisted Paths to European Integration: Comparing Agriculture and Transport Policies in a Transnational Perspective," *Contemporary European History* 20, no. 4 (2011): 383–403.
58 Gunnar Myrdal, "Twenty Years of the United Nations Economic Commission for Europe," *International Organization* 22 (1968): 617–628.
59 UN Department of Economic Affairs, Fourth Conference with the Regional Secretaries, Summary Record of the First Meeting held at Permanent Headquarters, New York, on Wednesday, 28 May 1952, RS/Conf.4/SR.1. United Nations Archives and Records Management Section (UNARMS): S-0441–0147–10.
60 Daniel Stinsky, "Western European vs. All-European Cooperation? The OEEC, the European Recovery Program, and the United Nations Economic Commission for Europe (ECE), 1947–1961," in *The OECD and the International Political Economy since 1948*, ed. Mathieu Leimgruber and Matthias Schmelzer, Transnational History Series (New York: Palgrave Macmillan, 2017).

with OEEC facilitating Western Europe and ECE maintaining a potential backdoor for defectors from the East, the UK sought to reduce ECE's activity to a minimum. In the East, communist proxy governments were installed and Western influence refuted. Poland and Czechoslovakia in particular had been instrumental in the creation of ECE, but under Communist rule both countries began to abstain from its technical committees.[61] After the death of Czechoslovak foreign minister Jan Masaryk in March 1948, the Eastern countries did not fully take part in ECE's work again until 1954.[62] The absence of Eastern representatives further increased the problem of duplication with OEEC, as active membership in the technical committees at both venues was now effectively Western.

ECE thus had to reinvent itself: it had to become an organization seeking to bridge rather than prevent the division of Europe. With OEEC facilitating a Western bloc, "it was up to us in Geneva to use our 'bridgehead' and try to save East/West cooperation," Myrdal wrote, convinced that "not even a lavish ... flow of US dollars could make up for the supplies which had of necessity to come from Eastern Europe."[63] Trade with the East was never a huge proportion of Western Europe's economic performance. Its significance was not about volume, but about specific goods. Grain, timber, coal, oil, manganese, nickel, and chrome were among the materials Western countries had to import from the East. Likewise, Eastern Europe needed manufactured goods from the West to achieve its industrialization targets. Despite its goal to achieve strategic autarky, the USSR still sought to exchange foodstuffs and raw materials for manufactured goods and know-how.[64] The foreseeable reemergence of German production would aggravate problems for both sides, as the Western zones' exports were increasingly directed toward Western Europe and the United States, instead of what the ECE secretariat regarded as their "natural" outlets in Eastern Europe. This view was harshly criticized in the UK Foreign Office:

> What the ECE Secretariat cannot bring themselves to realise is that Eastern Europe is a fundamentally different economic entity now ... and no amount of tinkering with trade ... will alter this fact. ... We cannot encourage the long-term developments of trade between West-

---

[61] Opening remarks of the Executive Secretary concerning Minister Jan Masaryk's death at the first meeting of the Manpower Sub-Committee, 11 March 1948. ARBARK: Václav Kosteleckýs arkiv, 3332–4–2–2 March-December 1948.
[62] Fagen, "Gunnar Myrdal and the Shaping of the United Nations Economic Commission for Europe," 427.
[63] Gunnar Myrdal, Report on development in relations with Paris Conference, 24 September 1947. ARBARK: Václav Kosteleckýs arkiv, 3332–4–2–1 1946–48.
[64] Gunther Mai, "Osthandel und Westintegration 1947–1957. Europa, die USA und die Entstehung einer hegemonialen Partnerschaft," 205–206.

ern and Eastern Europe on a basis which may change in four or five years . . . . This is, surely, the real case against the grandiose ideas put forward by the ECE Secretariat.⁶⁵

While the UK thus doubted the practicality of East-West cooperation, the Truman administration increasingly saw it as a security threat. Preventing the USSR from bolstering its military capacity through imports, however, took more than a ban on American military technology: "Don't forget," the former Hungarian minister and American exile Miklós Nyárádi told Myrdal, "you cannot differentiate between shipments of military or nonmilitary value. . . . This goes even for items like wood and glass if they are to be used for framing Stalin pictures . . . to lift the morale of Soviet soldiers."⁶⁶ To create effective export controls, the US thus had to apply a broad definition of the "strategic goods" affected by the ban, and ensure the cooperation of other countries. In March 1948, the US introduced export controls that drastically reduced trade with the USSR. ERP recipients had to comply with the American restrictions for goods and materials paid with Marshall aid.⁶⁷ Following the Soviet blockade of Berlin in September 1948, a Western counter-blockade shut down inter-zonal trade and German trade with Eastern Europe.⁶⁸ Other western countries were increasingly forced to comply with the American embargo.⁶⁹

ECE's self-declared aim to provide a bridge between East and West thus conflicted with American security interests. At an ECE Trade Committee meeting in May 1949, "a deadlock developed", wrote Myrdal's assistant Melvin Fagen, when "the eastern European countries stressed the futility of any efforts . . . as long as discriminatory export licensing policies were practiced against them."⁷⁰ The embargo policy became the dominating issue in ECE's annual Commission sessions, and rendered its Trade Committee almost useless. Walt Rostow, by now Myrdal's right hand man in the Secretariat, complained to American journalist Walter Lippman that the embargo "is a bad policy because it does not seriously affect the war potential of Eastern Europe, while at the same time it disrupts a commercial relationship on which the future position of Western Europe de-

---

65 E.A. Radice, untitled document, 20 July 1948. TNA, ECE and OEEC relations, FO 371–71802.
66 Nicholas Nyárádi, *My Ringside Seat in Moscow* (New York: Crowell, 1952), 211.
67 Frank Cain, *Economic Statecraft During the Cold War: European Responses to the US Trade Embargo* (New York: Routledge, 2007).
68 Mai, "Osthandel Und Westintegration 1947–1957. Europa, Die USA Und Die Entstehung Einer Hegemonialen Partnerschaft," 205–206.
69 Gunnar Adler-Karlsson, *Western Economic Warfare 1947–1967. A Case Study in Foreign Economic Policy* (Stockholm: Almqvist & Wiksell, 1968).
70 Fagen, "The Work of the Committee on the Development of Trade, 1949–1957," vii–2.

pends. It is denying the Western European countries one . . . method for ending their dependence on the US."[71]

The Korean War further increased American skepticism toward ECE. In a book published in 1952, Nyárádi warned American readers of "a strong trend in western European countries to reflect [Myrdal's] trusting attitude", adding that an ECE report dated May 6, 1951 "when the Russian-supplied Chinese Communist troops were busily killing the soldiers of the U.N. forces in Korea – disclosed that the European nations who were benefiting by Marshall Plan aid had doubled their shipments of engineering products to Russia!"[72] The secretariat's insistence on East-West trade thus risked American goodwill that was vital for ECE's survival. On the other hand, ECE's work was also threatened by the limitations posed on trade. Technical cooperation in ECE's committees, as Vincent Lagendijk has shown for the example of electricity connections, was severely hindered by the prevalence of trade obstacles.[73] A four-party deal to share energy resources involving Austria, Poland, and the transit countries Czechoslovakia and West Germany, was projected from 1949 onwards. While the project was not hindered by technical difficulties, it did not take off before the 1960s. Eastern absenteeism and the Western embargo on generating equipment made it impossible to fulfill the plans of ECE's Electric Power Committee during the 1950s. ECE succeeded, however, in keeping the idea alive and on the agenda. In this instance, Myrdal's dictum that a bridge between East and West "must be built, even if no-one crosses it for the time being" worked out.[74]

Besides trade, ECE sought to facilitate East-West cooperation through regular exchanges of expertise in the form of conferences, study tours, and a harmonization of statistics.[75] Groups of timber experts from East and West studied woodcutting methods in Finland or Switzerland, and housing experts were invited to Warsaw. These occasions were framed in academic terminology as "excursions," "seminars" etc., emphasizing their political neutrality through the link to academic research. The academic habitus was particularly prevalent in the ECE Re-

---

[71] Walt Rostow to Walter Lippman, 17 March 1949. UNOG Archives: ARR 14/1360 – Box 73 Folder "Germany".
[72] Nyárádi, *My Ringside Seat in Moscow*, 211.
[73] Lagendijk, "The Structure of Power: The UNECE and East-West Electricity Connections, 1947–1975," 57–63.
[74] Quoted in Anika de la Grandville to Václav Kostelecký, 28 April 1980. ARBARK, Václav Kosteleckýs arkiv, 3332/4/3/5 Övriga handlingar rörande ECE.
[75] Tom Griffin, "The Relationship of the United Nations Economic Commission for Europe (UN/ECE, Geneva) to the Organization for Economic Cooperation and Development (OECD, Paris) and the Statistical Office of the European Communities (Eurostat, Luxembourg)," *Statistical Journal of the United Nations ECE* 13, no. 1 (1996).

search and Planning Division, the largest administrative unit of the Secretariat. "[O]ur research set-up here amounts to quite a faculty," Myrdal boasted to Ohlin, "we certainly keep up the academic spirit."[76]

The research work of its Secretariat became a crucial *raison d'être* for ECE. Western delegates discussing the future of ECE in 1953 agreed that it was "not accomplishing much of importance at present," but considered its "statistical and research work useful and want to keep it."[77] It proved difficult, however, to incorporate economists from all member states into Myrdal's "faculty." Not only did Myrdal hold a poor opinion over Eastern European university education, the governments usually presented candidates for UN service whose qualifications were political rather than academic. In 1948, ECE launched an In-Service Training Scheme for Eastern European economists, funded by the Rockefeller Foundation. Myrdal's goal was to train "bright young boys" for service in IOs directly at ECE.[78] Despite not achieving its original purpose, the scheme was considered a success at the UN and the Rockefeller Foundation. Of the 27 students who participated in the scheme until 1955, only two came from countries behind the Iron Curtain. The majority came from Yugoslavia, Austria, and Finland, and a few even from NATO states such as France, Norway, and West Germany.[79] Eventually, the scheme was redirected toward the developing world, and recruited participants in India and Ceylon.[80] When Rockefeller funding ran out in 1955, In-Service Training continued as part of the UN Technical Assistance program. The scheme failed to provide a loophole for recruitment from Eastern Europe, but it did help to mitigate the problem that personnel qualified for UN service was more readily available in some countries than in others.[81]

---

[76] Gunnar Myrdal to Bertil Ohlin, 15 August 1953. ARBARK: Václav Kostleckýs arkiv, 3332–4–2–5.

[77] Telegram, State Department to US Representation at the UN, New York, 26 March, 1953. National Archives and Records Administration (NARA): RG 59 Department of State Decimal File 340.240, 1950–54, Box 1349.

[78] Excerpt from letter to NSB from Gunnar Myrdal, 16 November 1948. Rockefeller Foundation records, projects, RG 1.2 (FA387), Series 100: International. Folder: Economic Commission for Europe – Scholarships 1947–1951, Box 7 Folder 49.

[79] Gunnar Myrdal, The Research work of the Secretariat of the Economic Commission for Europe (draft), Rockefeller Foundation records, general correspondence, RG 2, 1952–1957 (FA425). Subgroup 1956: General Correspondence: Series 1956/100: International. Folder: ECE (A-Z).

[80] Gunnar Myrdal, "The Research Work of the Secretariat of the Economic Commission for Europe," in *25 Economic Essays in English, German and Scandinavian Languages in Honour of Erik Lindahl*, ed. Ekonomisk tidskrift (Stockholm: Ekonomisk Tidskrift, 1956), 624.

[81] On other examples of ooperation in the social sciences across the Cold War divide, see Katja Naumann's contribution in this volume.

Despite rising international tension, declining Western support, and continuing Eastern absenteeism in its committees, the ECE secretariat upheld its commitment to East-West trade. Myrdal told ECOSOC that "[e]ven in the best event, I am not looking forward to rapid and spectacular accomplishments . . . . The maximum hope I have is that . . . it will be possible gradually to change a situation which is not good to a situation which is somewhat better."[82]

Seeing the futility of further regular Trade Committee meetings, the Secretariat introduced a practice of extraordinary trade consultations upon invitation. These trade meetings were prepared through consultations the Secretariat held directly with governments.[83] A meeting planned for September 1952 had to be cancelled after the Secretariat received no confirmation from the USSR. Myrdal had stepped on a lot of people's feet to get this meeting going, particularly at the US delegation in Geneva: ". . . the trade consultations will be held . . . only because Myrdal and the ECE Secretariat want them to be held and because no country is prepared to take a strong position against them," one official complained to the State Department.[84] The Secretariat's persistence during the early 1950s was thus, at least to some extent, hinged on Myrdal personally. When he was hospitalized after a severe car accident in 1952, sources in the Swedish government told the US embassy that Sweden could not provide a successor if Myrdal should resign. Assuming that "the member nations could not agree on any other national," the Swedes regarded it a likely outcome that ECE could be dissolved.[85] Myrdal's accident came at a critical time. For *The Manchester Guardian*'s correspondent, the failure of the 1952 trade meeting a few weeks earlier was "the end of [the Secretariat's] efforts to expand trade with Eastern Europe."[86]

Despite such seemingly bleak prospects, the trade consultations achieved a remarkable breakthrough in 1953/54. To a large degree, this was due to the change in Soviet leadership and subsequent policy changes toward the West

---

[82] Gunnar Myrdal's speech to the Economic and Social Council, 8 July 1953. UNOG Box 83, ECE Debate at 9th Session.

[83] Fagen, "Gunnar Myrdal and the Shaping of the United Nations Economic Commission for Europe," 431.

[84] Joseph Greenwald, Economic Officer, US Resident Delegation to ECE, to Ruth Philipps, State Department, July 10 1952. NARA: RG 59 Department of State Decimal File 340.240, 1950–54, Box 1349.

[85] Telegram, US Embassy Stockholm to State Department, 20 February 1953. Subject: "Future of Gunnar Myrdal as Secretary General of the Economic Commission for Europe". NARA: RG 59 Department of State Decimal File 340.240, 1950–54, Box 1349.

[86] London Embassy to State Deparment, Manchester Guardian Comment on the Economic Commission for Europe, 5 September 1952. NARA: RG 59 Department of State Decimal File 340.240, 1950–54, Box 1349.

and the Eastern Europe. Yet, even before Stalin's death in March 1953, Soviet officials at ECE had begun to carefully explore a change in trade policy. The enormous economic requirements of reconstruction, combined with the effects of land reform, forced industrialization, urbanization, and arms build-up brought the USSR's efforts to achieve strategic autarky to its limits.[87] Soviet planning and the economic exploitation of Eastern Europe did not replace the need to import Western manufactured goods. But it was only after Stalin's death that a trade consultation was held with the participation of the USSR at Myrdal's initiative.[88] The ECE secretariat facilitated informal, bilateral talks in a multilateral environment. It scheduled parallel, bilateral talks between experts from all participating countries in the many conference rooms of the *Palais des Nations*, even involving countries that did not entertain diplomatic relations with one another. "[S]eldom have the trade statistics so rapidly and decisively registered a big jump in response to what in effect was an intergovernmental meeting, although it was concealed as a consultation of the Executive Secretary with experts," Myrdal wrote later in a rather self-congratulatory article.[89] While the ECE trade talks did not restore trade to its pre-war level, they did give an impetus to a quantitative upturn in East-West commercial exchange.[90] More importantly, however, they reestablished a link for economic consultation between East and West that was not subsequently broken again.

Once the USSR's grip on the Eastern Europe weakened after Stalin's death, ECE provided existing institutions that allowed a rather quick restoration of East-West contacts, albeit on a limited scale. For the 1953 Commission session, a Czechoslovak chairman was elected for the first time. In 1954, the Eastern countries returned to the committee meetings, established permanent missions in Geneva, and began to take part in all of ECE's work. Among the files of the American resident delegation, several full-colored brochures advertising Czechoslovak products in English and German can be found – something almost unthinkable two years earlier. ECE's In-Service Training scheme, now financed by the UN Technical Assistance Administration, admitted Bulgarian and Romanian stipendiaries for the first time in 1956. "The change in the political situation has per-

---

[87] Mai, "Osthandel und Westintegration 1947–1957. Europa, die USA und die Entstehung einer hegemonialen Partnerschaft," 205.
[88] Fagen, "Gunnar Myrdal and the Shaping of the United Nations Economic Commission for Europe," 428.
[89] Myrdal, "Twenty Years of the United Nations Economic Commission for Europe," 621.
[90] Evgeny Chossudovsky and Jean Siotis, "Organized All-European Co-Operation: The Role of Existing Institutions," in *Beyond Détente: Prospects for East-West Co-Operation and Security in Europe*, ed. Nils Andrén and Karl E. Birnbaum (Leiden: A.W. Sijthoff, 1976), 161.

mitted us to realize the original intention of getting trainees from countries in Eastern Europe," [91] Myrdal wrote. With Eastern participation restored, ECE became a meeting space for experts from both parts of the continent. While East-West tensions in the face of Soviet military interventions in East Germany in 1953 and in Hungary in 1956 prevailed, ECE provided a niche for ongoing cooperation over de-politicized, technical issues. Evgeny Chossudovsky and Jean Siotis argue that "it proved possible to concentrate on programs which lent themselves to being 'de-politicized,' by reducing them to a series of narrowly circumscribed technical components (such as the supply of fertilizers and alkalis, and the classification of hard coal by types . . .) that could be dealt with by specialists."[92] Other practices – such as consensus-based, no-vote decision-making in the committees, and a system of East-West rotation of chairmanship – aimed to ensure ECE's usefulness. The price for this policy of re-focusing ECE on piecemeal, technical cooperation instead of ambitious trade agreements, however, was that it removed ECE from its central position on the more controversial questions of East-West coordination. During the détente of the 1970s, ECE was already entrenched in technical cooperation, and it and the UN played a secondary role to the Conference on Security and Co-Operation in Europe (CSCE).

Conclusion

In a speech to the American Psychological Association in 1952, Myrdal called for all social sciences (including psychology) to engage collectively with problems of international cooperation: "[T]he powerful tools of social engineering . . . are so badly needed in this field where more than anywhere else the practitioner must at present work by rules of thumb."[93] The firm belief in the capacity of rational planning and social engineering that was central to Myrdal's thinking as a public intellectual during the 1930s and 40s was thus transferred from Sweden to the international level. The relative independence of the ECE Secretariat from its superior bodies in the UN system and its member states meant that as Executive

---

91 Gunnar Myrdal, The Research work of the Secretariat of the Economic Commission for Europe (draft), Rockefeller Foundation records, general correspondence, RG 2, 1952–1957 (FA425). Subgroup 1956: General Correspondence: Series 1956/100: International. Folder: ECE (A-Z).
92 Chossudovsky and Siotis, "Organized All-European Co-Operation: The Role of Existing Institutions," 161.
93 Gunnar Myrdal, "Psychological Impediments to Effective International Cooperation," *The Journal of Social Issues* 8, no. 6 (1952): 5–31.

Secretary, Myrdal was able to adopt for ECE key agendas rooted in his own intellectual and political work. Myrdal's ideal representation of international civil servants was similar to the social engineers he saw in charge of modernization in Sweden and elsewhere: post-ideological, rational and problem-oriented planners acting on the basis of an assumed *volonté générale*. The self-styling of the Secretariat borrowed several elements from academia. Not only was the Research and Planning Division the biggest unit within the Secretariat, its research work became a *raison d'être* for the entire organization. Social scientists, in Myrdal's view, were naturally inclined to not only analyze and understand, but to improve and rationalize societies. On the international level, social science and in particular economic analysis should form the basis for action in what Myrdal perceived as a world interest toward détente and against bloc formation.

Founded as an organ for technical cooperation, ECE was a prolongation of the trend toward economic planning from the national to the international level. Acknowledging that the reconstruction plans of different European countries were at conflict with each other, ECE's founders at the UN sought to make it a venue for the international coordination of economic policy. As such, ECE was the first permanent post-1945 IO dedicated to general economic cooperation in Europe. The bottleneck problems to economic recovery – especially coal, food, housing, timber and transport – seemed to call for experts and planners. Other postwar IOs, like ECE's predecessors or OEEC, shared the mindset of technocratic internationalism that characterized ECE. Nonetheless, cooperation in these IOs remained intergovernmental; the international bureaucracies attached to them had only a limited capacity to start policy initiatives. The ECE Secretariat's continued push for a revival of East-West trade stands out as an exception.

Positing that the trend toward economic bloc formation in Europe was abnormal and detrimental to economic development on either side of the Iron Curtain, Myrdal stylized ECE as a champion of East-West cooperation. The preference for East-West trade over intra-mural economic integration was rooted in Myrdal's engagement during the 1940s with continental social democrats in the *Internationale Gruppe* and as Swedish minister of commerce. In both capacities, Myrdal had held the conviction that positively engaging the USSR in economic cooperation was both necessary and possible. ECE retained this position even in the face of growing hostility among Western governments, particularly in the United States. While the American embargo policy and the ongoing Eastern absenteeism in ECE's technical committees seriously threatened the organization's continued existence, the Secretariat was nonetheless able to considerably shape the agenda and keep the call for East-West cooperation alive. The deadlock that paralyzed the Commission for years could not be broken by Myrdal's policy of small steps, but only by Stalin's death and the subsequent changes in Soviet policy. The power of experts and planners in international bureaucracies thus had clear limitations. Their actions, however, indicated a direction and a place for limited cooperation on technical issues once contacts were re-established. Myrdal's stated intention to build a bridge between East and West "even if no one crosses it for the time being" was thus fulfilled, albeit not in the ambitious form of a full restoration of trade connections.

The example of ECE shows a trend toward rationalization and scientization in international relations. While the Secretariat tried very hard to disentangle trade and economic cooperation from foreign policy, geopolitics remained the defining force that shaped ECE. Nonetheless, ECE's preoccupation with technical cooperation allowed it to de-politicize complex problems by dissolving them into smaller, technical question addressed by experts instead of diplomats. The trend toward economic planning and the acute supply shortages of the postwar period encouraged this development. The breakthrough in ECE's deadlock, finally, took place within a broader development of careful détente after Stalin's death. The USSR began to engage with the UN on a broader scale. In the following year, the Soviet Union joined the International Labor Organization (ILO) and the United Nations Educational, Scientific, and Cultural Organization (UNESCO).[94] The Geneva Summit of 1955 – the last meeting that brought together the "Big Four" of 1940s summit diplomacy – was the climax of this development of careful rapprochement. Although the opportunity for a lasting détente passed with Soviet military interferences in the GDR and in Hungary, ECE was able to keep its "bridge" for technical cooperation on a limited scale open for the following decades.

As an intellectual, Gunnar Myrdal "could be characterized in terms of a number of antinomies", as Sven Eliæson suggested: "the parochial cosmopolitan, the patriotic internationalist, the compassionate 'nihilist,' the elitist egalitarian, the social Darwinist anti-racist, the male-chauvinist feminist, the ahistorical 'historicist', the conservative socialist."[95] One might add the post-ideological ideologue, the pan-European Cold Warrior, and the free-trading planner.

---

94 Wightman, "East-West Cooperation and the United Nations Economic Commission for Europe," 6.
95 Eliæson, "Gunnar Myrdal: A Theorist of Modernity," 331.

Part 2: **High Modernism Planning**

Isabelle Gouarné
Mandatory Planning versus Indicative Planning?
The Eastern Itinerary of French Planners (1960s-1970s)

> It is one of the ironies of this strange century that the most lasting results of the October revolution, whose object was the global overthrow of capitalism, was to save its antagonist, both in war and in peace – that is to say, by providing it with the incentive, fear, to reform itself after the Second World War, and by establishing the popularity of economic planning, furnishing it with some of the procedures for its reform.
> Eric J. Hobsbawm, *Age of Extremes: The Short Twentieth Century, 1914–1991*
> (London, Abacus, 1995 [1994]), 7–8

In his famous book *The Age of Extremes: The Short Twentieth Century,* Eric Hobsbawm invited readers to challenge the distinction made by economic historians between "mandatory planning" (i.e. the Soviet mode of organization of economy based on a strong hierarchical top-down decision process and a strict state control) and "indicative planning" (i.e. a "flexible" administrative mode of regulation, set up in a few capitalist countries after the Second World War in order to correct imperfections of the market). Instead, Hobsbawm examined the effects of "real socialism" on the political and economic structures of Western states. Through the fears and borrowings it elicited, he argued, the Soviet regime was a powerful accelerator of structural reforms in Western economies, thereby contributing to their "golden age". By contrast, the collapse of the socialist "bloc" precipitated the rise of neoliberalism by discrediting the project of a planned economy. Hobsbawm's argument was an invitation to study how the fate of Eastern societies influenced the trajectory of the welfare state in the West. This chapter takes up the challenge by looking into the case of France.

Sometimes presented as the only Western state with a genuinely planned economy, France opted for a centrally managed economy to rebuild and modernize the country in the wake of World War Two. A "culture of regulation and economic and social protection," initiated during the Popular Front, prevailed among French political and administrative elites, who supported the setting up of a "mixed economy" combining planning and market.[1] Based on the

---

[1] See the works of Michel Margairaz, in particular: *L'État, les finances et l'économie (1932 – 1952). Histoire d'une conversion* (Paris: Comité d'histoire économique et financière de la France,

model of a large company and supported by a comprehensive statistical information system, French planning was meant to ensure the coherence and feasibility of the country's projects. It relied on a process of negotiation and consultation (the commissions du plan included "social partners") to anticipate social conflicts. This socio-technical innovation was conceived as an original solution to the crisis of political representation that had led to the war.[2]

To what extent can the French system be considered as an "adaptation of Soviet ideas to a capitalist mixed economy," as Hobsbawm argued?[3] What type of dialogue did French planners engage in with the East, and for what purposes? What were the social uses and impact of these exchanges, in the East and in the West, during decades of crisis? To tackle these questions, I rely on an approach that highlights transnational circulations of ideas as well as their underlying social networks and discursive practices. The renewal of Cold War studies has indeed been based on the deconstruction of political categories such as "blocs," "iron curtain" and opposition between systems,[4] paving the way for the analysis of East-West circulations in the cultural, scientific and technological realms, and more recently regarding the very structures and forms of government of states.[5]

The Cold War's "mental map" effectively shifted substantially, being alternatively based on the idea of an irreducible "opposition" and "competition" be-

---

1991, 2 vol.); "Rénovation," in *Dictionnaire De Gaulle*, ed. Claire Andrieu, Philippe Braud, Guillaume Piketty (Paris: Laffont, 2006), 1000–1005; "La faute à 68? Le Plan et les institutions de la régulation économique et financière: une libéralisation contrariée ou différée?", in *Mai 68 entre libération et libéralisation. La grande bifurcation*, ed. Michel Margairaz and Danielle Tartakowsky (Rennes: PUR, 2010), 41–62.

2 Alain Desrosières, "La commission et l'équation: une comparaison des plans français et néerlandais entre 1945 et 1980", *Genèses* 34 (March 1999): 28–52.

3 Eric J. Hobsbawm, *Age of Extremes*, 274.

4 See György Péteri, "Across and Beyond the East West Devide," *Slavonica* 10 no. 2 (November 2004); Sandrine Kott and Justine Faure (ed.), "Le bloc de l'Est en question," *Vingtième siècle* 109 (2011/2); Sari Autio-Sarasmo and Katalin Miklóssy (ed.), *Reassessing Cold War Europe* (London/New York: Routledge, 2011); Paul Boulland and Isabelle Gouarné (ed.), "Communismes et circulations transnationales," *Critique internationale* 66 (January-March 2015).

5 See recent research on East-West circulations in the area of planning and forecasting, including: Gil Eyal and Johanna Bockman (ed.), "Eastern Europe as a Laboratory for Economic Knowledge: The Transnational Roots of Neoliberalism," *American Journal of Sociology* 108–2 (September 2002): 310–352; Johanna Bockman, *Markets in the Name of Socialism. The Left-Wing Origins of Neoliberalism* (Stanford: Stanford Univeristy Press, 2011); Jenny Andersson and Eglė Rindzevičiūtė (ed.), *The Struggle for the Long-Term in Transnational Science and Politics: Forging the Future* (London/New York: Routledge, 2015); Eglė Rindzevičiūtė, *The Power of Systems. How Policy Sciences Opened up the Cold War World* (Ithaca/London: Cornell University Press, 2016).

tween political systems on the one hand and of a "convergence" on the other. Its definition was a constant subject of tension in the East and West alike, among intellectual and political elites whose internationalization strategies are never unrelated to national concerns, as Yves Dezalay has noted. While the international space of state expertise was structured on the basis of "resources acquired and accredited in national fields of power", the "mobilization of an international capital of competencies and relations" is also an "important asset in strategies of power in the national field".⁶

This chapter pursues this approach by studying an oft-neglected component of the internationalization of political and administrative elites – namely, the actual and symbolic relations between the French modernizing fractions and the Soviet Union and some Eastern European socialist countries, during a historical period (late 1950s-1970s) dominated by the idea of a "convergence of systems."⁷ It examines how this conception informed strategies of internationalization toward the East, which admittedly differed depending on the countries and their respective ongoing structural reforms, but enabled the emergence of economic expertise networks. Ultimately, a forgotten stage in the development of an international field of expertise will be documented – before neoliberalism became the new orthodoxy along with the US hegemony, when Europe and the Soviet Union formed a hub around the idea of a state-controlled economy.

---

6 Yves Dezalay, "Les courtiers de l'international. Héritiers cosmopolites, mercenaires de l'impérialisme et missionnaires de l'universel," *Actes de la Recherche en sciences sociales* 151–152 (2004/1): 4–35. See also Marion Fourcade, "The Construction of a Global Profession: The Transnationalization of Economics," *American Journal of Sociology* 112, no. 1 (July 2006): 145–194.
7 This article draws on a study of archival documents from the French and Soviet state institutions in charge of planning and from research centers in economics: in Russia, the Archive of the Academy of Sciences (ARAN) and the State Archive of the Economy (RGAE); in France, the National Financial and Economic Archive (CAEF) and the archives of scientific organizations such as the National Center for scientific research (CNRS) and the School of Advanced Studies in the Social Sciences (EHESS). This study of archival materials was complemented by memoir literature and also by a dozen face-to-face semi-structured interviews with French economists who took part in the exchanges with Eastern countries in 1960s-1970s. The interviews were focused on their professional trajectory (the successive positions held in the political-administrative and economic fields), on the different phases of their cooperation with Eastern economists, the conditions of work and dialogue, and on their visions and representations of Eastern socialist system.

Thinking beyond Cold War oppositions

Developed since the late 1930s, the convergence theory supported, with a number of variations,[8] the idea of a rapprochement between the "capitalist" "Western" systems and the Soviet Union's and Eastern Europe's "socialist" systems. Their respective evolutions, it argued, led to the same type of "industrial societies" (or "post-industrial") whose goals and operating methods were similar. This idea was largely popularized with de-Stalinization and the subsequent thaw, especially in US social science, where Soviet studies scholars fueled general considerations on modern society (Inkeles, Sorokin, Parsons, Rostow, Bell et al.).[9] According to David Engerman, however, it had limited interest to the US government.[10] In France, on the other hand, it resonated far beyond academic circles and into the political and administrative field itself, especially among its modernizing elements who had gathered within the "triangle" formed by the INSEE (National institute of statistic and economic studies), the national planning board (Commissariat au Plan) and the Ministry of Finance's economic and financial studies department (Service des études économiques et financières), later renamed Directorate of forecasting (Direction de la prévision).[11]

Between interest and sympathy:
French economists and the Soviet "model"

At a time when the French political and administrative field was experiencing sweeping changes, the outlines of this new institutional space were traced in the immediate postwar period by a group of senior officials with atypical backgrounds. Senior public service was rarely a family tradition for them. Many of

---

[8] For discussion of different formulations of this thesis, see Théofil I. Kis, "État des travaux sur la problématique de la convergence: théories et hypothèses," *Études internationales* 2, no. 3 (1971): 443–487. See also in this volume the contributions by Sandrine Kott, "The social engineering project," and Ondřej Matějka, "Social engineering and alienation."

[9] David C. Engerman, "To Moscow and Back: American Social Scientists and the Concept of Convergence," in *American Capitalism. Social Thought and Political Economy in the Twentieth Century*, ed. Nelson Lichtenstein (Philadelphia: University of Pennsylvania Press, 2006), 47–68.

[10] David C. Engerman, *Know Your Enemy. The Rise and Fall of America's Soviet Experts* (Oxford/New York: Oxford University Press, 2009), chap. 7.

[11] Alain Desrosières, *La Politique des nombres. Histoire de la raison statistique* (Paris: La Découverte, 1993); *Gouverner par les nombres. L'argument statistique* (Paris: Presses de l'École des Mines, 2008, 2 vol.).

them came from religious minorities (Jewish – for instance, François Bloch-Lainé, Étienne Hirsch, Simon Nora or Pierre Uri; or Protestant – as Claude Gruson and Jean Saint-Geours) or had modest social backgrounds (Claude Gruson, Robert Marjolin, Jean Serisé). At odds with the posture of apoliticism traditionally prevailing in the field, their trajectories had often been marked by intense political commitments, in the Resistance (Jean Serisé, for instance) or in left-wing parties – the Socialist Party (Pierre Uri, Jean Saint-Geours) and even the Communist Party (Claude Alphandéry, Jean Bénard, Jean Denizet, Jacques le Noane, Jacques Mayer, André Nataf; in the next generation: Philippe Herzog, Gaston Olive and others).[12] While their training (Polytechnique, École des Ponts et Chaussées, École des Mines) put them within the tradition of state engineers who are the bearers of economic knowledge,[13] they had also been deeply impressed by the crisis of democracy in the 1930s and 1940s and were eager to restore social bonds by implementing a political modernization project. This group of state economists thus brought forward an original response to the challenge of postwar reconstruction based on national planning and accounting.

United by the same ambitions for modernization, this community of senior officials was however divided as to the definition of the type of planning that should be implemented.[14] There had been heated debates on the subject at the time of the country's liberation. Under the helm of Jean Monnet, a soft, indicative and consultative form of planning had eventually prevailed against the more controlling approach envisioned by some, who considered the Soviet Union as a "model" from which France could draw inspiration (Pierre Mendès France and his adviser Georges Boris, and also Claude Gruson, Alfred Sauvy and other planners of the postwar period).[15]

---

12 Brigitte Gaïti, "Les modernisateurs dans l'administration d'après-guerre. L'écriture d'une histoire héroïque," *Revue française d'administration publique* 102 (2002/2): 295–306; *De Gaulle, prophète de la Cinquième République (1946–1962)* (Paris: Presses de Science Po, 1998), chap. 7. See also François Fourquet, *Les Comptes de la puissance. Histoire de la comptabilité nationale et du plan* (Paris: Encres, 1980).

13 Marion Fourcade, *Economists and Societies: Discipline and Profession in the United States, Britain & France, 1890s to 1990s* (Princeton/Oxford: Princeton University Press, 2009), especially chap. 4.

14 On this topic, see Vincent Spenlauher, *L'évaluation des politiques publiques, avatar de la planification* (Grenoble: Thèse de l'Université Pierre-Mendès France, 1998), chap. 1.

15 Philippe Mioche, "La planification comme 'réforme de structure'. L'action de Pierre Mendès France de 1943 à 1945," *Histoire, économie et société* 1, no. 3 (1982): 471–488; *Le Plan Monnet. Genèse et élaboration, 1941–1947* (Paris: Publications de la Sorbonne, 1987). See also Jean-Louis Crémieux-Brilhac, *Georges Boris. Trente ans d'influence. Blum, De Gaulle, Mendès France* (Paris: Gallimard, 2010).

Claude Gruson (1910 – 2000)

Often presented as the "father" of French national accounting, Claude Gruson was a long-time admirer of Soviet and East German planning. In the biographical interviews he published under the title *Programmer l'espérance* [Programming Hope] in 1976, he noted:

> The first reason for my admiration, which indeed I am not trying to hide, is that this system, which is completely different from capitalism, exists: it is capable of evolving and meeting complex goals. . . . From a political standpoint, the Soviet system has visible flaws. On the other hand, the Eastern system is arguably much more egalitarian than ours." Later, he adds: "We need to look for another model of society, as it is in Western Europe that this problem whose responsibility is ours arises. . . . Still, I don't want to completely rule out any form of application of the Soviet model in the future. Europe will certainly be threatened by a deep crisis within a few years. . . . Under that assumption, the only way out might be a system inspired by Eastern socialisms: a deeply troubled and disorganized Europe would find its salvation in the implementation of a simple and robust system, based on a centralism that wouldn't necessarily be Stalinist, being on the opposite capable of moving toward decentralization and democracy. But it all depends on how deep and lasting the crisis is.[16]

Gruson's interest in Soviet planning and Marxism was anchored in his vocation as a state engineer and a Protestant intellectual concerned with "programming hope" and bringing about the "future of brotherhood, justice and love" to which the world was "promised." An alumnus of the Ecole Polytechnique and a "self-taught" economist, he was one of the key actors of postwar French planning in the Ministry of Finance and as Director-General at the INSEE (1961–1967). Upon the liberation of France, he was tasked with setting up the Department for economic and financial studies at the Treasury and with coming up with information and analysis tools to guide the reconstruction's economic and social policy.[17] He viewed economic power as "oppressive" and "dictatorial," and remained a steadfast supporter of planning even after the 1960s, when state regulation of the economy in all forms was heavily criticized. He conceived planning not simply as a means to "reduce uncertainty," to use Pierre Massé's phrase, but as a "political support tool for policy-making" and an instrument of democratization.

---

16 Claude Gruson, *Programmer l'espérance* (Paris: Stock, 1976), 162–163 and 177–178.
17 Aude Terray, *Des Francs-tireurs aux experts. L'organisation de la prévision économique au ministère des Finances, 1948–1968* (Paris: Comité pour l'Histoire économique et financière de la France, 2002).

While the Khrushchev Thaw introduced a "peaceful coexistence" policy and allowed Soviet scientists to open up to the world, he actively participated in the first exchanges between French and Soviet planners and economists. In 1958, he was part of the delegation of French planners and economists sent to the Soviet Union to learn about the methods of Socialist planning. After leaving his post at the INSEE in 1967, he went on to work in the banking sector and drifted away from the East-West state expertise networks. Yet, he continued to carefully monitor attempts at reforming Socialist economic systems; during the "transition" years, he strongly opposed the economic orientations that were adopted. In his view, introducing a market economy in the former Socialist countries required an "adaptation effort" that demanded "not a centralized planning that would stifle initiative, but at least a powerful central apparatus of strategic regulation, capable of providing strong insights on economic activity and of correcting its inconsistencies".[18]

As we can see with Claude Gruson' case, communists were far from the only ones with an interest in Soviet planning. In the postwar period, it was very widely shared among this circle of state economists, characterized by a left-wing sensibility.[19] It had much to do with the engineer-state (or expert-state) model that the Soviet Union had managed to embody, especially after the trials of World War Two and the fight against Nazi Germany, as several French economists noted in interviews:

> It is necessary to understand the moment well. Russia is one of the great victors of the War, but maybe, seen from France, with a specific orientation, because the fight against the Germans was horrendous. Well, Stalingrad and so on. The Communist Party is the first party in France. Maybe it wasn't anymore at that time, but it had been until recently. Thus Russia has a special aura. And in particular, we are very impressed by its success in the area of planning. (Interview with Jean Serisé, 28 November 2012)

> We faced a planned economy, which had won the War. Well, they [the Soviets] were saying it, but it is true that they had a certain prestige. Soviet Russia had prestige, not only for having won the War against the Germans, but for having won with an economic base that they sort of managed to embellish enough, if you will, and so on. (Interview with Jean Saint-Geours, 19 November 2012).

---

18 Claude Gruson, *Propos d'un opposant obstiné au libéralisme mondial* (Paris: Éditions MSH, 2001), 73–81 and 79.
19 Aude Terray, *Des Francs-tireurs aux experts*.

French interpretations of the convergence theory

Having lost momentum in the early stages of the Cold War, the postwar interest in planning in the East was revived in the post-Stalinist period as the Soviet Union achieved a series of technological feats (including the launch of Sputnik, the first artificial satellite, in 1957, of the first man in space in 1961, etc.) and engaged in a set of structural economic reforms alongside other Eastern European countries.[20] Edmond Malinvaud (1923–2015), who embodied a model of success for French state economists, despite his great political restraint,[21] recalled:

> According to my tentative assessment, however, we overestimated the real performance in the USSR in 1960, and we also had for long a too favourable image of the changes since then. . . . I shall venture into giving two reasons explaining why propaganda achieved its aim to some extent. First, we were too much impressed by some Soviet successes: in Word War II, hence, we thought, by its war economy; and on the technological front, particularly in the nuclear and aerospace fields. Those successes were too easily accepted as such (we did not know their cost) and as more widely significant. Second, looking at the social problems in our part of the world we fell too much into mistake of the believing that "the grass was greener" in the other part. . . . Without accepting the Communist political project, whose political features were found by most to be too undemocratic, many were ready to concede that the Soviet system was performing better on the social front.[22]

From the late 1950s on, multiple initiatives were taken in France and in the other Western countries to get information not only on the content of those reforms and their political orientations, but also on the technical innovations they could bring in terms of planning and "economic information." That period also saw the rise of a generation of French academics who specialized in the Soviet economy (Charles Bettelheim, whose first works were already well known, but also Marie Lavigne, Basile Kerblay, Jean Marczewski, Henri Chambre, Georges Sokoloff and others), which reflected that wider interest.

---

20 For an overview, see Bernard Chavance, *Les réformes économiques à l'Est, de 1950 à 1990* (Paris: Nathan, 2000).
21 On his career path, see Frédéric Lebaron, *La Croyance économique. Les économistes entre science et politique* (Paris: Seuil, 2000), and especially 67–71. His election to the Collège de France in 1987 marks the culmination of his career as an economist, at the junction of research and high administration.
22 Edmond Malinvaud, "Introduction: Some Notes on Assessments about Economic Systems," in *Planning, Shortage, and Transformation. Essays in Honor of János Kornai*, ed. Eric Maskin and András Simonovits (Cambridge, Mass.: MIT Press, 2000), 1–14, 4–5.

The renewal of economic thinking in the East[23] was attentively followed by the "modernizers," who then faced "the experience of relegation," in the words of Brigitte Gaïti. The March 1952 appointment of Antoine Pinay as Prime Minister and the end of the Marshall Plan aid in 1953 had led them to be politically marginalized. Pierre Mendès France's political return allowed them to remobilize, but this was short-lived. Only by rallying to the support of General de Gaulle in 1958 did they manage to genuinely get back into the political and administrative game; this was the golden age of the French Plan.[24] The idea of a "convergence of systems" found a lasting echo in France during that political juncture. The call to move beyond the "outdated stereotype" of an opposition between socialism and capitalism became a leitmotiv in the discourse of these economists:

> First, let's give up on the all too common distinction between 'centrally planned economy' and 'market economy'. The image suggested by that distinction might be convenient for the sake of an argument, but it gives us a false view of reality. . . . It is trivial to note that the variety of regimes that exist in the world match neither of those two images [that of a central body determining an optimal program; that of the market]. Decision-making processes are actually far more complex. They require the effects of decentralized actions and of decisions taken at the highest national level to be combined everywhere.[25]

> Conceived in really different circumstances, for different, if not opposed, purposes, Soviet-type planning and Western-type planning, very dissimilar in the beginning, are slowly evolving toward a common model. . . . The most advanced socialist and capitalist countries have reached a very similar, if not identical, stage of development. They are consciously seeking the forms of economic management allowing to make the best use of resources, which are not fundamentally different, and with methods which are, indeed, practically the same. Is it surprising that they are gradually finding similar solutions?[26]

Such a comparative approach to the Eastern and Western systems may appear surprising. It was a departure first from the dominant discourse during the Cold War, which held that communism and capitalism were radically at odds; also, it clearly strayed from the idea of a "third way," which had been influential

---

23 Bernard Chavance, "La théorie de l'économie socialiste dans les pays de l'Est entre 1917 et 1989," in *Nouvelle histoire de la pensée économique*, ed. Alain Béraud and Gilbert Faccarello (Paris: La Découverte, 1993), vol. 2, chap. 19.
24 Brigitte Gaïti, *De Gaulle, prophète de la Cinquième République*.
25 Edmond Malinvaud, "Réflexions pour l'étude de la planification dans les sociétés occidentales," Presentation at the conference on long-term planning organized by the International Economic Association (Moscow, December 1972). INSEE Papers, Centre des archives économiques et financières (CAEF), France (B55.512).
26 Jean Marczewski, "Planification et convergence des systèmes," *Revue de l'Est* 2/4 (1971): 5–19.

to that generation of senior civil servants when they were young, in the 1930s.[27] In fact, even if it received the intellectual backing of French economists who were specialists of Eastern countries, its diffusion elicited strong criticisms, coming primarily from Marxist communist intellectuals, who faulted the convergence thesis for neglecting the fundamental differences between the two systems when it came to their "economic and social basis."[28]

The success of the convergence thesis among the "modernizers" is actually owed to the fact that it could be used as a tool in the legitimation struggles in which they were engaged, rekindled by the "uncertain configuration of the political game" opened with General de Gaulle's return to power (1958). Against the traditional powers of parliament and the political parties, these senior civil servants then sought to "diffuse a new representation of politics, in which technical management skills countered political representation, economic efficiency countered legal regularity, planning countered law, and the executive countered the legislative."[29] In these political rivalries, the convergence thesis offered a theoretical rationalization to the political interests supported by state economists. As it defined the most advanced societies as "mixed economies," it made planning a key feature of the social and political modernization process and even a backbone of the "French grandeur" that was so dear to de Gaulle: France, thanks to its original experience of planning, could play a prominent role in the field of international economic expertise.[30] The idea of convergence thus gave the "modernizers" a theoretical foundation for their alliance with Gaullism.

---

27 Antonin Cohen, "Du corporatisme au keynésianisme. Continuités pratiques et ruptures symboliques dans le sillage de François Perroux," *Revue française de science politique* 56 (2006/4): 555–592.
28 See, for example, the review written by the Marxist historian Jean Bouvier of *Choix et efficience des investissements* (Paris: École Pratique des Hautes Études, 1963) in *Annales. Histoire, sciences sociales* (January-February 1970, 144–145). On the positions of economists in the French Communist Party, see Nicolas Azam, *Le PCF confronté à "l'Europe". Une étude socio-historique des prises de position et des recompositions partisanes* (Paris : Dalloz, 2017).
29 Delphine Dulong, *Moderniser la politique. Aux origines de la Ve République* (Paris: L'Harmattan, 1997), 287.
30 It was this specificity, which, for instance, justified the organization in France of the IEA (International Economic Association) conference on public economics. In the introduction to the conference proceedings, Julius Margolis (Professor at Stanford University) noted: "It was fitting that the Conference on the Analysis of the Public Sector be held in France where there existed a tradition of economic analysis for public works planning and a remarkable renaissance of analysis in many branches of the public services. The French experiences are being duplicated in many nations of the world as increasing recognition has been given to the value of economic concepts and models to guide the operations of government." Introduction to Julius Margolis and Henri Guitton, *Public economics: an analysis of public production and consumption and*

Turning to the East

In the late 1950s, French planners and economists turned to the East, targeting the socialist countries that seemed to have made the most progress in reforming their planning systems and that were accordingly thought to be the most advanced in the "convergence" process. This worldview had thus a performative effect,[31] effectively shaping a space of East-West circulations that remains to be precisely mapped. Now eager to identify "common concerns" between "indicative planning" and "mandatory planning," the French economists seized every opportunity they could to engage in a dialogue with the East. This internationalization effort was primarily but not exclusively aimed at the Soviet Union. It included other socialist countries such as Poland and Hungary, where structural reforms had been attempted since the 1960s. However, these East-West networks were defined not only by the opportunities for exchange created by the reforms underway in socialist countries, but also by the degree to which political authorities in those states made opening up to the West possible and the ways in which they allowed it to happen.

Soviet economic science and the West: a negotiated opening

The development of these networks of expertise was in no way an easy process. Admittedly, the Thaw had marked a turn in East/West relations, starting with France and the Soviet Union,[32] but exchanges remained limited, including in the field of social science, where tensions still ran high in the East between the "defenders of the dogma" and "scholars concerned with studying 'real' society."[33]

---

their relations to the private sectors. Proceedings of a conference (New York: MacMillan/St Martin's Press, 1969), xi–xii, x. On this international conference, see Mathieu Hauchecorne, "L'État des économistes au 'miroir transatlantique.' Circulations et hybridation de l'économie publique française et états-unienne," in *Comparaisons franco-américaines*, ed. Daniel Sabbagh and Maud Simonet (Rennes: Presses Universitaires de Rennes, 2016).
31 Pierre Bourdieu, "Décrire et prescrire. Les conditions de possibilité et les limites de l'efficacité politique (1980)," in *Langage et pouvoir symbolique* (Paris: Seuil, 2001), 186–198.
32 Marie-Pierre Rey, *La Tentation du rapprochement. France et URSS à l'heure de la détente (1964–1974)* (Paris: Publications de la Sorbonne, 1991).
33 Martine Mespoulet, "La 'renaissance' de la sociologie en URSS (1958–1972). Une voie étroite entre matérialisme historique et 'recherches sociologiques concrètes,'" *Revue d'histoire des sciences humaines* 16 (2007): 57–86.

This applied to economics in particular. In the Soviet Union, the discipline was constructed as a detailed defense of socialism against capitalism (including in the form of political economics, "politèkonómiâ"). It had managed to gain more autonomy by turning to applied methods and mathematics. While debates remained heated, at the time of Khrushchev's reforms, a division of labor emerged between theory, which was assigned to the Marxist-Leninist ideologues, and practice (intersectoral and sectoral economies), which fell to the mathematical economists. This dividing line was sometimes challenged, in particular during political crises, as in 1968, when the entire discipline was again subjected to greater political control. Still, as Natalia Chmatko notes, "the adoption of that structure gave free rein to the economists: in theory they no longer contested the superior role of Marxism-Leninism and did not assert their autonomy from that ideology; but on the other hand they claimed to take interest in special disciplines, inferior levels."[34] Often originally trained in mathematics or engineering, the mathematical economists rarely took part in general theoretical debates, which were monopolized by the Marxist-Leninist political economists. Mathematical economics was reduced to applied mathematics, disconnected from theoretical generalizations. All references to the neoclassical school remained politically suspect, as Ivan Boldyrev and Olessia Kirtchik have shown.[35] The mathematical economists were mostly found in the research institutes created during the 1960s mainly by the Academy of Sciences and the Central Institute of Mathematical Economics [CEMI : Central'nyj èkonomiko-matematičeskij institut], as well as in the Siberian branch of the Academy,[36] the Institute of Economics and Industrial Engineering [Institut èkonomiki i organizacii promyšlennogo proizvodstva] and the research centers affiliated with the Gosplan, such as the Institute for Economic Research [Naučno-issledovatel'skij èkonomičeskij institut].

---

34 Natalia Chmatko, "Les usages des sciences économiques en Russie entre les années 1960 et 1990," *Histoire Économie et Société* 4 (2002): 583–603, 586.

35 See Ivan Boldyrev and Olessia Kirtchik, "The Culture of Mathematical Economics in the Post War Soviet Union," WP6 (Moscow: High School of Economics Publication, May 2015); "General Equilibrium Theory behind the Iron Curtain: The Case of Victor Polterovich," *History of Political Economy* 46/3 (2014): 435–461. On the uses of cybernetics in Soviet economy, see Slava Gerovitch, *From Newspeak to Cyberspeak. A History of Soviet Cybernetics* (Cambridge,Mass./London: MIT Press, 2002), chap. 6; Adam E. Leeds, "Dreams in Cybernetic Fugue: Cold War Technoscience, the Intelligentsia, and the Birth of Soviet Mathematical Economics," *Historical Studies in the Natural Sciences* 46, no. 5 (2016): 633–668.

36 On the Siberian branch of the Soviet Academy of Science, see Paul R. Josephson, *New Atlantis Revisited. Akademgorodok, the Siberian City of Science* (Princeton: Princeton University Press, 1997).

Even though it was limited to specific applications, the international opening up of Soviet economic science required constant negotiations to counter the political and ideological reluctances it elicited, but also to circumvent the regime of secrecy surrounding economic information. Much of the data on the Soviet economy indeed remained classified, and research centers such as the Gosplan's Institute for Economic Research fell under a special scheme that strongly limited opportunities for receiving foreign colleagues.

An argumentative strategy was however devised to justify the expansion of such exchanges. It used the discourse on the "scientific and technical revolution" led in the post-Stalin period by the "reformist" Soviet elites, taking up the idea of a "convergence of systems."[37] In this sense, the reports drafted by the mathematical economists following their first contacts with Western colleagues are a revealing read. Two arguments were systematically put forward: the East/West dialogue could meet the objectives of Soviet authorities concerning their political influence abroad and economic modernization. For instance, in the 1971–1972 memo of the CEMI research institute, the "great interest" of these exchanges was emphasized, first in terms of "propaganda for Soviet achievements abroad" and also of the "practical application of foreign experience." In a number of cases, these contacts would allow the Soviet Union "not to waste time and resources" in replicating the management and policy-making systems discovered abroad that could "successfully be applied in our country."[38]

Building a network of state expertise

These closely monitored international exchanges began gaining momentum in the late 1950s. Although France was not the only Western country to open a dialogue with Eastern economists, it probably acted as a driving force[39] due to the Gaullist policy of opening up to the Soviet Union and the planning community's

---

37 Eglė Rindzevičiūtė, *The Power of Systems*, chap. 1. On the Soviet planners' interest in the Western (and especially French) experience of economic governance, see also Eglė Rindzevičiūtė, "A Struggle for the Soviet Future: The Birth of Scientific Forecasting in the Soviet Union," *Slavic Review* 75/1 (2016): 52–76.
38 "Spravka ob effektivnosti meždunarodnyh naučnyh sviazej CEMI AN SSSR za 1971–1972 g." Central Mathematics and Economics Institute Papers, Russian Academy of Sciences Archives, Moscow (F. 1959, Op. 1, D. 384, L. 2–11).
39 See, for instance, Vladimir Alekseevič Vinogradov's memoirs: *Moj XX vek. Vosponimaniia* (Moscow: Izdatel'skij dom kalan, 2003), 132 on.

keen interest in Eastern reform attempts based on mathematical economics and computer science.

The mathematical economists were particularly sought after by the French economists who exchanged with the East. Jean Marczewski, a French economist of Polish origin, was for instance bitterly disappointed in the fifth international economic history conference held in Leningrad in August 1970, where he moderated a session on the history of planning: not only was the convergence thesis, of which he was one of the leading French theoreticians, officially disputed by the Soviets, but he was also unable to pursue the dialogue he had engaged a few years before with Soviet economists/planners:

> Defended by the author of this report, the thesis of the necessary convergence between Soviet and Western management systems provoked clearly negative reactions from the Soviet participants and also from some Romanian and East German colleagues. In contrast, it was received favorably by most Westerners as well as by Yugoslavian, Hungarian and Polish colleagues.[...]
>
> Conclusion:
> Contrary to their compatriots directly involved in planning action – with whom I had had long discussions during my three-month stay in the USSR, the Soviet economical historians seem not to have yet understood the significance of the evolution of the Eastern and Western economic systems under the pressure of technical progress.
>
> This difference may result partly from the fact that Soviet historians have much less contact with the contemporary reality than the economists involved in action.
>
> It may also come from a certain doctrinal hardening of the regime, whose instructions in the domain of intellectual relations with capitalist countries are currently stricter than in 1966, the year of my previous trip [to the USSR].[40]

To clear these ideological and political hurdles, forms of exchange other than large-scale international conferences were favored. These included workshops and seminars with small numbers of participants, focused on applied economics and avoiding ideological questions as much as possible, drawing on the support of international organizations and academic institutions. On the French side, the *École pratique des Hautes études* (EPHE) worked on developing regular institutional exchanges with the Soviet Union and Eastern European countries in the economic field, primarily through joint workshops. A director of studies at the EPHE since 1948, Charles Bettelheim, whose ties with the Soviet Union dated

---

[40] Jean Marczewski, "Rapport sur les résultats de la mission à Leningrad, Paris, 27 octobre 1970". CNRS Papers (National Center for scientific research)/French National Archives (19860367/16).

back to his years as a Communist activist (1933–1937),[41] played a key mediation role in the 1950–1960s. During several trips to the East, he made multiple contacts with Soviet Union economists – in the Central Institute for Mathematical Economics (CEMI) with N. P. Fedorenko and V. S. Nemčinov, at the Gosplan's Institute for Economic Research with A. N. Efimov, and at the Institute for Global Economics and International Relations (IMEMO) –, and more broadly with Eastern European economists, particularly in Poland.[42] In May 1960, for instance, he coordinated a Franco-Polish workshop at the EPHE in Paris, on the theme "Choice and efficiency of investments," featuring French academic economists and representatives of the Institute of Statistics-national planning board-Ministry of Finance triangle (Claude Gruson, Edmond Malinvaud, Jean Bénard, Joseph Klatzman, André Platier, Charles Prou).[43] The workshop offered not to revisit theoretical debates, but instead to adopt an "operational outlook" by focusing on concrete problems: how should the volume and distribution of investments be determined? How should the efficiency of investments be calculated? How should the discount rate be set? etc. In doing so, French economists were keen to highlight common ground between "indicative planning" and "mandatory planning" and overcome the reluctance that had been voiced on the subject.

After having presented the methods applied in France for the choice of public investments, Edmond Malinvaud noted:

> The above could suggest that the criteria adopted in France differ fundamentally from the criteria recommended in Eastern countries. That is not my opinion. I have already indicated that we deal with the problem in the same way that the economists working in the countries of mandatory planning. I will now try to show that in practice, in the simple situations, we arrive at formulas similar to some of those proposed by Polish and Russian authors.[44]

Charles Bettelheim stated also:

> The presentations of Gruson and Fedorowicz are complementary. Since in both cases fundamental financial problems of indicative planning and mandatory planning appeared, we

---

41 In 1936, he spent five months in Soviet Russia. On his life and career, see Fabien Denord and Xavier Zunigo, "'Révolutionnairement vôtre'. Économie marxiste, militantisme intellectuel et expertise politique chez Charles Bettelheim," *Actes de la recherche en sciences sociales* 158 (June 2005): 8–29.
42 See the manuscript of his memoirs filed in his archives: Charles Bettleheim Papers, EHESS Archives (École des Hautes études en sciences sociales).
43 Charles Bettelheim, *Choix et efficience des investissements* (Paris: Mouton & Co, 1963). The Polish delegation included H. Dunajewski, Z. Fedorovicz, K. Laski, B. Minc and K. Romaniuk.
44 Ibidem, 78.

could point to the common and the specific data and questions for both planning systems.⁴⁵

Another favored means of establishing dialogue between Eastern and Western experts consisted in organizing fact-finding missions. In 1958, a delegation of French economists, led by the Commissioner General of the national planning board Étienne Hirsch, went to the Soviet Union for a nearly three-week-long mission (11–30 May 1958). Put together with the assistance of the Ministry of Foreign Affairs, the team included planning administrators (François Bloch-Lainé, Claude Gruson, Simon Nora, Jean Sérisé, Jean Bénard), and academic economists who worked in relation with the political and administrative field (Jean Marchal, Jean-Marcel Jeanneney, Robert Goetz-Girey, Raymond Barre et Basile Kerblay). Its objective was to initiate in-depth talks on Soviet planning – not so much its results as its methods, institutions and mechanisms.

A report over 100 pages long was drafted after the mission.⁴⁶ Diplomatic precautions were obviously taken in the report's wording, since it was circulated to the Soviets, and it adopted a rather measured tone. It presented the successes and failures of Soviet planning, the challenges it encountered and the solutions envisioned. Mostly it showed how seriously the French delegation took these exchanges. An in-depth questionnaire had been developed and submitted to the Soviets before the mission. It included very specific questions on planning techniques – on the "logic" of planning (the consistency and balance of the objectives, the choice of objectives and optimums), economic calculation issues (relations between the plans, price-setting, evaluation of the investments, consumption studies, etc.) as well as the methods used to implement and monitor planning. Work sessions were organized to disseminate concrete information on Soviet planning at various levels: the Gosplan, the research institutes of the Academy of Sciences, the Republics,⁴⁷ the factories and the kolkhozes.

The impressions of the French delegation were probably rather lukewarm. In an interview, Jean Sérisé reported observing numerous discrepancies between the Soviet reality and the logic of the planning in the course of his mission: factory work stopped between noon and 2pm, the black market was expanding, access to consumer goods was difficult, etc. His account mostly conveys disillusion:

---

45 *Ibidem*, 121.
46 The report was written mostly by Jean Bénard, the youngest member of the delegation, but it was reviewed collectively. Interview with Jean Serisé, 28 November 2012.
47 The French delegation was divided in three groups for tours in Leningrad, Kiev and Tbilisi.

That vision of planning was rather different from the one we had at the start. That is, it was much more pragmatic; and essentially, they did not proceed the way we thought they proceeded. . . . My colleagues were quite sad. They sympathized. But finally, there was a little something that was beginning. (Interview with Jean Serisé, 28 November 2012)

Although this first-hand experience of the Soviet reality was a disappointment for some, the report's conclusions remained inconclusive:

A problem remains. We can glimpse paths toward a solution. We can be assured that Soviet economists are actually committed to exploring these paths with very powerful resources and a great deal of flexibility and inventiveness. But obviously, we have no right to predict the results of a research that is still in the realm of creative imagination. . . . All we can say is that if the Soviet planners follow through on their current research – even they manage to put the huge core production apparatus developed during the Stalinian period to work for a continuous and free improvement of living standards as well as the achievement of great collective objectives – the achievements of the Soviet economy will far exceed the remarkable ones we can already observe today.[48]

Lastly, in the 1960s, these exchanges of experts were boosted by De Gaulle's international policy of rapprochement with the East. They were institutionalized with the intergovernmental agreement on technical and scientific cooperation signed by France and the Soviet Union in 1966. The nuclear and spatial sectors were pilot areas in that cooperation, but it concerned numerous scientific fields, and included exchanges on planning and forecasting methods.

A "working group on economic information" was created in June 1967 within that framework.[49] On the French side, it mainly involved the Institute of Statistics-national planning board-Ministry of Finance triangle. On the Soviet side, it included participants from the Gosplan and its research institutes,[50] the central directorate for statistics,[51] as well as research institutes of the Academy of Scien-

---

[48] Report on May 1958 mission to the USSR. Direction du Trésor Papers, CAEF (B 594). See also the paper that Basile Kerblay published after this mission: "Entretiens sur la planification avec des économistes soviétiques," *Cahiers du monde russe et soviétique* 1/1 (1959): 174–179.
[49] Groupe de travail mixte franco-soviétique sur l'information économique réciproque, "PV de la première session, Moscou, 20–23 juin 1967". Direction générale de la Recherche scientifique et technique Papers/French National Archives (19770321/411).
[50] Especially the Council for Study of Productive Forces (Sovet po izučeniju prouzvoditel'nyh sil) and the Institute for economic research (Haučno-issledovatel'ckij ėkonomičeckij institut).
[51] On the history of the Soviet Institute for Statistics in the Stalinist period, see Alain Blum and Martine Mespoulet, *L'Anarchie bureaucratique. Statistique et pouvoir sous Staline* (Paris: La Découverte, 2003).

ces.⁵² Bringing together "high-level executives in planning and in economic and technical bodies," it was aimed at initiating a dialogue "in the fields of mathematics and of the information processing methods used for economic research, planning and management." Five themes were initially selected: the use of mathematical economics and computer science in corporate management; the preparation of the state's economic decisions; the issues relating to the processing of useful information for corporations and the state; the issues relating to the training of executives; the application of computer science to planning and management issues. In the 1970s, these themes were included in the "computer science" section of the cooperation. The signature of the intergovernmental scientific cooperation agreement enabled the intensification and diversification of forms of exchanges (seminars and workshops; exchanges of documents; long-term missions or internships) between French and Soviet planners, economists and statisticians.

Transnational circulations and planning reforms

Beginning in the late 1950s, a network of experts on economics and state was formed between France and Eastern countries, based on the participants' shared belief that they were working on "similar problems" and could identify "common solutions." In an interview, the French economist Jean-Michel Charpin stressed this sense of belonging to the same professional community:

> In the 1970s, well, during much of the 1970s, we considered them [Eastern economists] as colleagues. We considered them as colleagues, who were working in a very different country, of course, in an authoritarian regime, really different lifestyles . . . . However, fundamentally, we considered them as colleagues, who used methods of quantitative economics, at the service of their government. Besides, they were not so bad. Generally they had good training in mathematics. (Interview with Jean-Michel Charpin, 5 September 2016)

Should this be seen as a genuine circulation of ideas between East and West? What were the effects of these exchanges on planning practices in the East and in the West? These questions pave new avenues of research – I will only provide a few pointers for further research here, as taking comprehensive stock of the crisscrossing uses of these relationships remains to be done.

---

52 In particular, the Central Mathematics and Economics Institute (CEMI) and the Institute of economics and industrial engineering (Siberian branch of Soviet Academy of Sciences).

"Common solutions" to "similar problems"

One particular example is worth looking at – the discussions initiated with Soviet and Hungarian economists around the French macro-economic modeling experiment prepared for the Sixth Plan. Contacts had been made for that project within the framework of the Matheco program launched by the United Nations Economic Commission for Europe[53] with the assistance of the United Nations Development Programme. The project aimed at promoting cooperation on the application of computer science and mathematical methods in economics. A first cycle of study was held in Varna (Bulgaria) in September-October 1970 on the use of macroeconomic planning models. It brought together planners and economists from France (Seibel, Courbis), Norway (Spurkland, Sevaldson), the Netherlands (Van de Pas), as well as Hungary (Kornai, Norva & Bager), Bulgaria (Nikiforov), Czechoslovakia (Cerny) and the Soviet Union (Isaiev).

The Hungarian presentations particularly caught the French participants' attention; the decision was made to further pursue these talks in the form of Franco-Hungarian meetings held alternatively in Paris and Budapest in the early 1970s (a French delegation was in Hungary on 25 – 29 October 1971;[54] a Hungarian delegation was in Paris in June 1972; etc.):

> While friendly relationships have existed for many years between Hungarian and French planners, the starting point of the mission lies more precisely in the contacts that were established between the French and Hungarian delegations at the international seminar in Varna (October 1970) and results from the interest that the representatives of each of the two countries manifested for the economic research carried out in the other country. The current mission aimed to allow each partner to be informed of the most recent developments in each other's research (research, which in the Hungarian case seems promising and very instructive for French planning), and, on the basis of the experience gained in each country, to have an exchange of views on common problems.[55]

Regarding the French expectations of these exchanges with Hungarian planners, the initial goal was to find "lessons to draw" from the Hungarian experience, and more precisely to study how Hungarian techniques could be used to over-

---

[53] On the role of the Economic Commission for Europe, see the contribution of Daniel Stinsky in this volume.
[54] The French delegation included: Claude Seibel, Henri Guillaume, Bernard Ullmo (INSEE); Pierre Malgrange (CEPREMAP); Jean-Pierre Pagé and Alain Bernard (Division des études et synthèses quantitatives, Commissariat au Plan).
[55] Report of Commissariat au Plan, INSEE (Institute for Statistics), CEPREMAP (Center for the Economical Research and its Applications), "Mission in Hungary," 25 – 29 October 1971. Commissariat au Plan Papers/ French National Archives (1992 0270/1).

come difficulties encountered in models for planning, especially the FIFI (Physico-Financial) model devised by the directorate for programs at the French national institute of statistics (INSEE).[56] FIFI was introduced as a model for "simulating" economic policy. It proposed a description of "'spontaneous' economic developments" and possible variants based on the objectives "considered desirable." It was referred to as "physico-financial" because one of the technical innovations it attempted to introduce consisted in taking into account the interdependence between physical variables and value variables (based on the treatment of firms, prices and wages), an approach it shared with the Hungarian forecasting model:

> For our part, we were particularly interested in the way in which a very detailed and fully formalized model, such as the "mathematical model of the IVth Hungarian plan", could be inserted in the real planning process and also in the possibilities of using "dual price system" (or a system of implicit valuations) as reference indicators for sectoral studies. The attempts made in France in this domain revealed a number of difficulties that related to the double nature (financial and physical) of the FIFI model, a characteristic that we also find in the Hungarian model.[57]

The French had proposed three themes for discussion: establishing a function for state preference; the relations between micro- and macro-economics; the search for sector-specific optimization criteria.[58] It appears, however, that French planners mostly focused on the then crucial question of the integration of the international dimension and the development of an "international specialization model." By the late 1960s, the growing internationalization of the economy required coming up with forecasting models (such as FIFI) that distinguished between production sectors subject to international competition, "exposed sectors," and so-called "sheltered sectors." The Hungarian innovations were perceived as a potential source of inspiration in that respect, even though that appropriation required adjustments to be relevant to a "liberal economy":

> We need to examine how relations describing production costs . . . can be adapted to the accounting practices of French sectors and if necessary, to include on a sector-by-sector basis in the international specialization model relations of that nature (possibly by adding a supplementary constraint for the industry as a whole, which could be extracted from FIFI

---

56 Michel Aglietta and Raymond Courbis, "Un outil pour le Plan: le modèle FIFI," *Économie et statistique* 1/1 (1969): 45–65.
57 Commissariat au Plan, INSEE, CEPREMAP, "Mission en Hongrie, 25–29 octobre 1971". Commissariat au Plan Papers/French National Archives (1992 0270/1).
58 Letter from Claude Seibel to T. Norva, 27 May 1971. CAEF (H 1931).

results and would translate in indirect form the hypothesis of an economy affected by competition).[59]

However, another form of circulation quickly developed, consisting in the transfer of the FIFI model to the East. As the minutes of the Franco-Hungarian meeting held in Paris in May-June 1972 report:

> It was suggested that one country might use a model built in the other country; in this case the [French] model FIFI would be tested for the Hungarian economy. The [French] Institute for Statistics would transfer the computer program and provide technical assistance for the transcription, either by sending someone to Budapest or by receiving a Hungarian intern in Paris.[60]

The FIFI model was of interest to Hungarian planners in that it allowed them to conceive the volume-price relation in various production sectors. The underlying planning rationales in the French and Hungarian models were different, but in this respect complementary, as Claude Seibel explains:

> The Gosplan was ultimately a regulator in the Marxist sense. That is also why they took an interest in our business: in fact, we were trying to monitor movements in prices, whereas they had instructions in terms of quantity and quality, but not at all in terms of prices. So for Kornai and the Gosplan guys . . ., having a volume-price balance was a guide: prices were administered, so making a forecast, a projection on prices that would be closer to the company's economic reality was what interested them, because it was a sectoral model. There were only eight sectors, which wasn't a lot, but it allowed them to think: 'We've got planning on volume; but if we set too low a price, we're going to run into big problems in a number of companies'. That's what they were interested in: the volume-price verification. [61]

Mutual legitimizations of state expertise

Similar exchanges were developed with Soviet economists, who also took an interest in the macro-economic models built in France. Several Franco-Soviet meetings were held in the early 1970s within the framework of a cooperation agreement on "the problem of the elaboration and practical utilization of

---

[59] "Rapport sur la rencontre des planificateurs hongrois et français," 7 December 1971. CAEF (H 1931).
[60] Commissariat au Plan, Service économique, "Conclusion de la visite de la délégation hongroise," 20 June 1972. CAEF (H 1931).
[61] Interview with Claude Seibel, 13 April 2016.

macroeconomic models in planning". On the Soviet side, they involved economists from the Central Institute of Mathematical Economics (CEMI), who were then engaged in efforts to optimize and decentralize the Plan. The cooperation in France on that issue was considered "very effective," especially given that this country was "visibly the only one of the capitalist countries where this research [on the elaboration and practical utilization of interbranch and macroeconomic models in planning and forecasting] is a state endeavor." The report drafted following the French mission (6–27 January 1971) of CEMI deputy director Stanislav S. Šatalin and his aides states that the methods, models and procedures used in France can be "applied with great usefulness in the research conducted in our country."[62]

This recourse to foreign experience may have been legitimized by the Soviet discourse of the time on the "scientific and technical revolution" and the idea of a "convergence of systems" but was challenged by the "conservative" factions of Soviet economic science.[63] In 1973–1974, for instance, mathematical economists were the targets of harsh attacks, being accused of using "the formulas of bourgeois economists," particularly regarding the then central question of price-setting, an underlying issue in the appropriation of the French model FIFI for the purposes of Socialist planning.

These attacks had an impact on the uses of Western experience by Soviet mathematical economists. Their reforming efforts, aimed at decentralizing economic management and giving firms increased autonomy, met with much resistance at the time, not only among the ideologue economists who defended the Marxist dogma, but also among the bureaucrats whose role in the "top-down" control of the economy was challenged in the process. The mathematical economists had a narrow path for reform, as all references to "market socialism" had become politically suspect after the repression of the Prague Spring in 1968. The dialogue with the French was subject to limitations. It continued, but was refocused on economic quantification tools (modeling, operational research,[64] etc.). It happened for the most part within the framework of the "computer science" cooperation sector and primarily involved the research institutes of the Academy of Sciences on the Soviet side, beginning with the Central Institute of Mathemat-

---

[62] Report on the scientific mission in France (6–27 January 1971). Central Mathematics and Economics Institute Papers, Russian Academy of Sciences Archives, Moscow (F. 1959, Op. 1, D. 333).
[63] On the debates in Soviet economics in 1950s-1970s, see Sergei Alymov, "'This is profitable for all': Agrarian Economists and the Soviet Plan-Market Debate in the post-Stalinist period," *Jahrbücher fur Geschichte Osteuropa* 65/3 (2017): 445–474.
[64] Eglė Rindzevičiūtė, *The Power of Systems*.

ical Economics (CEMI), which had been appointed as the Soviet organization of reference for these collaborations in 1967. Under the umbrella theme "Automatization of information processing and application of mathematical and computer science methods in research on economics, planning and management," the exchanges of the Soviet economists with the French were structured in the 1970s and 1980s around two main clusters: "scientific methods for corporate management" and "the use of mathematical methods in macroeconomics." Like other East-West exchange networks, this cooperation became a means to acquire Western computer science technology and circumvent the embargo imposed by the CoCom (Coordinating Committe for Multilateral Export Controls).[65]

The refocusing of the exchanges on quantification and computer science issues was arguably a means to leave a space for dialogue open in the West in the context of the ideological and political tightening of the Brezhnev years, once the debates on future structural reforms had been closed.[66] Drawing on a long tradition of state engineering, the French tradition remained of interest to Soviet economists. However, only during the so-called "transition" years were some Russian economists able to cite "indicative" French planning as a model and a source of inspiration for pursuing a moderate, progressive reform agenda.[67] The Franco-Soviet dialogue, which since the late 1950s had revolved around a reflection on combining planning and market mechanisms, took on a new relevance then, even though the networks that had also for several decades brought together US and Eastern economists enabled a quick and enthusiastic embrace of neoliberal economic policies.[68]

Indeed, by the 1960s, Eastern socialist countries had become testing grounds for French planners, allowing them to validate and perfect the models they were elaborating, such as the strategy devised by Wassily Leontief, a US economist with Russian roots, to promote his input-output model.[69] In doing so French planners were legitimizing their economic expertise and more broadly their role at a time when they were being increasingly marginalized in the French state apparatus. As Claude Seibel noted in an interview on the subject of the diffusion of French macroeconomic models in the East, the point of these exchanges was "to validate our work from a scientific standpoint: it was a form of validation."[70]

---

65 See the contribution by Sandrine Kott in this volume.
66 Gil Eyal and Johanna Bockman, "Eastern Europe as a Laboratory."
67 Interview with Dmitrij B. Kuvalin, 20 February 2017.
68 Gil Eyal and Johanna Bockman, "Eastern Europe as a Laboratory."
69 Ibid.
70 Interview with Claude Seibel, 13 April 2016.

Introduced after World War Two, the "sociopolitical consensus" across the aisle on the need for an "administered mode of regulation" using a planning board started to fall apart by the mid 1960s. Reports of a "disenchantment" or "disaffection" with the *Plan* became routine. French planning then faced a double challenge.[71] First, within the political field, mounting criticism against the culture of economic regulation came from both right and left.[72] Then, within the political and administrative apparatus, after an income policy was abandoned in 1965, the Plan was increasingly conceived as a management tool and no longer as a political project.[73] Additionally, the importation in France of PPBS (Program, Planning, Budgeting System), a US technology for rationalizing public policy, resulted in a loss of power for the planners, as the Ministry of Finance took this opportunity to reassert its control over the planning board.[74] These criticisms intensified in the 1970s, as the oil crisis called into question the balance between short-term and long-term approaches, and led to a growing gap between a management logic (focused on managing economic crises as they arise) and a planning logic (focused on long-term control).

In response to these intensifying challenges, state economists developed an intense reflection on the planning board, its methods, models and political role for the advent of an "economic democracy," documented in multiple books, articles and leaflets on the subject. Following the reform momentum in the East was a response to expectations in terms both of technical upgrading and political legitimization. Each sign of disinterest manifested by Soviet economists toward these exchanges was therefore bitterly disappointing, despite the asymmetries that characterized them. In 1973, for instance, the French delegation's report following the Moscow meeting of the French-Soviet group on economic information read:

> According to the French participants present at previous meetings, and in particular the President of the delegation, a number of small facts suggest that [the French-Soviet economic information group] would be losing its value in the eyes of GOSPLAN. A slight bitter-

---

71 Henry Rousso, *La Planification en crises* (Paris: Éditions CNRS, 1987).
72 Michel Margairaz and Danielle Tartakowsky (ed.), *Mai 68 entre libération et libéralisation*.
73 On this transformation, see Thomas Angeletti, "Faire la réalité ou s'y défaire. La modélisation et les déplacements de la politique économique au tournant des années 1970," *Politix* 95 (2011/3): 47–72.
74 Vincent Spenlehauer, "Intelligence gouvernementale et sciences sociales," *Politix* 48 (1999): 95–128. See also: Aude Terray, *Des Francs-tireurs aux experts*, 466 on; Philippe Bézès, *Réinventer l'État. Les réformes de l'administration française (1962–2008)* (Paris: Presses universitaires de France, 2009).

ness appeared in the concluding remarks made by President Huet during the signature of the memorandum.[75]

Conclusion

This research on the relations between French planners and economists with their Eastern counterparts offers some insights into the broader and as of yet still very much incomplete study of East-West economic science networks during the Cold War. It shows at least that alliances were set up during the 1960s in Europe to redefine the role of economic expertise in the state apparatus.

This dialogue served different national strategies. For the French state economists, the chief objective was to reformulate and legitimize the role of the country's planning board and to validate its methods, as the postwar consensus on the need for a regulated form of economic management was breaking down. For the Eastern economists, the goal was to propose a new expertise based on a "neutral" economic science and acquire some degrees of autonomy from the political and ideological communist authorities. For some time, an alignment of interests was possible. Faced with the rise of neoliberal discourse,[76] these East-West networks conveyed another definition of economic science, open to social science, in favor of combining planning and the market, and attentive to mechanisms of decentralization and democratization of economic power.

The intensity of this dialogue has been largely forgotten today. The history of French economic science largely reflects the scope of the exchanges with the United States, but entirely neglects those with the East. This relates to what can be described as the "failed" internationalization of French economic science, which did not succeed in asserting its state expertise on the long term despite having forged ties with the East at a very early stage. While the East was becoming a field for experimenting and a key stake in struggles over the definition of economic science, the economists who opposed any form of state interventionism were the ones who managed to rally East European and Soviet econ-

---

75 INSEE, Service des programmes, "Compte rendu de la IXᵉ Session du Groupe de travail mixte franco-soviétique (Moscou, 21–29 mai 1973)," 7 June 1973. INSEE Papers, CAEF (B 57 701).
76 See such recent works on the history of neoliberalism as: Serge Audier, *Néo-libéralisme(s). Une archéologie intellectuelle* (Paris: Grasset, 2012); Philip Mirovski and Dieter Plehwe, *The Road From Mont-Pèlerin. The Making of the Neoliberal Thought Collective* (Cambridge, Mass.: Harvard University Press, 2009); François Denord, *Néo-libéralisme version française. Histoire d'une idéologie politique* (Paris: Demopolis, 2007).

omists to their cause and impose an authoritarian interpretation of neoclassical economics.[77]

Translated from the original French by Jean-Yves Bart

---

[77] Gil Eyal and Johanna Bockman, "Eastern Europe as a Laboratory."

Katja Naumann
International Research Planning across the Iron Curtain: East-Central European Social Scientists in the ISSC and Vienna Centre[1]

The production of applicable social knowledge by a professionalized body of researchers developed in tandem with the idea of planning research itself. International research coordination became a field of action and policy because its development coincided with the emergence of multiple international organisations at the end of the nineteenth century. Planning is, therefore, not only an outcome of social science research but also its prerequisite.[2] It is the planning of social science research, much more than research for the sake of social planning, that I will unpack.

This chapter addresses cross-border cooperation in the social sciences, focusing on two organizations set up by the United Nations Educational, Scientific, and Cultural Organisation (UNESCO): the International Social Science Council (ISSC) – which was a coordinating body for international disciplinary organisations, such as the International Sociological Association – and the European Co-ordination Centre for Research and Documentation in Social Sciences (Vienna Centre) – which was created as one (of many) regional centers whose aim was to coordinate collaborative work of research institutes, in this case from both sides of Cold War-divided Europe, and to develop what has been called comparative social science studies.

The two organizations were spaces of encounter, of cooperation and competition across the Iron Curtain, *and* they were spaces in which East-Central Europeans proactively participated – contrary to the popular belief that Soviet (USSR) domination of the overall geopolitical constellation left hardly any room for self-

---
[1] I want to thank Geert Castryck for his comments on earlier versions of this article.
[2] In recent years, the history of social scientific knowledge (and its application for social planning) has gained momentum, see for example: Peter Wagner, "Social Science and Social Planning during the Twentieth Century" in *Cambridge History of Science: The Modern Social Sciences*, vol. 7, ed. Theodore M. Porter and Dorothy Ross (Cambridge: Cambridge University Press, 2003), 591–607; Kerstin Brückweh, Dirk Schumann, Richard F. Wetzell, and Benjamin Ziemann, *Engineering Society* (Basingstoke: Palgrave, 2012), Christiane Reinecke, Thomas Mergel, *Das Soziale ordnen: Sozialwissenschaften und gesellschaftliche Ungleichheit im 20. Jahrhundert* (Frankfurt am Main: Campus, 2012).

directed action, effectively generating a self-contained Eastern bloc.³ Scholars from that region could enter the ISSC as individuals by invitation, or via their countries' official membership. This "double ticket" strengthened their position, and Polish scholars, in particular, made use of this opportunity. As a result, membership in the ISSC and its executive committee (EC) broadened from 1954 onwards,⁴ and this led to innovations in the agenda. In a similar vein, scholars from the Eastern part of Europe proactively engaged in the Vienna Centre, by suggesting and co-directing large research projects with collaborators from all over the continent. The fact that they made intensive use of these institutionally provided spaces of participation are signs and evidence that the two institutions were not completely captured by the Cold War constellation.⁵

Therefore, histories of these two institutions demonstrate (once again) that international organizations during the Cold War were much more than instruments for and under complete control of the two superpowers; they were used as platforms to connect and exchange, and became spaces where it was possible to move beyond nominal participation and marginality, resulting from the dynamics of the confrontation between the two superpowers. Scholars from

---

[3] Drawing inspiration from Global Cold War Studies and new research on international organisations, the idea of an isolated and sealed off Eastern bloc has been disproved, and entanglements across the East-West divide have been shown: Tobias Rupprecht, "Die sowjetische Gesellschaft in der Welt des Kalten Krieges: Neue Forschungsperspektiven auf eine vermeintlich hermetisch abgeschottete Gesellschaft," *Jahrbücher für die Geschichte Osteuropas* 3 (2010): 381–99. Michel Christian, Sandrine Kott and Ondřej Matějka, "International Organisation in the Cold War: The Circulation of Experts beyond the East-West Divide," *Acta Universitatis Carolinae Studia Territorialia* 17 (2017): 35–60; György Péteri, "Sites of Convergence: The USSR and Communist Eastern Europe at International Fairs Abroad and Home," *Journal of Contemporary History* 47 (2012): 3–12; in this volume the article by Stinsky.

[4] In 1954, after Stalin's death, the Soviet Union (USSR) joined UNESCO. That same year, Poland, Czechoslovakia, Hungary, and Yugoslavia resumed their membership (they had been founding members but ceased their relations with the organization in 1952).

[5] A Cold War orientation also resonated in studies of Eastern European sciences, which are treated separately, creating the impression of scientific and scholarly isolation. The bipolar structure of the geopolitical and ideological confrontation shaped the view, and consequently scientific organisations, networks, and individuals that may have interacted, connected, and communicated across the Iron Curtain have been "under-explored." This is changing, and unlike earlier works that considered mainly platforms of unofficial exchange, newer works show professional societies and other scholarly institutions as sites of encounter and negotiation between increasingly diverse group members, see: Maxine Berg, "East-West Dialogues: Economic Historians, the Cold War, and Détente," *Journal of Modern History* 87 (2015): 36–71, Thibaud Boncourt, *A History of the International Political Science Association* (Quebec: Association internationale de science politique 2009); Johanna Bockman, *Markets in the Name of Socialism: The Left Wing Origins of Neoliberalism* (Stanford: Stanford University Press, 2011), 50–75.

throughout East-Central Europe engaged in these institutions with their own academic and political agendas, and helped the harboring and advancement of intentions that extended beyond the rationale of the belligerent hegemonic powers. The Vienna Centre's raison d'être, for example, was to bridge the East-West divide, and in the way it was used even thwarted the bipolar logic.

Among the reasons that enabled East-Central European experts to participate in their own right is a long tradition of transnationally connected social science research and the institutional opportunities offered by international organizations in the field, after the end of World War Two (WWII). Substantively, the professional exchange despite (much more than across) the East-West divide introduced innovations in the design and conduct of comparative social science research, and it consequently contributed to the transcendence of the bloc-divide.

To substantiate this argument, this chapter will sketch two dimensions of the development of the ISSC and Vienna Centre respectively: First, the institutional possibilities and structural framing of the participation of East-Central European actors will be explored, by describing the politics of membership and internal modes of operation. Second, based on biographical and other evidence of individual experiences and interests – which included engaging as experts and being on equal footing with their colleagues from other parts of Europe – I will highlight the scope and direction of East-Central European scholars' involvement in the research planning of these institutions.[6]

Addressing infrastructure and research, planning means several things in this context: It involved setting up an institutional platform to increase contact and exchanges between scholars from countries all over Europe; coordinating the joint work of different research institutions, which includes developing guidelines for collective work (i.e. regulations for the composition of teams, workflows, or joint meetings); organizing funding from governments and foundations; building infrastructure for large-scale social science research, such as databases, and supporting the development of common research designs, which involves provisions to secure the comparability of the collected data and the possibility for coherent interpretations of the results. At the heart of

---

6 This chapter is based on published materials (progress reports, evaluations, etc.), and it is supplemented by literature on key actors. These sources do not allow for an in-depth evaluation of the connections between the internal politics of these bodies and the course of the programmatic work. They also do not display the direction of the actual research undertaken, for example the decision to opt for certain types of methods, and they are rather silent about conflicts and confrontations. They are, however, a valuable source for reconstructing the institutionally provided spaces for participation and demonstrating that Eastern European scholars filled them.

the endeavor was the advancement of social science methods towards a comparative social science studies methodology, which could explain the differences in the ideologies and socio-economic systems in Europe (and beyond); in addition, its ultimate goal was to establish a general theory of development.[7] However, initially and for quite some time thereafter, the idea and concept of international comparative research remained vague, and its planning headed in different directions.

The last section of this chapter will briefly address the place of Cold War entanglements between Eastern and Western social scientists, in the longer history of transnational scientific relations. WWII and the onset of the Cold War are still understood as introducing a marked rupture in continuities and legacies from the pre-war era. However, the postwar activities of East-Central European scholars, who participated in the ISSC and the Vienna Centre, clearly relied on contacts, networks, and experiences that originated in the 1920s and 1930s. The rapidly developing cooperation across Europe, also globally, in social science research planning since the mid twentieth century is, in my view, closely connected to entangled European scientific relations of the previous period.

Through this essay, it should become clear that the international production of social knowledge from the 1960s through the 1980s had a strong Polish and East-Central European imprint, and that this imprint resulted as much from new institutional settings emerging after the onset of the Cold War as from intellectual traditions and networks from the pre-war period. Both dimensions undercut the idea that the East-West divide was the prime and all-encompassing logic of the time. Recognising this may help to contextualize the period of the Cold War confrontation between the United States (US) and the USSR in longer trajectories, and to understand the Cold War not as a bipolar confrontation but as a plural and layered constellation.

---

[7] See, among other things, the report on the inspection of the Vienna Centre by UNESCO in 1971: Lucio Garcia del Solar, European Coordination Centre for Research and Documentation in the Social Sciences, JIU/HBP/71/13, GE.72–1890; see also the Statutes of the Centre, and: Pierre Feldheim, introduction to *International Cooperation in the Social Sciences. 25 Years of Vienna Experience*, ed. František Charvát, Willem Stamation, Christiane Villain-Gandossi (Vienna: European Co-ordination Centre for Research and Documentation in Social Sciences, 1988), 9–16.

The ISSC: Spaces of participation and Polish organizational power

During the Cold War, international research planning increased; older institutions were reorganized and new ones were founded, such as the World Federation of Scientific Workers. Research coordination expanded, too, especially through UNESCO and its institution-building. A double structure emerged, consisting of self-organized scholarly bodies, based on individual membership, and bodies that represented national research institutions (often government sponsored), in which relations were at times close and at other times strained.

By incorporating "Science" into UNESCO's name, the founders sought to promote their understanding of an open society, in a time of sharpening ideological competition over the best form of social organization.[8] The competing universalisms of the two blocs, for which international organizations were prime sites of cooperation and competition,[9] were a driving factor behind scientific internationalism from the 1950s to the 1980s; decolonization processes and the resulting demands for representation by newly independent nations were another. Therefore, UNESCO's written agenda specified the planning of social science research, which would become an ongoing issue of negotiation and contestation by policymakers and scholars from Europe, the US, and, later, other world regions.

The division of social sciences (DSS) was one of eight divisions of UNESCO's secretariat. Admittedly, the social science program had always been one of the smallest in the organization.[10] However, until at least the early 1970s, the DSS was effective, especially in terms of building a network of institutions that would broaden, anchor, and shape international social science research planning. It initiated disciplinary international organizations for economics, sociology, and political science in which respective national associations would collaborate. It helped establish permanent regional coordination centres: The first was the Vienna Centre (in 1963); later followed by CODESRIA (Council for the Development of Economic and Social Research in Africa), UNAPDI (UN Asian and Pa-

---

[8] Aant Elzinga, "Unesco and the Politics of International Cooperation in the Realm of Science," in *Les Sciences Coloniales: Figures et Institutions*, ed. Patrick Petitjean (Paris: Orstom, 1996), 163–202.
[9] Sandrine Kott, "Cold War Internationalism," in *Internationalisms: A Twentieth-Century History*, ed. Glenda Sluga and Patricia Clavin (Cambridge: Cambridge University Press, 2016), 340–362.
[10] Peter Lengyel, *International Social Science: The UNESCO Experience* (New Brunswick: Transaction Books, 1986), 2.

cific Development Institute), CLACSO (Consejo Latinoamericano de Ciencias Sociales), and FASRC (Federation of Arab Scientific Research Councils).

The secretariat also established two bodies: the International Committee for Social Science Documentation (in 1950), which aimed at bringing together technicians to prepare international bibliographies and catalogues of periodicals, journals, and other reference works, and the International Social Science Council (in 1952).[11] The activities and publications of the ISSC triggered the founding of national counterparts; for instance, the Polish Academy of Science, beginning in 1958, published the *Quarterly Review of Scientific Publications* in English, in order to make Polish research available to a broader audience. These developments indicate the emergence of an infrastructure for mutual observation and exchange, which in its scope and technical sophistication did not exist in the first half of the twentieth century.

UNESCO was by no means the only actor operating in this domain. By the mid 1950s, more than a dozen international organizations played an active role in shaping the social sciences.[12] However, it played a substantial role in catalyzing institutional expansion for the planning, coordination, and exercise of social science research. These efforts evolved into a globally connected network of national, regional, and international organizations.

The idea of creating a (new) international social science institute was first voiced in 1948 by a United Nations (UN) committee of experts, who were charged with designing research institutes for wings of the UN. Two years later, the World Congress of Sociologists supported the initiative, and in 1952, the ISSC was established through a resolution by UNESCO's Sixth General Conference. It was assigned three tasks: (1) to advance "the social sciences throughout the world"; (2) to promote the application of social sciences "to the major problems of the present day," and (3) to facilitate internationalization of the social sciences through policies oriented towards organizing comparative research and the interpretation of data. The hope was that it could be achieved by establishing contacts and collaboration between existing organizations in the field, creating new international structures for subjects not yet institutionally anchored, and by disseminating publication information, making recommendations to funding agencies, as well as by designing and conducting research. In summary, the ISSC

---

11 The establishment of national centres, schools, or institutes, and the linking of local institutions with UNESCO spurred the worldwide spread of social sciences (in particular the US-inspired method of social theory building). See S.P. Agrawal and J.C. Aggarwal, *UNESCO and Social Sciences: Retrospect and Prospect* (New Delhi: Concept, 1988), 52–54.

12 See T.H. Marshall, *International Organizations in the Social Sciences*, revised edition (Paris: UNESCO, 1965),

was founded as an instrument for coordinating social science research planning and policy.[13]

In 1953, it began operating as an autonomous body funded by UNESCO. The membership procedure specified that two-thirds of the members would consist of recommended representatives from the six professional associations that constituted its council.[14] The remaining third would be individuals chosen based on their professional standing, rather than their affiliation with any association.

These specifications came out of an intensive debate on what form the new institution should take: a federation of the major social science organizations, or a consultative body of individual members acting in their personal capacity. This seemingly technical discussion was in fact crucial, as it would affect the relationship between disciplines in the ISSC, the nature of authority, and the balance of power between different actors – i.e. alliances of scholars, professional associations, and international organizations, such as UNESCO's DSS – engaged in field research. Broad international involvement was also crucial, including participation by Eastern European scholars. The final decision gave the ISSC limited powers, in relation to international disciplinary associations, but the membership criteria also allowed the council to involve experts on subjects not yet institutionalized, and people who, for interdisciplinary or political reasons, could not otherwise participate.

Given the six-year limit on membership, and the requirement that half of all council members must retire every three years, the ISSC was constructed as a dynamic body. At the same time, its structure allowed for continuity in personnel, since terms of office for the EC were not limited. For example, Jean Piaget, the first president of the council, remained in office until 1961. Conversely, the EC, which consisted of roughly 10 researchers, saw an influx of new people from both sides of the Iron Curtain from 1957 onwards; before this time, members exclusively came from France, Britain, and the US, sparking criticism. Scholars

---

[13] Statutes in Marshall, *International*, 79. See also Jennifer Platt, *Fifty Years of the International Social Science Council* (Paris: International Social Science Council, 2002), 7–10. In parallel with the ISSC, the General Conference provided for an "International Social Science Research Centre for the study of the implications of technological change"; it was established by the ISSC and, in 1960, incorporated into it.

[14] Report on the Constituent Assembly of the Provisional International Social Science Council, October 1952, *International Social Science Bulletin* V, no. 1 (1953): 143–148. Founding members were the International Sociological Association, International Economic Association, International Political Science Association, International Union of Psychology, International Association of Legal Sciences, and the International Union of Anthropological and Ethnological Sciences.

from East-Central Europe began taking part in 1959, when Józef Chałasińky (Poland) was appointed to the council.[15]

Chałasińky (1904–1979) was one of the foremost internationally recognized Polish sociologists of the second half of the twentieth century. His international profile, relations, and skills dating back to the interwar period shaped the role he played in the ISSC. Born in Lublin into a rural civil-servant family, he studied sociology in Poznań with Florian Znaniecki, one of the founders of the field in Poland following World War One. In 1931, after completing his first and second thesis, he received a grant from the Rockefeller Foundation, and went to the University of Chicago where he worked with Ernest W. Burgess on a study that addressed living conditions of a Polish workers' colony in South Chicago. In 1936, he accepted both a position at the University of Warsaw and the chairmanship of the National Institute of Rural Culture, a recently established extra-university research unit. He used the institute to unite and further institutionalize sociological research in Poland, by, among other things, organizing and leading a collective study on the Polish countryside. The study was still under way when war broke out, and some research was destroyed during warfare. However, four volumes of *Young Generation of Peasants* written by Chałasińky had already been published in 1936. The volumes were later criticized for offering a mythical narrative of Polish peasantry, and Chałasińky's aim had indeed been to mobilize Poles in rural areas to take part in the development of the Polish nation. The collective study, however, had another agenda, namely a critical move away from the main concern of contemporary sociologists in Western Europe and the US. Unlike Western sociologists, whose studies focused on workers and the functioning of industrialized societies, Chałasińky wanted to better understand and advance rural society. Although industrialized production had emerged in certain regions of Poland, agriculture remained the primary occupation. Thus, Chałasińky wanted to broaden the narrow focus of established sociological research. Following WWII, he moved to the University of Łódź, where he continued to institutionalize his discipline, while also maintaining his international connections through, among other things, his engagement with the ISSC. In 1961, he was made a full member.[16]

---

[15] Platt, *Fifty Years*, 11–12.
[16] Late in his career, he lost his right to teach for criticizing the influence of Stalinism on Polish sociology at the 1959 World Sociological Congress. He also lost his strong academic standing when a new style of sociology, based on the neo-positivist turn in American sociology, gained momentum. See Wlodzimierz Winclawski, "Józef Chalasińky: A Classic of Polish Sociology," *Eastern European Countryside* 13 (2007): 169–178.

The programmatic principle that Chałasińky used to advance sociology in Poland also guided his international work. Postwar Polish sociology, as practiced by Chałasińky, aimed at understanding societal development in agrarian societies. Other Polish sociologists studied the mobility of peoples, and these studies appear to have been prompted by the need to understand and deal with people, living in areas of East Poland, who were gained after WWII. These two lines of inquiry met and found expression in the research the ISSC planned and coordinated.

Thus, the exemplary case of Chałasińky instructively shows how the ISSC became a platform for people whose ideas thwarted the opposing official discourses of the time. The presence of "Polish"-minted academic interests in international research planning hints at academic logic outweighing geopolitical logic (which does not exclude competition over who produces the most convincing sociological explanations and social theories).

In 1961, the council was enlarged and statutes were changed so that no more than two members of the EC could be of the same nationality; the council also had to consist of "scholars representing the principal cultural regions of the world".[17] The change in statutes resulted in substantial changes in personnel: Sjoerd Groenman, a Dutch sociologist, was elected president; E. Pendleton Herring, a US political scientist, became vice president, and Kazimierz Szczerba-Likiernik became the new secretary general. (Szczerba-Likiernik was of Polish origin and had just retired as head of UNESCO's DSS, where he had worked with Alva Myrdal to found the ISSC.) In addition, Adam Schaff (Poland), René König (West Germany), and Stein Rokkan (Norwegian-born residing in the US) became members of the council. This pluralization, as well as the share of scholars from Eastern Europe is also clearly indicated in Jennifer Platt's data.[18] As Table 1 indicates, the number of council members from North America (mostly from the US) and from Western Europe had declined considerably by the early 1980s. The 1960s witnessed an influx of Eastern European scholars, whose numbers remained stable until 1989–1990, while the 1970s saw an expansion in scholars from the global South. Regarding the composition of ISSC officers, a similar trend is visible in Table 2. Until the end of the Cold War, officers from Eastern and Central Europe increased, becoming the largest represented group.

---

17 Statutes, in Marshall, *International Organizations*, 81.
18 Platt, *Fifty Years*.

Table 1: Representation by region in the executive committee[19]

	1950s	1960s	1970s	1980s	1990s
North America	23	19	13	8	13
Western Europe	71	56	42	40	45
Eastern Europe (incl. GDR)	0	19	18	20	15
Asia	6	5	10	7	6
Latin America	–	–	13	15	10
Africa	–	–	6	8	5
N	35	73	72	84	99

Table 2: Representation by region among ISSC officers[20]

	1950s	1960s	1970s	1980s	1990s
North America	33	33	11	0	20
Western Europe	67	53	43	33	49
Eastern Europe (incl. GDR)	–	13	25	40	9
Asia	–	–	14	0	4
Latin America	–	–	7	27	13
Africa	–	–	–	0	4
N	24	30	28	30	45

With the addition of Szczerba-Likiernik and Schaff, the council had two highly committed members from Poland within its ranks. Together with Rokkan, they immediately began pushing the organization in new directions, especially towards cross-national comparative research.

Schaff and Rokkan, in particular, made use of the opportunity within the ISSC to develop both the infrastructure for comparative studies and a policy for internationalizing comparative social science research.[21] Two major strategies were agreed upon: (1) the creation of a long-term program of meetings, workshops, and training to develop skills and resources for comparative research,

---

[19] Ibid, 55.
[20] Ibid.
[21] Stein Rokkan, "Cross-Cultural, Cross-Societal and Cross-National Research," *Historical Social Research* 18 (1993): 6–54, here 7 (originally published in *Main Trends of Research in the Human and the Social Sciences*, Paris: UNESCO/Mouton 1970, 645–689). For an overview of the activities until 1972, and reflections on how the program was received in the different social science disciplines, see Stein Rokkan, *A Quarter Century of International Social Sciences: Papers and Reports on Developments, 1952–1977* (New Delhi: Concept Publishing, 1979).

and (2) the establishment of an organization to promote systematic research across cultural and political boundaries. In short, ISSC activities were directed towards the development of infrastructure services (for the social sciences at large and for comparative studies), which, in the first place, targeted existing data, materials, and expertize. The Vienna Centre, then, was conceived as the instrument and space for creating new comparable data and knowledge.

When, in 1965, the ISSC evaluated its program, it confirmed the double structure but expanded its own work. On the one hand, it continued to focus on the institutional and infrastructural foundations of research, namely the development of data archives in different countries, especially of statistical data that could be processed using computers; on the other hand, it decided to engage more directly in stirring the direction of research. It entered three new fields to facilitate systematic comparisons: work on qualitative cross-cultural methods, analyzes of historical change, and analyzes of processes of modernization.

Historical investigations, jointly conducted by historians and sociologists, addressed nation-building, urbanization, industrialization, and demographic transformation in Europe and the East. These themes were specifically chosen in view of pressing social and political challenges. The hope was that knowledge could make the social world more predictable and could improve it. Research for the sake of social planning and the planning of social science research are often interrelated. In a similar vein, the analysis of contemporary changes focused on regional disparities in development in South Asia, Western Europe, and Eastern Europe. Here, insights into general patterns of social and political change were hoped for.

Notions of development, directional change, and modernization had already been discussed extensively within the ISSC, but mainly based on quantifiable data that could be coded and processed (levels of growth, spread of innovations, and the speed of economic, social, and political mobilization). The work was guided by the belief that the developmental course of societies could and should be directed, which emerged within the wider process of the "scientification of the social."[22] They wanted to organize research that analyzed such data in a broader historical context, considering chronology and other variables. As Rokkan explained, "The social sciences can only become 'developmental' through close

---

[22] Lutz Raphael, "Embedding the Human and Social Sciences in Western Societies, 1880–1980: Reflections on Trends and Methods of Current Research," in *Engineering Society: The Role of the Human and Social Sciences in Modern Societies, 1880–1980*, ed. Kerstin Brückweh, Dirk Schumann, Richard F. Wetzell, and Benjamin Ziemann (Basingstoke: Palgrave, 2012), 41–58.

co-operation with the students of the time dimensions of social life, the historians."²³

Additionally, the ISSC supported projects that allowed for the participation of Polish scholars not involved in the council, and who fostered concrete ties in divided Europe. For example, it supported research projects, such as the interaction between social values and the responsibilities of local political authorities, which entailed fieldwork in Poland, Yugoslavia, the US, and India, and which was planned and conducted by teams from all four countries.²⁴

The strong involvement of Polish sociologists faltered at the end of the 1960s. Following the death of Szczerba-Likiernik (in 1969) and the departure of Chałasińky out of the EC, fewer Polish scholars participated in the council. Although Chałasińky had taken steps to ensure continued Polish influence, convincing his colleague Jan Szczepański to replace him, Szczepański left the EC after four years, abiding by new rules that limited EC participation to four years. There were also structural and political reasons for declining Polish participation: In 1968, the Polish government partly blocked collaboration with UNESCO. In 1972, the council became a federation of international disciplinary associations, ending individual membership based on expertize. From then on, participation in the ISSC depended upon having a strong international position within one's discipline, and to be delegated to the ISSC by one of the international disciplinary associations.²⁵

The Vienna Centre: An infrastructure for planning and cooperation in social science research across the blocs

After the ISSC had voiced the need for a new institution devoted to planning comparative studies by scholars from both blocs, expert talks and political negotiations began immediately. In 1962, UNESCO's general assembly adopted a resolu-

---

23 Stein Rokkan and Kazimierz Szczerba-Likiernik, introduction to *Comparative Research across Cultures and Nations*, ed. Rokkan Stein (Paris: Hague Mouton), 1–13, 6.
24 See the description in Alexander Szalai and Riccardo Petrella, in collaboration with S. Rokkan and E.K. Scheuch, *Cross-National Comparative Survey Research: Theory and Practice* (Oxford: Pergamon Press, 1977), 231–278.
25 It was not until the mid-1980s that there was another Pole, Leszek Kosinki, in the executive committee. Kosinki had previously served as secretary general of the International Geographical Union, and it was his involvement in this organization that qualified him for the ISSC.

tion, presented by delegations from Austria, Belgium, Czechoslovakia, Italy, Poland, and Yugoslavia, that gave the ISSC responsibility for setting it up. In May 1963, the council implemented the resolution, and in early 1964, the Austrian government and UNESCO reached an agreement that it would be based in Vienna; it was motivated by the country's neutrality. Co-funded by the ISSC and UNESCO, the non-governmental organization (NGO) would operate autonomously.

The Vienna Centre's primary function was that of a platform for cooperation of scholars from leading European institutions, which have (in UN terminology) "different social and economic structures"[26] in the field of comparative studies; its purpose was to devise respective methodologies and research techniques. The Vienna Centre was a coordinating agency – not a research institute; it was concerned with research planning, selecting general themes for projects that would be carried out by multinational teams, nominating scientific directors and participants for these projects, and directing the teamwork.[27]

Another motive of the initiators (Schaff, Stein, and others) was to Europeanize the cross-national survey research of the time. Until the early 1960s, US scholars had dominated the field. Their superior access to funding had given them control over field operations and coding in each country. In Europe it was perceived as "American data imperialism," leading to "a variety of distortions: too many of the questions were phrased and too much of the analysis was carried out in ignorance of the cultural intricacies and socio-political realities of each of the systems covered."[28] The Vienna Centre also clearly came into being as a joint effort of East-Central and Northwestern Europeans to counter the American hegemony in the field. Here, again, one can grasp that the confrontation and geography of the Cold War was more complex than the bipolar axis of East-West suggests.

In a larger sense, the Vienna Centre was set up in the spirit of détente and the policy of peaceful coexistence of the early 1960s; it was premised on the idea that rapprochement between the East and the West could be supported by understanding the social problems and challenges on each side. The effort to ap-

---

[26] European Coordination Centre for Research and Documentation in the Social Sciences, JIU/HBP/71/13, GE.72–1890, 5; Ricchardo Petrella and Adam Schaff, *Une expérience de coopération européenne dans les sciences sociales: Dix ans d'activités du Centre de Vienne, 1963–1973* (Vienna: Centre européen de coordination de recherche et de documentation en sciences sociales, 1973), 7–11 and the Statutes.
[27] Adam Schaff, "The Foundations of the Vienna Centre: Their Development and Prospects," in *International Cooperation in the Social Sciences. 25 Years of Vienna Experience*, eds. František Charvát, Willem Stamation, Christiane Villain-Gandossi (Vienna: ECCRDSS, 1988), 17–33.
[28] Szalai and Petrella, *Cross-National Comparative Survey Research*, ix.

prehend the social structures and conditions that existed in countries with different ideologies and sociopolitical systems would also help each country to reflect inwardly. This enhanced knowledge would allow more informed contributions to social theory-building. In essence, the Vienna Centre was a manifestation of the belief in progress and social engineering, and in the capacity of social science expertize to transcend the antagonism of the Cold War. To achieve this, an NGO seemed to yield better results than UNESCO's DSS or the ISSC.

Finally, the Vienna Centre's founding was motivated by professional competition. Demographers and economists, it was believed, had already organized internationally through their work in organizations like the UN, World Bank, and the Organisation for Economic Cooperation and Development (OECD). In contrast, sociologists, anthropologists, and political scientists, despite their extensive work interpreting data from a large number of countries and producing models of the socio-economic order, did not yet have any infrastructure for cross-national studies and large-scale theories.[29]

Cooperation across the East-West divide brought together different and, in fact, rival values, research orientations, and practices, sparking confrontations and challenging ideological ambitions. Competing agendas, vocabularies, and geopolitical rationales clashed, tensions arose, and efforts at concrete collaborative research projects were derailed.[30] Nevertheless, within the Vienna Centre, scholars observed and learnt about one another, and this triggered the circulation of knowledge.[31] The main domain was the development of comparative methodologies and research designs, which would substantiate theory-building. Although much of the debate was about how to count, these debates were, in fact, about how to interpret and, thus, about prognosis and social planning.

The Vienna Centre's ability to present itself as a space for conceptualizing a kind of European social science arose from the fact that it did not openly contradict Cold War rationales. Governments, for example, had a stake in the Centre's agenda. The research it initiated was done at the involved research institutes, which were financed by their states; several countries also supported the centre

---

[29] Rokkan and Szczerba-Likiernik, 8.
[30] Ricchardo Petrella and Adam Schaff, *Une experience*, 100–105.
[31] For a similar incident at UNESCO in which the trajectory went from confrontation to common learning, see Katja Naumann, "Avenues and Confines of Globalizing the Past: UNESCO's International Commission for a "Scientific and Cultural History of Mankind" (1952–1969)," in *Networking the International System: Global Histories of International Organizations*, ed. Madeleine Herren (Heidelberg: Springer, 2014), 187–200.

directly.³² However, political concerns seemed not to have outweighed the idiosyncrasies of the leading figures at the centre. Additionally, the institutionalized spaces for exchange and collaboration prevented and prohibited politically motivated interventions.

In what follows, I outline the substantial spaces of manoeuvre that existed within the Vienna Centre for East-Central European scholars and experts, which are visible in their level of involvement in the director's committee, work procedures, and programs. To repeat, I understand their positioning and contributions as expressions of the Centre's power to cut through the already porous Iron Curtain.

The Vienna Centre's organizational chart was simple, consisting of the director's committee and a fairly small administrative and technical staff. Scientific collaborators were involved only for the duration of a project, and the director's committee was the nucleus of decision-making; at the beginning, it consisted of 10 members, and by the 1980s it increased to 20.

In 1978, six of the director's committee of 18 members came from East-Central or Southeast Europe.³³ Crucial for the influence of scholars from that region was the presidency of Adam Schaff, which lasted almost 20 years (1964–82) and encompassed the entire initial stage, the program's evaluation c. 1972–73, and its restructuring in the early 1980s. After his retirement in 1982, Pierre Feldheim (Belgium) took over.³⁴

Adam Schaff (1913–2006) was a controversial academic figure, whose career path was shaped by the changing ability of the Communist Party to control the social sciences, and by a generational shift in Polish sociology that ushered in an American-inspired form of empirical research. Schaff had studied law and economics at the École Libre des Sciences Politiques in Paris, and philosophy in Warsaw and Moscow, where he received a doctorate. In 1948, he was awarded the first chair in Marxist philosophy at the University of Warsaw, after which his academic stature, as well as his standing in the Communist Party climbed

---

32 In the period from 1964–1972, Hungary, Poland, Czechoslovakia, the USSR, and Yugoslavia covered 14.9% of the Vienna Centre's expenses; Western European countries paid 34.4%, while Austria as the host country covered 15.5%. UNESCO had the largest share with 34.4% (Petrella and Schaff, *Une expérience*, 71). Things changed in 1973 when UNESCO terminated its subvention, resulting in its share having to be shouldered by member states or other funding sources.
33 Petrella and Schaff, *Une Une expérience*, 8, and Marshall, *International Organizations*, 77. See also the entry for the Vienna Centre, in *International Directory of Social Science Research Councils and Analogous Bodies, 1978–79*, 134–5.
34 The president was assisted by a director; the post was filled, among others, by Oskar Vogel (German Democratic Republic) from 1982–86, who was followed by František Charvát (Czechoslovakia/Canada).

steadily. He quickly gained influence and received political support for his efforts at establishing a Marxist perspective on Polish history.[35] In his writings from the 1960s, he demonstrated openness to less orthodox positions.[36] In 1968, however, he was dismissed from his teaching post and removed from his leading positions in the Communist Party (he was later also excluded). However, because of his international standing, he was able to leave Warsaw for Vienna, where in 1971 he was given an honorary position as professor of social philosophy at the University of Vienna.[37]

The choice of location for international-organization meetings is not an insignificant matter; when a nation is chosen as host, it signals and recognizes that nation's stature. By looking at the cities where the directorate met, one can observe a shift to the East: In 1964, the first board meeting was held in Vienna, followed by Paris (1965), Constance (1966), Moscow (1968), Budapest (1969), and Ljubljana (1970). Between 1964–1972, the Vienna Centre organized approximately 130 official meetings for project directors and participants; a total of 1,600 people attended. Austria hosted the most meetings (25), followed by France (22), Poland (18), Czechoslovakia (13), Hungary (10), and Yugoslavia (9).[38]

East-Central Europe's presence in the directorate and in the symbolic politics of the Vienna Centre can be attributed to policies during the early years aimed at maintaining a strict equilibrium between East and West, both in terms of the composition of the board and of the multinational research teams. As difficult as it must have been to uphold, the Centre remained committed to balanced participation; the principle was also a "protective shield" against accusations of political misuse.

The director's committee was charged with maintaining that balance in the research projects sponsored by the Vienna Centre; it reviewed, selected, and revised proposals for joint research projects submitted by scientific institutions and by individual researchers. Once approved, research secretaries established contacts with potential partners, so that international working groups could

---

[35] Maciej Górny, *Die Wahrheit ist auf unserer Seite: Nation, Marxismus und Geschichte im Ostblock*, (Cologne: Böhlau 2011), 177. See also Marcin Kula, *Mimo wszystko bliżej Paryża niż Moskwy. Książka o Francji, PRL i o nas, historykach* [Closer to Paris than to Moscow. About France, the Polish People's Republic and about us, historians] (Warsaw: Wydawnictwa Uniwersytetu Warszawskiego 2010).

[36] He even participated in Christian-Marxist dialogical enterprises, see Ondřej Matějka, "Social Engineering and Alienation between East and West," in this volume.

[37] On Schaff, see Armando Montanari, "Social sciences and comparative research in Europe: Cross-national and multi-disciplinary projects for urban development. The role of geography," *Revue belge de géographie* 1–2 (2012), http://belgeo.revues.org/6085 (accessed 19 June 2017).

[38] Petrella and Schaff, *Une expérience*, 18–19.

be formed. The working groups, then, determined the methodological approach and identified the reference concept. Concomitantly, the chair nominated two research directors for the project, one from each of the blocs. The chair also approved the project's budget, which could only be used for the "international part" of the work (group meetings and publications). Data collection, fieldwork in the participating countries, and the comparative analysis of results then followed.[39]

The scope of the collaboration is noteworthy: During the first decade, scholars from 25 European countries, including researchers from eight Eastern European academies, were involved in the program; 11 non-European countries also participated.[40] Typically, 4–7 experts collaborated on a project; the number could exceed a dozen in larger projects. Participation was, however, not evenly distributed: In the 80 projects and conferences directed by the Vienna Centre in its first 25 years (until 1988), six countries from the East (Bulgaria, Czechoslovakia, Hungary, Poland, the USSR, and Yugoslavia) and five countries from the West (France, West Germany, Italy, the Netherlands, and the United Kingdom) had the highest levels of involvement. Researchers from these countries took part on 26 or more occasions. Poland was involved the most (46, see also Table 3).[41] Looking at the number of participating institutions in the period 1964–69, Poland is also at the top (14 institutions), followed by Czechoslovakia (13), and France and the USSR (9 each).[42] Thus, it is no surprise that Warsaw was chosen to host the First International Seminar on Cross-national Comparative Review (in 1980), and that Polish researchers would utilize the occasion to highlight their role in the field.[43] Overall, the Vienna Centre's research network up to 1972 was far-reaching and dense, including 216 institutes in Europe and 22 outside of Europe, with 165 Eastern European research institutions involved.[44]

---

[39] Chantal Kourilsky, Armando Montanari and G. Vyskovsky, *Vienna Centre Report of Activity 1979–80*, no.10–11 (Vienna: ECCRDSS, 1980): 1–44.
[40] Petrella and Schaff, *Une expérience*, 16.
[41] Willem Stamatiou, "International Cooperation in the Social Science: The Vienna Centre," *International Social Science Journal* 118 (1988): 597–603.
[42] European Coordination Centre for Research and Documentation in the Social Sciences, JIU/HBP/71/13, GE.72–1890, 10.
[43] Manfred Niessen and Jules Peschar, *International Comparative Research Problems of Theory, Methodology and Organisation in Eastern and Western Europe* (Oxford: Pergamon, 1982).
[44] Petrella and Schaff, *Une expérience*, 16.

Table 3: Vienna Centre, Past and Current Projects, 1972[45]

	Title	Directors	Participation (countries / institutes)		Duration
1	Comparative forms of aid to developing countries	V. Kollontai E.A.G. Robinson	5	6	1964–66
2	Absorptive capacity for foreign aid of developing countries and problems of transference of techniques	E. Boserup I. Sachs	8	9	1965–68
3	Automation and industrial workers	F. Adler	16	40	1968–
4	Time-budgets and industrialisation	A. Szalai	12	20	1964–72
5	The costs of urban growth	R. Drewett M. Metelka	8	9	1971-
6	Juvenile delinquency and economic development	H. Michard P. Wierzbicki (later S. Walczak)	4	6	1964–72
7	Comparative study of legislation concerning fertility	M. Livi Bacci E. Szabady	16	20	1971–
8	Training of students from developing countries	R.V. Kerschagl O. Klineberg	4	4	1967–70
9	University graduates: Their training and conception of life	H. Peisert W. Markiewicz	6	7	1967–
10	Effects of organisational hierarchy	A. Tannenbaum K. Dóktor (later T. Rozgonyi)	12	12	1970–
11	Images of a disarmed world	J. Stoetzel	3	3	1964–65
12	Images of the world in the year 2000	J. Galtung	14	14	1966–72
13	Criteria for choosing between market and non-market (public) ways of satisfying population needs	V. Cao-Pinna S. Chataline	9	14	1968–
14	Location of new industries	V. Raskovic M. Penouil	8	8	1968–

---

[45] Petrella and Schaff, *Une expérience*, 15. I have added information from later progress reports. The figures are taken from reports produced by the Vienna Centre, which undoubtedly assembled them to highlight their achievements. Thus, some institutes included in these figures most likely collaborated only on paper, or for a brief period. Nevertheless, the figures indicate that the contacts and connections that the Vienna Centre developed across Cold War Europe were extensive.

Table 3: Vienna Centre, Past and Current Projects, 1972 *(Continued)*

	Title	Directors	Participation (countries/institutes)		Duration
15	Backward areas in industrialized countries	S. Groenman P. Turčan	12	14	1964–70
16	Diffusion of innovation in agriculture	B. Galeski (Poland) H. Mendras (France)	7	7	1965–70
17	The future of rural communities in industrial societies	B. Galeski O. Grande H. Mendras H.H. Stahl	16	30	1970–
18	Sources of law: Variety and evolution	E. Melichar I. Szabo	2	2	1972–
19	Economic and social problems of tourism in Europe	P. Barucci R. Galecki B. Jansson D. Prielozny	13	17	1972–

The research projects initiated and led by Czechoslovakian, Polish, and Hungarian scholars also display that they played a significant role in planning the substantive direction of comparative social science research. They had the coordinating power needed to negotiate and conduct projects involving scholars from up to 20 institutions, half from each side of the Cold War, who had to synchronize their data, adjust their methodologies for data production to obtain comparable data, and debated their interpretations.

In selecting its program of research, the Vienna Centre, at first chose topics based on existing research, and decided to pursue long-term comparative studies on three broadly defined fields of inquiry: "planning in global comparison," "basic concepts of aid to developing countries", and the "economic and social consequences of disarmament."[46]

The second field listed above (internally described as "backward areas") opened with the project "Backward regions in industrialised countries," co-directed by Sjoerd Groenman and Pavel Turčan (Czechoslovakia). In its third year, researchers collaborating on the project decided to organize a conference, in order to promote dialogue with economists who had studied the subject in

---

46 Petrella and Schaff, 12–13.

other European countries and other parts of the world. In partnership with the International Economic Association, approximately 40 scholars were invited to the 1967 conference in Varenna, including Ota Šik (Prague), B. Winiarski (Wrocław), and Imre Vajda and L. Koszegi (Budapest). Conference discussions prompted the project members to develop a new research line focusing on problems of urbanization. Based on a proposal by Gaston Gaudard and Jean Valarché (Switzerland), the new research line "The Costs of Urban Growth" began in 1973.[47]

In 1964, two of the main and best-known projects of the Vienna Centre started: The first, "Time-Budgets and Industrialization," was conceived and directed by Alexander Szalai (Budapest).[48] The second, "Images of a disarmed world," originated in Polish studies of the future, in particular on public opinion concerning the consequences of disarmament and the future course of foreign policy. Involved in this research was Julian Hochfeld, who later became director of UNESCO's DSS, and who in that role encouraged an international study on the topic. It began with a pilot project and fieldwork in France, Poland, and Norway, under the direction of Jean Stoetzel (Paris). Shortly thereafter, in 1966, a follow-up investigation led by Johan Galtung (Oslo) was approved, which involved 10 countries.[49]

Many projects in the initial years dealt with social change under conditions and consequences of industrialization and modernization; once again, the nexus between planning social science research and social science-based social planning is at hand. It included a study of juvenile delinquency in France, Hungary, Poland, and Yugoslavia, which was led by Stanislaw Walczak (Warsaw); it was prepared at a meeting in Warsaw in 1964, with sociologists from 11 countries.[50] In parallel, comparisons on agricultural settings and developments were organ-

---

[47] See the list of participants and introduction in E.A.G. Robinson, *Backward Areas in Advanced countries: Proceedings of a Conference held the International Economics Association at Varenna* (London: Melbourne MacMillan, 1969); Petrella and Schaff, *Une expérience*, 52–5; Montanari, 9–10.
[48] See the description in Szalai and Petrella, *Cross-National Comparative Survey Research*, 201–231.
[49] Helmut Ornauer and Johan Galtung, *Images of the World in the Year 2000: A Comparative Ten Nation Study* (Atlantic Highlands: Humanities Press, 1976); see also, Jenny Andersson and Eglė Rindzevičiūtė, *The Struggle for the Long-Term in Transnational Science and Politics* (Routledge: New York, 2015).
[50] See the description in Szalai and Petrella, *Cross-National Comparative Survey Research*, 131–168; ECCRDSS, *La délinquance juvénile en Europe. Actes du Colloque de Varsovie, octobre 1964* (Université libre de Bruxelles: Brussels, 1968).

ized. Based on a joint initiative by Schaff (for the Vienna Centre), Bogusław Gałęski, and Henri Mendras, the "Diffusion of innovation in agriculture" became a subject of investigation in 1965. The origins in this collaboration were regular meetings of Polish and French sociologists from about 1960s onwards.[51] In the program line "planning in global comparison" the project initiated by Włodzimierz Brus (Warsaw) started working on "Criteria for choosing between market and non-market (public) ways of satisfying population needs." Brus, who was also involved in the UNESCO study "Main trends of research in the Social and Human Sciences," had to cancel his participation in both projects in 1968, after he and other colleagues were not permitted to continue their engagement with UNESCO.

Several other topics for which the Vienna Centre organized collaborative research had been co-directed by scholars from East-Central Europe: Comparisons of university graduates, suggested by Helmut Peisert (Constance) and conducted with Władysław Markiewicz (Poznań); comparisons of legislation concerning fertility, directed by Massimo Livi Bacci (Florence) and Egon Szabady (Budapest), involved the International Union for the Scientific Study of Population, and comparisons of the effects of organizational hierarchy, which was developed by Arnold S. Tannenbaum (Ann Arbor) and co-directed with Kazimierz Dóktor (Warsaw). In 1970, the first project based in the region, namely in Bratislava, dealt with problems of tourism in Europe.

Upon the suggestion of Imre Szabó, the Vienna Centre prepared an international round-table discussion on the methodology of international comparative research, which evaluated the Centre's activities and decided on its future course. As a consequence, the policy shifted strongly away from planning large collective projects towards more shorter projects, as well as topical conferences; furthermore, the training of young researchers was added.[52]

New subjects came in and non-European colleagues were invited.[53] With this new orientation, the Vienna Centre sought to address the internal criticism that the national framework had hardly been transcended, and that the applicability

---

[51] Bogusław Gałęski, Wacław Makarczyk, Lili M. Szwengrub, *Cross-national European Research Project on the Diffusion of Technical Innovations in Agriculture* (Vienna: International Social Science Council, 1969).

[52] Training was offered in a series of International Seminars on Cross-national Comparative Research, see among others the documentation in Manfred Niessen, Jules Peschar, Chantal Kourilsky, *International Comparative Research: Social Structures and Public Institutions in Eastern and Western Europe* (Oxford: Pregamon Press, 1984).

[53] Jan Berting, Felix Geyer, Ray Jurkovich, *Problems in International Comparative Research in the Social Sciences* (Oxford: Pergamon Press, 1979).

of the results had been higher than the explanatory value of the studies.⁵⁴ Planning the research was valued more than the research of planning. The output should not be underrated: Over 70 books, published on both sides of the Iron Curtain, and several periodicals through which research circulated throughout Cold War Europe, were written.⁵⁵

Situating the post-WWII period within longer transnational scientific relations

Polish sociologists and philosophers, who together with colleagues from other parts of the socialist bloc proactively participated and indelibly influenced the ISSC and Vienna Centre, were not the only scholars from the region involved in international scientific institutions. From the mid 1950s onwards, and especially in the 1960s, a large number of intellectuals from East-Central Europe took part in such organizations. Hochfeld (1911–66), another key figure in the establishment of Polish sociology, was elected deputy director of the UNESCO DSS. Oskar Lange, a prominent Polish economist, participated in the study "Main trends of research in the Social and Human Sciences," coordinated by the DSS. Witold Kula, a seminal figure in Polish historiography, was on the board of the International Commission for a Scientific and Cultural History of Mankind, which was contracted by UNESCO to produce a six-volume world history, and also presided over the International Economic History Association. Erik Molnár, a prominent Hungarian historian, served with Kula on the board of the world-history project. To this list, one could add the Polish sociologist Stanisław Ossowski, one of the founders of the International Sociological Association.⁵⁶ As more studies on this topic are undertaken, it is likely that this list is only the tip of the iceberg.

The scope of East-Central European engagement raises the question: How was this high level of participation possible? Two processes, I believe, were essential: the extensive institutionalization of research coordination in the second half of the twentieth century, which I sketched before, and East-Central Europeans' previous experience with international cooperation. To this second aspect, I will now turn briefly.

---

54 Willem Stamatiou, *Vienna Centre*, 600; Charvát, *International Cooperation*.
55 Stamatiou, *International Cooperation*, 601.
56 Maxine Berg, "East-West Dialogues: Economic Historians, the Cold War, and Détente," *Journal of Modern History* 87 (2015): 36–71.

The rapidly developing European-wide, and later global, cooperation in the mid twentieth century was closely connected with scientific entanglements from the 1920s and 1930s. The speed with which the institutional expansion took place later makes it unlikely that it emerged from scratch; rather, it was made by people who were experienced with international cooperation from before WWII, people who had been well connected with colleagues working on similar topics at other places, and who as academic teachers had introduced their students to practices of transnational scientific exchanges.

Acting confidently and successfully on the international stage is demanding and requires specific skills and expertize. It also, often, requires permission from the state, which presupposes that the ruling powers recognize the value of international participation – an attitude that forms over time, as a society learns to see itself as part of a connected world. Instead of seeing the war as marking a rupture in scientific relations across Europe, I argue that earlier connections were channelled and found expression in the postwar institutional setting, albeit in indirect ways. The trajectories of East-Central European social scientists and historians are instructive here. If one looks closer at the academic biographies of those involved in the ISSC, the Vienna Centre, and related undertakings, one detects few newcomers to the international scene and many whose careers began in the first half of the twentieth century. For example, Chałasińky and Szczepański studied under the founding fathers of Polish sociology, Znaniecki and Stefan Czarnowski (1879–1937). The extensive scientific networks of their mentors, which spanned across Leipzig, Paris, Geneva, and Chicago, left a lasting impression on the two men.

The interwar years had been a time in which academic disciplines were consolidated as part of nation-building efforts. During the 1920s, Polish sociologists tackled contemporary challenges, writing commentaries on modern ideologies, mass movements, sudden social dislocations, economic depressions, as well the question of how to modernize Poland's predominantly peasant society. One of the major issues of the day was the Minority Treaty, which Poland had signed at the Paris Peace Conference. The treaty sparked a nationwide debate on how, or even if, national minorities could be integrated into the Polish state. This issue gave the social sciences increased stature in Poland and facilitated its institutionalization.[57]

---

[57] Stephan Stach, "The Institute for Nationality Research (1921–1939): A Think Tank for Minority Politics in Poland?," in *Religion in the Mirror of Law: Eastern European Perspectives from the Early Modern Period to 1939*, ed. Yvonne Kleinmann (Frankfurt am Main: Klosterman, 2015), 149–179; Olga Linkiewicz, "Scientific Ideals and Political Engagement: Polish Ethnology and the 'Ethnic Question' Between the Wars," *Acta Poloniae Historica* 114 (2016): 5–27; Martin Kohlrausch,

However, parallel to the nexus of scientism, professionalization, and nation-building, intensifying movements across disciplinary and national borders also shaped the social sciences in interwar East-Central Europe. Intellectual exchanges at conferences, fellowships, and visiting appointments, some of which were supported by American philanthropic foundations, were taking place across Europe. Emigration resumed in the 1920s, taking scholars across Europe and the Atlantic. Over the next decade, hundreds of social scientists emigrated from Central Europe, in the process accessing and building scientific networks. Others took advantage of access to international organizations made possible by the (re-)establishment of nation states in the region. For example, Marceli Handelsman, one of the doyens of Polish historiography, built extensive personal contacts across Europe. More importantly, he utilized them to help convince the International Committee of Historical Sciences to hold its seventh congress in Warsaw (in 1933).[58]

Consequently, the entangled processes of nationalization and internationalization turned out to be good preparation for the postwar constellation. One had the intellectual background needed to engage proactively with postwar studies on processes of nationalism and modernization, and one knew how to institutionalize new fields of studies and participate in existing international structures.

The pre-war transnational contacts and experiences that East-Central European scholars had cultivated were certainly altered by WWII, diminishing them in number and, in some cases, altering their influence. Some protagonists lost their lives, such as Handelsman who died in a German concentration camp. Wars, however, also produce new transnational dynamics. Znaniecki left Poland for the US in 1939, and many others fled, or chose to leave their homelands during WWII, which also redrew national boundaries, and, thus, shifted people nominally and practically to new national contexts. Against the backdrop of this upheaval, resettling and integrating into new surroundings took precedence, at least, temporarily over previous intertwinements. Within East-Central Europe, the situation was particularly complex, in part because the new ruling powers

---

Katrin Steffen, and Stefan Wiederkehr, *Expert Cultures in Central Eastern Europe: The Internationalization of Knowledge and the Transformation of Nation States since World War I* (Osnabrück: Fibre, 2010).

58 Dorothy Ross, "Changing Contours of the Social Science Disciplines," in *Cambridge History of Science*, vol. 7: *The Modern Social Sciences*, ed. Theodore M. Porter and Dorothy Ross (Cambridge: Cambridge University Press, 2003), 205–237, 224–237; Helke Rausch, "Akademische Vernetzung als politische Intervention in Europa. Internationalismus-Strategien US-amerikanischer Stiftungen in den 1920er Jahren," *Jahrbuch für Universitätsgeschichte* 18 (2015): 165–188.

pushed for radical new beginnings. There were other dynamics of change, for example the pre-war practice of studying abroad for an extended period of time in multiple countries, popular from roughly the turn of the century to the 1930s, which became less common. Postwar international institutions and expanded networks made shorter research trips more practical and enhanced long-distance communication. International periodicals and bibliographies achieved widespread circulation, making it possible for scholars to keep abreast of international research developments without leaving home; they also allowed authors to publish abroad more easily. When, in the 1950s, the political and institutional context in Eastern Europe created new possibilities for connecting, the skill sets required for developing international connections and the general attitude of valuing cross-border exchange already existed. It seems in many cases, East-Central Europeans were able to swiftly reactivate their scholarly connections and networks.

Conclusion

This chapter dealt with the planning of social science research as a particular domain of social planning. Contributing to social reform was not the predominant aim; often, however, it was closely related to it, either by dealing with the same social and political topics, and/or by being used at some stage for government and policy purposes. The ISSC and the Vienna Centre have been investigated as institutions, which developed European-wide research planning that was not limited by the East-West divide. The East-Central European experts, who made use of the institutionally given spaces of participation, testify that the Vienna Centre not only provided nominal cooperation but was perceived and used as a space in which they could follow their professional calling – to design and to conduct social science research in scholarly competition with colleagues from other places. Even more so, as part of the governing and administrative structure, they had organizational power and could co-determine the programmatic direction and the further institutionalization of international collaboration from the 1950s onwards.

Situating the post-WWII developments within a larger history of European scientific cooperation has shown that the 1950s introduced a massive process of institutionalization at the national *and* international level, aimed at providing the means for cross-border exchange and competition across the Cold War divide (while the institutionalization of cross-border exchange had begun at least half a century earlier).[59] The fact that institutionalization was not new meant that it could draw upon previous international experiences that facilitated the successful expansion of international scientific institutions and the participation of East-Central European experts. International planning activities multiplied, and older mechanisms of connectivity were gradually replaced. One finds in the 1950s, I want to argue, a complex constellation in which remnants of an interwar internationalism based on personal contacts, networks, and experiences have been transferred to a new setting created by the expansion of institutions of international research coordination

---

[59] Frank Greenaway, *Science International. A History of the International Council of Scientific Unions* (Cambridge: Cambridge University Press, 1996).

Sandrine Kott
The Social Engineering Project. Exportation of Capitalist Management Culture to Eastern Europe (1950 – 1980)

In their important book *The New Spirit of Capitalism* Luc Boltansky and Eve Chiapello describe management as a set of prescriptive indications which give direct access to the real spirit of capitalism.[1] In the same perspective, scholars have often studied management as a means to produce or reproduce a social order in which labor is treated and used as a commodity.[2] Therefore, the story of the "exportation" of the management culture from the US to Western Europe has been widely studied as a triumph of US capitalism and one feature of the Americanization of Europe.[3] This point of view has been recently challenged by scholars who have studied the exportation of this management culture to European peripheries and countries where the economic, social and ideological context differed drastically from that in the US and Western Europe. The question of the reception and above all the translation of this US management culture has thus become a central question.[4]

This chapter seeks to address this issue although from a different point of view by studying the rather counter-intuitive circulation of Western managerial knowledge to Eastern Europe during the Cold War. In order to grasp the deep meaning of this exchange we first have to look at management as part of a broader social engineering or social planning project. In that broader meaning, management is a set of prescriptions aiming to organize and rationalize human be-

---

[1] Luc Boltanski, Eve Chiapello. *The New Spirit of Capitalism* (London; New York: Verso, 2005) see also Luc Boltanski, "America, America...: Le Plan Marshall et l'importation du 'management,'" *Actes de la recherche en sciences sociales* 38, no. 1 (1981): 19 – 41.
[2] Marie-Laure Djelic, *Exporting the American Model: The Post-War Transformation of European Business*. Oxford: Oxford University Press, 1998.
[3] Matthias Kipping, "The U.S. Influence on the Evolution of Management Consultancies in Britain, France, and Germany Since 1945," *Business and Economic History* 25, no. 1 (1996): 112-123; Terry Gourvish and Nick Tiratsoo, *Missionaries and Managers: American Influences on European Management Education, 1945 – 60* (Manchester: Manchester University Press, 1998), Bent Boel, *The European Productivity Agency and Transatlantic Relations, 1953 – 1961* (Copenhagen: Museum Tusculanum Press/University of Copenhagen, 2003).
[4] Michal Frenkel, "The Americanization of the Antimanagerialist Alternative in Israel: How Foreign Experts Retheorized and Disarmed Workers' Participation in Management, 1950 – 1970," *International Studies of Management & Organization* 38, no. 4 (2008): 17-37.

https://doi.org/10.1515/9783110534696-007

havior and conduct in order to make human activity and more specifically human work more effective.[5] By forging predictions and strengthening coherence in human activity, management can certainly be interpreted as a social planning tool even if the actors themselves do not use the language of planning. With that in mind, management cannot be reduced to a mere product of capitalism.[6] As a social engineering project, management should be dated back to the end of the nineteenth century but became a field of study in its own right during the First World War. Already in the interwar years, social planners crossed the boundaries between political and economic systems, as in the case of the sociologist and social worker Mary Van Kleeck, executive director of the Russel Sage foundation.[7] While conceptualizing management both as a social and economic project she turned her attention to the Soviet Union to find new inspiration.

Two conclusions should be drawn from this example. First, as already argued by the recent historiography of the Cold War, in the interwar years circulations and convergence between both economic and social systems were taking place and models of economic and social planning were exchanged.[8] That leads to my second point: in order to understand these exchanges, we should be aware of the longer continuities. This chapter will show that the circulation of knowledge in the field of social planning was deeply rooted in the longer history of the relationships between Western and Eastern European countries, between the center of Europe and its (at first) less developed periphery.

To that purpose, I will use the sources produced by the International Labour Organization (ILO), which was set up in 1919 and has been both an actor in and a platform for these exchanges from the 1920s onward. For the post- World War Two period I will mainly analyze the documents produced by the management

---

[5] See the important book by Thibault Le Texier, *Le maniement des hommes: essai sur la rationalité managériale* (Paris: la Découverte, 2016).

[6] Thomas Etzemüller, "Social Engineering als Verhaltenslehre des kühlen Kopfes. Eine einleitende Skizze, " in *Die Ordnung der Moderne. Social Engineering im 20. Jahrhundert*, ed. Thomas Etzemüller (Bielefeld: Transcript, 2009), 11–39.

[7] Guy Alchon, "Mary van Kleeck and scientific management" in *A Mental Revolution. Scientific Management since Taylor* ed Daniel Nelson (Columbus: Columbus State University Press, 1992) 102–130.

[8] Among a very rich list and fast growing body of works Sari Autio-Sarasmo and Katalin Miklóssy, *Reassessing Cold War Europe* (NY: Routledge, 2011), Sandrine Kott, "Par-delà la guerre froide: Les organisations internationales et les circulations Est-Ouest (1947–1973)," *Vingtième Siècle. Revue d'histoire*, 109 (1 Jan., 2011): 143-154. Akira Iriye, "Historizicing the Cold War," in *The Oxford Handbook of the Cold War*, ed. Immermann, Richard H, and Petra Goedde (Oxford: Oxford University Press, 2013) 15–32.

projects set up by the ILO in the framework of the United Nations Development Programme (UNDP).[9]

I will first present how management became an important development project in the ILO and how it was exported to the Eastern part of Europe as a modernizing tool. Second, I will try to understand who were the players and stakeholders of this story, who was implementing and receiving this managerial culture. Third, we need to ask to which extent these players formed a "transbloc" new technocratic class, which has produced and used a common global language based on the same values.

Management as a development project from West to East

Management has been an important aspect of the activity and philosophy of the ILO since the 1920s, this led to the creation of the International Scientific Management Institute in 1926.[10] During the interwar years the organization encouraged management training in Western Europe as part of a larger ideal of social engineering seen as "scientifically" guided social planning.[11] Management would foster an increase in labor productivity and open the road to welfare capitalism.[12] During the 1950s, in the framework of the Expanded Programme of Technical Assistance, the ILO began to extend its management activities to European peripheries, first to Israel in 1952, then to Yugoslavia in 1955.[13]

---

[9] The UNDP started in 1965 taking over the Expanded Programme of Technical Assistance (1946–1966). Craig Murphy, *The United Nations Development Programme : A Better Way?* (Cambridge; New York: Cambridge University Press, 2006).

[10] See Thomas Cayet, "Travailler à la marge: le Bureau International du Travail et l'organisation scientifique du travail (1923–1933)," *Le Mouvement Social*, 228 (1 Sept., 2009): 39-56. Interestingly names differ in the various languages. The French say "Organisation scientifique du travail" and the Germans "Rationalisierung."

[11] Laak Dirk van, "Planung. Geschichte und Gegenwart des Vorgriffs auf die Zukunft [Planning. The past and presence of advancing the future]," *Geschichte und Gesellschaft* 34, no. 3 (1 July, 2008): 305-326. Jon Alexander, Adam Podgorecki, Rob Shields, *Social Engineering*, (Beaconsfield, Quebec: Carleton University Press, 1996).

[12] Thomas Cayet, *Rationaliser le travail, organiser la production : le bureau international du travail et la modernisation économique durant l'entre-deux-guerres* (Rennes: Presses universitaires de Rennes, 2010).

[13] An overview of this can be found in International Labour Office, *The effectiveness of ILO management development and productivity projects*, Report and conclusions, Management Development Series, 3 (Geneva: International Labour Office, 1965).

In 1962, ILO Director General David Morse emphasized the relationship between economic modernization and social management: "Successful industrialisation implies a social revolution. To set up industry . . . is not only acquiring capital and a knowledge of new techniques. Modern industry calls into being its own kind of society. It requires attitudes towards work different from those of traditional rural communities."[14] In 1958, in his opening speech to the International Labour Conference, he had already insisted on making "the ILO a real clearing house for information in the labour management field : a world centre for the exchange of information and research techniques and results and for the dissemination of labour management experiences to employers, workers and governments in all countries."[15] In the same year, the International Labour Conference voted for a resolution to set up a programme on management development, "more especially in the industrially less advanced country."[16] This task was taken over by the Management Development Branch of the ILO in 1960. Between 1960 and 1965, the number of professionals employed in this branch rose from one to 12. These professionals were engaged in special research projects and nine worked full time on the supervision and administration of field projects including recruitment and briefing of management experts.[17] One of the most visible results of this politics was the setting up in 1964 of the ILO Training Center in Turin. Its objective was to provide vocational training for future economic and social elites from newly decolonized countries. With the Turin Center, the ILO could really globalize its approach and become the vehicle of a broader exportation of this management culture. The first survey mission of the new ILO Management Programme was sent to Poland in 1958[18]; it later served as an inspiration for other undertakings of this kind in Eastern Europe and then in newly decolonized countries. The development of the ILO's management activities in Eastern Europe was an attempt to diffuse management tools in the first periphery of the Western World as part of a larger development programme, which was launched in Eastern Europe during the 1960s.

---

14 International Labour Office, *The ILO and Asia*, (Geneva: International Labour Office, 1962).
15 *Director General report* (Geneva: International Labour Office, 1958), 29.
16 *Record of Proceedings of the International Labour Conference* (ILC) (Geneva: International Labour Office, 1958), 777–778.
17 International Labour Office, *The effectiveness of ILO management development and productivity projects, Report and conclusions*, management development series, 3, (Geneva: International Labour Office, 1965) 6.
18 International Labour Organization Archives (ILOA) OTA/Poland/R.1 Report to the government of Poland on a survey mission in connection with management, productivity, supervisory of vocational training.

At the end of the 1950s and during the 1960s, all Eastern European countries except the GDR received development aid through international development programmes, a reality which cannot be understood without taking into account the longer economic history of these countries. As part of the European first periphery, Eastern European countries had already been the target of 'development' projects during the interwar period. In the 1930s, the League of Nations had commissioned a study on peasants and nutrition with regard to agricultural development.[19] Under the guidance of the Polish medical Doctor Ludwik Rajchman and with the help of the Rockefeller Foundation, the League of Nation's Health Organization got involved in sanitation and rural hygiene projects.[20] The ILO carried out technical assistance to various southeastern countries in the field of social insurance and labor law. The Second World War left a tragic imprint on this already less developed part of Europe with some countries losing from one third to 40% of their national wealth. With the end of the United Nations Relief and Rehabilitation Administration and the launching of the Marshall Plan in 1947, Eastern European actors felt threatened by the rapid reconstruction of Western Germany, and they turned to UN agencies for help. Already in 1947 the Polish government requested that the Food and Agriculture Organization send a mission to Poland "to investigate the economic and technical problems linked to the reconstruction of Poland's agriculture and related industries."[21] In the wake of destalinization, the Polish government applied for a training programme for disabled people[22] and between 1957 and 1960 several Polish Fellows went to West Germany, France, Great Britain and Sweden to study rehabilitation programmes for disabled people and invalids.[23] Following the Polish example Hungarian, Romanian and Bulgarian officials requested assistance in developing their agriculture (in the case of Bulgaria) or their tourist industry. During the 1960s and the early 1970s, almost all state socialist countries in Europe (apart from the Soviet Union and the GDR) applied for development programmes to various UN agencies. Unlike newly decolonized countries, Eastern European govern-

---

[19] Sunil Amrith and Patricia Clavin, "Feeding the World: Connecting Europe and Asia, 1930–1945," *Past & Present* 218, no. 8 (2013): 29-50.
[20] Iris Borowy, *Coming to terms with world health: the League of Nations Health Organisation, 1921–1946* (Frankfurt am Main/New York: Peter Lang, 2009).
[21] United Nations Archives (UN-A) 507–2–10–1 (S-0472/67/5) Letter David Weintraub to Mac Dougall 3 April 1947.
[22] ILO-A Z 3/64/2 see the demand addressed to Morse during his March 1958 mission to Warsaw: "Mr Rosner recalled that the office had been informed through Miss Fidler that the Polish government would be interested in participating in the ILO technical assistance scheme."
[23] ILOA OTA 50–1 (A).

ments did not request important financial support but they did call for Western expertise and technology.

This request for expertise increased in the 1960s in the dual context of the détente and the economic reforms implemented throughout the Eastern Bloc. The communist countries had to face labor shortage and needed to increase labor productivity. Throughout the Bloc, reforms were implemented to introduce more flexibility into central planning, while giving more autonomy to the top and middle management. This required new training for these managers who beside political loyalty had to develop economic and managerial skills.[24] As Zdeněk Mošna, a Czechoslovak economist put it very clearly in 1967: "One of the most difficult problems which the socialist countries are now facing is that the new models of management are being applied to managers formed under the centralised economic system. This is why there is a certain discrepancy between the content and objectives of the new economic systems and the present qualifications of managers. . . . The level of education of Czechoslovak industrial directors compares very unfavorably with that of directors in industrially developed countries in the West."[25]

It is in this context that the ILO began testing its new management programme in Poland. As it would be the case in the other socialist countries during the 1960s, the Polish project combined a fellowships programme and the setup of a management center. Forty-three fellowships for a total cost of $100,000, on the basis of 18 long-term periods of six months and 25 short term periods of two months were granted over three years. The host countries were all situated in the Capitalist West: primarily the United Kingdom, France and Sweden, secondly the Federal Republic of Germany and Belgium; three fellows went to Australia and one to Japan. Twelve fellowships were also awarded to members of the new Centre's staff, which had already been established in 1960 with the help of ILO experts. The national Management Development Centre (CODKK), the first of this kind in Eastern Europe was installed in a proper Building at the end of 1960. In 1962, more than a thousand people could attend the courses including senior executives from ministries and leading industries. In 1965, a computer was purchased through the United Nations Development Programme (UNDP), and was installed after a long negotiation under the supervision of a British team.[26]

---

24 Andrzej Korbonski, "The politics of economic reforms in Eastern Europe: The last thirty Years," *Soviet Studies*, 41, no. 1 (1989): 1–19.
25 See Zdeněk, *Mošna*, "The New Economic System and Management Development in Czechoslovakia," *International Labour Review*, 3 (1967): 61–81.
26 For a brief history of the Centre, see *National Management development Centre Poland. Report prepared for the Government of Poland by the International Labour Organisation acting as*

This undertaking was, as David Morse had recommended in his 1958 report, a joint project between the ILO and local agencies. At the end of the 1960s, the last ILO experts left and the Centre became completely independent[27].

Drawing from the Polish experience, emphatically celebrated as a successful model, ILO officials developed programmes of this kind in other Eastern European and later on in newly decolonized countries. The setup of the UNDP in 1965, while allowing governments to contribute in their national currency, facilitated applications from socialist countries.[28] The same year the Bulgarian and Romanian Government requested the newly founded UNDP/Special Fund (UNDP/S) to provide technical assistance in establishing management training centers in Sofia and Bucarest. Both projects started in 1967, and both were very large in scope: Four hundred and 57 expert's man-months were allocated to Bulgaria and 202 man-month fellowships were distributed. The Romanian Management Center (CEPECA) was set up in 1967 thanks to a UNDP allocation of 1,985,900 USD and a government contribution of 4,307,867 USD.[29] The Hungarian government applied for the same kind of programme in February 1966 and – in anticipation – a management development center (OVK) was set up in April 1966 under the direction of Imre Laszlo and the supervision of the Minister of Labour. The UNDP Governing Council approved the project in June 1967 and provided 228 man-month experts and 195 man-month fellowships. The ILO was responsible for the recruitment of the international experts teaching in the center and organized the fellowships programme, which was mostly reserved for the centre's staff. For the ILO, "the creation of the Management Development Centre in Hungary was an essential factor for the development of the country's economy," and instrumental to prepare the economic reforms of 1968.[30] Unlike the other countries already mentioned, Czechoslovakia, the most developed Eastern Bloc country (alongside with the GDR) could build on a long tradition of scientific manage-

---

executing agency for the Special Fund Sector of the United Nations Development Programme (Geneva: International Labour Office,1966).
27 *National Management Development Centre Poland, Report for the government of Poland* (Geneva: International Labour Office, 1966): 29.
28 For the larger context of "bridge building" in the mid-1960s and the exchange of know how in the field of cybernetic and management, see Leena Riska-Campbell, *Bridging East and West: The Establishment of the International Institute for Applied Systems Analysis (IIASA) in the United States Foreign Policy of Bridge Building, 1964–1972* (Finnish Society of Science and Letters, 2011), Eglė Rindzevičiūtė, *The Power of Systems: How Policy Sciences Opened up the Cold War World* (Ithaca, London: Cornell University Press, 2016), and Michael Hutter's chapter in this volume.
29 ILOA UNDP ROM/67/502. Report on project results, conclusions and recommendations, Geneva, Sept. 1972.
30 ILOA UNDP 7/B09/256 Report in Project results conclusions and recommendations, July 1971.

ment.³¹ The first international congress of scientific management of work had been held in Prague in 1924, under the supervision of the newly founded Masaryk Academy of Labour.³² During the 1930s, the Shoe factory Bata was regarded among experts of labor management as an exemplary place where the combination of scientific organization of labor and democratic management in small teams had been successfully implemented. The reformist communist regime inherited this expertise and could establish its own Institute of management without asking for international support.³³ Faculties of Management were set up at the Schools of Economics in both Prague and Bratislava.³⁴ Nevertheless, intellectual exchanges with the West were still vital for the Czechoslovak experts and strongly encouraged by the political authorities during the 1960s. In this period, there was a marked interest in two issues: the teaching of the workforce to adapt to automation and the training of top managers. In 1965, the Czechoslovak authorities applied for fellowships to send their top managers to the newly opened Turin center. By 1969 they could already participate in high-level management courses.³⁵ These exchanges were not stopped by 'Normalisation': in 1972–1974 seminars for top managers on rationalization in industrial enterprises were organized in Prague, Bratislava and Ostrava under the supervision of the ILO.³⁶ Conversely, with the financial and logistic support of the UNDP, in 1970 Czechoslovak authorities were able to organize a seminar on management in Jiloviste (close to Prague), in which 45 top managers and academics, mainly from developing countries participated. In a nutshell, in the 1960s Eastern European countries became involved in a larger and global circulation of management knowledge.

Moreover, even after the communist elites put an end to the economic reforms initiated in the 1960s and reinforced central planning (at least in Czechoslovakia, Romania, Bulgaria and the GDR) these management centers remained active, but functioned in closer association with the party and state apparatus. In 1971, the Romanian CEPECA was absorbed by the Stefan Gheorghiu academy led

---

31 Regarding this, see also the contribution of Vítězslav Sommer in this volume.
32 http://www.mua.cas.cz/en/masaryk-academy-of-labour-masarykova-akademie-prace-685 (accessed January 2017).
33 See also the contribution of Vítězslav Sommer in this volume.
34 *Report on the Seminar Management Development in Practice, Jiloviste, Czecholsovakia*, January, ILO, Management Development Series, 9, 1970 (Geneva: International Labour Office, 1970).
35 ILOA TAP 0–17
36 ILOA UNDP 17–2-B-1–1

by the Communist party[37] and "brought under the control of the political machine."[38] The same holds true for the Bulgarian management center which was included in the Academy of Social Science and Social Management[39] as early as 1969.

These institutions were used as training centers for the new generation of cadres. During the second phase of economic development in all socialist countries, political loyalty was no longer sufficient to attain leading economic positions; technical and managerial competencies were bitterly needed. The new cadres of the socialist regimes were thus largely trained in these institutes, which functioned in close symbiosis with Western managerial culture. In Bulgaria the management training center was supervised by Mr Tsankov, first deputy minister of the ministry of labor and social welfare, and became an Institute for training administrative cadres.[40] The Romanian CEPECA became one of three centers forming the Central Institute for Management Development for the Economic and State administration.[41] As a result, in all Eastern European countries a new class of internationalized technocrats began to emerge and could build a bridge between both Blocs.

A trans-bloc epistemic community?

The ILO Programme of Management launched in 1958 was drafted by Donald K. David, former Dean of the Harvard school of Business Administration and, at the time, Chairman of the Ford foundation. This clearly underlines the role played by two major actors: Harvard Business School and the Ford Foundation. They disseminated a particular US/Western managerial culture and continued to promote the scientific organization of work inherited from Ford.[42] Nevertheless, the Management Development Branch at the ILO was not directly linked to the powerful US management expert sphere, but was set up and led by the British expert Rhys

---

[37] For a closer contextualisation, see Anna-Maria Catanus,"Official and Unofficial Futures of the Communism System Romanian Futures Studies between Control and Dissidence," in *The Struggle for the Long-Term in Transnational Science and Politics Forging the Future*, ed. Jenny Andersson and Eglė Rindzevičiūtė (New York: Routledge, 2015), 170–192.
[38] ILO MI 221–11 C.R Wynnes-Roberts Report on mission to Romania 17–24 October 1971.
[39] ILOA UNDP, 10–2-B-2–1–1technical report 1, July 1971.
[40] ILOA MI 221–11 Wynne-Roberts' mission to Bulgaria October 1971.
[41] ILO MI 221–11 C.R Wynnes-Roberts' Report on mission to Rumania 17–24 October 1971.
[42] Giuliana Gemelli, *From imitation to Competitive Cooperation. Ford Foundation and Management Education in Western Europe (1950's-1970's)* (Florence: EUI, working papers, I and II, 1997).

Wynne-Roberts.[43] Under his leadership, the ILO developed a model largely inspired by the relatively new-born British management culture.[44] Wynne-Roberts' *Manual of Management* used by the ILO experts and republished in 1969, was "based on the *British Standard Glossary of Terms in Work Study* published in 1959."[45] The people acknowledged in the introduction all belonged to the same circle[46].

Moreover, experts sent to Eastern European countries to set up the management centers or organize seminars largely (but not exclusively) came from the UK and only secondarily from the US. Among the seven experts invited to give a lecture in the seminar held in Jilovitse (near Prague) in 1970, four came from the UK and one from the US. As for the remaining two, one was programme manager of the IBM International School in the Netherlands, and the other one the sales training manager of Caterpillar in Geneva. Between 1972 and 1975, the famous British Cranfield School of Management in Bedford subcontracted the three seminars on the rationalization of industrial enterprises in Czechoslovakia.[47] In the Hungarian case, even if the experts originated from 12 countries (including USSR, Poland, Czechoslovakia and Bulgaria) the three successive project directors as well as the computer specialists were British.

This centrality of British management in the ILO is astonishing considering that management education was comparatively underdeveloped in the UK. Beside the personal role played by Wynne-Robert himself and the linguistic requirements imposed by the programme, which gave an immense advantage to the English-speaking experts, three structural reasons can explain this situation. First, in the interwar years, with Lyndall Urwick[48] as a director of the International Scientific Management Institute between 1929 and 1933, the British manage-

---

43 ILOA P file 7045

44 Mildred Wheatcroft, *The Revolution in British Management Education* (London: Pitman, 1970), and John F Wilson and Andrew Thomson, *The Making of Modern Management: British Management in Historical Perspective* (Oxford: Oxford University Press, 2006).

45 International Labour Office, *Work study*, (Geneva: International Labour Office, 1969),vii–viii.

46 Dr. T. U. Matthew, formerly Lucas Professor of Engineering Production, Birmingham University, Mr. F. de P. Hanika of the Royal Technical College, Glasgow, and Mr. Winston M. Rodgers of the United Kingdom Department of Scientific and Industrial Research, an agency which was set up by the British government during the First World War.

47 ILOA UNDP.17–2-B-1–1–1.

48 On Urwick see Edward Brech, and alii, *Lyndall Urwick, Management Pioneer: A Biography* (Oxford: Oxford University Press, 2010). More precisely on the importance of Urwick in the UK see Wilson R Guerriero, "The struggle for management education in Britain: The Urwick Committee and the Office Management Association," *Management and Organizational History* 6, no. 4 (2011): 367–389.

ment culture and networks had already played an important role in the ILO. Second, the Glossary, to which Wynne-Roberts referred to justify the exclusive use of British terminology, was established by a tripartite committee in which employers and the British Trades Union Congress (TUC) had a seat and "represent[ed] the outcome of their collective thinking." [49] This tripartite collaboration was in line with the ILO culture and in tune with the way scientific management had been conceived by its officials. From the 1920s onward, the French first Director of the ILO, Albert Thomas, and his British deputy director Harold Butler tried to find ways to involve the trade unions in the management process. Unlike some of the members of the American Management Association close to Rockefeller and US big business, Thomas and Butler did not limit management to a technical tool in the hands of engineers or salaried managers. In close cooperation with Mary van Kleeck and the International Industrial Relations Institute, they approached management as intrinsically linked to industrial relations, a field that, since the pioneering work of Beatrice and Sidney Webbs at the end of the nineteenth century, had a long tradition in the UK.[50] Inside the ILO machinery, this approach of management through industrial relations could set the basis of a consensus between workers and employers, a consensus which was even more necessary, as there was a long tradition of hostility toward scientific management in a large part of the trades union movement, in particular in Southern Europe. [51] By contrast, British trade unionists viewed themselves and their mode of action as a necessary condition for the achievement of industrial democracy, which relied on well-managed industrial relations. In the management development programme presented in 1958, the articulation between organization of work, the training of managers, and industrial relations was again mentioned, but the industrial relation dimension of the project became clearly marginalized and the emphasis was put on the training of managers.[52] Moreover, that is the third reason which has to be mentioned, employers were deeply involved and interested in the development and spread of a new management culture. For their part, British employers and managers stressed the importance of using the new technology of computers to implement a scientific management programme. Since the end of World War Two operational research which had been widely devel-

---

49 International Labour Office, *Work study*, (Geneva: International Labour Office, 1969), viii.
50 As for the role of the Webbs, the British tradition and the paradoxical late institutionalisation of management studies in British higher education institutions, see Bruce E. Kaufman, *The Global Evolution of Industrial Relations: Events, Ideas and the IIRA* (Geneva: International Labour Office, 2004) 81–217.
51 Cayet, *Rationaliser le travail*, 109–135,
52 *Report of the Governing Body* (Geneva: International Labour Office, 1959, 143) 112–115.

oped by the British Army during the war,⁵³ made its entry into the business sector, and the *British Operation Research Quarterly* launched in 1950 was the first journal in this emerging research field⁵⁴. The new computational industry was heavily involved in and was pushing for the recognition of "management science," as it was called.⁵⁵ Thus, it does not come as a surprise that most of the management training centers set up in Eastern Europe by the ILO received computers financed and installed through the UNDP by British firms, beginning with the Poles, which purchased computer equipment from the International Computers and Tabulators, Ltd. in London (later ICL) for $209,000. The same company installed the computer of the Hungarian management-training center. As stated in the report, the use of the computer was modelled after the British example.⁵⁶ In Bulgaria the Manpower Development Programme was managed by John Mc Donald, a US civil servant. McDonald was working with a local team consisting of eight people, among them five experts from the UK.⁵⁷ He entertained very good relationships with the local representative of the British International Computers limited (ICL) which was also in charge of the computerization of the hotel booking system.⁵⁸

On the other side, there was a consensus among the experts sent by the ILO that the success of the project was tightly linked to the possibility of developing good contacts with local experts and the possibility of working together as a team.⁵⁹ In Eastern European countries, a group of people already internationally connected established the first contacts. In the 1950s and at the beginning of the 1960s experts who hade developed a close relationship with international or-

---

[53] Dominique Pestre, "Understanding and assessing complex systems to wage total war. OR and the Prime Minister Statistical Branch in the United Kingdom, 1939–1942," in *Engaged. Science in Practice from Renaissance to the Present*, ed. Mario Biagioli and Jessika Riskin (London: Palgrave, 2012), 83–102 and Dominique Pestre, "Repenser les variantes du complexe militaire – industriel – universitaire," in *Les Sciences pour la guerre, 1940–1960*, ed. Dominique Pestre and Amy Dahan (Paris: Presses de l'EHESS, 2004), 195–221.

[54] Dominique Pestre, "La recherche opérationnelle pendant la dernière guerre et ses suites, la pensée des systèmes,", *Revue scientifique et technique de la défense* 54 (2001), 63–69.

[55] See the PhD thesis of Cédric Neumann, *De la mécanographie à l'informatique. Le relations entre catégorisation des techniques, groupes professionnels et transformations des savoirs managériaux*, Thèse (Paris: ParisX, 2013), 172–244.

[56] ILOA UNDP 7/B09/256 Report in Project results conclusions and recommendations, July 1971, p.37.

[57] As an example, see Robert Hyman, "The historical evolution of British industrial relations," in *Industrial Relations, Theory and Practice*, ed. P. Edwards (Oxford: Blackwell, 2003).

[58] ILOA MI 221 Wynne-Roberts Report on mission to Bulgaria, 10–17 October 1970.

[59] ILOA TAP14–130.

ganizations in the interwar years, like the Polish ergonomist Jan Rosner, played an important intermediary role. In this regard, a common socialization within the ranks of social democratic parties seems to have helped to maintain the links since socialist exiles in the West could easily reconnect with former party members who had been forced to join the communist parties after 1947. Anton Zelenka was one of these figures; as an ILO official he declined the invitation to go back to Czechoslovakia after 1947 but was able to maintain links to his home country through his relations with Evzen Erban. A former member of the social democratic party, Erban had joined the Communist Party and become a minister for social affairs in the new Czechoslovakia. [60]

In general, in the 1960s, the reformers who could also have been former social democrats were crucial for the start of negotiations with the international organizations and the setting up of these management programmes. This was the case of what ILO experts labelled the "Men of October" in Poland. In Czechoslovakia, Karel Padevĕt, member of the State Committee for Technical Development, professor Pernica from the Prague School of Economics, or Zdeněk Mošna, dean of the faculty of management, Prague School of Economics, all reformers, played crucial roles. [61] The same holds true for Romania, where the mathematician and philosopher Mircea Malița, at that time deputy of the Foreign Ministry, was instrumental in the launching of CEPECA.[62]

However, the number of people who got involved in these programmes went well beyond this narrow group. As stated in a report for Bulgaria,

> Shortly after the project was approved by the UNDP, the Government established a scheme for management training for virtually everyone in a responsible position in the country including party, trade union, Komsomol managing staffs, local leaders, managers of state and cooperative farms, heads of functional divisions of ministries, district people's councils. The management Development Centre was designated to carry out courses at the first three levels of management, namely Ministers, Vice-Ministers and Director-general of trusts and state enterprises.[63].

---

60 See ILOA SI-0 – 17 correspondence about social security between Zelenka and Erban.
61 Zdeněk Mošna, "The New Economic System and Management Development in Czechoslovakia," *International Labour Review* 3 (1967): 61–81.
62 Anna-Maria Catanus, "Official and Unofficial Futures of the Communism System Romanian Futures Studies between Control and Dissidence," in *The Struggle for the Long-Term*, ed. Andersson, and Rindzevičiūtė, 173.
63 ILO UNDP, 10 – 2-B-2 – 1 – 1 Technical report 2, November 1971.

Between 1967 and 1972, 16,000 managers participated in training programmes run by the Romanian CEPECA.⁶⁴ In Hungary, between 1969 and 1971, 1,454 individuals – company directors, chiefs of section in ministries as well as chief engineers and assistant company directors – attended courses offered by the Management Centre in Budapest. Taking into account the fact that experts who wrote the reports were not bound by the use of "diplomatic" language, which prevailed among international civil servants, it is worth mentioning that the relations between foreign experts and the trainees were generally defined as "excellent."

A global language for planning economic progress

In fact Western experts and Eastern trainees shared a common "modern" belief in the possibility of planning and engineering the economy and society. Apart from some remarks concerning Bulgaria,⁶⁵ Western experts barely mentioned the fact that they were acting in a different economic system. In 1977, ILO officials even played with the idea of transforming the Bulgarian center into a Regional institute for the Balkans that they could use to train managers from Greece, Turkey, Romania, Bulgaria and Yugoslavia, regardless of their country of origin.⁶⁶

This common language was based on two assumptions. First, the increase of productivity was a non-questioned prerequisite and was regarded as a precondition for the general increase of wealth. In socialist countries in which the Communist Party was supposed to represent the workers and to lead the country in their interest, the increase of wealth generated by the productivity gains was supposed to be redistributed by the state; it was a technical and not a social issue. Second, all social discontent and conflicts were to be solved within the existing economic and social framework by applying good management tools without really questioning the verticality of the power relations within the enterprises.⁶⁷ In that respect, socialist countries in which the trade unions played the role

---

64 ILOA UNDP, 52–2-B-1–1 Review mission, Schiefelbusch, 18/04/1975.
65 "In contrast to Rumania the Bulgarian authorities want to ensure that management and management training in particular remain fully within the Marxist Leninist framework." ILOA MI 221 Report, Wynne-Roberts, Oct. 1970.
66 ILOA UNDP 10–2-C-2–2, report July 1977
67 Johanna Bockmann, *Markets in the Name of Socialism : The Left-Wing Origins of Neoliberalism* (Stanford, California: Stanford University Press, 2011) and Yves Cohen, *Le siècle des chefs: une*

of transmission belts – in the Leninist language – of the party and the state were very convenient partners for the ILO experts.

In general terms, from the experts' point of view, there was no doubt that the Western expertise should be exported to countries, which were not primarily perceived as socialist but as less developed. Wynnes Roberts made it clear in 1971 during a stay in Hungary: "There are a lot of things they [the leadership] still do not understand. In two years' time, I hope, they will have come to grip with reality and have understood better the sort of recommendations which the ILO experts including myself have been making to them and which they have tended to reject largely from sheer ignorance"[68].

In return, precisely because Eastern European countries were seen as being in a position of relative backwardness, their newly trained experts were considered particularly well suited to re-export the newly acquired knowledge to the decolonized and underdeveloped countries, and thus to become bridge builders between the First and the Third World. In 1964 the medical adviser, Dr. J. Nowacki of the Polish CODKK in Warsaw was already seconded as an adviser to the Ghanaian government.[69] This function became institutionalized during the 1970s in the framework of the UNDP; Bulgaria and Romania played the role of go-between, a role that the communist leadership endorsed easily.[70] The Romanian CEPECA developed as an international center in 1973 and managers coming from developing countries could follow the programme free of charge. In 1974, 53 participants from 19 African and Asian countries attended courses at the CEPECA; ILO experts stressed that the Romanians were in a better position to understand the problems that developing countries had to face when acquiring and implementing new management methods.[71] When the ILO expert George Boulden taught management courses in the Bulgarian city of Varna in 1983, ILO officials encouraged the Bulgarian authorities to export this knowledge to Cuba.

However, the existence and circulation of a common language on management did not mean that the various stakeholders used it for the same purposes. When the Ford Foundation developed a programme of fellowships in 1968–1969

---

histoire transnationale du commandement et de l'autorité (1890–1940) (Paris: Éditions Amsterdam, 2013).
68 ILOA MI 221 Report, Wynne-Roberts on mission to Hungary 17–24 January 1971.
69 *National Management Development Centre Poland, Report prepared for the government of Poland by the ILO acting as executing agency for the Special Fund Sector of the United Development Programme* (Geneva: International Labour Office, 1966), 30.
70 See also in this reagard the role played by the United Nations Industrial Development Organization.
71 ILOA UNDP 52–2-b-1–1, Rabenold to Stig Andersen (UNDP Regional Bureau).

to train Hungarian[72] as well as Czechoslovak[73] top managers in the US,[74] it was clearly a way to subvert socialist values. This led to tense discussions among the Eastern European countries at the beginning of the 70s. The GDR, which was the most developed country in the Bloc and the most identified with "socialism," heavily criticized the use of these training management centers, which for its leaders were just a way to spread capitalist management culture in a socialist economy.[75]

Meanwhile communist managers knew how to use this international management-culture for their own needs. After having taken advantage of management development programmes to train their cadres in the context of the economic reforms, the communist leadership began to pursue other objectives, as made clear by the Hungarian authorities. In 1972, with the beginning of the new Five Year Plan, they decided to put an end to the training course programme but remained interested in computerization. More generally, it seems that one main objective of the communist leadership was to acquire computers. If the Soviet Union as well as the GDR did produce computers, they never mastered this technology at the level of the capitalist West. The UNDP offered a relatively easy way for both Eastern European regimes and Western businessmen to bypass the embargo on Western technology imposed by the Coordinating Committee for Multilateral Export Controls (CoCom).[76] This was facilitated by the fact that, unlike the Expanded Programme of Technical Assistance, all countries could contribute to UNDP in their own currencies this solved the difficult problem of paying for technology in very scarce hard currencies. Thus, through UNDP, Eastern European countries could get access to computers, which, for their communist

---

72 Berlin-SAPMO (Archives oft the Party and mass Organizations of the FRG in the Federal archives) DY 3023–802 Bl. 204. Information der Botschaft der DDR in der UVR. Wirtschaftspolitische Abteilung. Budapest, den 7.3.1968
73 ILOA Z 1/17/1.
74 On the Ford foundation, see Peter D Bell, "The Ford Foundation as a Transnational Actor," *International Organization* 25, no. 3 (1971): 465-478 and Berman, Edward H. *The Ideology of Philanthropy: The Influence of the Carnegie, Ford, and Rockefeller Foundations on American Foreign Policy* (Albany: State University of New York Press, 1983) and above all Gemelli, *From imitation*.
75 SAPMO DY 34 / 12515. Information über die Konferenz der Vertreter der Ministerien für Arbeit der RGW-Staaten am 19 4 1973 in Bukarest zum Tagesordnungpunkt-Fragen der ILO.
76 On the CoCom in its earlier phase see Egil Førland, *Cold Economic Warfare: CoCom and the Forging of Strategic Export Controls, 1948–1954* (Dordrecht: Republic of Letters, 2009) and Michael Mastanduno, *Economic containment: CoCom and the politics of East-West trade* (Ithaca, N.Y: Cornell University Press, 1992). Even if the CoCom never succeeded in organizing a full embargo, it was nevertheless an obstacle for economic exchanges, in particular for high technological products.

leadership, were a crucial tool to make the central planned economy run properly. As clearly stated in the Bulgarian case in 1982 : "The task of analysing and collecting the mass of information required in a planned economy would be enormously facilitated by the use of electronic data processing methods. State ownership and control of industry produce conditions which are particularly susceptible to treatment and analysis by computers, which can assist management decision-making in many ways."[77] But if centrally planned economies, which relied on processing very large amounts of data, were in particular need of computers, both capitalist and socialist societies alike shared the belief that computers should be an essential tool to run the economy as well as to engineer society and manage people in enterprises. In Western countries, it became a widespread conviction in the 1960s that management could be a scientific activity, based on collecting and circulating information and not just on charismatic leadership.[78] Operational research, which developed along with the computerization of big firms, is a perfect example of the rise of this new common managerial culture. For Western engineers, computers should help to decentralize authority, to promote participation and to ensure that each manager or cadre becomes accountable for his/her achievements. Management by objectives and on specific projects were promoted simultaneously in Eastern European industrial combines.[79]

So one can wonder whether and to what extent this circulation of knowledge had, in return, an impact on Western management culture, and if socialist countries became a testing ground for the exportation of management techniques from the private to the public sector. Until the end of the 1970s, there was still a large public industrial sector in most Western European countries. In France, Polish or Romanian fellows were first sent to public and nationalized enterprises.[80] In Great Britain as well as in Norway, the public sector was the first to push for the implementation of management schools, while private business was rather reluctant.[81] In France, the planning authority (*Commissariat général au plan*) strongly supported the development of operational research. In all countries, the

---

[77] ILOA UNDP 10–2-B-2–1–1 Report, George Boulden March 1985.
[78] See the contribution by Isabelle Gouarné in this volume.
[79] Norman Giles, *Management by objectives* (Bucharest/Paris: International Labour Office, 1970) 70B09/472.
[80] ILOA UNDP 52–2-b-1–1 Chevron to Tidmarsh May 1973.
[81] Amdam Rolv Petter and Gunnar Yittri, "The European Productivity Agency, The Norwegian Productivity Institute and Management Education," in *Missionaries and Managers: American Influences on European Management Education, 1945–60*, ed., Terry Gourvish and Nick Tiratsoo (Manchester: Manchester University Press, 1998) 121–140.

military was one of the driving forces behind these social engineering projects. Rather than the sheer exporting of a Western model of management, we should rather describe this process as an encounter between managerial cultures based on deep technocratic convergences.

Conclusion

This chapter has shown that an important exchange and circulation of expertise in the field of management between Western and Eastern Europe developed between the 1960s and the 1980s. This circulation took several forms: fellowships programmes, organization of seminars and above all the creation of large management centers in the framework of the UNDP, and with support coming from the Ford Foundation's management programmes. All these contributed to the exportation of a Western management culture to Eastern Europe; a large part of the top and middle management of socialist Eastern European countries ended up being trained in seminars and courses taught by Western and US European experts. One first and early conclusion of this finding could be that long before the opening of the wall, capitalist values had already penetrated the socialist East. We have shown, however, that the reality is much more complex; the following concluding remarks open wider questions, which open new fields of research.

First, management should be interpreted as part of a larger social engineering and social planning project deeply rooted in common modernist objectives. In both Blocs, management was expected to help raising productivity and to produce wealth. For the capitalist West it was an essential part of the Fordist compromise and the pre-condition of welfare capitalism. For the socialist East, management was a crucial tool in the proper functioning of the state planned economy. In both Blocs it was a way to enforce discipline and control within companies and state enterprises.

Second, management implemented in the Eastern European Bloc countries by Western European experts should also be seen as part of the operational research and cybernetic turn, which went hand in hand with a belief in the possibility of the computerization of decision-making.[82] A wider circulation of computers is closely linked to this conception of management. On one side, Eastern European countries could obtain computers, which were not easily avail-

---

[82] See the contributions of Michael Hutter and Jenny Andersson in this volume

able in the Bloc through the UNDP. On the other side, Western European (mainly British) firms could enter new markets.

This – a third conclusive point – stands in line with longer term dependencies. Since the nineteen century Eastern Europe has been regarded by the West as a European periphery, the newly founded countries received relief and aid for rehabilitation (in the aftermath of both wars) as well as development aid. At the beginning of the Cold War, this aid dried out while these countries went through a period of rapid industrialization and a development phase connected to the "construction of socialism." In the eyes of international organization experts, they became a semi-periphery, and were very well suited to becoming a bridge between the fully developed West and the newly decolonized countries.

On these grounds – and this is the fourth conclusive point – this knowledge transfer was made possible thanks to the rise of a new class of Eastern European managers or cadres, who were ready for the changes which would occur after the fall of the Berlin wall[83].

In order to grasp the deep meaning and consequences of this circulation, more research should be done in the archives of the Eastern European countries themselves. This could help us to decipher how Eastern European cadres as well as the workers on the shop floor took up – or, on the contrary, rejected – this Western management culture. Conversely, important questions remain unanswered regarding the precise intellectual context in which Western expertise was shaped and the political and economic motivations of the experts. Finally yet importantly, one can wonder to what extent this exchange also had an impact in the West and could have fostered the long-term success of the New Public Management.

---

[83] Bockman, *Markets*, Gil Eyal, Iván Szelényi, Eleanor R Townsley, *Making Capitalism without Capitalists: Class Formation and Elite Struggles in Post-Communist Central Europe* (London; New York: Verso, 1998); Gil Eyal, *The Origins of Postcommunist Elites: From Prague Spring to the Breakup of Czechoslovakia* (Minneapolis: University of Minnesota Press, 2003).

Sari Autio-Sarasmo
Transferring Western Knowledge to a centrally planned Economy: Finland and the Scientific-Technical Cooperation with the Soviet Union

Super power competition, the arms race, division and conflict between different socio-economic systems determine our understanding of East-West relations during the Cold War era. The US-led high technology embargo, CoCom, which controlled all technology transfers that might have had strategic importance between the West and the Soviet Union, dominated the state of affairs in the field of technology and trade. In this context, the attempt by the Soviet Union to modernize[1] seemed impossible. In spite of the hindrances created by the East-West division, the Soviet Union managed to create a system of technology transfers with Western European states that was functional, even during the coldest phases of the Cold War era. Through the system of scientific-technical cooperation (STC), the Soviet Union was able to establish official and inter-governmental connections with Western European states, which created a vivid sphere of East-West interaction in Europe.[2] In spite of the East-West divide, the Soviet Union was an attractive trade partner, which helped to cooperate through the STC with West European states during the Cold War decades.[3]

The Soviet STC with the Western European states was possible because it took place "behind the scenes" that made the Soviet STC, in spite of the ideological-political differences, functional and active from the mid-1950s until the end of the Cold War. The STC is an interesting case study because it was launched with a clear purpose to solve the problem of technology and related knowledge in the situation when technological modernization was an imperative for the So-

---

[1] The author's research has focused on the technological modernization in the Finnish Centre of Excellence in Russian Studies "Choices of Russian Modernisation" coordinated by the Aleksanteri Institute, University of Helsinki, Finland.
[2] Sari Autio-Sarasmo and Katalin Miklóssy, "The Cold War from New Perspective," in *Reassessing Cold War Europe*, ed. Sari Autio-Sarasmo and Katalin Miklóssy (Abingdon: Routledge, 2011), 1–15.
[3] By the end of the 1970s, there were agreements with, among others, West Germany, France, Italy, Japan, the UK, Austria, and Finland. M. Maksimova, "Economic Relations between the Socialist and the Capitalist Countries," in *Finnish-Soviet Economic Relations*, ed. K. Möttölä, O.N. Bykov and I.S. Korolev. (London: Macmillan Press, 1983), 23.

https://doi.org/10.1515/9783110534696-008

viet Union. The STC – and the East-West interaction based upon it – has been missing from the Cold War historiography that has focused almost solely on the macro level developments. The Soviet STC was practical cooperation on micro level and remained thus nearly invisible at the level of superpower politics. In order to make the Soviet STC visible, the focus has been placed on case studies. Neutral Finland, the first STC partner of the Soviet Union, offers a good case study to investigate the STC cooperation in practice. During the Cold War, Finland became one of the major mediators of Western technology and related knowledge with the Soviet Union. State regulation and planning,[4] which were closely connected to the system of the Finnish-Soviet trade and the Soviet-Finnish STC, supported the process of mediation. This chapter aims to analyze what kinds of processes of technology and knowledge transfers took place between Finland and the Soviet Union during the Cold War. What kinds of Western technologies were transferred, and how were the transfers disseminated into the Soviet system? The following is based on materials collected in Russian and Finnish archives, on contemporary studies, research literature, and the author's prior publications.

The Soviet technological modernization and the system of STC

The Soviet scientific-technological cooperation (STC), launched in mid-1950s was connected to the technological modernization of the Soviet economy project, which was based on the acquisition of foreign technology and related knowhow. As a leader of the new superpower, Nikita Khrushchev (1956–1964) followed the model adapted by Peter the Great and the strategy that had been determining factor in the modernization project by Lenin and Stalin, that is, to borrow advanced Western technology in order to move quickly forward. Khrushchev's successor Leonid Brezhnev (1964–1982) continued on the same path in order to maintain the Soviet superpower status amid hardening East-West competition. The technological modernization was needed to strengthen the resilience of the Soviet economy and to transform extensive economic growth into intensive one. The Soviet Union had to compete with the United States as an equal com-

---

[4] In this chapter, planning is understood through the system of mixed economy in Finland and Finnish-Soviet clearing trade, i.e. the balanced flows of goods that were fixed to match with the Soviet five-year plans. The five-year planning horizon proved to be beneficial for the research and development (R&D) activities of the Finnish enterprises.

panion in order to prove the superiority of the socialist system and to be a credible leader for the socialist bloc.⁵ Being far from autarky, the Soviet Union had to seek interaction with Western states.⁶ The adopted modernization plan was based on serious planning, and on taking advantage of the existing connections with Western states in Europe with the aim to "catch up."

The key objective for the Soviet STC "to faster exploit the achievements of science and technology and the new methods of production"⁷ set the goals, and illustrates well the Soviet aims in its cooperation with the West. The main actor in the Soviet STC was the State Committee of Science and Technology (GKNT),⁸ which organized and coordinated all technology and know-how transfer and mediated information, propagated new practices, and took care of the diffusion of new technologies and related knowledge in the Soviet Union.⁹ The STC created a system of reciprocal and bidirectional transfers of technology and related knowledge between the partners.

The Soviet technological modernization project was an extraordinary endeavor. The Soviet military-industrial complex was capable of creating the competitive high technology of which the successful space program was a good example. Technology transfers from abroad were needed because there were hardly any ties between the high-prioritized military sector and civilian industry, which

---

5 Sheila Fitzpatrick, *The Russian Revolution*, 2nd edition, (Oxford: Oxford University Press, 1994), 19; P. Gregory and R. Stuart, *Soviet and Post-Soviet Economic Structure and Performance*, 5th edition, (New York: Harper-Collins, 1994), 8; See also Philip Hanson, *The Rise and Fall of the Soviet Economy: An Economic History of the USSR from 1945* (London: Longman, 2003), 62; Sari Autio-Sarasmo, "Soviet Economic Modernisation and Transferring the Technologies from the West," in *Modernisation in Russia since 1900*, ed. Markku Kangaspuro and Jeremy Smith (Helsinki: Finnish Literary Society [Studia Fennica Historica], 2006), 104–123.
6 Oscar Sanchez-Sibony, *Red Globalization. The Political Economy of the Soviet Cold War from Stalin to Khrushchev* (Cambridge: Cambridge University Press, 2014).
7 M. Kaje and O. Niitamo, "Scientific and Technical Cooperation Between a Small Capitalist Country and big Socialist Country," in *Finnish-Soviet Economic Relations*, ed. K. Möttölä, O. N. Bykov and I.S. Korolev. (London: Macmillan Press, 1983), 143–144.
8 The establishment of GKNT was an outcome of a chain of reorganizations during 1957–1965. The idea of the state committee remained much the same, in spite of different names. The final name *Gosudarstvennyi komitet po nauki i tekhnologii SSSR* (GKNT) was the final result and existed between 1965–1991. Russian State Archive of the Economy (RGAE) fond 9480, opis' 2. The GKNT was part of the wider structure of collection of information in the Soviet Union together with KGB and military intelligence GRU that were in charge of the illegal transfer of technology.
9 Russian State Archive of Contemporary History (RGANI), fond 5, opis' 40, delo 52, list 1–6; RGANI fond 5, opis'. 40, delo 52, list 13–19; RGANI fond 5, opis' 40, delo 121, list 29–30.

was not able to benefit from the innovations in the military-industrial complex.[10] In order to enhance the resilience of the economy, the Soviet leadership adopted the Western post-World War Two model of economic growth. The model was based on the transformation of extensive economic growth on an intensive one with the help of developed technology, especially automation. Due to the relatively low level of technological knowhow in the socialist bloc, the Soviet Union needed foreign technology in order to keep up with extremely fast technological development.[11] Transfer of technology through the system of the STC was a solution for that problem.

In this context, the major benefit was that the Soviet STC was based on intergovernmental agreements and thus an official way to transfer Western technology and technology-related knowledge to facilitate the Soviet modernization project. Through the system of the STC, the Soviet Union was not only able to gain technology but also knowledge and expertize connected with the technology that was needed to facilitate technological development and to boost domestic innovations in the Soviet Union. In spite of the CoCom, there were ways to obtain the desired technology through illegal trade and spying.[12] These channels, however, did not further the modernization project of the Soviet Union. In order to profit from the transferred technology, it needed knowledge to use,

---

[10] The Soviet military-industrial complex, the prioritized nine ministries, *devyatka* 'group of nine' in the 1960s and 1970s included ministry of aircraft industry, defence industry, general machine building industry, medium machine industry, radiotechnology industry, electrotechnical industry, ship building industry, machine building and communication device industry. In the 1960s, the priority was on rocket technology. N.S. Simonov, *VPK SSSR: Tempy ekonomicheskovo rosta, struktura, organizatsija proizvodstvo, upravlenie* [Military-industrial complex SSSR: Tempo of economic growth, structure, organisation of production and management]. Izdanie 2, (Universitet Dmitria Pozharskovo, Moskva 2015), 482; Irina B. Bystrova, *Sovetskij voenno-promyshlennij kompleks: problemy stanovlenija i razvitija 1930–1980 gody* [The Soviet military-industrial complex: problems of structuration and development 1930–1980] (RAN: Institut Rossijskoi Istorii Moskva, 2006).

[11] Sari Autio-Sarasmo, "Khrushchev and the challenge of technological progress," in *Khrushchev in the Kremlin. Policy and Government in the Soviet Union, 1953–1964*, ed. Jeremy Smith and Melanie Ilic (Abingdon: Routledge, 2011),133–143.

[12] Philip Hanson, "The Soviet Union's acquisition of Western technology after Stalin; Some thoughts on people and connections," in *Reassessing Cold War Europe*, ed. Sari Autio-Sarasmo and Katalin Miklóssy (Abingdon: Routledge, 2011), 28–30; For an overview, see Christopher Andrew, "Intelligence in the Cold War," in *The Cambridge History of the Cold War*, vol II, ed. Melvyn P. Leffler and Odd Arne Westad (Cambridge: Cambridge University Press, 2010), 430; In this chapter, illegal transfers are not investigated.

diffuse and refine it.[13] The STC enabled the transfer of the technology-related knowledge but it was also a way to establish bilateral cooperation that helped to maintain and continue the knowledge transfers and the technology trade in the future.

For the Soviet Union, neutral Finland was an easy choice as the first partner for the STC. Finland was part of the Russian Empire as an autonomous grand duchy from 1809. In 1917 Finland became independent and the two states continued the long tradition of bilateral trade until the "Winter War" broke out in 1939.[14] After the peace treaty in 1945, the Soviet Union demanded Finnish war reparations to focus on a certain type of technologies, which forced Finland to develop a machine-building industry. This served the Soviet plan well of turning Finnish production more in the direction of technology that was desired and needed in the Soviet Union.[15] The war reparations and the signing of the treaty of friendship, cooperation and mutual assistance (FCMA) between Finland and the Soviet Union in 1948 directed postwar relations and created the basis for the Finnish-Soviet trade.

Finland became the first market economy country to sign a five-year agreement on the exchange of goods with the Soviet Union; this was for the years 1951–1955.[16] In 1955, three years after the completion of war reparations, the FCMA treaty was prolonged and the agreement of the Soviet-Finnish STC was concluded.[17] The Soviet-Finnish STC agreement was the first treaty between

---

13 Philip Hanson, *Trade and Technology in Soviet-Western Relations* (London: Macmillan, 1981), 223; Gary Bertsch, "Technology Transfers and Technology Controls: a Synthesis of the Western-Soviet Relationship," in *Technical Progress and Soviet Economic Development*, ed. Ronald Amann and Julian Cooper (Oxford: Oxford University Press, 1986), 127–128; Ian Jackson, *The Economic Cold War. America, Britain and East–West Trade, 1948–1963* (London: Palgrave, 2001).
14 The Soviet Union attacked Finland on 30 November 1939 and the short war was called the "Winter War." After a short period of peace, the conflict started again in 1941 and lasted until 1944. The "Continuation War" was part of World War Two. After the peace in 1945 large areas of Eastern Finland were annexed to the Soviet Union and Finland had to pay heavy war reparations to the Soviet Union.
15 Tatiana Androsova, "Economic interest in Soviet post-war policy in Finland," in *Reassessing Cold War Europe*, ed. Sari Autio-Sarasmo and Katalin Miklóssy (Abingdon: Routledge, 2011), 33; Markku Kuisma, *Kylmä sota, kuuma öljy. Neste, Suomi ja kaksi Eurooppaa* [Cold War, hot oil. Enterprise Neste, Finland and the divided Europe] (Helsinki: Werner Söderström Ltd, 1997).
16 Juhani Laurila, *Finnish-Soviet Clearing Trade and Payment System: History and Lessons* (Helsinki: Bank of Finland Studies A: 94, 1995), 30.
17 "Sopimus tieteellis-teknillisestä yhteistoiminnasta Suomen tasavallan ja SNTL:n välillä, 16.8.1955" [Agreement on scientific-technical cooperation between the Republic of Finland and the Soviet Union], http://www.finlex.fi/fi/sopimukset/sopsteksti/1955/19550030 (accessed 15 September 2017).

any two states with different economic systems to agree upon scientific-technical cooperation (STC) on a contemporary basis.[18] Since the main targets for the Soviet STC were the technologically more developed countries in Western Europe, in the 1950s cooperation with Finland served as a model to establish connections with the West and rehearse East-West interaction in practice.[19] In spite of the fact that during the early years of cooperation Finland served as a testing site for the Soviet cooperation with the West, the STC agreement set the direction of the Finnish-Soviet technology cooperation for years to come.

State regulation and planning: Finnish-Soviet trade and the STC

The STC was strongly intertwined into the Soviet-Finnish trade. The trade was based on state regulation and planning through the mixed economy system of Finland. The Finnish-Soviet trade was based on the bilateral clearing system, that is, the balanced flows of goods was fixed to match the Soviet administrative and central management and planning system but in a way that did not hamper the workings of the Finnish market economy. The clearing arrangements consisted of five-year agreements and annual trade protocols. Each agreement determined the volume and content of trade for the forthcoming five-year period. These agreements focused on the exchange of goods and set concrete targets for trade by containing lists of imports and exports and specifying the value and volume of delivered goods. The lists were prepared in cooperation with the Finnish firms and Soviet foreign trade organizations. The prices of individual deliveries were negotiated and contracted between a supplier and a purchaser. The positive side of the system was that trade was foreseeable due to the long

---

[18] A. Romanov, "Suomen ja Neuvostoliiton välisen tieteellis-teknisen yhteistyön tuloksia," in *Suomen ja Neuvostoliiton välinen tieteellis-tekninen yhteistoiminta 30 vuotta* [The results of the Finnish Soviet scientific-technical cooperation in Soviet-Finnish STC 30 years] (Helsinki, 1985), 8.

[19] The main target in the West in the 1960s for the Soviet Union was technologically developed West Germany. RGAE fond 9480, opis' 7, delo 805, list 9; RGAE fond 9480, opis' 7, delo 805, list 39–41; The Soviet-West German trade agreement was concluded in 1958 and cooperation was widened after the agreement of cultural and scientific-technical cooperation in 1959. Archive of the Russian Academy of Sciences (ARAN) fond 579, opis' 13, delo 147, list 1–15; About the case of West Germany, see Sari Autio-Sarasmo, "Knowledge through the Iron Curtain: Soviet Scientific-Technical Cooperation with Finland and West Germany" in *Reassessing Cold War Europe*, ed. Sari Autio-Sarasmo and Katalin Miklóssy (Abingdon: Routledge 2011), 66–82.

agreements with secure payments. The drawback of the arrangement was that trade became very bureaucratic.[20]

The development of Finnish-Soviet trade presents a good picture of the structure of the Finnish-Soviet trade (import/export) in the 1970s and the simultaneous intensification of the STC.[21] Finnish exports to the Soviet Union took a remarkable leap in the mid-1970s. This was due to the worldwide oil crisis in the early 1970s that prompted almost inexhaustible Soviet demand for Finnish goods: the higher the oil price, the greater the export possibilities for Finland.[22] The value of Finland's exports to the Soviet Union almost doubled from 1974 to 1975.[23] The share of exports from Finland to the Soviet Union was 13.8% in 1971–1975 but in 1976 the exports were 20.2% in one year. Due to the clearing trade, import from the Soviet Union increased correspondingly: in 1971–1975 import was 14.7% but in 1976 the share was 18.5%. In 1978, the Soviet Union was the biggest trade partner of Finland and Finland was the third biggest trade partner of the Soviet Union.[24] Finnish-Soviet trade was at its highest in the first part of the 1980s. In 1982–1983, the share was over 25%, which was the peak year of the trade. For a short period of time, Finland was the most important trading partner for the Soviet Union.[25] Finnish-Soviet bilateral trade is a good example of "the commerce between countries with different economic and social systems" and thus Finnish-Soviet trade resonates well with the aims of the TRADESOC section in UNCTAD analyzed by Michel Christian in this volume. If not the most traditional one, there were several elements in the trade that were advocated in the Finnish-Soviet trade. At the same time, however, the Finnish-Soviet trade

---

20 Laurila, *Finnish-Soviet Clearing Trade and Payment System*, 18–21, 60–62, 100–103.
21 Pekka Sutela, *Trading with the Soviet Union. The Finnish Experience 1944–1991* (Helsinki: Kikimora Publications Series B 39, 2014), 42.
22 Sutela, *Trading with the Soviet Union*, 44–45. This also worked the other way round: when the oil price was low, Finland benefitted in terms of income, but had to accommodate decline in exports to the Soviet Union.
23 "Value of Finnish imports and exports by country 1856–1975" (Table 5.14.) in *Suomen taloushistoria. Historiallinen tilasto*, osa 3 [Economic History of Finland. Historical Statistics, part 3], ed. Kaarina Vattula (Helsinki: kustannusosaekyhtiö Tammi, 1983), 240; One explanation for the increase of exports was the oil crisis during which upward oil prices increased Finnish exports to the Soviet Union due to the bilateral balancing of Finnish-Soviet trade. Sutela, *Trading with the Soviet Union*, 64.
24 *Suomi-SNTL: Tieteellis-teknisen ja taloudellisen yhteistyön vuorovaikutus. Raportti Suomen ja Neuvostoliiton välisen yhteistyön metodologiaa koskevasta tutkimuksesta. Osat 1–2* [Finland-SSSR: Scientific-technical and economic interaction. Report on the methodological study of the Soviet-Finnish cooperation. Part 1–2] (Helsinki: Suomen ja Neuvostoliiton välisen tieteellis-teknisen yhteistoimintakomitean julkaisusarja 7, 1980), 15–16.
25 Sutela, *Trading with the Soviet Union*, 49, 64. On a per capita basis.

is a good example of the Soviet Union willingness to focus solely on bilateral trade.[26]

It is possible to see the interconnectedness of the Finnish-Soviet trade and the STC in the development of trade and the organization of the STC. The permanent Soviet-Finnish commission on economic cooperation based on the model of the STC was established in 1967 to support the development of the trade. Two years later the scientific cooperation was strengthened by establishing discipline-based working groups under the structure of the STC. In 1971, the treaty to develop economic, technological, and industrial collaboration between Finland and the Soviet Union was signed. In 1974 and 1975, long-term programs to increase economic and industrial collaboration between the two states were approved. In 1977 a long-term program was signed to deepen and develop the economy and trade in the field of industrial and scientific-technical cooperation between Finland and the Soviet Union until 1990. From the 1970s, the main aim of the joint programs was to increase technology transfers and especially technology trade between the two states.[27]

The Finnish mixed economy system enabled planning and state regulation that maintained the strong connection between the trade and STC. Many of the large conglomerates participating in the Finnish-Soviet trade and the STC were owned by the state, which made the regulation and planning even easier. In addition, actors in the trade and the STC were the same: intergovernmental working groups, trade delegations, Finnish enterprises, and the Soviet foreign trade organizations.[28] The five-year agreements and secured payments made the Finnish-Soviet trade attractive for Finnish enterprises. The trade possibilities in the Soviet Union and the whole socialist bloc offered huge possibilities for Finnish partners. Through the system of bilateral trade, Finnish enterprises were able to export upgraded goods to the Soviet Union and in exchange Finland was able to import oil and energy.[29] At the state level over-dependence on Soviet trade and Soviet oil was seen as problematic. That is why Finland tried to trade with the West and diminish its energy dependence on the Soviet Union by cooperating with Western oil suppliers. Still, the share of the trade was high and the

---

26 Michel Christian, "It is not a question of rigidly planning trade" in this volume.
27 *Suomi-SNTL: Tieteellis-teknisen ja taloudellisen yhteistyön vuorovaikutus. Part I*, 16–17.
28 Riitta Hjerppe, "Teollisuus" in *Suomen taloushistoria. Teollistuva Suomi*. Osa 2 [Economic history of Finland. Industrializing Finland, Part 2], ed. Jorma Ahvenainen, Erkki Pihkala, Viljo Rasila (Helsinki: Kustannusosakeyhtiö Tammi 1982), 412–413; Laurila, *Finnish-Soviet Clearing Trade and Payment System*, 61.
29 *Suomen ulkomaankauppatilasto 1971* [Export statistics of Finland 1971] (Helsinki 1972), 82–83.

share of the Soviet oil was at least half of Finnish oil imports.³⁰ Due to the fact that the clearing trade was based on a balanced flows of goods, it was difficult for Finland to find marketable goods to import from the Soviet Union. During the years of Finnish-Soviet trade, the imbalance of export/import was the major problem, but as a whole the trade with the Soviet Union was beneficial for Finland. The disadvantage of the clearing trade with the Soviet Union was that it cast a shadow on Finland's desired image in the West as a free, modern and developed Western market economy.³¹

Soviet STC and Finland – focusing on practical cooperation

The commission of Soviet-Finnish scientific-technical cooperation was established in 1955 as a state-level organization comprising of the Finnish ministry of foreign affairs, the Academy of Finland, and in the Soviet Union, the State committee of science and technology (GKNT) and the Soviet Academy of Sciences. The early years of the cooperation mainly consisted of reciprocal visits to the basic industrial production units that were possible to organize without overly complicated official arrangements. Soviet experts visited Finnish production units where the experts in *komandirovka* 'assignment' wrote reports about their observations, which were very practical, such as details related to the equipment used, lighting, and the organization of work.³² This information was collected in order to develop the organization of work at home and was based on interaction with the experts; Soviet experts asked questions and hosts shared information with their guests. During the late 1960s, when the technological development in Finland was fast, the STC started to divide into two: scientific cooperation and technological cooperation. The scientific cooperation consisted of experts from Finnish and Soviet universities, research institutes and ministries (in the Soviet Union). Finnish and Soviet experts met and exchanged information during the reciprocal visits, seminars, workshops, and conferences organized on the basis of the STC. In the bilateral meetings current scientific issues were discussed

---

30 Kuisma, *Kylmä sota, kuuma öljy*, 257, 275.
31 Laurila, *Finnish-Soviet Clearing Trade and Payment System*, 100–103.
32 A Soviet delegation visited the city of Tampere in August 1958 in local factories. Noted in the report was, for example, the quality of machinery (mainly American and West German). Russian State Archive of Scientific-Technical Documentation, branch in Samara (RGANTD) f. 18, op. 2–6, d. 205, l.1–12; Similar examples in West Germany, see RGANI, f. 5, op.40, d. 67, l. 1–2.

(such as new trends and technologies). Scientists conducted joint research projects and wrote books together.[33]

The technological cooperation consisted of the experts but also of Finnish enterprises and the Soviet trade organizations. In the export-oriented Finnish firms, it was understood that participation in the STC helped to widen economic and industrial cooperation with the Soviet Union.[34] In the field of technology cooperation, the system was closely connected to the Finnish-Soviet trade.[35] Technological knowhow had diversified in Finland because of the active collaboration with the Western enterprises, of which the electronic industry and oil refining industry were good examples.[36] These areas were also the primary interest of the Soviet partners. When Finland's connection and access to the Western technology and knowhow increased, the Soviet partners' interest in collaboration with the Finnish enterprises increased too. From the late 1960s, the visits of the Soviet partners were much better prepared than before. To enhance the process, the GKNT organized the collection of in-advance information, which increased Soviet specialists' ability to adapt knowledge during their visits. Soviet technology advisors in the Soviet embassies in respective countries collected the information available in technology fairs, such as brochures and advertisements, but also through specialized literature that was used to plan and specify the target enterprises to visit.[37]

---

[33] A good example is the Finnish-Soviet STC in the field of computer science. ARAN f. 579, op. 13, d. 162, l. 72–73; Concerning the Soviet delegations visits, see: ARAN f. 579, op. 13, d. 162, l. 17–34. From Finnish side, see Selostus suomalais-neuvostoliittolaisesta symposiumista 13.5.1975 [Report from Soviet-Finnish symposium 13.5.1975)]. Commission of the Finnish-Soviet scientific-technical cooperation: travelogues. Archive of foreign ministry of Finland (FMA).
[34] *Suomi-SNTL: Tieteellis-teknisen ja taloudellisen yhteistyön vuorovaikutus*, Part I, 11.
[35] In the case of Finland, see for example, Tieteellis-teknistä yhteistoimintaa varten Suomen tasavallan ja Sosialististen Neuvostotasavaltain liiton välille asetetun suomalais-neuvostoliittolaisen komitean pöytäkirja 17.-25.2.1956 Moskovassa pidetystä istunnosta (jäljennös) [Copy of the protocol of establishment of the commission on scientific-technical cooperation between Finland and the Soviet Union]. Commission of the Finnish-Soviet scientific-technical cooperation (STC), Archive of Finnish foreign ministry (FMA).
[36] Martti Häikiö, *Fuusio. Yhdistymisen kautta suomalaiseksi monialayritykseksi 1865–1982* [History of the enterprise Nokia 1865–1982, part 1] (Helsinki: Edita, 2001), 99; Kuisma, *Kylmä sota, kuuma öljy*, 255.
[37] RGANI fond 5, opis' 61, delo 55a, list 45–55. Soviet *sovetniki*, 'technology advisors' worked as coordinators between the GKNT and foreign enterprises; Instruction of the use of foreign journals: RGAE fond 9480, opis' 7, delo 805, list 81–86. Collected information was administered and translated into Russian by the All-Union Institute of Scientific-Technical Information, (*Vsesoyuznyi institut nauchnoi i tekhnicheskoi informatsii*, VINITI). RGANI fond 5, opis' 33, delo 46, list 15–16, 21. VINITI was established in 1952. It collected and produced summaries from 22,000 sci-

The Soviet specialists were assigned clear plans of action for their visits. On the basis of the information collected in advance, the GKNT drew up a list of questions about technological processes to be answered during the visit, based on detailed knowledge of the production of the receiving enterprise.[38] After demand for the new technology increased remarkably in the Soviet Union in the 1960s and 1970s, the cooperation started to focus on technology related-knowledge. It is possible to observe this phenomenon in the archival materials for instance when the Finnish partners brought to the discussions problems with the Soviet experts who were eager to get information about technology that was forbidden by strict license and patent agreements.[39] The cooperation became challenging for Finnish partners who did not want to risk problems in their contacts with their Western partners.

By focusing on the practical cooperation, the Soviet Union was able to keep the STC cooperation bilateral and use it in a way that served the needs of the Soviet side without creating tensions in the superpower politics. A good example of the target-oriented STC activity in the field of high technology was the establishment of the working group in cybernetics, later a working group on computer technology. During Khrushchev's leadership, cybernetics was given an important

---

entific journals and publication series, and about 8,000 books from 130 countries in 70 different languages. It was re-organized under the jurisdiction of the GKNT and the Academy of Sciences. Seppänen, Jouko, *Tieteellis-tekninen informaatio Neuvostoliitossa* [Scientific-technical information in the Soviet Union] (Helsinki: Suomen ja Neuvostoliiton tieteellis-teknisen yhteistoimintakomitean julkaisusarja 2, 1978).

38 RGAE fond 9480, opis' 7, delo 805, list 57.

39 Neste Oy:n vastaus TT-komission tiedusteluun 16.10.1961 [Reply from enterprise Neste to the enquiry sent by the commission of scientific-technical cooperation]. 13/647–55, FMA. The letter referred to the earlier experiences; In West Germany, the Soviet experts were accused of industrial espionage and Soviet experts' visits to the West German enterprises were suspended. RGAE fond 9480, opis' 7, delo 805, list 138. Illegal trade and spying were organized in more effective ways e.g., through military intelligence (GRU) and KGB. Additionally, dummy firms were established in Europe to acquire desired technology. *Report. Soviet acquisition of Western technology* (Library of Congress, 1. April 1982); Collection of information during the Cold War was easily connected to technological espionage. In the STC spying was not – at least not openly– an expressed aim because the desired information was available freely; Kuisma, *Kylmä sota, kuuma öljy*, 276. Finnish oil refining enterprise Neste collaborated with American technology enterprises; Although Finland was not a member of the CoCom embargo, enterprises were unwilling to share knowhow that was in conflict with the CoCom lists; Niklas Jensen-Eriksen, "CoCom and Neutrality: Western Export Control policies, Finland and the Cold War, 1949–58," in *Reassessing Cold War Europe*, ed. Sari Autio-Sarasmo and Katalin Miklóssy (Abingdon: Routledge, 2011), 49–65.

role in technological modernization.[40] The position of cybernetics changed in the mid-1960s when Leonid Brezhnev took over the leadership. In spite of the previous existence of Institutes of Cybernetics and efforts to develop Soviet computer technology, the Soviet leadership made a decision to give up the development of its own computer systems and to copy IBM 360[41] technology in 1969. Coinciding with the decision, the Soviet STC partner suggested the establishment of the working group of cybernetics through the system of STC to Finnish counterparts. The timing was impeccable because through the Finnish cooperation, Soviet experts gained access to the software that was needed to make the copied computers work.[42] Computer technology remained one of the major interests in the STC until the end of the Cold War.

The Cold War context created frameworks for the Soviet technology cooperation with the Western partners. Furthermore, it explains the ways in which the cooperation was motivated and organized. The Soviet-Finnish STC was based on individual projects, which helped to keep the cooperation bilateral and motivated on both sides. The Soviet partners were willing to strengthen the state-level cooperation and trade that would have supplied the economic, technological, and scientific demand in the Soviet Union. As a capitalist country, Finland was motivated by economic profit, marketing possibilities, and possibility to enhance domestic R&D. For the Finnish STC partners, especially export-oriented enterprises, the main motivator was direct contact with the Soviet partners.

---

[40] A good example of this was the establishment of the Tallinn Institute of Cybernetics, which was part of Tallinn University of technology. Sampsa Kaataja, "Expert Groups Closing the Divide: Estonian-Finnish Computing Cooperation Since the 1960s," in *Beyond the Divide. Entangled Histories of Cold War Europe*, ed. Simo Mikkonen and Pia Koivunen (Oxford: Berghahn books 2015), 103. According to Kaataja, Tallinn Institute of Cybernetics did not participate in fully classified projects but was a category B institution. There is an increasing number of studies focusing on Soviet cybernetics, see for example Slava Gerovitch, *From Cyberspeak to Newspeak. A History of Soviet Cybernetics* (Cambridge, MA: MIT Press, 2002); An important contribution to the field of cybernetics but also technology transfers is Egle Rindzeviciute, *The Power of Systems. How Policy Sciences Opened up to the Cold War World* (Ithaca and London: Cornell University Press, 2016).
[41] About IBM in Finland, see Petri Paju and Thomas Haigh, "IBM rebuilds Europe. The curious case of the transnational typewriter," *Enterprise & Society* 2(2015); Petri Paju, "Monikansallinen yritys ja siteet länteen. IBM Suomessa ja Länsi-Euroopassa 1940-luvun lopulla ja 1950-luvulla" [A multinational corporation and ties to the West: IBM in Finland and in Western Europe during the post-war years and the 1950s], *Historiallinen aikakauskirja* 3 (2015).
[42] Autio-Sarasmo, "Knowledge through the Iron Curtain," 72; For a discussion about the benefits of the cooperation, see ARAN, fond 579, opis' 13, delo 162, list 72–73. Other contributions in this volume thematize the East-West dimension of the computerization process – i.e. Sandrine Kott, "The social engineering project" and Ondřej Matějka, "Social engineering and alienation between East and West."

When they had direct contacts, firms were able to collaborate outside the official STC organs.[43] The Finnish enterprises were able to negotiate directly with their Soviet partners and agree, for example, on the prices.[44] The "technological turn" in the STC and the Soviet-Finnish trade took place in the 1970s when the technological level had markedly increased in Finland.

Finland as a mediator of Western technology to the Soviet Union

The Finnish enterprises in Soviet trade were mainly large conglomerates. The five largest accounted for almost 40 % of all exports from Finland to the Soviet Union because of the clearing trade system. Due to the long-term contracts, the privately owned profit-maximizing enterprises actively participated in the trade.[45] Finnish exporters were able to use the Soviet markets' springboard to the Western markets because Finland was able to develop and produce exports for which there was no demand in Finland. Long-term contracts and trade agreements and secured payments increased security in Finland and Finnish exporters were protected from external competition.[46] In the 1970s, when it was difficult to get into the Western market, the Soviet Union offered several trading possibilities and strict payments. Among especially successful enterprises were conglomerates that could offer a large assortment of products to supply Soviet demand.

A good example of an enterprise like this was Nokia, a conglomerate that became a member of the Soviet-Finnish STC in 1957. Nokia's cooperation and trade with the Soviet Union illustrates the development of the STC from the 1950s until 1991. During the Cold War era, Nokia had two major export lines to the Soviet Union: cables and communication devices.[47] Although Nokia became well known for communication devices, especially mobile phones in the

---

[43] These organs were the STC Commission and Economic Commission in Finland and in the Soviet Union Ministry of foreign trade, State Committee of Foreign Trade (GKES), ministries, and commercial missions of the Soviet Union in Finland. *Suomi-SNTL: Tieteellis-teknisen ja taloudellisen yhteistyön vuorovaikutus. Part I*, 40–43.
[44] Laurila, *Finnish-Soviet Clearing Trade and Payment System*, 60–62.
[45] Sutela, *Trading with the Soviet Union*, 65–66.
[46] Laurila, *Finnish-Soviet Clearing Trade and Payment System*, 100–103.
[47] Martti Häikiö, *Sturm und Drang. Suurkaupoilla eurooppalaiseksi elektroniikkayritykseksi 1983–1991. Nokia Oyj:n historia*. osa 2 [History of enterprise Nokia 1983–1991, part 2] (Edita: Helsinki, 2001), 195.

1990s, it was cable production that created the cornerstone for Nokia's beneficial trade with the Soviet Union. Soviet industry was not able to produce enough cables to meet the increasing demand, which opened large and widening trade possibilities for Nokia with the Soviet Union. Nokia had to follow the export quota defined in the state-level trade protocols for the exchange of goods, but being a privately-owned, profit-maximizing enterprise, Nokia's main aim was to make the export quotas as high as possible in order to gain maximum benefit from the trade with the Soviet Union.

In 1971 a protocol of exchange of goods was signed. It included the export of high technology cables. This profitable deal was important for enhancing the R&D and furthering other units at the Nokia conglomerate. The mid-1970s represented an especially beneficial time after the oil crisis when the Soviet Union wanted to import more cables than Nokia was able to produce. As a conglomerate, Nokia could exploit the positive turnover in the other units. One of the reasons for the possibility to develop R&D in Finland was the system of bilateral trade, which included the pre-pay system. When the product was partly paid in advance, it gave Finnish partners the advantage of developing their products, especially technology which was not only for the Soviet trade but targeted at Western markets as well. Thus, the Soviet trade was a useful stepping stone for new and expanding firms such as Nokia, but it also secured markets for other Finnish enterprises.[48]

Nokia Electronics started in the 1960s and developed on the basis of the Soviet trade. For Nokia – as well as other Finnish enterprises – connections to technologically-advanced Western countries were extremely important. The Finnish firms sent personnel to work in the electronic firms in the United States in order to learn to use the newest technologies in this sphere. Nokia bought electronic devices from West Germany (Siemens) and delivered the provided technology to Finland. The share of electronics in Nokia's exports was 40%, of which 30% was directed to the Soviet Union and COMECON countries and 10% to the West. In the 1970s, computer technology and computer systems became part of Nokia's portfolio and Finnish banks ordered computers and computer systems from Nokia.[49] Simultaneously the interest of the Soviet partners started to focus on these systems and STC visits focused on enterprises using these technologies.[50] These visits were partly connected to the work of the STC working

---

48 Sutela, *Trading with the Soviet Union*, 67, 73.
49 Häikiö, *Fuusio*, 93, 156, 161,164.
50 ARAN fond 579 opis' 13, delo 162, list. 17–34; Neuvostoliittolaisen delegaation Suomen vierailu. TT-komitea: saapuneet kirjeet [Soviet delegation in Finland, letters]. 1/1–30/6–71 FMA; Se-

group of cybernetics. The cooperation bore fruit decades later when Nokia delivered digital phone exchanges to the whole Soviet communication system.[51] The Soviet Union clearly played a crucial role in the development of Nokia Electronics.

Personal contacts and mutual trust were essential in the cooperation with the Soviet Union. These factors were especially important in the technology trade. That is why the role the commission of STC was fundamental when building contacts between Finnish enterprises and Soviet partners. In the 1980s when the Nokia's trade with the Soviet Union was at its highest, Nokia's CEO was a member of the Soviet-Finnish Commission on STC. Because of the bureaucratic and slow Soviet system, personal contacts were demanded at every level to enhance the collaboration. Trust was earned through the long partnership and good reputation but in Nokia's case the physical presence of its representatives in the Soviet Union proved to be very beneficial for trade. Nokia opened an office in Moscow in order to organize exhibitions and to facilitate negotiations with Soviet partners.[52] When the Cold War cooled down, personal contacts became even more important. Individual approaches and personal connections were used whenever it was needed to bypass the official and politically embedded macro (state) level politics.

After the Soviet invasion of Afghanistan in 1979, the CoCom restrictions were tightened remarkably. Although not a member of the CoCom embargo, Finland followed the strict trade restrictions.[53] Nokia had to adjust to Finland's economic policy and to take into account the changing situation. Finnish electronic industry needed American components and thus could not ignore the US geopolitics. Especially in the late 1970s and 1980s, the Finnish STC with the Soviet Union was viewed by the United States as suspicious and problematic.[54] The concern and suspicion in the United States was certainly partly justified, because besides the trade with the Soviet Union Nokia also delivered technology to the Finnish army. This became alarming in the 1980s when the CoCom embargo was signifi-

---

lostus suomalais-neuvostoliittilaisesta symposiumista 13.5.1975. TT-komitea: matkakertomuksia [Report from the Finnish-Soviet symposium. ST commission, travelogues] 1956–1978. FMA.

51 Häikiö, *Sturm und Drang*, 54–55.
52 Sutela, *Trading with the Soviet Union*, 2014, 88; Häikiö, *Sturm und Drang*, 47–48, 50, 53; Häikiö, *Fuusio*, 120, 157–158, 182. Nokia's CEO Kari Kairamo was an important figure in Finnish trade in the 1980s.
53 Jensen-Eriksen, "CoCom and Neutrality," 58–61.
54 *Report: Soviet Acquisition of Western Technology* April 1 1982 (Library of Congress). The report did not mention Nokia or Finland but similar activities were defined as "suspicious."

cantly tightened.⁵⁵ In order to get American components, Nokia had to get approval from the United States to continue trade with the Soviet Union. The solution was that Nokia's CEO made a personal agreement with the Pentagon to provide them with information about technological progress in the Soviet Union.⁵⁶ The fact that Finnish enterprises were always technologically one step ahead of the Soviet Union, kept the cooperation on track. In the late 1980s, Finland concluded a secret, state-level agreement with the United States about how to continue trade in the both directions.⁵⁷ By this time, however, Soviet-Finnish trade was reaching its final stage.

It is possible to argue that Nokia was able to continue trade with the Soviet Union under surveillance because the technology traded to the Soviet Union did not threaten the military strategic equilibrium. Nevertheless, the other branch of advanced technology in Finland, the ship building industry and especially the construction of icebreakers, was followed more closely during the Cold War.⁵⁸ A good example of the Cold War restrictions directly influencing Finland is connected to the case of Finnish mini-submarines in the 1980s. The Soviet Academy of Sciences ordered two deep-sea mini-submarines able to dive down to six kilometres from the Finnish conglomerate Rauma-Repola. At the beginning, the project was not objected to by Finland's Western allies, because they believed that Finland was not able to master the advanced technology needed for the project. Still the project was closely followed by the United States. After finishing the order successfully, the United States started to pressure the shipyard Rauma-Repola Oceanics by threatening the mother company Rauma-Repola with bank-

---

55 Full technological information was delivered only after the next generation device was created. Häikiö, *Sturm und Drang*, 126–127.

56 Interviews with Former Deputy Minister of Defence Richard Perle in the documentary film "Kauppasotaa pinnan alla" [Trade war under water]. Presented by Channel One YLE on Finnish Television 7 December 2008. Assistant Secretary of Defence in the Bush Administration in the US, Richard Perle was in charge of the negotiations with Nokia. The existence of the agreement was confirmed by Stefan Widomski, former Senior Vice President International Trade Affairs in Nokia corp. Discussion with Widomski in Helsinki in 21 May 2014.

57 Autio-Sarasmo, "Knowledge through the Iron Curtain," 74. Clearing trade between Finland and the Soviet Union/Russia ended in 1991.

58 For the political dimension and techno-politics of the Soviet-Finnish icebreaker trade, see Saara Matala, "Flashy flagships of Cold War cooperation – The Finnish-Soviet nuclear icebreaker project," *Technology & Culture*, 4/2018 forthcoming. Saara Matala, "The Business of Foreign Affairs. Unrealized visions of joint business, technology and politics in Finnish -Soviet shipbuilding at the end of the Cold War". (Paper presented in the ICOHTEC International Committee for the History of Technology) in *Proceedings of the 41th ICOHTEC Symposium 2014 Technology in times of transition*, ed. Helerea, E., Cionca, M, Ivănoiu, M (Brasov: Transylvania University of Brasov, 2014), 65–70.

ruptcy. In the end, two ready-made vessels were delivered to the Soviet Union but Rauma-Repola was forced to abandon Oceanics and the whole branch of the deep-sea industry.[59]

Transferred technology in the centrally planned economy

The main aim of the Soviet economic modernization project was the dissemination of the transferred technology and related knowledge into the Soviet R&D and industry to boost domestic innovations and thus facilitate the modernization of the Soviet (civilian) industry. Dissemination of the transferred technology and knowledge was essential for the process of diffusion,[60] the next phase of the modernization process that would have created a strong basis for the use of new applications and the emergence of domestic innovations. This process was expected to change the technological basis of the Soviet economy and to transform its extensive economic growth into an intensive one. From the perspective of Soviet leaders, the intensification would have increased the resilience of the USSR economy, and domestic innovations would have enabled the independent development of the Soviet industry and so lead to modernization.[61]

In the 1960s and 1970s, the main organ in the dissemination of the transferred technology and knowledge was the State Committee of Science and Technology (GKNT). It was in charge of new technologies and methods of developing science and technology in the Soviet Union. Thus the GKNT also coordinated the transfers channelled through the STC.[62] The process of dissemination and implementation of the transferred technologies had been evaluated in the mid-1950s. Due to its poor outcomes, the whole system was reorganized in the late 1950s in order to improve the process. One of the major changes was that GKNT's role in

---

59 Sutela, *Trading with the Soviet Union*, 93.
60 Diffusion is the process by which new technology and related knowledge is transferred through certain channels among the members of social system. Everett M. Rogers, *Diffusion of Innovations*, Third Edition (New York: The Free Press of Glencoe, 1983). Rogers refers also to the transfer of knowledge and technology.
61 Intensification, growth and innovation have been the main concepts in the Soviet and Russian modernization discussion. For an overview of the modernization discussion, see Joachim Zweynert and Ivan Boldyrev, "Conflicting patterns of thought in the Russian debate on modernisation and innovation 2008–2013," *Europe-Asia Studies* 69, No. 6 (2017), 921–939.
62 *Suomi-SNTL: Tieteellis-teknisen ja taloudellisen yhteistyön vuorovaikutus.* Part II, 37, 163; Rogers, *Diffusion of Innovations*, 335.

the dissemination of the collected information to the Soviet R&D and industry were clarified and strengthened. In order to make the process more effective, the GKNT was given authority to sign international contracts with foreign enterprises and organizations.[63] In addition, the GKNT was subordinated more clearly to the centralized planning system.

The Soviet planning system was seen as a booster for the dissemination process by determining how much and where the resources (including transfers) were to be allocated and how the allocations were controlled.[64] In spite of the obvious advantages of the planning system in resource allocation and mission-oriented projects, the main problem was that the innovation emphases and plan fulfilment were almost always in conflict. A major innovation often required several years before it began to operate successfully. The planning horizon in the Soviet Union was short and did not enable experimentation that would last several years. Any new technology also required considerable new resources and new suppliers, which represented a fundamental problem because of the lack of horizontal connections[65] between industries in the USSR. All branches of civilian industry needed to compete for the same materials, which resulted in departmental barriers being set up. The prices of new products were often set at a level that provided a lower rate of profit and counted for less towards plan fulfilment than the older, standard products. Hence, if plan fulfilment was threatened, the tendency was to shift away from new products toward the safe, old ones. There was a great gap between Soviet scientific and engineering achievements and the capacity to transform them into economically

---

[63] *Suomi-SNTL: Tieteellis-teknisen ja taloudellisen yhteistyön vuorovaikutus. Part II*, 165; A good example of this kind of contract was the one signed with West German enterprise Siemens in 1971. RGAE fond 9480, opis' 9, delo 2509 A, list 18–26 L; See also RGAE fond 9480, opis' 7, delo 816, list 57.

[64] Joseph Berliner, *Soviet industry from Stalin to Gorbachev. Essays on management and innovations* (Aldershot: Edward Elgar, 1988), 225; E.P. Hoffman & R.F. Laird, *"The scientific-technological revolution" and Soviet foreign policy* (Oxford: Pergamon Press, 1982), 82. Scientific research work was connected to the planning system in the 'thirties and 'forties. Loren Graham, *Science in Russia and the Soviet Union. A short History* (Cambridge: Cambridge University Press, 1993), 181; See also Alec Nove, *An Economic History of the USSR, 1917–1991* (London: Penguin books, 1992), 350.

[65] In the cases where horizontal connections were created, the outcome of the process was also more successful. A good example is the case of the Kirov *kolkhoze* in Estonia. Antti Sarasmo, "The Kirov Fishing *kolkhoz*. A Socialist Success Story" in *Competition in Socialist society*, ed. Katalin Miklóssy and Melanie Ilic (Abingdon: Routledge, 2014), 53–70.

competitive innovations.⁶⁶ Paradoxically, it was the same centralized control that enabled impressive mission-oriented projects, such as the Soviet space program, yet blocked innovation in many other fields.⁶⁷

It was paradoxical that the process of transfer was very functional and included tools that could have enhanced the dissemination and diffusion of new technologies. One of the tools was the system of organizing expert visits through the STC. These visits were not only channels for communication between Finnish and Soviet experts, but also a way to obtain the knowledge necessary for the successful diffusion process. During their visits, based on their own expertize, specialists collected different kinds of knowledge about the technology, but also about how to use it. After their visits, they wrote reports based on their observations and returned the questionnaires they were expected to fill during their visits to the GKNT. The GKNT was expected to deliver the information to the Soviet R&D and industry in order to develop further transfers and diffusion of the technologies and related knowledge. Practical information that was collected and reported by the specialists in their travel reports would have been easy to adopt in everyday work. However, the adaptation at the shop-floor level proved to be poor. The futility of the personal contributions to the process and the inability of individuals to utilize the imported models in their own work created an atmosphere of deep discontent among Soviet specialists. This brought the aspect of unintended consequence to the transfer process.⁶⁸

There are various explanations for the problems in dissemination, implementation, and diffusion of the transferred technology and related knowledge. The dissemination might have taken place but the diffusion was not realized and in many cases the transferred technology was implemented into use as such. This was especially the case when there was an urgent demand for certain technology. It was easier to start production by directly using the technology rather than to launch time-consuming experiments based on the new technology in order to enhance domestic innovations. Furthermore, there were departmental barriers created by the system of a planned economy but also institutional and personal barriers that hindered the process of diffusion and also implementation.

Such barriers were visible for instance in the Soviet forest industry that was one of the many modernization projects in the Soviet Union carried out during

---

66 Hoffman & Laird, *The Scientific-Technological Revolution*, 98; Berliner, *Soviet industry from Stalin to Gorbachev* 203, 218.
67 Graham, *Science in Russia and the Soviet Union*, 201.
68 Sari Autio-Sarasmo, "Technological Modernisation in the Soviet Union and Post-Soviet Russia: Practices and Continuities," *Europe-Asia Studies* 68, no.1 (2016): 79–96.

the Khrushchev leadership in the 1950s and 1960s. In the forest industry transferred technology filled technological gaps and helped the branch to be more competitive. At the same time there were clear failures in implementing transferred technologies and supporting innovations either based on the transferred technologies or genuine domestic innovations.[69]

The case of continuous pulp cooking[70] provides a good example in which different techniques had been innovated in the West but also in the Soviet Union. This genuine Soviet innovation did not succeed and the Western technology was implemented in the Soviet pulp mills. The Soviet pulp mills are a good example of the role of Finland as a mediator of the new technology. A major part of the most advanced pulp mills in the Soviet Union were originally Finnish but became Soviet when the Karelian Isthmus was annexed to the Soviet Union after World War Two. The original Finnish technology was used in the mills until the demand for more modern technology emerged. In the beginning, the Soviet innovation was introduced to the pulp cooking but due to severe problems in implementation, the home technology was replaced by foreign technology. Finland, again, had an important role in the mediation of the new technology and related knowledge. The Soviet forest industry specialists visited Finland through the STC and collected information. The existing knowledge and the implementation of the new technology did not solve the problem of the low quality pulp. The main reasons for the poor outcome were the quality of the raw material, problems in maintaining technology, the lack of spare parts, and horizontal connections and problems in sharing information. The system did not support providing enough resources for complicated technology.[71]

Similar problems emerged in other complicated systems of technology. In the 1980s, Nokia participated in the Finnish-Soviet protocol of an exchange of goods channelled through the STC with the project of the automatic phone exchange system DX 200. The DX 200 project was Nokia's production collaboration with the Soviet partner, that is, cooperation on an enterprise-production unit level. In the project, there was a conflict between the expectations and practical cooperation from the Soviet side. The Soviet partners seemed to be interested in

---

[69] Elena Kochetkova, "The Soviet Forestry Industry in the 1950s and 1960s: A Project of Modernization and Technology Transfer from Finland," *Publications of the Faculty of Social Sciences* 52 (2017).

[70] The pulp cooking is an interesting case because it had a dual meaning. Pulp was also needed in the military industry (especially in the production of ammunition) that explains the resource allocations to the field.

[71] Elena Kochetkova, "A history of failed innovation: continuous cooking and the Soviet pulp industry, 1940s-1960s," *History and Technology* 31, no. 2 (2015), 108–132.

the long-term collaboration in order to "learn-by-doing." But even though the system was based solely on planning in Nokia (Finland) and all the components came from the West (from the US, Japan or Germany) the Soviet partners were not able to benefit from the collaboration as expected. The Soviet partners complained that Nokia had not sent the necessary information to them and thus they had not been able to "sovietize" the production, that is, to produce equipment and components in the Soviet Union. Nokia replied to the accusations saying that all technical information was shared with the Soviet partners well in advance. The reply brought to the fore the fact that the problem was at the technological level of the Soviet partners and not in the actions of Nokia. In spite of the occasional problems, Nokia continued its projects of production collaboration with the Soviet Union. Among others, Nokia exported communication systems, robotics, and computer technology to the USSR.[72]

Conclusion

The Soviet system of the scientific-technical cooperation created an active network of bilateral connections between the Soviet Union and the Western European states. The Soviet-Finnish STC is a good example of how "behind the scene" East-West cooperation developed during the decades of Cold War division. When the Soviet-Finnish STC began in the mid-1950s the contacts were relatively modest and consisted mainly of reciprocal visits and the transfer of basic information. During the 1970s and 1980s, the cooperation started to focus on high technology and joint projects between Finnish and Soviet partners. The Soviet-Finnish STC was specific because it was connected and supported by the Finnish-Soviet clearing trade, regulated by the state and based on planning. For Finland, the role as mediator of Western technology and its cooperation with the Soviet Union proved to be beneficial. The Finnish export-oriented enterprises learned quickly to cooperate with the Soviet Union and to adjust their supply to the demand of the Soviet partners. With long trade agreements and secured payments from the Soviet trade, Finnish enterprises were able to focus on R&D and develop their products for the Western markets as well. Finland learned to "play" the Cold War and to balance trade with Soviet Union according to its own goals to increase Western trade. Thanks to this capacity Finland was able to diversify its economy and to transform into a technologically-oriented, modern state during the Cold War decades.

---

[72] Häikiö, *Sturm und Drang*, 56–57, 196–198, 254.

On the other side, from the point of view of modernization, economic diversification or domestic innovations, the outcome did not meet the aims of the Soviet Union. The main aim of the Soviet STC and its trade with Finland, i.e. the transfer of technology and related knowledge to boost domestic innovations and to enhance economic modernization, was not fully realized. The practical transfers through the bilateral STC proved to be very effective. Technologies and related knowledge were transferred to the Soviet Union through the STC according to the plan created by the GKNT. However, the dissemination, implementation and especially the diffusion of transferred knowledge to the Soviet R&D and industry proved to be difficult. Transfers, including new production models, technology and related knowledge, were processed in the system of GKNT, but the dissemination to the production level was not realized as planned. Technologies were not adapted at the shop-floor level as expected and the Soviet R&D was not able to boost domestic innovations. The system of the Soviet planned economy favored the fulfilment of the plan and the lack of horizontal connections created barriers that hindered the introduction of new technologies and technological experiments.

Technology transfers during the Cold War substantially influenced the innovation policy in the Soviet Union with obvious consequences for contemporary Russia. The Soviet Union acquired new technology from abroad and paid for the transfers with raw materials and energy. This created a basis for the one-sided, raw material-based economy that has proved to be one of the major obstacles for economic development in contemporary Russia. Current discussions about the economic modernization of Russia follow the same discursive patterns today as they did in the 1970s. The road towards the diversification of the economy presupposes competitive domestic innovations and intensive economic growth that would enhance resilience in the economy which in the Soviet-Russian case has remained an elusive objective.

Ondřej Matějka
Social Engineering and Alienation between East and West: Czech Christian-Marxist Dialogue in the 1960s from the National Level to the Global Arena[1]

In April 1968, the World Council of Churches (WCC), the most important international organization in the field of international ecumenical relations, organized a two-day debate among elite Christian theologians, Marxists from both sides of the Iron Curtain (some of whom were highly-placed representatives of the Communist Parties of the East), and scholars from Third World countries as well. This event attracted attention of both Western and Eastern observers of worldwide church affairs. *The Times, L'Humanité, Swiss Weekly Tribune* and even the Czechoslovak *Literární listy* offered relatively extensive coverage of this "unique debate" between "old ideological enemies," who were trying to find common ground on issues related to "the humanization of technical and economic development."[2] Reporters particularly emphasized the "global proportions and impact" of this dialogue.[3]

The surprising amount of interest in this enterprise is quite understandable when one keeps in mind that ever since its beginning, the Cold War was perceived and theorized as one of "great religious wars" by an important number of its protagonists, as well as by those who analyzed its history.[4] Communist leaders did not conceal their belief that it was imperative to overcome religion (and at times to actively fight against it), regarding it as an essential part of the *ancien ordre*. Western, and in particular, US political elites tended to base their anti-communist stance on an analogous "global conflict between the god-fearing and the godless."[5]

---

[1] I would like to thank the FNS (project "Shared modernities or competing modernities? Europe between West and East 1920s-1970s," based at the University of Geneva) and the PRVOUK research scheme (P17) at Charles University, Prague for support in different stages of this project.
[2] "Marxists in Talks with Christians," 17 April 1968, *The Times*; "Marxists, Christians Theorize Together," 28 April 1968, *Swiss Weekly Tribune*; "Un colloque international entre marxistes et chrétiens s'est tenu a Genève," , 22 April 1968, *L'Humanité*.
[3] Jan Milíč Lochman, "Dialog překračuje meze," *Literární listy* 14 (1968): 13.
[4] Dianne Kirby, *Religion and the Cold War* (Houndmills: Palgrave, 2013), 1.
[5] Ibid.

The Geneva meeting in the Spring of 1968 was an obvious break with this dominant pattern of antagonism. This chapter argues that this rupture with the past constituted the most visible manifestation of the existence of a particular "channel" of East-West exchange that had evolved in various European countries from the late 1950s. Over time, this channel was more and more explicitly described by its proponents as a reaction to the "de-humanizing" and "alienating" effects of various kinds of social engineering and planning in Europe's highly developed industrial societies. Questions about the "place of the human being" in an ever more regulated and technicized society seemed fundamental to both Christians and Marxists of the time across the Iron Curtain which justifies the relevance of the analysis of their debates for a more general reflection on planning and social engineering between East and West. Both camps found surprisingly compatible language that was inspired, on the one side, by the Gospel and, on the other, by the young Karl Marx, who first addressed the issue of alienation in his 1844 *Manuscripts*. Anthropocentric resistance to the "de-humanizing" effects of both "Stalinist techno-bureaucracy" and "capitalist productivism" led the protagonists of the Christian-Marxist encounters to consider themselves as "two minority sects." They saw themselves as struggling against a "technicized indifference" linked to ever more computerized planning and management practices, and for "a more human world of man – today and tomorrow."[6]

Different countries could be chosen as the field of observation of these phenomena. The Czech case is especially interesting and relevant for several reasons. First, in the 1950s the Czech lands became a site for experimentation in various forms of social engineering focused on rapid social transformation (i.e. the construction of a "socialist society"). An important component of those initiatives was the attempt to accelerate the atheization of society in a planned manner. Projects aimed at "getting rid of religious obscurantism" were imposed on Czechoslovakia with a heavier hand than in other countries of the Eastern bloc. Such projects were aided by the particularly weak position of institutionalized religion in the country and a stable grounding of local free-thinking and anti-church movements.[7]

---

[6] These concepts were frequently referred to by both Eastern and Western proponents of dialogue, including Jan Milíč Lochman, *Church in a Marxist Society: A Czechoslovak View* (Evanston: Harper & Row, 1970), 192; Roger Garaudy, *L'alternative* (Paris: Éditions R. Laffont, 1972); Milan Machovec, *Smysl lidského života: studie k filosofii člověka* (Praha: Nakladatelství politické literatury, 1965).

[7] Antonín K. K. Kudláč, *Příběh(y) Volné myšlenky* (Praha: Nakladatelství Lidové noviny, 2005); Martin Schulze Wessel, *Revolution und religiöser Dissens: der römisch-katholische und russisch-*

At the same time, there was the tradition of debate between Czech Marxists and Protestant elites about issues of modernity and modernization that dated from the interwar period and created favorable conditions for national and international exchanges, despite deepening political differences after 1948.[8] Last but not least, Czech intellectuals of various confessions and political backgrounds profited from past connections to different Western networks that were established during the interwar period or even earlier. These networks were the basis of the infrastructure of the East-West intellectual exchanges[9] in which Czech actors played a remarkable role.[10]

My analysis will begin at the national level and in the first part will examine the so-called "executive phase" of one particular campaign of anti-religious offensive: it is an example of social planning in practice where the actors themselves (in this case communist apparatchiks) used the then trendy P-word. Their effort in the mid-1950s had the objective of limiting the social influence of institutionalized religion in the public realm and hastening development towards a "communist society" in a "scientifically controlled" way. I will then reconstruct the process by which a Czech Christian-Marxist space of exchange (a "channel") was created, which appeared, in part, in reaction to this campaign. In fact, certain planners of atheization campaigns became progressively disenchanted with "administrative" anti-church measures, began to reflect upon the shortcomings of their own social-engineering practices and finally (at least some of them) opened themselves to inspiring debates with their former principal ideological adversaries (Christian theologians). In its third part, the chapter will explore the internationalization of this channel of interaction during the 1960s, taking into account the different motivations of the main Czech and West-

---

orthodoxe Klerus als Träger religiösen Wandels in den böhmischen Ländern und in Russland 1848–1922 (München: Oldenbourg, 2011).

8 For this aspect see Ondřej Matějka, "A generation? A school? A fraternity? An army? Understanding the Roots of Josef Lukl Hromádka's Influence in the Czech Protestant Milieu 1920–1948," *Communio Viatorum. A Theological Journal* 3 (2012): 307–320.

9 I offer a perspective of *longue durée* on this aspect of the Czech Protestant milieu in my article "'Unique Connections': Uses of the Transnational Social Capital of Czech Pastors, 1860s–1960s," to be published in *Cultural and Social History* in 2019. This article connects my research to the type of reflection introduced by Katja Naumann and Sandrine Kott in this volume.

10 The Geneva Christian-Marxist meeting held in April 1968 offers a particularly striking illustration of this phenomenon. There were four Czech participants among 41 elite representatives of the principal world denominations and prominent East and West European Marxists. See Conference on Trends in Christian and Marxist Thinking About the Humanization of Technical and Economic Development – List of Participants (April 1968), File 994.3.50.12, World Council of Churches Archives, Geneva.

ern actors, as well as the inner dynamics of one international organization, the World Council of Churches (WCC), which was struggling for relevance in a secularizing world.

This field of research in East-West dialogue has so far remained rather unexplored.[11] This chapter is therefore based almost entirely on primary sources (both published and unpublished) which come from different places: the relevant files in Czech National Archives covering the development of communist social engineering projects in the religious field; the archives of the Czechoslovak secret police, which closely followed all kinds of East-West contacts; the private papers of influential actors; and the testimonies of local participants in dialogue activities. I was able to analyze the international aspect of these contacts thanks to my gaining access to relevant files in the WCC archives in Geneva.

Planning a society without religion

It is undeniable that the vision of a society free of institutionalized religion was an important part of the project of communism in the Soviet bloc. In the late 1940s, the builders of socialism all over Central and Eastern Europe endlessly quoted the passage from Karl Marx's *Contribution to the Critique of Hegel's Philosophy of Right* where he famously stated that religion "is the sigh of the oppressed creature, the heart of a heartless world, and the soul of soulless conditions. It is the opium of the people."[12] In the 1940s and 1950s, in the rising European communist dictatorships, Marx's words were frequently instrumentalized as a battle call against religion. One of the main aims the builders of socialism had was to achieve, as quickly as possible, a state of development where such an "opiate" would be unnecessary, thanks principally to the benefits of scientifically planned economic management.[13] The big question of that time was

---

11 The first collective volume on this subject (emphasizing the philosophical dimension of the dialogic phenomenon) appeared recently in Czech Ivan Landa and Jan Mervart, *Proměny marxisticko-křesťanského dialogu v Československu* (Praha: Filosofia, 2017). I presented the first results of my research on Christian-Marxist dialogue in my article "Dialogues on Religion in a 'Socialist Society' under Construction: Marxist Social Scientists and Czech Protestants, 1940s-60s," in *Reconstructing Communities in Europe, 1918–68*, ed. Stefan Couperus and Harm Kaal (London: Routledge, 2017), 238–259.
12 For a historical contextualization of this thought, see Andrew McKinnon, "Reading 'Opium of the People': Expression, Protest and the Dialectics of Religion," *Critical Sociology* 1–2 (2005): 15–38.
13 Erika Jindřichová-Kadlecová, "Úloha křesťanství v historii třídních bojů" (PhD diss., Charles University in Prague, 1949), 1–2.

whether a direct, centrally planned campaign against the churches was a necessary part of such a process.

In the Czechoslovak case, in August 1948 a group of influential young apparatchiks prepared substantial materials on religious affairs for the deliberation of the Central Committee of the Communist Party of Czechoslovakia (*Komunistická strana Československa* [KSČ]). They proposed a series of measures laying out explicitly the need to "take all necessary steps," including direct anti-church policies, with the objective of achieving the "final and definitive liquidation of religion."[14] Zealous Czech Stalinists in their early twenties fervently admired the social engineering practices of their Soviet comrades, who had succeeded in "rapidly spreading the scientific world view among the masses" thanks to centrally-planned atheization campaigns undertaken in the USSR in the interwar period.[15]

However, early Cold War tensions and postwar socio-economic difficulties meant that the Czechoslovak communist leadership had to create as vast a consensus as possible for their project of building socialism. They could not antagonize an important segment of the population. Consequently, all believers (except for the "treacherous hierarchy" of the Catholic church and its religious orders[16]) were invited at the end of the 1940s to join the "joyful socialist enterprise."[17] While Catholics (mainly in the traditionally religious areas of Moravia and Slovakia) regarded this invitation with trepidation, an important number of Czech non-Catholics more or less enthusiastically embraced the socialist project, arguing that "when one reads Marx and Lenin, one can hear resonance of what was announced by the Old Testament prophets and New Testament apostles."[18]

Nevertheless, the idea of doing away with institutionalized religion (always a reminder of the incompleteness of the "new socialist reality") did not disappear

---

14 Návrh na řešení náboženských otázek v ČSR (30 August 1948), fond Generální sekretariát ÚV KSČ 1945–1951 (100/1), National Archives (NA) Prague.
15 Erika Kadlecová, interview by Ondřej Matějka, 15 January 2008.
16 See on this point Karel Kaplan, *Stát a církev v Československu 1948–1953* (Brno: Doplněk, 1993).
17 Ondřej Matějka, "La religion est devenue l'affaire privée des citoyens. La construction du socialisme et les milieux religieux dans les Pays tchèques," *Histoire@Politique* 7 (2009).
18 Josef Lukl Hromádka, *Komunismus a křesťanství: o nápravu věcí lidských* (Hradec Králové: Evangelické dílo, 1946), 34–35. A more detailed analysis can be found in Ondřej Matějka, "'Správný komunista má také býti správným křesťanem, jako byli křesťané první.' Vztah českobratrských evangelíků ke Komunistické straně Československa 1921–1970," in *Český a slovenský komunismus (1921–2011)*, ed. Jan Kalous and Jiří Kocian (Prague: Ústav pro studium totalitních režimů, 2012), 284–296.

from the to-do lists of the leading Czech communist ideologues. This goal resurfaced with new vigor in the second half of the 1950s, when the dictatorship already seemed socially and economically stabilized. In fact, in the late 1950s, the Czechoslovak communist leadership, always struggling for the prestigious position of "Moscow's best pupil," decided to accelerate the construction of a socialist society in an organized, thoroughly-planned manner, so that they could legitimately proclaim Czechoslovakia to be the second "pure" socialist state in the world.[19]

Antonín Novotný, then the First Secretary of the KSČ, outlined the roadmap in his opening address to the Party's eleventh congress, held in Prague in June 1958. He emphasized the necessity of forging "moral and political unity" among the Czechoslovak people and closely linked this kind of unity with the process of "finishing the cultural revolution."[20] He further called for a resolute and "carefully planned" campaign that would "speed up the cultural development" of the Czechoslovak population. Manifestations of "religious backwardness," and those who espoused them, soon became the main targets of this policy.[21]

This ambitious social-engineering offensive proceeded in several steps. It always combined a great deal of chaos with minutely planned bureaucratic measures that targeted important crossroads of social life. The most socially conflictive action was limiting the visibility and influence of practicing Christians in public spaces and more importantly, in the field of education. Following several rather ambiguously worded messages from the top level of the KSČ hierarchy,[22] regional and local Party officers decided that teachers at all levels of the educative system should be obliged to sign a document proclaiming their "successful coming to terms with religious prejudice" if they wanted to keep their positions.[23] Numerous witnesses agree that at the turn of the 1950s and 1960s, an alarming shortage of teachers resulted in some regions as many hyperactive school headmasters set for themselves the objective of attaining a purely atheist staff as soon

---

19 "Usnesení XI. sjezdu," *Rudé právo*, 23 July 1958, 1.
20 Antonín Novotný, *Zpráva o činnosti ústředního výboru KSČ XI. sjezdu a současné hlavní úkoly* (Praha: Ústřední výbor KSČ), 1958.
21 *11. sjezd KSČ – dovršení výstavby socialismu v naší vlasti* (Praha: ÚV ČSM, 1959). For a previous position of the Central Committee of the KSČ on this issue, see: "Zásady zkvalitnění ideologické a politické práce mezi učiteli všeobecně vzdělávacích a odborných škol," 18 September 1957 published in *Od X. do XI. sjezdu: Usnesení a dokumenty ÚV KSČ* (Praha: SPNL, 1958), 593.
22 This ambiguity arose from the fact that from 1954 on, the religious affiliation of Czechoslovak citizens was not recorded in any kind of official materials: file 3, archival unit 3, p. 23, fond 1261/0/14 (Secretariat of the Central Committee of the CPC 1954–1962), NA Prague.
23 Reports from 1958, 1959; XXI/2, file 11, fond SC, XVII/5, Central Archives of the Evangelical Church of Czech Brethren Prague (CA ECCB).

as possible.²⁴ As a "logical" outgrowth of this policy, applications by devout students for study programs at pedagogical faculties were systematically turned down. The justification was that a teacher in a socialist society must be wholly identified with a "scientific world view" that was incompatible with a religious confession.²⁵

In addition to these negative, discriminatory measures, which reduced the social influence of believers, the "positive" side of the social-engineering effort to "finish the cultural revolution" was the cultivation of "scientific atheists" through education and propaganda. The Politburo decided to systematically support the institutionalization of a new field of research, "scientific atheism." Its mission was to educate experts who could produce and disseminate "scientifically based propaganda" and, last but not least, "plan necessary steps in the process of finishing the cultural revolution."²⁶

Thanks to generous state funding, several research groups appeared in the field of "scientific atheism" in the late 1950s. Two centres gradually acquired dominant positions: the Department of Scientific Atheism at the Czechoslovak Academy of Sciences, headed by Erika Kadlecová (born 1924),²⁷ and the Department of Philosophy at the Faculty of Arts of Charles University, where an assistant professor, Milan Machovec (1925–2003), began to publish numerous writings on "methods of education in atheism."²⁸ These "experts" systematically collaborated with the KSČ apparatus, which substantially increased their political and social impact and at the same time allowed KSČ officials to claim the "scientific legitimation" of their positions in the field of religion and the policies they implemented.²⁹

In this regard, Czechoslovakia's communist dictatorship basically followed a wider European pattern of pursuing social and economic development. In an era

---

24 Karel Kaplan, *Kronika komunistického Československa. Doba tání 1953–1956* (Brno: Barrister & Principal, 2005), 630–631.
25 Draft of a letter to the regional committees of the CPC about current ecclesiastical situation, 27 September 1958, f. 132, a.u. 232, p. 18, fond 1261/0/14 (Secretariat of the Central Committee of the CPC 1954–1962), NA Prague.
26 More on this institutionalization in Ondřej Matějka, "Between the Academy and Power: Czech Marxist Sociology of Religion (1954–1970)," in *Sociology and Ethnography in East-Central and South-East Europe. Scientific Self-Description in States Socialist Countries*, ed. Ulf Brunnbauer, Claudia Kraft and Martin Schulze Wessel (Munich: Oldenbourg, 2011), 107–133.
27 See also Zdeněk R. Nešpor, *Ne/náboženské naděje intelektuálů: vývoj české sociologie náboženství v mezinárodním a interdisciplinárním kontextu* (Praha: Scriptorium, 2008), 293–313.
28 The most extensive text of this kind is Milan Machovec, "O metodách ateistické výchovy," *Filosofický časopis* 5 (1959): 678–694.
29 Ladislav Prokůpek, interview by Ondřej Matějka, 20 October 2007.

of "planned modernization," expert solutions were fundamental sources of social and political legitimacy.[30] Hence, in the 1950s and 1960s, the Czechoslovak communist leadership sponsored various "expert committees" focused on analysis of all sorts of economic, social and political issues.[31] The histories of these committees follow an almost universal pattern. In the first phase, experts where chosen on the basis of their loyalty to the original framework devised by the KSČ Politburo. Then, the experts progressively emancipated themselves and, to the dismay of the conservative Party leadership, began to spread an independent and critical discourse in their field of expertize, thanks to their access to forbidden literature and their contacts with Western science. Ota Šik's team in economics, Zdeněk Mlynář's team in political science and Radovan Richta's group devoted to "scientific and technological revolution"[32] all actively prepared the way for the reformist Prague Spring.

So did the above-mentioned "scientific atheists." After a period of docile fulfilment of the tasks formulated for them by the Ideological Committee of the KSČ, Kadlecová, Machovec, Sviták, Hranička and other scientific atheists began to reflect in an independent way upon the alienating effects of social engineering initiatives in the field of religion. With their ambitions to scientifically understand social reality, they launched a project for a standardized sociological survey on the religiosity of Czech population (carried out in 1963). This survey provided a background for reflection on the paradoxical outcomes of social planning in the sphere of human consciousness carried out in the 1950s.[33] Unsurprisingly, these growingly independent thinkers soon attracted the attention of their former "ideological opponents" on the Christian side, who eventually formed a stable coalition with them and a "channel" that created space for mutual exchange of ideas, as well as useful contacts and support.

---

30 Peter Wagner and Hellmut Wollmann, "Social Scientists in Policy Research and Consulting: Some Cross-National Comparisons," *International Social Science Journal* 4 (1986): 601–617. See also the introduction to this volume.
31 Zdeněk Mlynář, *Nightfrost in Prague: The End of Humane Socialism* (New York: Karz Publishers, 1980), 57.
32 A research project has been recently completed at the Institute for Contemporary History of the Czech Academy of Sciences, funded by the Czech Science Foundation: *History of Czechoslovak Scientific Interdisciplinary Teams in the 1960s* (principal investigator: Jiří Hoppe).
33 Erika Kadlecová, *Sociologický výzkum religiozity Severomoravského kraje* (Praha: Academia, 1967).

Launching the dialogue:
Formation of the national channel

In order to understand the logic of rapprochement between the Marxist and Protestant intellectual elites in the late 1950s in the Czech lands, it is first important to retrace the principal turning points in the trajectory of the communist "scientific atheists." Thanks to their strong social and political capital inside the dictatorship, they were able to secure and institutionalize space for Christian-Marxist exchanges at the national level.

Most of the scientific atheists started their intellectual journeys as enthusiastic young Stalinists, replacing the "old bourgeois cadres" in philosophy departments and sociological institutes from the late 1940s onward – often after participating in extensive University purges in the early 1950s. They entered academia with a firm belief in the omnipotence of the Party, the universal validity of Marx-Leninist teachings and the unlimited potential of social engineering practices in all spheres of activity. Their motto was "the future of the world is in our hands" thanks to "scientific planning."[34] This self-confident attitude was complemented by a strong sense of loyalty towards the KSČ, which permitted an otherwise unlikely acceleration of their academic careers. Many of them were sent to study in the USSR at elite Party institutes in order to be educated at the very source. Even though they brought back the "seeds of disenchantment" based on their opportunity to observe closely the dysfunctionality of Soviet social engineering practices,[35] they were still considered reliable enough to be given access to Western social-scientific literature and forbidden parts of the Marxist canon (such as Marx's early writings) in the early 1950s. Their discovery of the "young Marx" and his 1844 manuscripts, together with Khrushchev's 1956 revelations (for many of them "a genuine existential earthquake"[36]) and their contacts with Polish and Yugoslav revisionists, led them to substantially re-evaluate their own self-image and the socialist project.[37]

Nevertheless, the scientific atheists did not renounce that project altogether. Quite to the contrary, they invested enormous energy into trying to find out "what went wrong," in part because they remained deeply identified with social-

---

34 Ibid, 256. Erika Kadlecová, interview by Ondřej Matějka, 15 January 2008.
35 Mlynář, *Nightfrost in Prague.*
36 Erika Kadlecová, interview by Ondřej Matějka, 15 January 2008.
37 Ivan Sviták, *Devět životů: konkrétní dialektika* (Praha: SAKKO, 1992).

ism and felt personal responsibility for its failures in the Czech context.[38] In their field of expertize, based on intense study of Eastern and Western sociological literature, they carried on frequent debates with colleagues from other socialist countries. Because of their opportunities to observe what was going on at the local level,[39] they became persuaded that social engineering with the objective of hastening the demise of religious faith simply did not work, and furthermore, sometimes was outright alienating to believers.

That critical reflection found its way into the national media and reached a wider public. This was possible because of the solid social and political capital the scientific atheists had accumulated in the first years of the socialist regime, and because the post-Stalinist moment opened a wholly new discursive space where criticism of "the remnants of the cult of personality" was expected. Hence, the scientific atheists were authorized to publish in influential reviews such as *Nová mysl* or *Filosofický časopis* their revisionist thoughts about the inefficiency of "bureaucratic methods" used in the process of "finishing the cultural revolution" and the problem of "producing a sense of life" in a highly developed, centrally planned society.[40]

Protestant intellectual elites who suffered from the socially marginalizing measures of social engineering aimed at "finishing the cultural revolution" were quick to react. The first contact with Machovec was established by two young Protestant pastors, Karel Trusina and Milan Opočenský, who began attending Machovec's seminars at the Faculty of Arts in the late 1950s. They soon proposed arranging a discussion for Machovec with professor Josef L. Hromádka, dean of the Comenius Protestant Theology Faculty in Prague.[41] In this encounter, Machovec made a "great discovery" that "influenced the rest of his life."[42] He met a group of Christian intellectuals holding dogmatically sound

---

[38] For deeper reflection on this aspect, see Ondřej Matějka, "We are the Generation that Will Construct Socialism: The Czech 68ers Between Manifest Destiny and Mark of Cain," in *Talkin' 'Bout my Generation. Conflicts of Generation Building and Europe's 1968*, ed. Anna von der Goltz (Göttingen: Wallstein Verlag, 2011), 118–139.

[39] They were employed by the KSČ apparatus as lecturers for regional officers responsible for church policy. Ladislav Prokůpek, interview by Ondřej Matějka, 20 October 2007; Erika Kadlecová, interview by Ondřej Matějka, 15 January 2008.

[40] Some examples: Erika Kadlecová, "Ateismus bojovný a trpělivý," *Nová mysl* 10 (1962): 1254–1262; Machovec, "O metodách;" Milan Machovec, "Je naše vědeckoateistická výchova správně orientována?" *Filosofický časopis* 3 (1964): 354–361.

[41] Olga Nytrová and Milan Balabán, "Rozhovor s profesorem Milanem Machovcem. Jak tomu bylo s vaším křesťanstvím a marxismem?" *Křesťanská revue* 7 (2000): 176; Diaries 1958–1959, J. L. Hromádka papers, Archives of Evangelical Theological Faculty.

[42] Nytrová and Balabán, "Rozhovor," 176.

theological principles who nonetheless sincerely identified with the socialist project and had been well-acquainted with Marxist thought since the 1920s.[43] Furthermore, the Protestants' contacts and connections in the West opened a new and attractive space for the predominantly Eastern-oriented Marxist thinkers.

In the late 1950s, the first Christian-Marxist conversations took place regarding principally specific religious topics. For example, Machovec was working on a research project on Barthian dialectic theology and he found in his Protestant counterparts excellent informants and discussion partners.[44] Progressively, however, the growing group of Marxists and Christians that formed around Hromádka and Machovec cleared common ground for debate on more general topics, most notably about the alienation and dehumanization evoked by the then-current phase of Czechoslovak socialism. Personal experience with social engineering operations constituted an important reference point for them all. In the words of Jan Milíč Lochman, one of the main Protestant participants, the topic they examined with the most passion was the place of man "within the alienating structures of institutional manipulations as they evidently appeared within the centralized structure of socialist society."[45]

Christian intellectuals did not contest the fact that "a house for a new society was being built" or that Marxism offered "knowledge of social laws enabling effective management of social development."[46] Nevertheless, they shared a common concern with their atheist counterparts about the "manifold alienation of modern man [that] has not yet been overcome by the socialist structure of society."[47] The revisionist Marxists agreed that regulation and planning of different dimensions of social life often produced "fatalism," especially when such policies were carried out with "bureaucratized indifference," and thus could result in a "dehumanized world" where man played only the role of "a cog in a vast machine."[48]

---

43 On this aspect, see for instance Jiří Hájek, *Paměti* (Praha: Ústav mezinárodních vztahů, 1997).
44 As a result of this project, Milan Machovec published a book entitled *O tak zvané "dialektické" teologii současného protestantismu* (Praha: ČSAV, 1962).
45 Lochman, *Church*. See also Josef Lukl Hromádka, *Gospel for Atheists* (Geneva: WCC–Youth Department, 1965).
46 Milan Machovec, *O smyslu lidského života* (Praha: Orbis, 1957), 81.
47 Milan Opočenský quoted in Paul Mojzes, *Christian-Marxist Dialogue in Eastern Europe* (Minneapolis: Augsburg Publishing House, 1980), 119.
48 Milan Machovec, "Dialog v procesu humanizace člověka," *Osvětová práce* 15 (1965): 10–11; Lochman, *Church*, 192.

Since the early 1960s, these discussion partners became more attached to each other as they formed a coalition against the conservative Party apparatus. Its representatives observed, with a sense of shock, how the former brain trust of the atheization campaigns had become a nest of well-thought-out criticism of all attempts at "bureaucratic" social engineering in the field of religion.[49] Machovec, Prokůpek, and Kadlecová were furthermore ready to support Protestant protests against repressive measures aimed at limiting church activities. They also opposed social discrimination against believers, for example in admission procedures to the university.[50]

From the mid-1960s, the scope and resonance of this continuing dialogue widened and became even more general. Machovec, for instance, explicitly began to refuse to acknowledge social engineering attempts as a "so-called historical necessity" (related to the "inevitable march" towards a communist society without religion) and as an infallible guarantee of a brighter future. Quite the reverse. Referring to incidents of forced atheization, he contended that the idea that "the future human being can be planned in every respect" was "something quite crude and vulgar."[51] Machovec formulated sophisticated hypotheses about the origin of specific forms of alienation produced by the construction of socialism and called for deep reflection about the need for a "sense of life" in a society that was on its way toward communism.[52]

Machovec found his main source of inspiration in the work of the Marxist psychoanalyst and philosopher Erich Fromm, with whom he met for the first time in the context of the Christian-Marxist dialogue in Prague in the mid-1960s.[53] After that, Machovec and his Christian friends became ardent proponents of Fromm's ideas about what he called a "historical irony," where the "spirit of capitalism, the satisfaction of material greed," so typical of Western consumer societies, was infecting the socialist countries of East-Central Europe as

---

49 See the angry reports by Karel Hrůza from 1962–1963, fond IV ČCE, Archives of Ministry of Education, Prague.
50 Erika Kadlecová, "Socialismus a náboženství," *Rudé právo*, 28 May 1968.
51 Machovec, quoted in Hans-Joachim Girock, *Partner von morgen?* (Stuttgart: Kreuz-Verlag, 1968), 67; Milan Machovec, "Die Zukunft als Drohung und Chance," *Der Kreis, Sonderreihe*, 5 (1966): 31.
52 The first edition of Machovec's *O smyslu lidského života* from 1957 was followed by an enlarged version with a chapter on the dialogue in 1965: Milan Machovec, *Smysl lidského života: studie k filosofii člověka* (Praha: Nakladatelství politické literatury, 1965).
53 Benjamin B. Page, "Dialogues…," in *Mistr dialogu Milan Machovec. Sborník k nedožitým osmdesátinám českého filosofa*, ed. Kamila Jindrová, Pavel Tachecí, and Pavel Žďárský (Praha: Akropolis, 2006), 148–150.

well.⁵⁴ Fromm understood the logic of this process in the following way: the material success of capitalism was immensely impressive to poorer countries in Europe where communism triumphed. The attractiveness of socialism had become identified with its success in the competition with capitalism. According to Fromm and his followers, this competition was, nevertheless, being taking place on capitalist terms. Fromm warned that socialism "with its planned economy was in danger of deteriorating into a system which can accomplish the industrialization of poorer countries more quickly than capitalism, rather than of becoming a society in which the development of man, and not that of economic production, is the main goal." According to Fromm, but also Machovec, this danger was becoming ever more acute as Eastern regimes accepted a "crude version" of Marxism, divorced from "the humanist spiritual tradition of which Marx was one of the greatest representatives." What followed from this distortion, as diagnosed by Fromm in both East and West, was a society managed and planned "by giant enterprises, giant industrial, governmental, and labour bureaucracies" which produced alienated individuals.

The French philosopher Roger Garaudy (a member of the politburo of the French Communist Party between 1956 and 1970) was another key source of inspiration for Czech revisionist Marxists and their Christian counterparts. Garaudy gradually sharpened his criticism of the "Stalinist techno-bureaucracy" over time. He contended that it reproduced (and at times enforced) a "dualist structure" of governing/governed, dominating/dominated, and limited socialism to "a specific system of economic planning."⁵⁵ His critiques encountered an enthusiastic response in Prague among proponents of the Christian-Marxist dialogue. In the early 1960s, he repeatedly went there to present his thoughts on socialism as "a project of civilisation" leading to "a richer and more creative" life. This opinion was very much in tune with the reformist thinking then mushrooming in Prague, which Garaudy himself had already in 1963 baptized as the "Prague Spring."⁵⁶

At that time, Fromm and Garaudy were frequently referenced by the continuously expanding Czech circle of dialogical Marxists and Christians. It is possible to observe the progressive institutionalization of their debate in two places where the basic contours of the Christian-Marxist "channel" on the national level were being defined. On the one hand, more theologically oriented discus-

---

54 All quotes in the following paragraph come from Erich Fromm, *Socialist Humanism: An International Symposium* (New York: Doubleday, 1965), 214–216.
55 Garaudy, *L'Alternative*, 76–77. But see also Roger Garaudy, *From Anathema to Dialogue: The Challenge of Marxist-Christian Cooperation* (London: Collins, 1967).
56 Roger Garaudy, "Kafka et le Printemps de Prague," *Lettres françaises* 981 (1963): 1.

sions, which had started in Hromádka's apartment in the late 1950s,[57] moved to the Protestant theological faculty in the autumn of 1963. There, several dozen Protestants, Catholics and Marxists who were open to dialogue met every other Thursday in the refectory of the faculty. The topics they presented and discussed ranged from medieval theology to the issue of alienation in socialist society.[58]

The second space, more philosophically oriented, originated in discussions which first took place in Machovec's apartment in Košíře. The main participants were Hromádka's students Opočenský and Trusina, Machovec, and some of Machovec's closest philosophical partners, like Zbyněk Fišer. According to Milan Opočenský, "our debates were exciting, honest and often tough. I remember that we encouraged ourselves by reflecting on the fact that dialogue helps us not only in finding a way towards other people but also in engaging in dialogue with ourselves and with our mortal essence".[59]

Profoundly spiritual debates were soon to be confronted with more earthly preoccupations. After the birth of Machovec's second child in 1963, Mrs. Machovec presented her husband with a clear ultimatum: either Machovec, Opočenský, Trusina and their growing circle of Christian and Marxist partners would find a more suitable space for their noisy encounters than the Machovec family's kitchen or they would have to stop.[60] At that critical moment, Machovec decided to transfer the debates onto academic territory. In that way, he founded the "Monday Dialogic Seminar" at the Faculty of Arts, which later became famous and through the end of the 1960s attracted students and intellectuals from all faculties of Charles University and the Academy of Sciences.[61]

---

[57] Diaries 1957–1959, fond J. L. Hromádka, Archives ETF Prague.
[58] Reports from 1964–1966, File Jiří Němec, Archives of security services Prague.
[59] Milan Opočenský, "Velice jsem po tobě teskliv," in *Mistr dialogu Milan Machovec. Sborník k nedožitým osmdesátinám českého filosofa*, ed. Kamila Jindrová, Pavel Tachecí, and Pavel Žďárský (Praha: Akropolis, 2006), 215.
[60] Pavel Žďárský, "Milan Machovec a jeho filosofická antropologie v 60. letech 20. století" (PhD Diss., Charles University in Prague, 2011), 51.
[61] Jiřina Šiklová, "Dialogický seminář na Filozofické fakultě UK v šedesátých letech," in *Mistr dialogu Milan Machovec. Sborník k nedožitým osmdesátinám českého filosofa*, ed. Kamila Jindrová, Pavel Tachecí, and Pavel Žďárský (Praha: Akropolis, 2006), 50, 56.

The dialogue goes global

Despite Hromádka's and Machovec's adroit manoeuvring in the context of communist dictatorship (and family dynamics), the Czech Christian-Marxist channel did not remain unnoticed by the conservative wing of the KSČ leadership and the secret police (*Státní bezpečnost* [StB]). This was partly because of its subversive political rhetoric but even more because of its progressive internationalization. StB files document in great detail the growing number of international observers and participants attracted by these Prague dialogues. They also show how StB officers continuously sounded the alarm for the upper levels of the KSČ about what they considered a danger of "foreign ideological infiltration."[62]

In this particular case, the reports of the agents and collaborators of the secret police, despite a frequent tendency to produce conspiracy theories and interpret the world in terms of the games of intelligence agencies, probably did not overestimate the rapid internationalization of the religious dialogue. The dialogue was undoubtedly closely linked to a global context: in the mid-1960s, Christian-Marxist dialogues "broke out" almost simultaneously in a number of European countries, including Czechoslovakia, Italy, West Germany, and France.[63]

The Czech group became an intensely courted partner for Western participants. It was attractive because it had grown up autonomously in the Eastern, socialist part of the European continent, thus constituting a sort of "laboratory." It offered Western counterparts original and "indigenous" thinking from the "Second World" about problems of alienation that were relevant to modern bureaucratic societies, where new forms of social regulation and management (as interpreted by Fromm) were being introduced.[64] The group's members' influence also rested on their "impressive intellectual performance," which was reported with a sense of admiration not only by political allies like Garaudy and Fromm but by critical observers and opponents of communism as well, such as those from Radio Free Europe.[65] Furthermore, in its conquest of Western audiences, the Czech dialogic group enjoyed a unique advantage: the international

---

[62] General report for the CC – 1965, Archives of security services Prague.
[63] Leonard Swindler, *The Age of Global Dialogue* (Eugene: Pickwick Publications, 2016), 297.
[64] For a further instrumentalization of the Czechoslovak reformist experience, see Garaudy, *L'alternative*.
[65] Christians and Marxists in Marianske Lazne, 10 July 1967, 300–8–3–13449, Records of Radio Free Europe/Radio Liberty Research Institute, Publications Department, Background Reports, Open Society Archives at the Central European University, Budapest.

social capital of Czech Protestants, who had traditionally possessed close connections to the West.

From the very beginning of Cold War détente, Czech Protestant elites were able to rapidly (re-)establish contacts and networks and even enlarge them. The scientific atheist Machovec's career trajectory constitutes a perfect example of the benefits. "The Protestants made me leave my Prague quietness and forced me to start travelling," he amusedly confessed in the 1970s.[66] In fact, thanks to the Protestants' recommendations, Machovec was invited to several international Christian debating fora in the early 1960s. In the wake of his first Western trip, to Graz for the World Student Christian Federation conference in 1962, he became "a genuine dialogue magnet." His foreign lectures and discussion tours, which emphasized the alienating impact of modernization in both the East and the West, always met with great success.[67]

Machovec was not alone in profiting from the dynamics of international interfaith dialogue as Protestant networks opened the gates to the West. In the second half of the 1960s, his Marxist colleagues Vítězslav Gardavský and Julius Tomin were "exported" to the USA, thanks to sponsorship by the National Council of Churches, in order to inform the overseas intellectual public about the Christian-Marxist dialogue. Tomin even earned a visiting professorship at the University of Hawaii as an outcome of that trip.[68] Thanks to Protestant connections, Ladislav Prokůpek, a member of Kadlecová's Department of Scientific Atheism at the Czechoslovak Academy of Sciences in the 1960s, obtained a scholarship from the World Council of Churches and spent a semester in Geneva in the academic year 1969–70.[69]

These increasingly more intense exchanges gradually led to the establishment and stabilization of spaces for dialogue at the international level. Regular international dialogic conferences organized by the *Paulus Gesellschaft* probably represented the earliest manifestation of this stabilization in the 1960s. The West German association, whose name refers to the Apostle Paul's mediation efforts

---

66 Opočenský, "Velice jsem po tobě teskliv," 213.
67 Helmut Beth, "Im Dialog mit Milan Machovec," in *Mistr dialogu Milan Machovec. Sborník k nedožitým osmdesátinám českého filosofa*, ed. Kamila Jindrová, Pavel Tachecí, and Pavel Žďárský (Praha: Akropolis, 2006), 184–199. Opočenský, "Velice jsem po tobě teskliv," 213. Petr Pokorný, "Vzpomínky na Milana Machovce," Ibid., 208–209. The first book introducing Machovec's thought in the West, *Marxismus und dialektische Theologie: Barth, Bonhoeffer und Hromádka in atheistich-kommunistischer Sicht*, was published in 1965 in Zurich by the Evangelische Verlags Zollikons (EVZ). Its translator, Dorothea Neumärker, was a German Protestant participant in the Prague-based Christian Peace Conference and the author of a monograph on Hromádka.
68 Lubomír Miřejovský, *Dopisy z XX. století* (Praha: Nuga, 2004), 312, 316–325.
69 Ladislav Prokůpek, interview by Ondřej Matějka, 20 October 2007.

between the Jews and the Gentiles, was founded in 1956 by Erich Kellner, a West German Catholic priest and theologian who was interested in re-thinking the position of Christianity in the "scientific age." In the early 1960s, Kellner noticed the new intellectual movement among East European Marxists and decided to offer *Paulus Gesellschaft* as a mediator and moderator of discussions between the two ideological camps. The first East European who was authorized to attend a *Paulus Gesellschaft* conference was the Polish philosopher Adam Schaff in 1964.[70] In the following years, the *Paulus* initiative continued to develop. In 1965, a much more numerous delegation of Eastern Marxists came to Salzburg to discuss the theme of the "Christian and Marxist Future." They returned again in 1966 to Herrenchiemsee, where they compared "Christian Humanity and Marxist Humanism."[71]

The international reputation of these encounters grew with every meeting and it seemed only logical to try to organize one in the East. It is significant that the Czech team of Marxist sociologists, headed by Erika Kadlecová, offered to co-sponsor the 1967 *Paulus Gesellschaft* congress. It took place in the Czech resort town Mariánské lázně (Marienbad) and marked the apogee of the dialogic movement with over 220 participants and extensive media coverage (mainly in the West).[72]

The central topic of the debate in Marienbad was "Creativity and Freedom in a Human Society." This clearly marked a continuation of East-West reflection on the alienating effects of bureaucratically-managed societies in high modernity and the limited possibilities for development of freedom and creativity in such contexts. The participants, irrespective of the ideological camp from which they came, agreed that it was necessary "to protect the individual against all attempts to reduce him merely to a medium for the construction of a technologically over-rationalized future" and warned against "new forms of alienation" in developed capitalist and socialist societies. At the end of their deliberations, they tried to strengthen their message by asserting that they represented "the two most important ideologically-oriented groups [i.e. Christians and Marxists] in modern society", which felt "a special responsibility for the future of man."[73]

Who contributed most to such an ambitious claim? On the one hand, there were leading Catholic and Protestant theologians such as Karl Rahner, Johann

---

[70] Katja Naumann introduces Schaff more extensively in her contribution to this volume.
[71] Mojzes, *Christian-Marxist Dialogue*, 158 ff.
[72] "Christians and Marxists in Marianske Lazne," 10 July 1967.
[73] "Christians and Marxists in Marianske Lazne," 10 July 1967. Nevertheless, the two groups were also systematically presented as "minority sects" in a "sea of indifference" (Lochman, *Church*, 192).

Baptist Metz, Giulio Girardi, Yves Congar, Jürgen Moltmann and Georges Casalis. On the other hand, the most active Western European participants from the Marxist field included Manuel Azcarate, a respected member of the Spanish Communist Party in exile, Lucian Gruppi, the head of the Ideological Section of the Central Committee of the Italian CP, Walter Hollitscher, a professor of philosophy at the University of Leipzig and a consultant to the Central Committee of the Austrian Communist Party, and of course, Roger Garaudy.

The encounters facilitated by the *Paulus Gesellschaft* produced even more offspring, which further enhanced the East-West channel of communication. In particular, two journals became spaces for intense intellectual exchange on various topics opened up by the Christian-Marxist dialogue. The Austrian journal *Neues Forum* started to play a role as the "official review" for Christian-Marxist dialogue in the mid-1960s. Ironically, it was first financed by the decidedly anticommunist North American "Congress for Cultural Freedom." As it emancipated itself and added a subtitle, "International Review for Dialogue," it became one of the liveliest journals specializing in East-West dialogue. It had wide recognition in Europe, and was led by an international editorial committee staffed by "dialogic stars" from both sides of the Iron Curtain, including Moltmann, Bloch, Metz, Fromm, Hromádka, Machovec, and also Eric Hobsbawm.[74]

In 1967, the prominent Catholic theologian Karl Rahner founded yet another journal with a similar background and purpose. It was entitled the *Internationale DIALOG Zeitschrift* and first appeared in 1968. It constituted a more theologically oriented platform for continuing exchange between Christians and Marxists with an international audience.[75]

It is possible to identify even lower-level ramifications of the Christian-Marxist channel between Eastern and Western Europe, which had a concrete impact on the ground of academia. Exchanges between the *Collegium Academicum* of the University of Heidelberg and Charles University offer such an example. In fact, thanks to his growing fame in West European Protestant circles after the Graz conference in 1962, Milan Machovec (together with Czech Protestant historian Amadeo Molnár, another proponent of the dialogue) was invited to the annual conference of the *Evangelische Akademie Berlin* in September 1963, to contribute to the topic "Neighbours in the Centre of Europe." In the early 1960s, this was still quite a unique opportunity for dialogue with the West German students who were members of the *Collegium Academicum* of Heidelberg. Representatives of

---

[74] *Neues Forum – Dialog* (1968–1969); David McLellan, "Christian-Marxist Dialogue," *New Blackfriars* 577 (1968): 462–467.
[75] Svein Rise, "Karl Rahner," in *Key Theological Thinkers: From Modern to Postmodern*, ed. Staale Johannes Kristainsen and Svein Rise (London: Routledge, 2013), 225–238.

this academic association decided to use their newly formed contacts to gain an invitation for 15 students to stay in Prague in 1964. In the months that followed, they established a regular series of semester-long exchanges between Heidelberg and Prague for a dozen students, which lasted until the end of the Prague Spring and allowed a much wider circle of students to enjoy opportunities originally only available in the Christian-Marxist channel.[76]

Finally, in the mid-1960s, the public importance of these encounters, as well as the influence of certain Czech actors in the World Council of Churches, attracted the WCC's attention to the dialogue.[77] We can observe a double motivation for the organization's interest. First of all, the early 1960s were marked by the WCC's effort to find new ways to legitimize its existence and purpose in an ever more secularized Euro-Atlantic context (which still remained the centre of gravity of the WCC).[78] At the same time, the WCC was looking for more intense connections to the Second and Third Worlds. Both of these logics converged at the moment the WCC was preparing to hold a "Conference on Church and Society" in Geneva in 1966.[79] Of the 420 participants, about equal numbers came from the Third World, socialist countries, North America and Western Europe, making it the first large ecumenical conference in which the participants from the Western countries were not in a majority.

One of the outcomes of the conference (co-organized and co-chaired by Czech dialogic theologian Lochman) that was explicitly emphasized in the final report for the WCC's Central Committee, was an accent on the necessity to develop all kinds of dialogic initiatives, with a special focus on contacts with Marxism. "We urge that the WCC seek to initiate a formal dialogue with Marxists on an international basis, in each region of the world."[80] The justification for that effort underlined the fact that "many Christians and Marxists have common social concerns," arising from "the emergence of a pluralistic and technological society in both East and West."[81]

---

76 Beth, "Im Dialog mit Milan Machovec," 185–193.
77 File 42.11.04, WCC archives Geneva.
78 File 994.3.50.12, WCC archives Geneva. One of the principal coordinators of the dialogue in Geneva, Lukas Vischer, insisted that "the World Council's Church and Society Conference, and the Christian Peace Conference are shattering the chains of the Constantinian era in which the church was considered the champion of the existing order whatever it might be. The church is vitally interested in the thoughts and problems of THIS world".
79 For more on this conference, see Katharina Kunter and Annegreth Schilling, *Globalisierung der Kirchen: der Ökumenische Rat der Kirchen und die Entdeckung der Dritten Welt in den 1960er und 1970er Jahren* (Göttingen: Vandenhoeck & Ruprecht, 2014), 38–41.
80 Minutes of Central Committee 1967 (205), WCC archives Geneva.
81 Ibid.

On the basis of that suggestion (symbolically presented to the Central Committee of the WCC by Lochman himself), the WCC decided to co-finance a series of Christian-Marxist meetings. It also tried to actively contribute to the spread of dialogue among students – for instance, by co-organizing dialogic seminars in Geneva. Unsurprisingly, one of the first invitees came from Prague. In 1967, Josef Smolík, a professor of Protestant systematic theology and an active participant in the Prague Christian-Marxist meetings, used the seminars to introduce, together with his colleague Richard Shaull (a professor at the Princeton theological seminary deeply influenced by Josef L. Hromádka during his studies[82]), elaborate thinking on the dangers (and challenges) of the computerized cybernetic society then arising both in the West and in the East as the result of the "scientific and technological revolution." Smolík analyzed the "introduction of cybernetic models for management of economic and social life" and explicitly argued, in line with ideas discussed at Marienbad and in the *Neues Forum*, that "the danger that cybernetics represents consists of stealing the fundamental dimensions of humanity from a man," which "leads to the complete disintegration of the human being deprived of his freedom." Shaull warned, in quite the same vein, that the danger of a "technicisized civilization," characterized by ever more rationalized and computerized management, was resulting in "a new form of slavery." The only way out that Shaull and Smolík could imagine required a "new revolution" substantially inspired by emancipatory movements in the Third World.[83]

This line of thought, which consistently emphasized connections with the South and consequently globalized the whole dialogic enterprise, dominated the most important international manifestation of the Christian-Marxist channel. This was the conference organized by the WCC in Geneva in April 1968 mentioned in the introduction of the chapter. The organizing committee invited speakers with special care, including representatives from South America, Africa and Asia. The WCC then announced with triumphant jubilation that its conference was the first occasion when theologians and philosophers coming from the First, Second, and Third Worlds would simultaneously take part in debates.[84] The organizers stated with great satisfaction that the conference dialogue "reached global proportions" and engaged with "pressing and practical prob-

---

[82] Angel D. Santiago-Vendrell, *Contextual Theology and Revolutionary Transformation in Latin America* (Pickwick Publications: Eugene, 2010), 17.

[83] Josef Smolik and Richard Shaull, *Consommateurs ou révolutionnaires* (Association du Foyer John Knox: Genève, 1967), 12–13, 18.

[84] WCC Information, 16 April 1968, file 994.3.50.12, WCC Archives Geneva.

lems" on the world level – most importantly, the issue of the dehumanizing consequences of scientifically managed social and economic development.[85]

Conclusion

Geneva 1968 can thus be seen as the conference that confirmed the globalization of the dialogic enterprise, which had grown out of several sources. In this chapter, we followed one of those sources, reaching back to the Czechoslovakia of the late 1950s. There, observation of the dysfunctionality of social engineering practices in the sphere of religion (and a common interest among Christians and Marxists alike in finding a remedy for this situation) brought together elite Marxists and Protestant theologians. They progressively began to share their reflections on wider issues connected with rationalized scientific management and the planning of social life in developed industrial societies, along with the alienating effects of such phenomena. The national dialogue in Czechoslovakia found enthusiastic partners and supporters in the West and thus became a space of interaction, a channel through the Iron Curtain.

Nevertheless, the April 1968 Geneva meeting marked the limits of this channel. The attempt to integrate the South into the East-West debates backfired in the end. Critical observers rightly stated that although it was certainly impressive to see how smoothly Czech and Hungarian Marxists communicated with Western Christians about social engineering and alienation, the presence of Third World delegates only accentuated the declining relevance of this European intellectual harmony in a global context. The Indian delegate to the conference put it in blunt terms when he noted that original solutions to "the old East-West ideological conflicts do not bring anything interesting for contemporary Indians."[86] Representatives of the South therefore systematically attempted to turn the focus towards the problems relevant to them: revolution and liberation struggles in the Third World, and ambiguous theological justifications for violence. This "revolutionary arrogance,"[87] which scandalized both Eastern and Western habitués of the dialogue channel, was a clear signal to the leadership of the WCC. In the following years, they shifted their focus to debates on revolutionary and liberation

---

85 "Bilan et perspective du dialogue" (by Roger Garaudy, May 1969), file 994.3.50.12, WCC Archives Geneva.
86 "Dialogue entre chrétiens et marxistes à Genève" (by Van der Bent, 1968), file 994.3.50.12, WCC Archives Geneva.
87 Ibid.

theology. After one more attempt to continue the global Christian-Marxist dialogue in 1969, the WCC ceased to support that kind of activity.

The rapid end of the dialogic effort in the international ecumenical arena was closely connected with its decline in the national (Czech) context as well. The Geneva meeting took place only four months before the invasion of Czechoslovakia by Warsaw Pact troops, which crushed the Prague Spring. Czech actors in the dialogue all identified with the reformers' attempt to find a "third path" between socialism and capitalism, and so their fate was sealed once "normalization" in occupied Czechoslovakia picked up speed. At the beginning of the 1970s, Machovec, Kadlecová, Prokůpek and their colleagues were singled out as proponents of a "theological form of the anti-communist theory of convergence."[88] They lost their jobs in the academic sphere and spent the following 20 years in the dissident intellectual underground.[89] In a sense, however, the channel opened up by the Czechoslovak dialogic encounters of the late 1950s bore helpful fruit in the 1970s. Ironically enough, Milan Machovec (one of the founding fathers of Czech scientific atheism in the early 1950s) earned most of his income for the greater part of the 1970s from his part-time job as the organist at Saint Antonin's church in Prague-Holešovice, which he obtained thanks to his dialogic reputation in Catholic circles.

---

[88] Ladislav Hrzal and Jakub Netopilík, *Ideologický boj ve vývoji české filozofie* (Praha: Svoboda, 1983), 376.

[89] Their intellectual heritage continued to be praised in certain Western intellectual circles in the following decade: Roger Garaudy for instance referred to the Prague Spring and the Christian-Marxist dialogue in his synthesis *L'Alternative*, published in the early 1970s. He used the Czechoslovak version of "humanized socialism" from the 1960s as an inspiration for the future (which he connected to the project of *auto-gestion*). On the Yugoslav dimension of this phenomenon, see Benedetto Zaccaria in this volume.

Simon Godard
The Council for Mutual Economic Assistance and the failed Coordination of Planning in the Socialist Bloc in the 1960s

Planning has long been deeply associated with socialist economies, although capitalist countries have been influenced by this idea and have experimented, to different degrees, government interventionism in the economy over the short twentieth century.[1] Thus planning the economy is not a specifically socialist idea, and even though central planning was a shared characteristic of most Eastern European countries during the Cold War, the entanglement between planning and socialism can still be questioned. Already in the 1960s, Polish economist Wlodzimierz Brus considered the association of economic planning and socialism "not as a definitive solution, but as a choice among possible alternatives."[2]

Even though the Gosplan was established in the USSR soon after the October Revolution, the first five-year plan was only adopted in 1928. A model of socialist planning was indubitably shaped in the USSR, but never remained unchallenged[3] nor incapable of evolution.[4] The persistence of market-like institutions in the Stalin era, analyzed by Paul Gregory and Mark Harrison,[5] or the Yugoslav path to economic development after 1948, show how misleading and inaccurate a strong opposition between centrally planned economies and markets would be. Indeed, the functioning of the economic system started to be challenged again in the German Democratic Republic (GDR) in 1956 and in the USSR in

---

[1] Secrétariat général de l'ONU, *Planification en vue du développement économique* (New York: Nations Unies, 1963); Jan Tinbergen, *La planification* (Paris: Hachette, 1967), 220–235; Claude Gruson, *Origine et espoirs de la planification française* (Paris: Dunod, 1968).
[2] Wlodzimierz Brus, "Rapports entre politique et économie en régime socialiste," *L'Homme et la société* 6 (1967): 70; see also Wlodzimierz Brus, *Problèmes généraux du fonctionnement de l'économie socialiste* (Paris: Maspéro, 1968), 36–46.
[3] Naum Jasny, *Soviet Economists of the twenties. Names to be remembered* (Cambridge: Cambridge University Press, 1972); Alessandro Stanziani, *L'économie en révolution. Le cas russe, 1870–1930* (Paris: Albin Michel, 1998).
[4] Jacques Sapir, "L'économie soviétique: origine, développement, fonctionnement," in *Retour sur l'URSS. Économie, société, histoire*, ed. Jacques Sapir (Paris: L'Harmattan, 1997), 99–144.
[5] Paul Gregory and Mark Harrison, "Allocation under Dictatorship: Research in Stalin's Archives," *Journal of Economic Literature* 43, no. 3 (2005): 721–761.

1957.[6] The centrally planned economy, which had been considered a monolithic model by the Western European countries and the USA, proved to be more flexible in the 1960s than had been assumed. Following the liberalization initiated by the USSR, most of the people's democracies in Eastern Europe engaged in economic reforms. Central planning was strengthened but limited to the establishment of major macro-economic indicators, whereas basic economic actors – such as the enterprises – were given more room for manoeuvre, in order to allow them to implement the plan at their level and to coordinate themselves with other economic actors involved in the production process.[7]

Defining a common model for the socialist economy in the 1960s proves to be more difficult, as market incentives were being reintroduced in the planned economy by these national economic reforms.[8] However, under the combined influence of destalinization and Western European integration, the USSR and the people's democracies engaged in redefining their international cooperation in a more multilateral way during this decade, in order to tackle the decline of development strategies based on extensive growth. Thus the 1960s at the Council for Mutual Economic Assistance (COMECON) start and end with two major debates over attempting to create a regional economic integration that could have shaped a transnational socialist economic model. This contribution analyzes how the socialist countries members of the COMECON, who officially shared a common economic model, dealt with the specific issue of the international coordination of their economic plans. In spite of the adoption of the "basic principles of the international socialist division of labor" in 1962, and the setting of the "integration" of the national economies as the Council's main goal in 1971,[9] various economic and political actors in the socialist world doubted that a common international plan and regional integration would be the most promising way to develop their national economies. Eventually, parallel evolutions towards planning the economy at national level led neither to a convergence of these econo-

---

6 Helmut Steiner, "Das Akademie-Institut für Wirtschaftswissenschaften im Widerstreit wissenschaftlicher, ideologischer und politischer Auseinandersetzungen," *Sitzungsberichte der Leibniz-Sozietät* 36, no. 1 (2000): 89–109 ; Peter C. Caldwell, "Productivity, Value and Plan: Fritz Behrens and the Economics of Revisionism in the German Democratic Republic," *History of Political Economy* 32, no. 1 (2000): 103–137.
7 Michael Kaser, *The Economic History of Eastern Europe. 1919–1975*, volume III (Oxford: Clarendon Press, 1986).
8 Bernard Chavance, "La théorie de l'économie socialiste dans les pays de l'Est entre 1917 et 1989," in *Nouvelle histoire de la pensée économique*, vol. 2, ed. Alain Béraud and Gilbert Faccarello (Paris: La Découverte, 1993), 235–262.
9 Jozef Van Brabant, *Economic Integration in Eastern Europe. A Handbook* (New York, London, Toronto: Harvester Wheatsheaf, 1989), 63–102.

mies, nor to the international coordination of their development within the framework of the COMECON. There the transnational approach and international comparison allow to challenge Paul Gregory's hypothesis about Stalin's economic policy, according to which political dictatorship was intrinsically rooted in the structure of planned economies since the system could only be functional with political coercion over the economy.[10] What might have been true for Soviet economics under Stalin may be interpreted differently while looking at the international coordination of planned economies.

Most of the historiography on the international organization focuses on its failure to develop a teleological argument. Since the international coordination of planning at the COMECON indeed failed, it would be the sign that socialist economies were unable to promote an attractive development model at international level.[11] Thus the organization would be deemed a mere empty shell established by the Soviet Union to ensure its power over the bloc. The following analysis argues that the COMECON was not a mere transmission belt for the USSR, aiming at transferring its economic model to the socialist countries in Eastern Europe.[12] Rather than concentrating on the meager results of the multilateral attempts at coordinating economic planning within the COMECON, in order to disclose structural weaknesses of the system and explain the allegedly impossible enforcement of economic common planning in the socialist world, I will consider the reasons why the COMECON failed, while looking at how the coordination process of the national plans of its member states took place. Following the international negotiation process in its different steps allows a reinterpretation of the so-called "failure" of the Council. Indeed, planning cannot be reduced to its economic dimension in the socialist world, nor exclusively be considered a technical process intended to rationally allocate scare resources.[13] It is also a political statement of sovereignty. Beyond the apparent economic failure of the COMECON, a political process of constant negotiation ought to be highlighted, during

---

[10] Paul Gregory, *The Political Economy of Stalinism* (New York: Cambridge University Press, 2004).

[11] André Steiner, "The Council of Mutual Economic Assistance – An Example of Failed Economic Integration?," *Geschichte und Gesellschaft* 39 (2013): 240–258.

[12] For the first analysis of a complex balance of power within COMECON, see Randall Stone, *Satellites and commissars: Strategy and Conflict in the Politics of Soviet-Bloc Trade* (Princeton: Princeton University Press, 1996); See also Martin Dangerfield, "Sozialistische Ökonomische Integration. Der Rat für gegenseitige Wirtschaftshilfe (RGW)," in *Ökonomie im Kalten Krieg, Studien zum Kalten Krieg, Band 4*, ed. Bernd Greiner, Christian Müller, and Claudia Weber (Hamburg: Hamburger Edition, 2010), 350.

[13] Andrew Sloin and Oscar Sanchez-Sibony, "Economy and Power in the Soviet Union, 1917–1939," *Kritika* 15, no. 1 (2014): 22.

which the governments of the people's democracies needed the failure of international cooperation in order to promote a paradoxical discourse on the necessity to reform and empower the Council. Thus failure was manipulated in order to shift the balance of power within the Eastern bloc and to favor the people's democracies.[14] The multilateral forum established by the COMECON was a showcase of socialist solidarity and efficiency during the Cold War competition, and constituted a configuration of international relations much more beneficial to the smaller states than the bilateral negotiations with the Soviet Union, allowing the former to safeguard some room for manoeuvre in shaping their economic development.

Eventually, the failed coordination of economic planning at the COMECON seems to have had an economic, as well as a political interest for several actors in the socialist world.[15] In order to analyze this strategic manipulation of failure, I will explain how the debate on supranational planning at the COMECON failed in the first half of the 1960s, before going on to analyze the parallel transnational economic networks that emerged out of this failure. Lastly, I will show how the "economicization" of international relations, as well as other concepts borrowed from the Western European regional integration process were introduced, before being circulated through the East, as a means to depoliticize a very political game played by the people's democracies in order to control their own economic development.

The failed supranational turn of the COMECON

After the establishment of the communist regimes in Eastern Europe, all countries of the socialist bloc had turned to a planned model of economic development. In the second half of the 1940s and in the 1950s, planning was not specific to the socialist world, and neither did sharing the same model favor international co-operation among socialist countries. Each communist government understood planning as a tool for a global transformation of the new socialist society: it had to promote the industrialization of mostly agricultural countries, and to

---

14 For an analysis of power relations between the USSR and the people's democracies within COMECON, see also: Suvi Kansikas, "Room to manœuvre? National interests and coalition-building in the CMEA, 1969–1974," in *Reassessing Cold War Europe*, ed. Sari Autio-Sarasmo and Katalin Miklossy (London: Routledge, 2011), 193–209.
15 Natacha Coquery and Matthieu de Oliveira, *L'échec a-t-il des vertus économiques* (Paris: Comité pour l'histoire économique et financière de la France, 2015).

create the proletarian basis needed by the regime to legitimate its policy.[16] Under these circumstances, co-operation in the field of economic planning could only be understood, at first, as an unacceptable loss of sovereignty by the COMECON member states. Even though the people's democracies stood, after 1945, under the strong influence of the Soviet economic model of the 1920s[17] and of its evolution into a planned economic system in the 1930s, plans remained elaborated in a national framework. The adoption of a socialist regime, economic planning, and forced industrialization were considered a magic tool that would equalize the development levels of the different COMECON member states. According to the less developed countries, such as Romania, a discourse on the economic irrationality of the parallel development of industrial capacities at national levels was unacceptable. Despite the diffusion of the Soviet planning model, any plan-coordination had to take into account the political rationale of national development strategies, until each member state had reached an equal level of development. In July 1966, Nicolae Ceaușescu still stated that "mission is given to the socialist world-system to develop interstate relations based on mutual respect, and on the preservation of the reciprocal interests. The socialist world-system develops as a system of *national economies*."[18]

Besides, the organization was founded in January 1949 as a direct answer to the Marshall Plan. It represented a political answer to the OEEC and had not been initially conceived as an alternative and integrated economic area. The first topic on the agenda during the formative years of the COMECON was the coordination of its member states' foreign trade toward the West, in order to foster East-West economic relations.[19]

However, in spite of the original rejection of any plan coordination by the Polish representative at the bureau of the Council in 1950, Moscow managed to transform it into the main goal of the organization after 1954. This indicates how economic cooperation among socialist countries was progressively regarded as a possible stimulus for economic development. Its members never considered

---

16 Peter Rutland, *The Myth of the Plan* (London: Hutchinson, 1985).
17 Lars Haga, "Imaginer la démocratie populaire: l'Institut de l'économie mondiale et la carte mentale soviétique de l'Europe de l'Est (1944–1948)," *Vingtième Siècle. Revue d'histoire* 109 (2011): 13–30.
18 Bundesarchiv (German Federal Archive, hereafter BArch) BArch DC 20–19575, *Entwicklung der Arbeit im Rat für gegenseitige Wirtschaftshilfe. 1964–1969*, "Information über den Meinungsaustausch der Ersten Sekretäre der kommunistischen und Arbeiterparteien und der Vorsitzenden der Ministerräte zu Fragen der Arbeit des Rats für gegenseitige Wirtschaftshilfe," 1966, f. 19.
19 BArch DE 1–21734, *Protokolle und Berichte des Ständigen Vertreters der DDR im RGW über Beratungen des Büros des RGW vom 8.12.1950 bis zum 27.11.1955*.

the COMECON an exclusive and alternative economic area in Europe, and the Council started with the sole *ex-post* coordination of foreign trade plans. Yet its importance grew stronger for the socialist countries in the second half of the 1950s. Thanks to the implementation of a multilateral clearing agreement, the elaboration of model contracts for foreign trade, the institutionalization of multilateral co-operation with the creation of standing commissions responsible for different fields of the production or dealing with transversal issues – such as currencies, foreign trade, etc. – the COMECON achieved a real reorientation of trade flows in Europe until the mid-1960s. East-West trade still represented 49% of the foreign trade of the people's democracies in 1948, before East-East trade became dominant in the foreign trade balances of the COMECON member states. It accounted for two-third of their exports in 1953, 55% in 1956, before it stabilized at a little over 60%.[20] In parallel, the Council's institutions increased their role in the international co-ordination of economic planning. From 1955 onwards, the COMECON was indeed given the task of coordinating the five-year plans of its member countries.[21]

Economic historians have explained why this co-operation was doomed to fail from an economic point of view.[22] The differences in the levels of economic development of the member countries were too pronounced, and the most industrialized members, such as the GDR or Czechoslovakia, were reluctant to subsidize the industrial development of future competitors within the bloc, while accepting low quality products in return. The USSR was not willing to subsidize the development of its allies at its own costs, especially from the 1970s onwards.[23] Eventually, the coordination remained mostly limited to foreign trade plans and did not promote the elaboration of transnational production cycles. Due to the state monopoly on foreign trade and to the lack of real economic competition induced by the missing convertibility of prices and currencies, the COMECON was thus unable to shape a regional model and to integrate the national economies of its members the way the EEC did.

This analysis, which mainly focuses on the late 1960s and on the 1970s, overshadows the vivid debates about the goals and the methods of multilateral eco-

---

20 Wlodzimierz Brus, *Histoire économique de l'Europe de l'Est (1945–1985)* (Paris: La Découverte, 1986), 154.
21 Tibor Kiss and George Hajdu, "International Cooperation in Planning within COMECON," *Eastern European Economics* 14, no. 4 (1976): 12.
22 Steiner, "The Council of Mutual Economic Assistance"; Ralf Ahrens, "Spezialisierungsinteresse und Integrationsaversion im Rat für Gegenseitige Wirtschaftshilfe: Der DDR-Wekrzeugmaschinenbau in den 1970er Jahren," *Jahrbuch für Wirtschaftsgeschichte* 2 (2008): 73–92.
23 Marie Lavigne, "The Soviet Union inside COMECON," *Soviet Studies* XXXV/2 (1983): 135–153.

nomic co-operation, which regularly animated the COMECON. Most of these debates mirrored the discussions on the evolution of the EEC in the West, and ended up with no practical and measurable outcome at the COMECON.[24] Leaving the field of the sole quantitative measurement of the success or the failure of multilateral economic co-operation, we can raise other issues. Which theoretical and political contents were at the core of these economic debates? Is it possible to identify failure as a logical outcome, intended by some actors pursuing a political goal, rather than an economic rationale through economic discourses? This contribution is not looking for the economic explanation of the failure of plan coordination, but for the strategic process of negotiation, which led to this failure, as well as its impact on shaping international relations within the socialist bloc.

In the early 1960s, the construction of the Berlin Wall and the missile crisis in Cuba led to a closing off of the socialist bloc. Confronted with this evolution of the international context, which affected their economic relationship with capitalist countries, the members of the COMECON were forced to close ranks and to commit to the organization in order to find new impulses, which would sustain their economic growth. This diplomatic framework, as well as the new spirit of multilateral co-operation with the allies following the destalinization in the USSR, were decisive in the adoption by the Council's members in 1961/1962 of the "basic principles of the international socialist division of labor", which had been discussed since 1957.[25] According to the "basic principles," the USSR and its partners would engage in the so-called "specialization" of their productions and progress toward an economically rational division of labor at bloc scale. Khrushchev used this important turn, and the deepening of multilateral co-operation it promoted, in order to formulate, in a speech delivered to the Central Committee of the Communist Party of the Soviet Union in November 1962, a concept for the evolution of the COMECON.

While discussing the Soviet economic reforms implemented since 1957, alongside their implications in terms of international co-operation, the Soviet leader mentioned his project to turn the COMECON into what he called a "unified

---

24 Suvi Kansikas, "Acknowledging Economic Realities: The CMEA Policy Change vis-a-vis the European Community, 1970–1973," *European Review of History* 21, no. 2 (2014): 311–328; Angela Romano, "Untying Cold War Knots: The EEC and Eastern Europe in the long 1970s," *Cold War History* 14, no. 2 (2014): 153–173.
25 Van Brabant, *Economic Integration in Eastern Europe*, 66–71; The text of the "basic principles" is reproduced in Alexander Uschakow, *Integration im RGW. Dokumente* (Baden-Baden: Nomos, 1983), 1018–1036.

planning organ."²⁶ Khrushchev saw his proposal as a twofold opportunity. The transformation of the COMECON into a "unified planning organ" would lead to the strengthening of the Council and its institutions. Thus, the international organization would be appropriately staffed and able to conduct its own economic expertize, without having to subcontract it to the Gosplan. This would dismiss direct criticism against any "imperial" influence of Soviet planning over the other member states. Instead, the Soviet Union would keep an indirect influence through the quantitative domination of Soviet experts in the international staff, as well as through its tradition to educate the elites of other member states, some of whom were delegated to work for the COMECON.

For a moment, between 1962 and 1964/1966, the coordination of economic planning within the socialist bloc was genuinely a priority on the COMECON's agenda. However, even though the people's democracies, except for Romania, officially endorsed the Soviet proposal, the debate immediately escalated at the cost of the USSR itself. For different reasons, but using the same methods, Bucharest and the other Eastern European countries manipulated the debate, and managed to shift the balance of power within the bloc in their favor, while playing on the failure of common economic planning. The Romanian delegation in the Council voluntarily rephrased Khrushchev's proposal as an evolution toward "supranational planning." Even though Khrushchev himself participated in the Executive Committee meeting of the COMECON in February 1963, in order to clarify what he meant by "unified planning organ," the actors would discuss for the next two years the opportunity of empowering the COMECON to organize supranational planning.

The semantics used by the Romanians and other Eastern European countries transformed the issue of plan coordination from a technical one, related to economic rationality, into a political one. Since the COMECON was a showcase for socialist international solidarity in the Cold War competition, the USSR could not afford to impose its will to the organization, as long as its partners were putting the whole legitimacy of the socialist world at stake in the debate. As a means to pre-empt the transformation of the Council into a supranational plan commission, Romania adopted the opposite strategy to the one that France chose, confronted with the strengthening of the EEC Commission's powers in the mid-1960s. While De Gaulle opened the "empty chair" crisis to resist the evolution of the

---

26 Stiftung Archiv der Parteien und Massenorganisationen der DDR (Foundation for the archives of the parties and mass organizations of the GDR, hereafter SAPMO-BArch) DY 30 – 3407, *Protokoll und Anlagen der XVII. Tagung des RGW*, "Bericht über die wichtigsten Fragen der XVII. Tagung, der 3. Sitzung des Exekutivkomitees und der 3. Sitzung des Büros des Exekutivkomitees," 12.1.1963, f. 95 – 96.

EEC, Romania engaged in a very legal guerrilla warfare and participated in as much co-operation projects as it could, in order to bloc them. Bucharest's representatives referred to all COMECON legal documents: mostly the founding communiqué of 1949 and the charter adopted in 1959, to highlight the recognition of each member state's sovereignty, guaranteed by the USSR since 1949. Underlining the equality of all partners proclaimed by the charter, Romania made great use of the so-called "principle of interest" which governed the negotiations at the COMECON. According to this rule, no country could be obliged by its partners to participate in a common project. However, when it had proclaimed its interest in participating, any agreement had to be achieved unanimously. In declaring its interest in all projects dealing with common planning, Romania *de facto* gained the right to veto all decisions agreed upon by its partners.

Transforming the economic issue of international plan coordination at the COMECON into a political game played a great role in shaping room for manoeuvre for Romania in its "national communist" course in the 1960s.[27] Significantly, Ceaușescu used the same strategy to veto the evolution of the Warsaw Pact into a more integrated and formalized alliance in the second half of the decade.[28] Bucharest used the socialist international organizations during the Cold War to instrumentalize their constant failure to its own benefit, while officially advocating the respect of the COMECON and the Warsaw Pact's procedures[29]. The USSR, who needed to present socialist solidarity in public discourses on the international stage, could uneasily denounce the Romanian legalist strategy.

Confronted with a debate which revealed diverging opinions on supranational planning and the rationale – economic or political – to be put forward in the cooperation taking place at the COMECON, Moscow was risking disqualifying the legitimacy of the socialist alliance with the failure of the organization. Consequently, the USSR soon withdrew from the supranational planning debate, to the great dissatisfaction of its closest allies, such as the GDR and Poland. As early as 1963, East-Germans experts of the COMECON wrote a confidential report on the situation at the Council according to which,

---

[27] John Michael Montias, "Background and origins of the Rumanian dispute with COMECON," *Soviet Studies* XVI, no. 2 (1964): 125–151; Irina Gridan, "Du communisme national au national-communisme. Réactions à la soviétisation dans la Roumanie des années 1960," *Vingtième Siècle. Revue d'histoire* 109 (2011): 113–127.

[28] Laurien Crump, *The Warsaw Pact Reconsidered. International Relations in Eastern Europe, 1955–1969* (London: Routledge, 2015), 170–213.

[29] Laurien Crump and Simon Godard, "Reassessing Communist International Organisations: A comparative Analysis of COMECON and the Warsaw Pact in relation to their Cold War Competitors," *Contemporary European History* 27, no. 1 (2018): 85–109.

> no steps have been taken towards common planning, proposals for the establishment of interstate unions [of production] . . . have not been adopted . . . The Soviet party always tries to conciliate the other parties and not to contradict anyone . . . After the communist parties' meeting of July 1963, the Soviet representatives were very cautious . . . The greatest confrontations happen between the representatives of the people's democracies, without any active support from the Soviet comrades.[30]

The East-German deputy secretary of the COMECON even stated that, if the USSR had such a passive attitude in the debate, it was because the Soviets "probably had no concept for the improvement of the work at the Council."[31] Eventually, Moscow officially renounced its proposal in 1964, but in the meantime other countries, especially the GDR and Poland, had engaged in the conflict with Romania. Berlin and Warsaw used the same strategy as Bucharest and inclined to use legal arguments in their statements. They insisted on defining more clearly the "principle of interest." In 1966, Gomulka referred to article four of the statute of the COMECON in front of its counterparts from the USSR and the people's democracies, in order to deny any country a veto right.[32] He directly tackled Romania and even officiously threatened the USSR with a withdrawal of Poland from the COMECON, if the organization "did not satisfy the legitimate interest of the majority of its countries."[33]

For different reasons, but with the same methods, all people's democracies played the failure of common planning at the COMECON against the superpower of the Soviet Union within the bloc in the first half of the 1960s. They manipulated the debate on the international coordination of economic planning, not while aiming at its failure in the short term, but in the *longue durée*. An immediate break with the COMECON could have caused the exclusion of a country from the bloc, which was an outcome that neither the people's democracies, nor the USSR could afford shortly after the Sino-Soviet split in 1961. On the contrary, the long debate on supranational planning and its organized failure had an economic and political interest. It helped the smaller allies develop a legal strategy that would challenge the solidarity of the socialist bloc, while officially seeking its strengthening. Thus fighting for the failure of supranational planning was

---

[30] BArch DC 20–19577, *Wirtschaftliche und technische Zusammenarbeit im Rat für gegenseitige Wirtschaftshilfe. 1964–1969*, "Einige Probleme der Zusammenarbeit der Länder im Rahmen des RGW in den letzten zwei Jahren," f. 9–12, f. 16.
[31] SAPMO-BArch DY 3023–801, *Zusammenarbeit mit dem Rat für gegenseitige Wirtschaftshilfe. 1962–1963*, "Zu einigen Hauptfragen der Arbeit des Rats für gegenseitige Wirtschaftshilfe," 8.01.1965, f. 221.
[32] BArch DC 20–19575, *Entwicklung der Arbeit im RGW, 1964–1969*, f. 25–28.
[33] SAPMO-BArch DY 3023–795, *Tagungen von Fachorganen des RGW, 1966–1967*, f. 100–106.

not proving incompatible with a discourse advocating more planning, but refusing the dominant influence of the Soviet model, while remaining within the COMECON framework. The USSR had to make compromises in order to maintain its role as a global Cold War player, which was partly legitimized by the cohesive image of the socialist bloc that the COMECON was embodying.[34]

Scales and spaces of transnational economic planning in the socialist world in the 1960s

In order to legitimate their criticism about supranational planning, without being accused of causing the failure of the socialist model of development, the governments of the COMECON member states agreed upon strengthening the organization's institutional structure and its staff of international civil servants. Between 1962 and 1968, the secretariat's staff increased from less than 100 to a little more than 600 international civil servants. The great majority of these specialists were recruited for their technical expertize in planning, in different industrial fields, in finance, and their knowledge of Russian, the working language of the Council. They were no trained diplomats and formed, in the technical divisions of the secretariat, a series of epistemic communities.[35]

Until the international secretariat was appropriately staffed, Soviet institutions clearly influenced the practice of plan coordination within the organization. In 1957, the ambassador of the Polish government at the Council, Piotr Jaroszewicz, still expressed a critical opinion about the working arrangements of the COMECON. According to him, "in view of formal considerations, the completion of the work on the coordination of the national economic plans by the Gosplan of the USSR, and not by the apparatus of the COMECON, was not entirely appropriate."[36]

What has been the real impact of this major criticism, not only on the planning practice but also on the planning culture of the Council, as well as on the

---

[34] A similar process characterizes the contemporary evolution of the Warsaw Pact, see Crump, *The Warsaw Pact Reconsidered*.
[35] Simon Godard, "Le Conseil d'aide économique mutuelle et la construction d'une diplomatie économique parallèle dans l'Europe socialiste (1962–1989)," in *Réinventer la diplomatie. Sociabilités, réseaux et pratiques diplomatiques en Europe depuis 1919*, ed. Vincent Genin, Mattieu Osmont, and Thomas Raineau (Brussels: Peter Lang, 2016), 171–187.
[36] BArch DE 1–21257, *Arbeitsweise der Ratsorgane und wissenschaftlich-technische Zusammenarbeit 1956–1959*, "Brief von P. Jaroszewicz an A. A. Pawlow, Sekretär des RGW," 12.04.1957, f. 5.

ultimate meaning of the success or the failure of its coordination of national plans? The fact that the secretariat of the Council internalized sufficient economic expertize in the first half of the 1960s helped the international organization move away from its practical dependency on the technical support of Soviet institutions. However, a question still remained partially unanswered: What about the influence of national planning cultures in the work of the COMECON? Could the project of plan coordination only be successful under the condition that a new transnational planning culture would be established in the Council? To what extent did the international organization actually favor the re-branding of the Soviet planning model as a common model for the whole socialist camp and in whose interest?

From the 1960s onwards, most experts delegated by the people's democracies to work for the COMECON in Moscow belonged to a small elite of former foreign exchange students, who had studied in the Soviet Union.[37] This international socialization acquired prior to the delegation at the COMECON explains why the majority of the experts, coming from different national spaces with their own specificity in defining planning and in planning economic development, had no difficulties working together in the framework of the international organization. Whether in the permanent representations of the member states at the COMECON or in the technical divisions of the secretariat, "one knew each other," as a former East-German specialist said. Peter H., one of the most important brokers between the GDR and the COMECON, who was in charge of the cooperation of his country with the international organization between 1962 and 1990, even talks about the milieu of international civil servants as a "mafia." This socialization, as well as the common working and living experience in Moscow, proved crucial in shaping a transnational culture among the COMECON experts. In the 1960s, these claimed public recognition by their governments of some room for manoeuvre for the international secretariat and the permanent representations, which would allow them to develop transnational projects involving plan coordination. In 1963, the leaders of the basis organization of the East-German experts at the COMECON wrote in their report on past activities that "the permanent representation of the GDR at the COMECON cannot be considered as a mere 'post office' . . . but should be [considered as] an international office of

---

[37] Simon Godard, "Une seule façon d'être communiste? L'internationalisme dans les parcours biographiques au Conseil d'aide économique mutuelle," *Critique internationale* 66, no. 1 (2015): 69–83.

the GDR, active in the field of economic policy, which has to complete important political and economic tasks."[38]

This statement, which can be considered a direct criticism of the way COMECON experts were treated by their national authorities, advocated more autonomy for the international civil servants and the recognition of the importance of their job. Two years later, the Polish ambassador at the COMECON, Piotr Jaroszewicz, emphasized this analysis in stating in front of its counterparts: "We do not delegate our comrades to the secretariat so that they defend the interests of our country, but in order for them to analyze objectively the issues raised by our co-operation."[39]

Most of the international civil servants working for the COMECON's institutions in Moscow were really eager to coordinate economic planning in their field of expertize and to elaborate multilateral co-operation projects. They enjoyed a form of "autonomy by abandonment." Regular and up to date inputs from the member states' planning organs and governments were rare. COMECON agents repeatedly mentioned their disappointment with the fact that they often had to act without knowing what the position of their country would be on a co-operation project. According to the same Jaroszewicz, "most of the time, the collaborators of the secretariat are not aware of the actual opinions of the member countries, particularly how far they can go to bear compromises. Eventually, they more or less defend their personal opinion, hoping that it will match the official opinion of the country concerned."[40]

However, this situation of abandonment, in which the governments anticipated at best no positive outcome of planning coordination at the COMECON, and consequently cared very little about it, gave the opportunity to the Council's experts to engage in the relatively autonomous elaboration of such projects for common planning.

---

38 SAPMO-BArch DY 30 – IV A 2–20–193, *SED-Grundorganisation Rat für gegenseitige Wirtschaftshilfe*, "Rechenschaftsbericht der Parteileitung der APO der SED im RGW in Moskau," 18.4.1964, f. 7.

The "basis organization" is a party organ that united all party members in the workplace to organize and control their political and social life. In 1961, the group of East German experts at the COMECON (working for the permanent representation as well as in the international secretariat) split from the "basis organization" of the GDR embassy in the USSR to found an autonomous basis organization, acknowledging and defending the specificity of their work in Moscow.

39 BArch DE 1–51766, *Schriftwechsel betreffend Rat für gegenseitige Wirtschaftshilfe*, "Bericht über die Tätigkeit des Sekretariats des RGW in Moskau," 25.5.1965.

40 Ibid.

Although they were able to reflect on the economic rationale of plan coordination at bloc scale, COMECON experts were never able to transfer their transnational acculturation to the planning organs at national levels. There, international plan coordination was always being considered an extra amount of work.[41] International planning agreements, which, until 1966, were only coordinated *ex-post* by the COMECON after the completion and the adoption of the different national plans[42] – not to speak of supranational planning – were perceived by the national planning organs as having a disturbing and restrictive influence on the smooth execution of the plan at national level. This attitude did not favor the development, over the years, of a common planning culture among the socialist countries members of the Council. The brigade commissioned by the Central Committee of the Unified Socialist Party of the GDR (SED) to evaluate the activity of the basis organization at the COMECON noted in its report in 1964 that "the reports, analyses, etc. sent to Berlin [by COMECON experts] to the plan commission, the council of the national economy or the ministry for foreign and intra-German trade find virtually no resonance."[43]

All in all, debates about the necessity and opportunity of a multilateral coordination of economic planning were not completely evacuated at the COMECON. Even though this coordination failed because of a political strategy pursued by several people's democracies' governments and aimed at manipulating the international organization, in order to shape room for manoeuvre allowing them to control their own economic development, plan coordination was discussed at the Council. Only the micro-level analysis of the debates held by its servants allows us to describe a transnational public space, where the convergence of national plans was conceived.

In the strategic field of nuclear energy for example, mutualized investments and a coordination of the production plans of several national industries would have been economically rational at COMECON level. However, common planning in the nuclear industry always remained limited, despite the establishment in 1960 of a standing commission on the peaceful use of the atomic energy and

---

41 An actor-based description – from the factories' chief planners to the Kremlin's administration – of the planning process in the USSR, unwrapping the intertwining of its political and economic rationale and the difficulty of articulating national planning and international plan coordination is provided in the fascinating historical novel by Francis Spufford: Francis Spufford, *Red Plenty* (London: Faber and Faber, 2010).
42 Françoise Lemoine, *Le COMECON* (Paris: PUF, 1982), 103.
43 SAPMO-BArch DY 3023–81, *Untersuchungen des ZK der SED in den SED-GO in der UdSSR und im RGW in Moskau*, "Bericht über den Einsatz einer Brigade des ZK in der PO der SED im RGW und in den Vertretungen der DDR in Moskau in der Zeit vom 10.-20.12.1963," f. 35.

the relative success of common investment projects organized by the COMECON in the late 1970s in two nuclear plants in Ukraine, intended to share their production between the participating countries.[44] The participation in these technical projects often required massive investments in developing an industrial sector in the people's democracies and was obtained under Soviet pressure, since it disturbed the global architecture of national development plans. Nevertheless, Heidelore K., who worked as an expert for nuclear energy in the secretariat of the Council in the 1980s, explained how her general direction developed on its own initiative a project for the common planning of the decommissioning of nuclear plants. Since national governments were only interested in building an industry on their own territory, COMECON experts identified the field of decommissioning these production units as an opportunity for the international organization to conceive a common plan at the level of the socialist bloc, without being challenged by the governments of its member countries.

In the end, COMECON experts lacked the necessary networks of influence in their own countries, which would have allowed them to enforce the idea of planning coordination at bloc scale and to promote the role of the international organization in this process. However, if the Council failed to establish itself as the legitimate actor who would define a common and European model of socialist economic development, it did not completely fail to create a transnational economic space.

Focusing on the fiasco of the supranational planning debate or the resistance of the national planning organs to engage in the "integration" of their economies under the auspices of the COMECON, recent historiography[45] on the organization overshadowed the necessary analysis of the moving and blurry borders of the COMECON system. In 1963, confronted with the Romanian obstruction to any supranational coordination of plans at the COMECON, the ambassadors to the Council proposed to the first secretaries and heads of government of the member countries the creation of "industrial production unions" or "joint companies."[46] Even though the principle of joint companies was soon rejected, the idea of transnational production networks at the level of the socialist enterprises, associated to the COMECON but not integrated into the organization as

---

44 Sonja D. Schmid, "Nuclear Colonization?: Soviet Technopolitics in the Second World," in *Entangled Geographies. Empire and Technopolitics in the Global Cold War*, ed. Gabrielle Hecht (Cambridge: MIT Press, 2011), 125–154.
45 Steiner, "The Council of Mutual Economic Assistance"; Ahrens, "Spezialisierungsinteresse und Integrationsaversion."
46 BArch DC 20–19575, *Entwicklung der Arbeit im Rat für gegenseitige Wirtschaftshilfe. 1964–1968*, "Kurze Information über die Tagung des Exekutivkomitees," f. 10–13.

working bodies, lived on. This decentralized form of international co-operation, based on an economic rationale and on the coordination of the production between enterprises working in the same industrial field, matched the spirit of the national economic reforms of the 1960s in the socialist countries.

In 1964, Hungary, Czechoslovakia, Poland, the GDR, and Bulgaria, soon joined by the USSR, created the first Economic International Organization (EIO), whose aim was to coordinate the production of rolling bearings. A few months later, the same members extended their co-operation and created Intermetall.[47] This time, the EIO did not deal with a single product but with issues related to the whole sector of the steel industry. In 1967, all COMECON countries, except Romania, started to discuss the creation of an EIO in the field of chemical industry, Interchim, which was finally founded in 1970. In the second half of the 1970s, the EIOs had become influent purchasing organizations, steering the foreign trade of their partners and entrusted with the duty to improve the supply of their industrial sector, which would promote the equitable sharing of modernization efforts, in order to increase the production and to reduce the dependency on Western markets, while also promoting exchanges with Western Europe.[48] Even though they dealt essentially with the coordination of foreign trade, as well as research and development, but not directly with the production plans, the EIOs became successful competitors of the COMECON standing commissions. They mirrored the international organization's structure and sometimes even hired members of its staff. Yet they were positively considered by the national governments, whereas multilateral coordination of planning within the COMECON made little progress. Confronted with the possible overlapping of the Council's and the EIOs' activities, the Soviet deputy ambassador at the COMECON acknowledged a great autonomy for the latter: "The Council's organs should use the results achieved by the EIOs for their own work. As far as the EIOs are concerned, it is sufficient for them to make use of the Council in working under its general principles."[49]

Eventually, during the debate on the creation of Interchim in the late 1960s, the leader of the East-German delegation clearly explained the difference between plan coordination at the COMECON and in the EIOs:

---

[47] On the impact of the EIOs in networking the socialist bloc, see Dagmara Jajesniak-Quast, "'Hidden Integration'. RGW-Wirtschaftsexperten in europäischen Netzwerken," *Jahrbuch für Wirtschaftsgeschichte* 1 (2014): 179–195 (specifically 186–190).

[48] BArch DG 11–1261, *Gründungsmaterialien Interchim*, "Analyse der Tätigkeit des Intermetalls und Entwurf über die Verstärkung der Arbeit der DDR innerhalb der Organisation," 10 Oct.1966.

[49] BArch DG 11–217, *Interchim*, Teil 1, "Niederschrift über den Meinungsaustausch zur Tätigkeit und zur weiteren Richtung der Arbeit der internationalen Industriezweigsorganisationen."

> With the concept *economic organization*, as opposed to the usual designation as 'international organization', we want to express what is new in the forms and methods [of international co-operation]. The *innovation* must consist, amongst others, in that we succeed in solving all questions and problems first of all with economic methods . . . which does not mean that we should waive the principle of socialist internationalism or the comradely mutual assistance.⁵⁰

Thus, putting forward an economic rationale in advocating the coordination of economic planning in the socialist bloc was not impossible in the 1960s. Even though they rapidly evolved to embrace entire industrial sectors, EIOs were originally created to deal with a specific product and kept this focus on micro-level coordination. This resonated with the spirit of the economic reforms implemented at the national levels by the Soviet Union, the GDR, Czechoslovakia, and later Poland and Hungary. However, the COMECON was too exposed to constitute the adequate forum where this form of coordination could be implemented. The people's democracies saw the economic interest of such an international co-operation in planning, but they engaged in a political manipulation of the COMECON at the intergovernmental level, using its showcase position in the Cold War. The EIOs were not as exposed as the Council and delegated the international coordination of plans to representatives of socialist enterprises themselves, who enjoyed more flexibility than the governments to develop an economic analysis.

A transnational space for a partial coordination of economic planning, still limited to foreign trade, was eventually shaped in parallel to the COMECON and as a necessary diversion, considering the failure of the Council to play this role. If the COMECON failed, it is also because its members found ways to reach the positive economic outcomes of plan coordination without having to realize it within the Council's institutional system.

Circulation of regional integration models: the paradoxical 'economicization' of international relations in the socialist world

During the 1960s, the terms of the debate on the international coordination of planning in Eastern Europe borrowed a lot from the semantics used to character-

---

50 BArch DG 11–1261, *Gründungsmaterialien Interchim*, "Thesen und Argumente zum Statut von 'Interchim.'" Emphasis given by the original report.

ize the evolution of the European Communities in the West.⁵¹ Two main goals were successively attributed to the COMECON. The international organization had to promote the "specialization" of its member states' national economies in the first part of the decade, then to achieve their "integration" in the 1970s. In both cases, progress toward the establishment of a socialist economic model and the creation of growth incentives within the COMECON area were to be achieved through international planning coordination. However, a crucial institution of Western economic theory, which is the free market, was never openly mentioned within the framework of the COMECON.⁵²

If destalinization and the Soviet willingness to establish a more multilateral system within the bloc played a role in shaping a favorable environment for this transformation of the COMECON, the strategic evolutions of the Council nevertheless have to be considered in the light of the EEC's contemporary evolutions. Indeed, the latter circulated through the iron curtain and were put forward and manipulated by the governments of second rank economic powers in the East, in order to preserve their sovereignty over the elaboration of national economic policies. The discussions on the International Socialist Division of Labor (ISDL) started in 1957, when the Common Market was created in Brussels, and led to the adoption of the "basic principles" of the ISDL in 1962, when the EEC started to implement its first common policy, the Common Agricultural Policy. With the ISDL, the socialist countries members of the COMECON expected a positive economic effect of international co-operation based on economies of scale and increased productivity of national industries. Each country would have specialized in the production of several specific products, which it could have traded with its partners. Economists expected an improvement in the quality of industrial products and decreasing production costs. This analysis shared with the model of regional economic integration elaborated by the EEC the idea that the promotion of cross-border circulation of industrial goods would have a positive impact on the modernization of the national economies, which were members of this trade area. However, unlike the market-based *ex-post* adjustment of the interna-

---

51 This circulation of knowledge about economics owes a lot to the good relations established by the COMECON's secretariat with its counterpart at the United Nations Economic Commission for Europe, whose role as a bridge between East and West is well analyzed by Daniel Stinsky's contribution in this volume. See also Daniel Stinsky, "A Bridge Between East and West? Gunnar Myrdal and the UN Economic Commission for Europe, 1947–1957."
52 The reflection on markets is not absent from Eastern European debates at the national levels and in other frameworks than the COMECON, see Johanna Bockman, *Markets in the Name of Socialism: The Left-wing Origins of Neoliberalism* (Stanford: Stanford University Press, 2011).

tional division of labor that existed in the EEC, the members of the COMECON believed to be able to achieve the ISDL with *ex-ante* plan coordination.

Despite economic measures promoting the international circulation of goods between the COMECON countries, such as the adoption of a common unit of account (the transferable ruble) in 1963 or massive efforts to elaborate common industrial standards during the 1960s, intra-COMECON trade lacked a common price-basis and convertible currencies, which would have allowed it expand in proportions similar to the increase of the intra-EEC trade. Implementing the ISDL without market mechanisms, in a time when socialist enterprises were given more room for manoeuvre in organizing their own process of production, but never fully controlled foreign trade, was unrealistic.[53] This discrepancy between the new practice of planning the economy at national and at international level also explains the economic failure of the Council. Nevertheless, the COMECON took over the spirit of the economic reforms implemented in its member countries, which was to "catch up and overtake" capitalist countries in developing a socialist model of development mirroring the Western model, but suited to the specific framework of planned economies.[54]

In its attempt at copying Western European economic integration, the COMECON relied on several legitimate or illegitimate models. Created as an answer to the Marshall Plan in 1949, the COMECON was supposed to challenge the OEEC/OECD, more than the European Coal and Steel Community or the EEC, to which establishment it did not react at first. However, COMECON documents almost never mention the OEEC/OECD and focus until the late 1960s on strengthening the organization's contacts with the United Nations Economic Commission for Europe in Geneva (ECE), in order to achieve international recognition with the help of the UN regional commission. This strategy pursued a diplomatic goal defined by the Soviet superpower and did not take into account the economic interests of the people's democracies, which developed a growing interest for trade with EEC members in the 1960s, rather than for the deepening of a technical cooperation with the ECE. Thus the unofficial declaration by the EEC and the COMECON of their interest in opening reciprocal recognition negotiations in 1971, followed by the official recognition of the EEC by the socialist countries in

---

[53] R. Selucky, "The impact of the economic reforms on the foreign economic relations of the socialist countries," *Soviet and Eastern European Foreign Trade* 4, no. 3 (1968): 72–86.

[54] For the reverse case study of the influence of socialist economic knowledge on Western European countries, see the contribution by Isabelle Gouarné in this volume: Isabelle Gouarné, "Mandatory planning versus Indicative planning. Eastern Itinerary of French planners (1960s-1970s)".

1972,⁵⁵ led to two different sets of East-West dialogue. While the EEC Commission started bilateral commercial negotiations with each COMECON member state in 1974, enforcing its own official recognition and fostering bilateral trade, the COMECON secretariat opened a first round of negotiations with the EEC Commission in 1975, which was interrupted by Brussels in 1980. The COMECON was then forced to unilaterally recognize the EEC, which already dealt directly with its member states' governments. It managed later to reopen negotiations with Brussels, leading to mutual recognition of both international organizations in June 1988, when the COMECON was already crumbling down.⁵⁶

Eventually, the long diplomatic and largely unsuccessful process of mutual recognition cannot hide a real circulation of goods between the East and the West, but also of concepts about regional economic integration. Particularly after 1968, at a time when Soviet opening towards the EEC had made public debate possible, the EEC model worked as the main reference in the discourse on the necessary evolution of the COMECON.⁵⁷ Polish and Hungarian representatives in particular analyzed the evolution of market coordination within the EEC and used the perspective of the completion of the custom union by 1968 to urge their partners at the COMECON to progress toward a stronger coordination of their economies. As the Hungarian ambassador at the COMECON, Rezsö Nyers, said in 1968, "the integration that is happening in other parts of the world – especially in Western Europe – is so powerful, that the smaller socialist countries can demonstrate an equivalent economic potential only if they co-operate closer among each other and with the Soviet Union than has previously been the case."⁵⁸

Thus the COMECON, like other international organizations, appeared more and more as "a resource-place for political leaders, who were aware of the economic vulnerability of their country."⁵⁹ The strategy of the Polish and Hungarian

---

55 Vladislav Zubok, "The Soviet Union and European Integration from Stalin to Gorbachev," *Journal of European Integration History* 2, no. 1 (1996): 85–98; Marie-Pierre Rey, "L'Europe occidentale dans la politique extérieure soviétique de Brejnev à Gorbatchev, évolution ou revolution ?," *Relations internationales* 147, no. 3 (2011): 73–84.
56 SAPMO-BArch DY30–7090, *Tagung des politisch-beratenden Ausschusses des Warschauer Vertrages*, 1988.
57 Suvi Kansikas, *Socialist countries face the European Community. Soviet-bloc Controversies over East-West Trade* (Fankfurt am Main: Peter Lang, 2014).
58 SAPMO-BArch DY 3023–804, *Zusammenarbeit mit dem Rat für Gegenseitige Wirtschaftshilfe. 1968–1969*, "Brief von Rezsö Nyers an Boleslaw Jaszczuk," 4.6.1968, f. 249–250.
59 Sandrine Kott, "Par-delà la guerre froide. Les organisations internationales et les circulations Est-Ouest (1947–1973)," *Vingtième Siècle. Revue d'histoire* 109 (2011): 149.

governments was twofold.⁶⁰ Since they were increasing their economic relations with the West at that time, they needed a stronger integration of the socialist economic area in order to export their products in the East. This would have helped them finance the acquisition of Western technologies to modernize their national economies. Hungary for example took advantage of a COMECON-agreement achieved in 1963, making the Hungarian factory Ikarus responsible for the production of large buses for the whole bloc, to develop its mechanical constructions' sector and became one of the world's greatest bus producer.⁶¹ Besides, in pushing the international organization to endorse their reformist interpretation of the socialist economic model (including the development of new foreign trade relations, more autonomy given to the enterprises and the development of market incentives within the socialist economies), they were seeking protection against peer pressure aimed at forcing them to revoke their national economic reforms, which had been implemented after 1968. In the context following the Prague Spring, the USSR and its most conservative partners were indeed willing to block any evolution toward market socialism. While playing the EEC-threat at the COMECON and the urgent necessity to mirror Western European integration in the East, Warsaw and Budapest could paradoxically legitimize their national economic course in presenting it as a declination of multilaterally agreed COMECON goals.

Indeed, in 1971, the USSR and its partners engaged the COMECON in the so-called "global program", including the task to achieve the "integration" of its member states' national economies. The term "integration," directly borrowed from the Western European regional model, was deeply controversial and the agreement purely formal. The members of the COMECON never did manage to positively define what socialist economic integration should be. Alexei Kosygin gave a very vague definition of the term in his defense of this new goal of planning coordination at the 23rd Session of the COMECON in 1971: "The socialist integration will not be accompanied by the creation of supranational organs ... We do not interfere [in national planning], no supranational organs . . . Thus it is

---

60 P. G. Hare and P. T. Wanless, "Polish and Hungarian Economic Reforms – A Comparison," *Soviet Studies* 33, no. 4 (1981): 491–517.
61 The political rationale behind this strategy and its economic failure for the global modernization of the Hungarian economy is analyzed in Zsombor Body, "Enthralled by Size: Business History or the History of Technocracy in the Study of a Hungarian Socialist Factory," *The Hungarian Historical Review* 4, no. 4 (2015): 964–989.

different from the integration that is carried out nowadays in the capitalist countries".[62]

In associating the memory of the supranational debate with the idea of economic integration, in order to distinguish these two more clearly, the Soviet government tried to overcome the failure of the coordination of economic planning at the COMECON, which had characterized the 1960s. However, the concept of "integration" remained alien to the socialist world. According to Mikhaïl Lipkin: "The term 'integration' itself, which was before something like a swear word, in the official Soviet lexicon at least, associated with NATO, arms race and monopolistic markets, now became a major tool in the ideological struggle between the two systems in the environment of *détente*."[63]

Diverging interests converged to impose an 'economicisation' of international relations within the COMECON in the 1960s. The Council, which was created as a political answer to Western European integration, finally tried to adopt Jean Monnet's logic putting forward economic rationality as a means towards enforcing political integration. However, in a bloc where the partners were not politically equal, dysfunctional economic co-operation and the failure of planning coordination were crucial to the people's democracies, as they were striving to shape some room for manoeuvre vis-à-vis Moscow in their national development strategies. The imitation of the Western European model of economic integration, which was strongly promoted by the Hungarian and the Polish governments – seeking the modernization of their national economies through regional integration and the establishment of a socialist market, eventually aggravated the tensions between socialist economies at the COMECON in the long run and at the same time promoted their international autonomy in the short term.

Conclusion

It seems evident that the COMECON was structurally unable to organize an economically rational planning coordination among the socialist countries, in order to elaborate a common planned model of development at bloc scale. Not only because of internal problems specific to the socialist economic system did it

---

62 SAPMO-BArch DY 30 – 3415, *Protokoll der XXIII. Sonder-Tagung des Rates für Gegenseitige Wirtschaftshilfe*, "Protokollarische Niederschrift der Leiter der Delegationen der 23. RGW-Tagung am 26. April in Moskau," f. 55.
63 Mikhaïl Lipkin, "The Soviet Union, CMEA and the Question of First EEC Enlargement" (paper presented at the XIV International Economic History Congress, Helsinki, 2006).

fail, but also because the organization was pushed by its members to mirror more and more the evolutions of the EEC's regional economic integration in the 1960s.

However, the Council was not doomed to fail because socialist economic planning was irrational in itself,[64] or unable to be coordinated at bloc scale. It failed because the COMECON was created as – and always remained – a political organization, while officially pursuing economic goals. Oscar Sanchez-Sibony has shown how Soviet economics has to be analyzed in a global framework, taking into account the influence of parallel evolutions in the capitalist system.[65] We have stressed out in a similar way how the Cold War held sway over the shaping of the socialist world-economy after 1949. Considering COMECON's unique showcase position in the Cold War, it becomes evident that the USSR, playing its superpower role, could not afford to let the organization fail. According to the official equality of all member states, Moscow had to bear compromises with its partners within the framework of the COMECON, were it to maintain the image of socialist solidarity on the international stage.

Eventually, the failure of planning coordination at the COMECON was neither accidental nor structural, but intended and instrumentalized by the people's democracies, in order to create a "dynamics of dissent"[66] that shaped, within the bloc, political room for manoeuvre for the smaller states against the Soviet superpower. Romania, the GDR, Poland, Hungary or Czechoslovakia had an economic and political interest in nurturing the failure of planning coordination in the Council, in order to bargain long-term empty agreements against short-term real bilateral compromises from the Soviet Union. Looking at the learning process at stake in international economic cooperation among socialist countries, as has been done here, helps answer in a new way the question why the COMECON failed. Considering how international and national agents involved in the COMECON co-operation shaped common planning projects, it becomes clear that the structurally weak interest of economic co-operation does not explain alone the failure of the Council. Rather, common economic failure and political success of separate national development strategies were two sides of the same coin.

---

[64] For an overview of the debate, see Peter Boettke, *Socialism and the Market: The Socialist Calculation Debate Revisited*, vol. 5 (London: Routledge, 2000). A critical discussion of the strategic academic use of this debate in the capitalist world is provided in Johanna Bockman and Gil Eyal, "Eastern Europe as a Laboratory for Economic Knowledge: The Transnational Roots of Neoliberalism," *The American Journal of Sociology* 108, no. 2 (2002): 317–323.

[65] Oscar Sanchez-Sibony, "Depression Stalinism. The Great Break Reconsidered," *Kritika* 15, no. 1 (2014): 23–49.

[66] Crump, *The Warsaw Pact Reconsidered*.

Part 3: **Alternatives to Planning**

Benedetto Zaccaria
Learning from Yugoslavia? Western Europe and the Myth of Self-Management (1968–1975)

This chapter focuses on Western European reception of the Yugoslav model of self-management, based on social ownership of the means of production and the self-government of working people.[1] The self-management system, as it developed in Yugoslavia since the early 1950s – when it was first introduced – posited the decentralization of the state's functions to the largest possible degree. This system therefore distinguished itself from the Soviet model of state ownership which had characterized Yugoslavia's economy between the end of World War Two and the split between Tito and Stalin (1948): self-management was indeed not compatible with central planning. The self-managed system proposed an alternative vision of planning which represented a "third way" between the socialist and capitalist models.[2] Focusing on the management of enterprises, the Yugoslav leadership aimed at re-shaping the relationship between the state and the economic system. Starting from the 1950s, Yugoslavia gradually developed a model of "social planification" from "below," which was to be – at least in theory – an outward reflection of the preferences of producers and consumers. "Social planification" meant a shift from central planning to an "indicative" planning which, since the mid-1960s, had to provide forecasts and set forth the objectives to be pursued by government through non-administrative measures, without imposing legal or mandatory obligations to enterprises.[3] The bases of the "indicative" system of planning were to be the preferences of the enterprises which, maximizing their income according to the principles of the market economy and avoiding workers' alienation, would further the general in-

---

1 On the economic dimension of self-management, see Jaroslav Vanek, *The Participatory economy: an evolutionary hypothesis and a strategy for development* (Ithaca and London: Cornell University Press, 1971).
2 For an overview on the divergence between theory and practice of Yugoslav self-management, see Vladimir Unkovski-Korica, "Self-management, development and debt: the rise and fall of the 'Yugoslav experiment'," in *Welcome to the Desert of Post-Socialism: Radical Politics After Yugoslavia*, ed. Igor Štiks and Srećko Horvat (London: Verso, 2015), 21–45.
3 On simultaneous debates on social planning in the Soviet bloc, and in particular in Czechoslovakia, see Vítězslav Sommer's chapter in this volume.

terest.⁴ The notion of "self-management planning" was definitively sanctioned by the 1974 Yugoslav constitution, which sanctified self-management as Yugoslavia's cornerstone also in view of the death of its leader and symbol – Josip Broz Tito.⁵ Self-managed planning had to be developed within and among enterprises: coordination of individual plans was to be legally required, and such co-ordination was to be codified into legally binding agreements between the enterprises on specific obligations and undertakings. Self-management planning therefore posited that the harmonious development of the country's economy was to be based on labor-managed firms.

In recent years, several studies have highlighted the political and economic origins of self-management and its role in shaping the history of Yugoslavia during the Cold War.⁶ However, little attention has been paid to the influence of self-management beyond Yugoslav borders, and to the relationship between management and planning.⁷ This essay offers a preliminary historical analysis on how "labour management" came to be perceived in Western Europe as an alternative socialist way of planning, particularly in the domain of manpower. It also shows that the self-management model overcame the ideological boundaries of the Cold War through scholarly and intellectual networks, encouraged by the Yugoslav leadership, which influenced the zeitgeist of the late 1960s and early 1970s and, consequently, the agenda of policy-makers in Western Europe. This chapter is structured around three sections. The first focuses on the emergence of social and political unrest in Western Europe in the late 1960s, and the consequent need, for Western European policymakers, to look for new models of industrial relations. The second section deals with the role of Yugoslav scholars and intel-

---

4 Milojko Drulović, *L'autogestion à l'épreuve* (Paris: Fayard 1973); Cyrus Ardalan, "Workers' Self-Management and Planning: The Yugoslav Case," *World Development* 8 (1980): 623–638.
5 See Edvard Kardelj, *Pravci razvoja političkog sistema socijalističkog samoupravljanja* (Beograd: Komunist, 1978); Stefano Bianchini, *La Diversità socialista in Jugoslavia. Modernizzazione autogestione e sviluppo democratico dal 1965 a oggi* (Trieste: Editoriale Stampa Triestina, 1984).
6 On the origins of "self-management" see the recent contribution by Vladimir Unkovski-Korica, "Workers' Councils in the Service of the Market: New Archival Evidence on the Origins of Self-Management in Yugoslavia, 1948–1950," *Europe-Asia Studies* 66 (2014): 108–134.
7 The external influence of the Yugoslav model has been analyzed in connection with the Soviet bloc countries by Johanna Bockman, *Markets in the Name of Socialism: The Left-Wing Origins of Neoliberaism* (Stanford: Stanford University Press, 2011). For the French reception, see Frank Georgi, "A la recherché de l'autogestion. Les gauches françaises et le "modèle yougoslave (1948–1981)" https://lms.hypotheses.org/288 (accessed January 2018). On the link between management debates and the question of planning, see Vladimir Unkovski-Korica, *The Economic Struggle for Power in Tito's Yugoslavia: From World War II to Non-Alignment* (New York: I.B. Tauris, 2016); Dennison Rusinow, *The Yugoslav Experiment, 1948–1974* (London: C. Hurst for the Royal Institute of International Affairs, 1977).

lectuals in spreading in the West the idea that Yugoslavia's self-management system might be the solution to the improvement of democracy in industrial relations. The third and final section points at how the Yugoslav experience was a constant source of inspiration for the reforms on the labor market which were implemented in Western Europe throughout the 1970s.

Looking for a third way

On 17 December 1972, the President of the European Commission, Sicco Mansholt, went to the island of Brioni for an official visit to Yugoslavia's leader, Tito, and Edvard Kardelj, the main ideologue of the Yugoslav regime and the putative "father" of self-management. The visit was supposed to set the seal on the renewal of the trade agreement which the European Economic Community (EEC) and Yugoslavia had concluded in 1970 – the first to be signed between the Community and a socialist country since the constitution of the EEC in 1957. For the Yugoslav regime, affected as it was by the centrifugal tendencies which had emerged during the "Croatian Spring" of 1971 and its successive repression, the renewal of the 1970 agreement was of major economic importance, as it was meant to signal the EEC's willingness to open its markets to Yugoslav agricultural and industrial produce, thereby offering a guarantee to its future economic growth. The renewal of the agreement also had a political meaning, to confirm the Community's willingness to support the political stability of the Yugoslav federation: the 1970 agreement had indeed been negotiated in the aftermath of the Soviet invasion of Czechoslovakia, which had aroused Western fears about Soviet expansionism towards the Balkans. In other words, the 1970 agreement and its renewal – still under negotiation at the very moment when Sicco Mansholt arrived in Yugoslavia to meet Tito and Kardelj – were the means of keeping the Balkan country, once again, "afloat".[8] Yugoslavia was therefore the *demandeur* of trade concessions which the EEC, although reluctant due to its traditional agricultural protectionism, was ready to accept for political reasons.[9]

---

8 Yugoslavia had been supported by the West after the 1948 Tito-Stalin split through military and economic aid. See Lorraine M. Lees, *Keeping Tito Afloat: The United States, Yugoslavia and the Cold War* (University Park, PA: Penn State University Press, 1997), 43–119.
9 On the origins and development of EEC-Yugoslav relations during the 1970s, see Benedetto Zaccaria, *The EEC's Yugoslav Policy in Cold War Europe, 1968–1980* (London: Palgrave Macmillan, 2016).

However, Mansholt's visit was somehow paradoxical. Despite Yugoslavia's clear economic weakness, talks focused only partially on economic relations between Belgrade and the EEC. Instead, special attention was paid to the Yugoslav system of self-management. During the bilateral meetings with Tito and Kardelj, Mansholt praised the Yugoslav model of industrial relations which, in his opinion, represented an expression of genuine workers' democracy. After exalting the political and social virtues of the "Yugoslav model", Mansholt – a member of the Dutch Labour Party – also discussed the possible application of the self-management system to solve social conflicts in Western Europe. Ironically enough, Yugoslavia, which had requested the EEC's economic help in terms of trade and cooperation, was depicted by Mansholt as a valuable model of economic organisation.[10]

Why did Mansholt praise Yugoslavia? Was his admiration sincere, or was it the mere expression of diplomatic politeness vis-à-vis one of the oldest and highly influential leaders of the socialist and non-aligned worlds? The answers to these questions must be sought in a general trend of admiration for Yugoslavia's position in the international arena and its innovative socio-political model. As regards its international position, since the late 1940s Western diplomatic circles had recognised Yugoslavia's national "road to Communism" as a precious asset in terms of ideological confrontation with Moscow – the Tito-Stalin split in 1948 was in fact the first challenge to Stalin's hegemony in East-Central Europe[11] – but also in terms of prevention of Soviet influence in the Balkans and the Adriatic. In addition, Western diplomats and policy-makers recognised and admired Tito's role in making Yugoslavia – a country which lacked real economic and military weight – one of the leading and most influential countries within the Non-Aligned Movement.[12] As previously noted, in the course of the 1960s, Belgrade had also been able to play a winning card in the Moscow-Belgrade confrontation in developing relations with the EEC and its member states. This was particularly the case of Italy which, after the establishment of the first center-left coalition in 1963, had improved its relations with Belgrade, regarded as a precious political and economic partner in the Balkans. The Socialist Party of Pietro Nenni, an ad-

---

10 Arhiv Jugoslavije (AJ), KPR, I-3-b/42, Zabeleška o razgovoru Predsednika Republike sa g. Sicco Mansholtom, predsednikom Komisije EEZ, na Brionima, 17.12.1972; Zabeleška o razgovoru druga E. Kardelja sa Sikom Manšholtom, predsednikom Izvršne komisije Evropske ekonomske zajednice, 17.XII 1972. godine na Brionima.
11 See Jeronim Perović, "The Tito-Stalin Split: A Reassessment in Light of New Evidence," *Journal of Cold War Studies* 9 (2007): 32–63.
12 On Yugoslavia's non-alignment, see Tvrtko Jakovina, *Treća Strana Hladnog Rata* (Zaprešić: Fraktura, 2014).

mirer of Yugoslavia's road to socialism, played quite an important role in favouring Italian-Yugoslav relations in the late 1960s.[13] A similar role had been played by the Christian Democrats led by Aldo Moro, the first Italian Prime Minister to visit Yugoslavia in 1965.[14] And West Germany too had recognized the geopolitical asset represented by Tito's Yugoslavia after the entry of the Social-Democratic Party (SPD) into the coalition government and the demise of the Hallstein Doctrine.[15] The European Commission, the Community institution in charge of negotiating trade agreements by virtue of the Common Commercial Policy envisaged by the Treaty of Rome (1957), had recognised the political value of Yugoslavia as the first socialist country to enter into direct relations with the EEC (which the Communist rhetoric had traditionally depicted as an imperialist reality) and also for the importance attached by the Community to establishing good relations with developing countries within the G77. Mansholt himself, as the European Commissioner for Agriculture, had sponsored the establishment of the System of Generalised Preferences for members of the G77, including Yugoslavia.[16] In expressing his admiration for Tito's Yugoslavia, Mansholt was therefore following a well-established tradition of diplomatic admiration for the country's international status which eclipsed the reality of a weak federation characterized by a severe commercial deficit and centrifugal tendencies.

And yet, Mansholt's admiration for the Yugoslav model envisaging "indicative" state planning on the basis of enterprises' preferences and indications was not limited to a tradition of diplomatic regard for Yugoslavia's international role. In fact, it was linked to the socio-economic crisis undergone by Western European societies during the 1960s. Social and political unrest, mainly driven by students' and workers' protests, was a product of the *Trente glorieuses* – a period characterized by widespread social peace and marked economic growth – and started a process of change in social and political paradigms. Catchwords like

---

13 See Massimo Bucarelli, "Roma e Belgrado tra Guerra Fredda e Distensione," in *La politica estera italiana negli anni della Grande Distensione (1968–1975)*, ed. Pier Giorgio Celozzi Baldelli (Roma: Aracne, 2009), 144–157.
14 See Karlo Ruzicic-Kessler, "Italy and Yugoslavia: from distrust to friendship in Cold War Europe," *Journal of Modern Italian Studies* 19 (2014): 641–664.
15 See Milan Kosanović, "Brandt and Tito: Between Ostpolitik and Nonalignment," in *Ostpolitik, 1969–1974: European and Global Responses*, ed. Carole Fink and Bernd Schaefer (Cambridge: Cambridge University Press, 2009), 232–242. On the "Hallstein Doctrine" see Werner Kilian, *Die Hallstein-Doktrin. Der diplomatische Krieg zwischen der BRD und der DDR 1955–1973* (Berlin: Duncker & Humblot, 2001), 52–65.
16 On Sicco Mansholt's attitude towards the G77, see Giuliano Garavini, *After Empires: European Integration, Decolonisation, and the Challenge from the Global South 1957–1986* (Oxford: Oxford University Press, 2012).

"freedom" and "self-determination" spread throughout the world – from California to Mexico, to Poland, Czechoslovakia and Yugoslavia – through the powerful influence of the media and communication networks among activists. Traditional societal and economic practices were overwhelmed by new concepts concerning the place of individuals in society: protest movements across Europe called for new social and political rights.[17]

Reactions to the waves of political unrest affecting the Western hemisphere differed greatly. In the socialist bloc, the search for a new course of social and political relations was harshly repressed by communist élites – as epitomized by the Soviet intervention in Czechoslovakia in August 1968 – whereas in Western Europe political leaders were obliged to find a *modus vivendi* with the appeals for new education rights and improved working conditions which stemmed from their own societies. Social and political change obliged Western European élites at all levels – political, economic, academic – to search for new models of relations in society and, more in particular, in the education systems and workplaces.[18]

In the sphere of higher education, the 1968 movement and its aftermath spurred the governments of the EEC member states – the "Nine," after the entry of Great Britain, Ireland and Denmark in 1973 – to launch the first Community initiatives, for both education[19] and vocational training.[20] Instead, as regards labor, the Western European leaderships were confronted with the need to improve working conditions in the Common Market, from health to mobility. Within this framework, the idea developed of widening workers' rights and decisional powers in enterprises. This clearly emerges from the conclusions of the

---

[17] On the global implications of the 1968 movement, see Carole Fink, Philipp Gassert and Detlef Junker, *1968: the world transformed* (Cambridge: Cambridge University Press, 1998). See also Valentine Lomellini and Antonio Varsori, *Dal Sessantotto al crollo del Muro: i movimenti di protesta in Europa a cavallo tra i due blocchi* (Milano: FrancoAngeli, 2014).

[18] On the origins of the EEC social policy and its developments between the late 1960s and the early 1970s, see Antonio Varsori, "Alle origini di un modello europeo: la Comunità europea e la nascita di una politica sociale (1969–1974)," *Ventunesimo Secolo* 9 (2006): 17–47.

[19] See Simone Paoli, *Il sogno di Erasmo. La questione educativa nel processo di integrazione europea* (Milano: FrancoAngeli, 2010), 70–125; Anne Corbett, *Universities and the Europe of Knowledge: Ideas, Institutions and Policy Entrepreneurship in European Union Higher Education Policy, 1955–2005* (London: Palgrave Macmillan, 2005), 60–96.

[20] Lorenzo Mechi, "Du BIT à la politique sociale européenne: les origines d'un modèle," *Le Mouvement Social* 3 (2013): 17–30; Antonio Varsori, "La formazione professionale e l'educazione nella costruzione europea e il Cedefop," in *Sfide del mercato e identità europea. Le politiche di educazione e formazione professionale nell'Europa comunitaria*, ed. Antonio Varsori (Milano: FrancoAngeli, 2006), 173–212; Francesco Petrini, "The common vocational training Policy in the Eec from 1961 to 1972," *Vocational Training* 32 (2004): 45–54.

International Political Science Association (IPSA) round table held in Salzburg in 1968, according to which "one of the trends of the coming modernisation of politics is the trend towards increased participation in decision and policy-making processes."[21] Indeed, the late 1960s and early 1970s saw the rise of debate regarding the concept of industrial democracy, that is to say, the reproduction of democratic practices within companies, in order to allow workers to participate in governing bodies.[22] These developments were closely linked to the concept of "planning", i.e. the direct intervention of the state in the industrial domain, in order to regulate the relationships between employers and employees. It is therefore not surprising that academic and intellectual debates on how to reform industrial relations examined models of economic organization stemming from the Socialist world.[23] In terms of industrial relations, had socialist countries in Central and Eastern Europe something to teach in terms of economic planning which could also be applied to capitalist societies? The answer to this question indicated the Yugoslav experience of self-managed planning.

Spreading the Yugoslav model in Western academic circles

International interest in the Yugoslav model was effectively spurred thanks to the International Labour Organisation (ILO).[24] Within the ILO, debates on industrial management had been developing since the 1920s, and resulted in a series of international instruments covering certain aspects of industrial relations, including the "Freedom of Association and Protection of the Right to Organise Conventions" in 1948, the "Right to Organise and Collective Bargaining Convention" in

---

21 Historical Archives of the European Union, Florence (HAEU), Alexandre Marc papers (AM), Box. 488.
22 See Campbell Balfour, *Participation in Industry* (London: Croom Helm, 1973); Walter Kolvenbach, *Partecipazione e governo dell'impresa. I modelli europei* (Roma: Edizioni Lavoro, 1984); Ettore Maraschi, "Democrazia industriale e organizzazione del lavoro," *L'Impresa* 5 (1977): 491–496.
23 See Théofil I. Kis, "État des travaux sur la problématique de la convergence: théories et hypotheses," *Études internationales* 2 (1971): 443–487. On the positive attitude of French intellectuals towards the Soviet model, see, for example, Georges-Henri Soutou, "Teorie sulla convergenza nella Francia degli anni Sessanta e Settanta," *Ventunesimo Secolo* 9 (2006): 49–77.
24 On ILO's role in the exchange and circulation of expertise in the field of management between Western and Eastern Europe during the 1960s and 1970s, see Sandrine Kott's chapter in this volume.

1949, and the "Voluntary Conciliation and Arbitration Recommendation" in 1951. These instruments were supplemented in 1952 by the "Co-operation at the Level of the Undertaking Recommendation," which dealt with labor relations at enterprise level at a time when the term "workers' participation" was not yet a topical concept.[25] However, the ILO had not managed to draw definite conclusions from such recommendations, due to the great variety of national practices and approaches to the problem of workers' participation in the organization's member states. In the early 1960s, ILO rephrased the question of industrial democracy. In 1962, it financed a study on workers' management in Yugoslavia, in the conclusions of which it claimed that self-management had "undoubtedly strengthened the position of the collective *vis-à-vis* the management."[26] In 1966, the ILO adopted a new resolution concerning workers' participation in enterprises, as a result of which a technical meeting was convened in 1967, covering "methods used throughout the world to enable workers to participate in decisions within undertakings."[27] The meeting concluded that worker's participation was of prime importance and should constitute one of the ILO's long-term commitments. ILO sponsored the launch a major research project on "Worker participation in company management," which was carried out by the International Institute for Labour Studies (IILS) which the ILO had established in Geneva in 1960. The longest project ever carried out by the Institute, it became the top priority of IILS's research work for more than 20 years. The aim of this study was a critical and comparative examination of solutions to the main social and economic problems which had already emerged or were about to emerge in the spheres of economic development, job satisfaction, social welfare and industrial organization.[28] In 1967, Robert Cox, the Director of IILS, concluded that workers' participation in factories was a crucial element in the future development of Western societies.[29] Yugoslav experts had been actively involved in the definition of the working program since the early stages of the project. The first International Seminar on Workers' Participation in Decisions within Undertakings held within the IILS

---

[25] Walter Kolvenbach, *Partecipazione e governo dell'impresa*, 14.
[26] International Labour Office. *Workers' Management in Yugoslavia* (Geneva: International Labour Office, 1962).
[27] See Maryse Gaudier, The International Institute for Labour Studies: its research function, activities and publications, 1960–2001. www.ilo.org/wcmsp5/groups/public/—dgreports/—inst/documents/genericdocument/wcms_194523.pdf (last accessed 31 January 2017).
[28] Ibid.
[29] Robert Cox, "La participation des travailleurs à la gestion des entreprises. Etat et avancement du projet. I – Un champ d'enquête fertile," *Bullettin de l'Institut international d'études sociales* 2, February 1967.

project took place in Belgrade – upon the invitation of the Yugoslav government and in cooperation with the Yugoslav Commission for the ILO – in December 1969 and confirmed the prominent role of the "Yugoslav model" in policy debates on industrial relations.[30] The ILO research project stimulated the interest of international scholars on the Yugoslav model. The Czech sociologist Jan Vanek, who devoted many years to the study of Workers' Councils in Yugoslavia,[31] stimulated the interest of his brother, Jaroslav Vanek who, as a professor of economics at Cornell University, was to become one of the most influential scholars in the field of "labor managed economy" in the course of the 1970s.[32]

Following ILO's initiatives, Yugoslav scholars made great contributions to the creation of a critical networking system for international researchers and practitioners,[33] a pivotal role being played by Branko Horvat, the Yugoslav economist. Horvat was in fact a scholar with solid institutional links to the Yugoslav regime, which actively contributed to support his own efforts to make Yugoslavia's self-management a reference model for discussions on industrial democracy in Western Europe. This attitude has to be contextualized within Yugoslavia's aim at enhancing its relations with Western Europe in order to escape from the economic stagnation of the country and its serious commercial deficit. In 1965, Yugoslavia's ruling party, the League of Communists of Yugoslavia (LCY) had indeed taken a "liberal" turn, which consisted of a gradual process of economic liberalization in order to develop and modernise the country's industrial apparatus and link it to the Western European system.[34] Merging socialist and market principles, Belgrade aimed at reflecting the idea of "socialism with a human face" distinguishing itself from the Soviet model[35].

---

30 Activities of the ILO 1969. Report of the Director-General (Part 2) to the International Labour Conference, Fifty-fourth Session, 1970. International Labour Office, Geneva, 1970, 66. (www.ilo.org/public/libdoc/ilo/P/09383/09383(1970 – 54-part2).pdf (accessed 2 June 2017). See also: ILO Report on International Seminar (Belgrade, 1969) on Workers' Participation in Decisions within Undertakings, Geneva, 1970.
31 Jan Vanek, *The Economics of Workers' Management: A Yugoslav Case Study* (London: Allen and Unwin, 1972).
32 See the author's preface in Jaroslav Vanek, *The General Theory of Labor-Managed Market Economies* (Ithaca, London: Cornell University Press, 1970).
33 Steven Deutsch, "A Researcher's Guide to Worker Participation, Labor and Economic and Industrial Democracy," *Economic and Industrial Democracy* 26 (2005): 645–656.
34 Ivan Obadić, "A troubled relationship: Yugoslavia and the European Economic Community in détente," *European Review of History* 21 (2014): 329–348.
35 Archivio della Presidenza della Repubblica, Rome, Box 130, Jugoslavia, Appunto per il Presidente della Repubblica, 20 settembre 1968; See Ukandi G. Damachi, Hans Seibel, and Jeroen Scheerder, *Self-Mangement in Yugoslavia and the Developing World* (London and Basingstoke: The MacMillan Press, 1982), 1–5.

After studying economics, sociology and philosophy in Zagreb, Manchester and London, Horvat had become Research Director at the Federal Planning Bureau in Belgrade (1958–1963) and, between 1963 and 1970, had been the Director of the Institute of Economic Sciences, again in Belgrade. In 1967, he had founded the journal *Economic Analysis and Worker's Self-Management*,[36] which was to become the official journal of the International Association for the Economics of Self-Management (IAFESM), later officially established in Dubrovnik in 1978. Horvat made a great contribution towards stimulating the debate on workers' participation in Western universities, as a professor at the University of Michigan (1968), University of Florida (1970) and the American University in Washington (1970, 1972 and 1974). One of his first, major contributions was a journal article published as a supplement to the *American Economic Review* in 1971, entitled "Yugoslav Economic Policy in the Post-War Period: Problems, Ideas, Institutional Developments".[37] The article followed the mainstream idea of the "convergence of systems" – widespread among intellectual and political élites in both the West and the East, which posited the convergence between capitalism and socialism.[38] Indeed, Horvat argued that the Yugoslav model of economic and social planning could offer a number of advantages to Western enterprises, for at least three reasons:

> (1) it reduces uncertainty which is the basic restriction on free decision-making; (2) it increases the rate of growth, the market expands and so the number of available alternatives increases; (3) it equalizes success of a producer less dependent on external conditions which he cannot control and which are economically and socially irrational.[39]

Horvat's main conclusion concerned the "experimental" nature of the Yugoslav model, which could offer a solution to the "fallacious" dichotomy between planning and market.[40] His work reflected an impressive wave of scholarly contributions focused on what Horvat defined as the "Yugoslav social laboratory."[41] In

---

[36] Milica Uvalić, and Vojmir Franicević, "Introduction: Branko Horvat – Beyond the Mainstream," in *Equality, Participation, Transition: Essays in Honour of Branko Horvat*, eds. Vojmir Franicević and Milica Uvalić (Basingstoke: Palgrave Macmillan, 2010), XI.
[37] Branko Horvat, "Yugoslav Economic Policy in the Post-War Period: Problems, Ideas, Institutional Developments," *The American Economic Review* 61 (1971): 71–169.
[38] See Isabelle Gouarné's chapter in this volume.
[39] Horvat, 'Yugoslav Economic Policy', 159.
[40] Ibid., 159–161.
[41] See the literature review offered by Phillip I. Blumberg, "Selected Materials on Corporate Social Responsibility," *The Business Lawyer* 27 (1972): 1275–1299. See also Ichak Adizes, *Industrial Democracy: Yugoslav Style* (New York: Free Press, 1971); Deborah D. Milenković, *Plan and Market*

parallel with Horvat's activism in spreading the notion of self-management in the Western intellectual world, other Yugoslav scholars where engaged in an analogous mission. This is particularly the case of the Dean of the Faculty of Political Science in Belgrade – Nadjan Pašić – who, in the early 1970s, praised the virtues of the Yugoslav model in several international seminars in the United States and Western Europe[42].

Needless to say, the stream of academic debate regarding the Yugoslav model did also include critical views, which expressed scepticism about the applicability of the self-management system to Western capitalist economies. As Ellen Turkish Comisso was to argue in her comprehensive 1979 study on the country's self-management, discussion on the self-managed economy too often appeared "more intent on evaluating than in understanding, more anxious to package the Yugoslav experience with a seal of approval or disapproval than to explain and analyse its operation."[43] In this regard, the renowned American political scientist Robert Dahl was well aware of the unlikeliness of Western labor's support for any system of worker-owned industry.[44] And yet, in an article published in *The New York Review of Books* in 1970, Dahl himself argued that,

> Yugoslavia is the only country in the world where a serious effort has been made to translate the old dream of industrial democracy into reality – or into as much reality as dreams usually are. Let me add at once that in the government of its state apparatus, Yugoslavia is not, of course, a representative democracy. . . . Yet if Yugoslavia is less democratic than the United States in the government of the state, it is more democratic in the way industries and other enterprises are governed.[45]

---

in *Yugoslav Economic Thought* (New Haven: Yale University Press, 1971); A. Ross Johnson, *The Transformation of Communist Ideology: The Yugoslav Case. 1945–1953* (Cambridge, Mass.& London: The MIT Press, 1972); Gerry Hunnius, G. David Garson and John Case, *Workers' control: A Reader on Labor and Social Change* (New York: Vintage Books, 1973); Duncan Wilson, "Self Management in Yugoslavia," *International Affairs* 54 (1978): 253–263; Joop Ramondt, "Workers' self-management and its constraints: The Yugoslav experience," *British Journal of Industrial Relations* 1 (1979): 83–94.

42 See, for example, Marius J. Broekmeyer, *Yugoslav Workers' Self-Management. Proceedings of a symposium held in Amsterdam, 7–9 January, 1970* (Dordrecht: D. Reidel Publishing Company, 1970); G. David Garson, "Models of Worker Self-Management: The West European Experience," in *Worker Self-Management in Industry: The West European Experience*, ed. G. David Garson (New York: Praeger Publishers, 1977), 206.

43 Ellen Turkish Comisso, *Workers' Control under Plan and Market: Implications of Yugoslav Self-Management* (New Haven and London: Yale University Press, 1979).

44 Robert A. Dahl, *After the Revolution: Authority in a Good Society* (Yale: Yale University Press, 1970), 134–136.

45 Robert A. Dahl, "Power to the Workers," *The New York Review of Books* 15 (1970): 20–24.

1975 marked the apex of Western scholarly interest in the Yugoslav model of self-management. The Yugoslav leadership had just approved a new constitution (1974) which had brought a series of fundamental changes for the management of its economy which were based on a "self-management planning" requiring continuing participation by all economic and socio-political entities in the country. This new constitution had followed a period of profound instability in the country, due to the emergence of centrifugal tendencies in Croatia (1971), a severe economic crisis after the 1973 Oil Shock, and the still open question of Tito's succession. It was the aim of the Yugoslav leadership to exalt the model of self-management – one of the two pillars on which the Yugoslav federation was built, together with non-alignment – as a system which, in Pašić's words, may "offer a historical alternative to the trend of bureaucratization, an alternative for many millions of people who today are helpless in the face of huge bureaucratic organizations which determine the conditions of their lives"[46].

In 1975, the Executive Committee of the International Political Science Association (IPSA) decided to entrust to the Yugoslav Political Science Association the organization of a Round Table, to be held in Dubrovnik from 9 to 13 September. The objectives of the conference were: a) Participatory and Industrial Democracy and self-management as factors of modernisation of political systems; b) National and class interests in multi-ethnic societies. The Yugoslav model was therefore at the very core of the debate. Belgrade used the meeting to confirm self-management as a reference point for the question of industrial democracy to the many leading international political scientists gathered in its capital. The Yugoslav government took this opportunity for praising the system of self-management planning. As claimed by the regime's ideologue, Edvard Kardelj, at the inaugural speech of the round table:

> The very fact that the issue concerning the influence of self-management and participation on the development of contemporary political systems has attracted the attention of a large number of scientists from many different countries is a sufficient proof that this topic is reflecting one of the salient problems of the mankind. . . . Self-management theory and practice can, beyond any doubt, affect considerably further evolution of the social and democratic political systems in the world.[47]

---

[46] See Ichak Adizes, and Elisabeth Mann Borgese, *Self-Management: New Dimensions to Democracy* (Santa Barbara and Oxford: Clio Press, 1975), 118.
[47] HAEU, AM 488, Opening address by Edvard Kardelj at the Round Table Meeting, Dubrovnik, 9 September 1975.

From theory to practice?

Did any move from theory to practice in fact take place? Reforms in the field of labor in Western Europe suggest that the answer to this question is negative: nowhere these reforms tended towards a system of "socially-owned" enterprises according to the Yugoslav experience.[48] Conversely, they led to the introduction of the less-radical concepts of "participation" and "codetermination," which implied that decision-making power was shared with the management or the state.[49] However, the spread of academic works and debates on self-management described above did contribute towards bringing the problem of "labor management" to the top of the political agenda of Western European policy-makers. What could the West learn from the Yugoslav experience? The Yugoslav experience indicated that the state, through its normative intervention, could plan the role and prerogatives of manpower, and make it a driving force in the management of enterprises to solve social conflicts.

Who were the real promoters of the Yugoslav model? As suggested in previous section, the Yugoslav government played a crucial role in consciously exporting the self-management model in Western academic and intellectual circles. The impressive number of scholarly works, conferences and symposia addressing the issue of workers' participation with the direct involvement of Yugoslav leading ideologists – *in primis* Edvard Kardelj – shaped discussion of the crucial question on how to reform industrial relations in Western Europe.

Indeed, in the EEC member states, references to the Yugoslav model frequently recurred in political debates between governing and opposition parties, concerning in particular the development of industrial democracy. In West Germany, the constitution of the "Grand Coalition" in 1967 revived the debate on workers' participation, in order to expand the steel and coal discipline of co-determination (established in 1951) to all sectors of the economy. The Biedenkopf-Kommission, established at governmental level in 1968, confirmed the need to expand the practice of co-determination.[50] The Yugoslav model featured prominently in the West German debate on this topic, also as a consequence of the *Ost-*

---

[48] On the US experience, see Christopher Eaton Gunn, *Workers' Self-Management in the United States* (Ithaca and London: Cornell University Press, 1984).
[49] For a general overview on the evolution of labour relations in Western Europe in the mid 1970s, see Johannes Schregle, "Labour Relations in Western Europe: Some Topic Issues," *International Labour Review* 109 (1974): 1–22.
[50] David T. Fisher, "Worker participation in West German industry," *Monthly Labor Review* 101 (1978): 59–63.

politik launched by the FRG Chancellor Willy Brandt. The termination of Hallstein Doctrine meant the re-activation of diplomatic relations between Yugoslavia and the FRG, which had been interrupted in 1957 after Tito's decision to recognize the German Democratic Republic. Yugoslavia was therefore seen under a new light in Federal Germany. What was stressed by the Social Democratic party was its peculiar role as a bridge between East and West, and a representative of the non-aligned movement.[51] It is therefore not surprising that the Yugoslav model became a benchmark for the evolution of industrial relations in the country, being praised by the very political elites which were engaged in the *Ostpolitik* in the late 1960s and early 1970s. Needless to say, Yugoslavia's example spurred animated discussions in the country.[52] On one hand, self-management was repeatedly quoted by the representatives of the Christian-Democratic Party (CDU) and by the employers' associations as a threat to the FRG's economic and social order. On the other, large sectors of the Social Democrat Party (SPD), headed by the party's chairman at the Bundestag, Herbert Wehner, declared themselves as being inclined towards the Yugoslav model of socialism.[53] After the electoral success in 1969, Willy Brandt's SPD set the expansion of co-determination as one of its top priorities. During the party congress in Saarbrucken in 1971, the Young Socialist faction of the party used the Yugoslav model as a reference point, pleading for the introduction of Yugoslavia's model of workers' self-administration. The result of this debate was a compromise between the above-mentioned views. The government coalition eventually agreed, in 1974, on a co-decision system – which came into force on 1 July 1976 – which also envisaged parity in the Supervisory Board of enterprises even beyond the coal and steel sector.[54]

However, it was in Italy and France that, between the late 1960s and early 1970s, leftist parties and trade unions stimulated an unprecedented debate on the self-management system. In fact, scholarly attention of the Yugoslav model in Italy and France had originally developed in the late 1960s due to a number of representatives of the European federalist movement, which viewed self-man-

---

[51] See Hans-Dietrich Genscher, *Rebuilding a House Divided* (New York: Broadway Books, 1997), 488.
[52] See, for example, Roggemann Hervig, *Das Modell der Arbeiterselbstverwaltung in Jugoslawien* (Frankfurt am Main: Europaische Verlagsanstalt, 1970). This volume considered the Yugoslav solutions in relation to the problems arising in West Germany.
[53] 'Jugoslawien – Kein Modell für Uns', Spiegel-Gespräch mit Dr. Hanns Martin Schleyer, Vorstandsmitglied der Daimler-Benz AG *Der Spiegel*, 25.05.1970. See magazin.spiegel.de/EpubDelivery/spiegel/pdf/44906260 (accessed on 30 January 2017).
[54] Fisher, "Worker participation," 59–63.

agement as a system grounded on the political values of federalism. In Italy, the search for a third-way between political democracy and individual freedom was cultivated by Adriano Olivetti, a *sui generis* figure of industrialist wishing to change the paradigms of capitalist society. Olivetti's political thought was in line with that of another leading figure of the European federalist movement, namely the French philosopher and political activist Alexandre Marc.[55] The latter appreciated the decentralization of power to self-managed enterprises and the autonomy of workers' communities. For him, self-management coincided with the basic principle of federalism, namely autonomy. From his view point, the Yugoslav model challenged the Soviet model of almighty "State", replacing it with that of "Society." For Marc, this was an experiment to be followed with great attention.[56] Italian federalists had also started reflecting on the need to link the European ideal to an organic social and political doctrine starting from the first issue of the journal *Democrazia integrale*, first published in 1963. During its first years, this journal had concentrated on the experience of self-government in different contexts, including Yugoslavia's self-managed enterprises.[57] The scientific legacy of *Democrazia integrale* was in fact the deepening and development of analyses on the Yugoslav experience. One of the first thorough assessments of the Yugoslav self-management to be published in Italy – in 1965 – was indeed the work of the then young political scientist Tito Favaretto, one of the first collaborators of *Democrazia integrale*.[58] Favaretto would later became the Director of ISDEE – *Istituto di Studi e Documentazione sull'Est Europeo* in Trieste which, in the early 1970s, conducted a major comparative research on workers' participation in enterprises in Italy and Yugoslavia which aimed at increasing the knowledge of Yugoslavia's self-management in the Italian political scenario.[59] In late 1960s, scholarly interest on the Yugoslav model matched with the rise of collective bargaining as a consequence of the emergence of social unrest in the two countries.

---

55 See Ferdinand Kinsky and Franz Knipping, *Le fédéralisme personnaliste aux sources de l'Europe de demain, hommage à Alexandre Marc* (Baden Baden: Nomos, 1996); Gilda Manganaro Favaretto, *Il federalismo personalista di Alexandre Marc (1904–2000)* (Milano: FrancoAngeli, 2006).
56 Alexandre Marc, "Faillite de l'autogestion?," *Europe en Formation*, no. 141, 1971.
57 Tito Favaretto, "Autonomia e potere nella Repubblica Federativa Jugoslava," *Democrazia Integrale* 6 (1965): 4–24 and 7(1965): 3–21.
58 Ibid.
59 The result of this research, started in 1971, were later published in Cecilia Assanti, Luigi Meneghini and Rudi Kyovski, *La Partecipazione dei lavoratori alla disciplina dei rapporti di lavoro in Italia e Jugoslavia* (Trieste: ISDEE, 1976).

In Italy, the center-left coalition headed by the Christian Democrat and Socialist parties looked for new models of industrial relations also to face, at the same time, the rise of radical, leftist groups – included *Autonomia operaia* and *Lotta Continua* – which seemed to be able to gain control of workers' protests.[60] The Socialist Party– traditionally an admirer of Yugoslavia's non-aligned policy and self-managed system[61] – played a pivotal role in re-defining industrial relations in Italy together with the country's main trade unions, which feared that workers' participation in enterprises might endanger their own raison d'être[62]. Within this framework, the example of labor managed economy offered by Yugoslavia – already present in the country's debates since the mid-1960s – featured prominently. The Italian Communist Party (PCI) was to increase its attention towards the Yugoslav model after the appointment of Enrico Berlinguer as Secretary General in 1972 and the consequent, gradual emancipation of the party from the Soviet influence.[63] As noted by some of its leading figures, Giorgio Amendola and Giorgio Napolitano, the issue of labor-managed enterprises went back to the political thought of Antonio Gramsci with regard to the role of workers in enterprises.[64]

Union-controlled factory delegate councils emerged as a platform for workers' control demands, as stated in the Law on Workers' Rights, approved by the Italian Parliament in 1970 with the support of the Socialist Party and left-wings elements among the Christian Democrats.[65] Within this framework, the three major labour groups – CGIL (*Confederazione Generale Italiana del Lavoro*), CISL (*Confederazione Italiana Sindacati Lavoratori*) and UIL (*Unione Italiana del Lavoro*) concluded a Trade Union Agreement stating that workers' councils' function was to negotiate industrial agreements.[66] This marked the overcoming of reserved managerial prerogatives. For instance, as noted by G. David Gerson, a prominent American scholar of self-management models during the 1970s, the

---

60 Silvio Lanaro, *Storia dell'Italia repubblicana. L'economia, la politica, la cultura, la società dal dopoguerra agli anni '90* (Venezia: Marsilio, 1992), 364–386; Bruno Trentin, "L'autogoverno nella fabbrica e nella società," *Mondoperaio* 32 (1979): 109–114.
61 See the documents stored at Fondazione di Studi Storici Filippo Turati, Firenze, Fondo Mario Zagari, serie 5: Affari Esteri, "Yougoslavie," 31–03–1973/09–10/1973.
62 See Gino Giugni, *Diritto sindacale* (Bari, Cacucci editore, 1986), 45–46; Gian Primo Cella, *Divisione del Lavoro e Iniziativa Operaia* (Bari: De Donato, 1972).
63 Silvio Pons, *Berlinguer e la fine del comunismo* (Torino: Einaudi, 2006).
64 Giorgio Amendola, *Antonio Gramsci nella vita culturale e politica italiana* (Napoli: Guida Editori, 1978); Giorgio Napolitano, *Intervista sul PCI* (Roma-Bari: Laterza, 1976), 51–73.
65 See Paolo Mattera, *Storia del PSI 1892–1994* (Roma: Carocci, 2010), 192–196; G. David Garson, "Models of Worker Self-Management," 17.
66 See *Autogestione e lotta per il lavoro* (Roma: Nuove Edizioni Operaie, 1976).

labor contract regulating employees' rights in FIAT (*Fabbrica Italiana Automobili Torino*) "asserted unprecedented control affecting not only working terms and conditions but also location of investments and the basic plan of production . . . In general, the factory delegate system has brought about decentralised, detailed negotiations for collective agreements of unprecedented scope."[67]

After the spectacular events of May 1968, self-management became a central element in the political agenda of French unions and leftist parties. To seize upon the issue of workers' participation, the Government promoted a substantial expansion in the contents of collective agreements, combined with a trend towards "multi-industrial" bargaining at national level. This produced major agreements on job security (1969), training (1972) and guaranteed income for employees over 60 years of age without employment (1972).[68] The Yugoslav model echoed in French public debates on the issue of industrial democracy.[69] As noted by the French Foreign Ministry in March 1972: "French public opinion follows with sympathy the original experiment of Yugoslav socialism as some political groups are particularly interested in the possibilities opened by self-management".[70] These milieus – which gained large visibility in France and abroad after the strike at the LIP watch factory and the consequent attempt to install a self-managed rule in the firm – encompassed in particular the representatives of the French Socialist Party. The latter invoked a vision of "another society" making continuous references to the models proposed by Yugoslavia and, later, Algeria – a country which was emerging from France's recent colonial rule.[71] Like in Italy, a prominent role was played by the country's largest trade unions, such as the communist *Confédération general du travail* (CGT) and, in

---

[67] G. David Garson, "Models of Worker Self-Management."
[68] Jacques Chazal, "La participation des travailleurs aux décisions dans l'entreprise en France," *Revue syndicale suisse: organe de l'Union syndicale suisse* 66 (1974): 326–333.
[69] Marie-Geneviève Dezès, "L'utopie réalisée: Les Modèles étrangers mythiques des autogestionnaires français," in *Autogestion: La dernière utopie*, ed. Frank Georgi (Paris, Publications de la Sorbonne, 2003), 30–54. On French literature on self-management during the 1970s, see also Pierre Rosanvallon, *L'Age de l'autogestion* (Paris, Le Seuil, 1976); Edomond Maire, *Demain l'autogestion* (Paris: Seghers, 1976).
[70] "L'opinion publique française suit avec sympathie l'expérience originale du socialisme yougoslave, certains milieux politiques s'intéressant particulièrement aux possibilités ouvertes par le système de l'autogestion". See Archives du Ministère des Affaires Étrangères, La Courneuve, Europe 1971–1976, 3766, Ministère des Affaires Etrangères, Direction des Affaires Politiques, Note, La France et la Yougoslavie, Paris, 24 March 1972.
[71] Stephen Bornstein and Keitha S. Fine, "Worker Control in France: Recent Political Developments," *Worker Self-Management in Industry*, 152–191.

particular, the *Confédération française démocratique du travail* (CFDT).[72] The CFDT played a particularly important role in proposing a system of *socialisme autogestionnaire*, which developed out of close contacts with representatives of Yugoslav trade unions which would continue throughout the 1970s.[73] The campaign promoted by the CFDT was to shape the national debate on workers' representation in enterprises. According to a Report published by the Sudreau Commission, established in 1974 on the initiative of the French President Valéry Giscard d'Estaing to cope with popular response to the unions' platforms, a larger field of application was to be left to collective bargaining. The governmental Centre for the Coordination of Research on Self-Management (CICRA) played a strong role of advocacy which echoed the general call by the Socialist Party, firstly the opposition leader François Mitterrand, for self-management.[74]

In the mid-1970s, debates on industrial democracy in Great Britain were influenced by extensive reforms in the field of workers' participation in Europe, particularly in Yugoslavia[75]. The Employment Protection Bill, which came into force on 31 January 1975 at the initiative of the Labour Party, envisaged the right for trade unions to bring recognition disputes before a governmental authority, the Conciliation and Arbitration Service, which could recommend recognition by employers.[76] Within the Labour Party, debates on workers' participation took the Yugoslav model into serious account. This is shown, for example, by the role played by the Fabian Society – to which some of the Party's leading figures such as Harold Wilson and Roy Jenkins were politically close – in favoring debates on self-management. As maintained by Jeremy Bray and Nicholas Falk in the periodical *Fabian Tract*:

> Any discussion of workers' management is bound to take account of Yugoslav experience. It is impossible to transplant institutions from one society to another, differing in history, culture, psychology, education, state of development and political system. But the Yugoslav

---

[72] Daniel Chauvey, *Autogestion* (Paris: Editions de Seuil, 1970).

[73] On the CFDT's stance on self-managed enterprises, see Albert Detraz, Alfred Krumnov and Edmond Maire, *La CFDT et l'autogestion* (Paris: Les Editions du Cerf, 1974); See also Archives de la CFDT, Paris, CH/7/715, Relations entre la CFDT et la Confédération des Syndicats Yougoslaves, 1967–1970.

[74] Albert Deutsch, "Researcher's Guide," 4. François Mitterrand's support for self-management was highlighted by Sicco Mansholt to Edvard Kardelj during the December 1973 meeting quoted above.

[75] Derek C. Jones, "Worker Participation in Management in Britain: Evaluation, Current Developments, and Prospects," in *"Worker Self-Management in Industry,"* 145.

[76] "Employment Protection Bill," *House of Commons Bill* 119, 25 March 1975. See also "The Community and the Company." Report of a Working Group of the Labour Party Industrial Policy Sub-Committee, 1974.

experience raises important questions, and has served as a focus for an increasing volume of criticism and analysis of the economics of workers' control. Workers' management in Yugoslavia developed not as the application of an ideological blue-print, but as the practical means of industrial development of a country with strong internal antagonisms and well founded suspicions of central control, lacking an established industrial structure. This makes it more remarkable as a politico-economic invention.[77]

The developments described above constituted clear evidence of the increasing governmental recognition of the inadequacy of industrial relations systems and the need to avoid social confrontation. With hindsight, the increasing intervention of the state in regulating industrial relations confirms that Mansholt's praise of the Yugoslav system of self-management described at the beginning of this chapter was, in fact, not an isolated or exceptional attitude. In addition, Mansholt's words were set within the context of a general debate which took place at Community level about the problem of workers' democracy in the early 1970s. The importance of social provisions in this field was officially confirmed at the Conference of the Heads of State and Government held in October 1972 in Paris. In its "Guidelines for a Social Action Programme," presented to the Council on 18 April 1973, the European Commission declared that improvements in living and working conditions were the basic objectives of the Community.[78] Participation and industrial democracy was one of the three priority themes of the program. Indeed, one of the first effective decisions to be sponsored by the Mansholt Commission was the establishment of the European Foundation for the Improvement of Living and Working Conditions (EUROFOUND) in December 1973.[79] To draft its proposals in the sphere of labor, the Commission relied on a vast network of academic experts, which the institution consulted regularly during international round tables and conferences. This is the case, for example, of the Conference on Work Organisation, Technical Development and Motivation of the Individual, held in Brussels on 5–7 November 1974. In these circumstances, the Yugoslavia's Workers Councils had been quoted and discussed as reference points on the virtues of workers' participation by several researchers, including

---

[77] Jeremy Bray and Nicholas Falk, "Towards a worker managed economy," *Fabian Tract* 430 (1974): 1–30.

[78] Supplement 4/73 to the Bulletin of the European Communities, 1973. On the origins of the Social Action Programme see Varsori, "Alle origini di un modello europeo," 17–47; Jean Degimbe, *La politique sociale européenne du Traité de Rome au Traité d'Amsterdam* (Bruxelles: Institut Syndicale Européen, 1999), 20.

[79] HAEU, BAC-COM(1973)2026, Création d'une fondation Européenne pour l'amélioration des conditions de vie et de travail (Communication et proposition de la Commission au Conseil), Bruxelles, 5 December 1973.

Kenneth Walker of the IILS in Geneva.[80] In the following years, the European Commission published a number of documents affirming the need to create a Community discipline in the sphere of industrial democracy. On 12 May 1975, the Commission also presented a proposal for a Council Regulation on the Statute for an envisaged "European Company" to regulate, for the first time, workers' participation at European level.[81] The Commission's proposal included the creation of European "Work Councils," representing all the employees of "European Companies" with offices in various member states.[82] A few months later, the Commission also published a Green Paper on Employee Participation and Company Structure in the European Communities (the "Gundelach Report"), which sought to give new impetus to the continuing debate on the decision-making structures of industrial and commercial enterprises.[83] One year later, in 1976, a European Commission Communication on the Humanisation of Work insisted on the need to combat alienation in the workplace through the involvement of workers in decision-making processes: "The reform of work organisation is a continuing process, the full potential of which cannot be appreciated *a priori*, given that, essentially, it implies by definition a genuine participation of the employees and an increase in the value of their contribution to the smooth running of the enterprise."[84]

At Community level, the question of workers' participation was to represent a continual theme for discussion until the end of the decade, culminating in the proposition of the "Vredeling Directive" in October 1980. However, the attempt by the European Commission to harmonise rules concerning industrial relations at European level were doomed to fail. The Council of Ministers of the EEC took no decisive measures to create one single form of undertaking under company law in Europe; on the contrary, at the time the Commission's proposed "Statute" met with severe criticism from employers' associations and European trade unions. Only in September 1994, after more than 20 years of debate, did the Council

---

80 Archive of European Integration, University of Pittsburgh, (AEI), Commission of the European Communities, Conference on Work Organisation, Technical Development and Motivation of the Individual, Brussels, 5–7 November 1974, http://aei.pitt.edu/39679/1/A3935.pdf (Accessed 10 February 2018).
81 Supplement 4/75 to the Bulletin of the European Commission, 1975.
82 Jorn Pipkorn, "Employee Participation in the European Company." Paper for the International Conference on Trends in Industrial and Labour Relations, Montreal, Canada, 26 May 1976.
83 HAEU, European Commission Green Paper on Employee Participation and Company Structure in the European Communities, COM(75)570.
84 HAEU, Commission of the European Communities, Reform of the organisation of work (Humanisation of Work), Communication from the Commission to the Council, COM(76) 253 final., Brussels, 3 June 1976.

of Ministers adopt a Directive on the Establishment of a European Works Council for the purposes of informing and consulting employees.[85]

Indeed, the late 1970s witnessed a radical change in the models of socio-economic relations in Western Europe, as the focus of policy-makers shifted from industrial democracy to the fight against inflation and financial stability. At the same time, with the only exception of Mitterrand's first mandate as French President, the 1980s witnessed a reduction in national interventionism, which began in favor of greater liberalization of the economy, corresponding to the entry on the international scene of Ronald Reagan in the United States and Margaret Thatcher in the United Kingdom.[86] These international developments meant the decline of the age of industrial democracy and the gradual removal of this subject from the agenda of policy-makers. Such a political and cultural shift was paralleled by the simultaneous waning of Yugoslavia as a model of economic organization in Western European political debate, as the economic decline undergone by the country in the late 1970s and the acceleration of centrifugal trends in the federation after the death of Tito in 1980 emphasized the limitations of self-management.[87] In the early 1990s, the Yugoslav wars would turn the Yugoslav "dream" into a "nightmare."[88]

In fact, the academic literature on "labor management" and Yugoslavia's role in it continued to flourish.[89] What was the reason for such persistence?

---

[85] On the Vredeling Directive, see Laurent Warlouzet, *Governing Europe in a Globalizing World* (New York: Routledge, 2017), in particular Chapter 3; Francesco Petrini, "Demanding Democracy in the Workplace: The European Trade Union Confederation and the Struggle to Regulate Multinationals," in *Societal Actors in European Integration. Polity-Building and Policy-making 1958–1992*, ed. Wolfram Kaiser and Jan-Henrik Meyer (London: Palgrave Macmillan, 2013), 151–172; Jean-Jacques Danis and Reiner Hoffman, "From the Vredeling Directive to the European Works Council Directive – some historical remarks," *Transfer: European Review of Labour and Research* 1 (1995): 180–187; Michael Nelson, "The Vredeling Directive: The EEC's Failed Attempt to Regulate Multinational Enterprises and Organize Collective Bargaining," *New York Journal of International Law and Politics* 20 (1988): 967–992.

[86] See Richard Aldous, *Reagan and Thatcher: The Difficult Relationship*, (London: Hutchinson, 2012).

[87] See Sabrina P. Ramet, *The Three Yugoslavias: state-building and legitimation, 1918–2005* (Bloomington, IN: Indiana University Press, 2006), 325–340.

[88] Georgi, *Autogestion*, 8.

[89] See, for example, Nadjan Pašić, Stanislav Grozdanić and Milorad Radević, *Workers' management in Yugoslavia: Recent developments and trends* (Geneva: International Labour Office, 1982); Saul Estrin, *Self-management: Economic theory and Yugoslav practice* (London: Cambridge University Press, 1983); Chris Rojek and David Wilson, "Workers' self-management in the world system: The Yugoslav case," *Organization Studies* 8 (1987): 297–308.

The answer to this question is linked to the fact that the Yugoslav model was an abstract reference used to construct theoretical models which, in the end, were not tested in reality.[90] However, as shown in this chapter, Yugoslavia's self-management became an *Idealtypus* which, although not claiming validity in terms of correspondence with social reality, emerged as a reference point for the evolution of industrial relations in Western Europe.

Conclusion

In the late 1960s, Western Europe underwent a period of social and political turmoil which marked the end of the *Trente glorieuses*. To face social discontent, Western European leaderships looked for new models of relations in the field of labor: the idea of enhancing "labor management" was developed, in order to improve democracy at industrial level and reduce workers' alienation. Such reformist zeal developed out of an intense period of academic and political debate over the best way to reform industrial relations. Within this debate, the Yugoslav model of self-management featured prominently. Western European élites at all levels – political, economic and academic – focused in particular on a system of "self-management" based on direct participation of workers in the management of socially-owned enterprises. International organizations such as the ILO and academic networks focusing on the Yugoslav model contributed towards bringing the problem of "labor management" to the forefront of the political agenda of Western European leaders, as demonstrated by the exponential rise in state interventionism in the fields of manpower and industrial democracy. Although the constitutive principles of self-management were not applied in Western Europe, the Yugoslav experience frequently recurred in the political debate which surrounded the introduction of such new normative measures.

This chapter concludes that the Yugoslav model taught Western Europe a useful lesson, pointing to the "ideal" virtues of self-management planning in order to improve industrial relations. The impact of Yugoslavia's self-management was therefore mainly theoretical: it favored debates on industrial democracy and shaped Western European cultural and political zeitgeist of the early 1970s in the labor field. Yugoslavia represented a genuine "social laboratory" where self-management could be tested and implemented. The fortune of the Yu-

---

90 See Saul Estrin and Milica Uvalić, "From Illyria towards Capitalism: Did Labour-Management Theory Teach Us Anything about Yugoslavia and Transition in its Successor States?," *Comparative Economic Studies* 50 (2008): 663–696.

goslav-style managed economy was not linked to its performance – which retrospectively proved to be weak – but to the very fact that it proposed, at least in theory, a new way of planning which refused at the same time the centralised Soviet model and the indicative Western measures. However, as all theoretical models it was affected by the evolution of debates on industrial democracy, being overcome when the *nouvelle vague* of economic liberalism became the new reference model in the Western world, and Yugoslavia, due to its internal contradictions, foundered into its fatal crisis.

Vítězslav Sommer
Managing Socialist Industrialism: Czechoslovak Management Studies in the 1960s and 1970s[1]

The first issue of the Czechoslovak management studies journal *Modern management* (Moderní řízení) from March 1966 opened with an editorial stressing that the introduction of more efficiently organized management in socialism required the need "to know more."[2] In the 1960s, the effort to establish the so-called "new system of planned management of national economy" was a substantial part of economic reform strategies. Czechoslovak economists and reform communists in general shared the conviction that state-owned enterprises should have more independence in their decision-making and require more qualified and competent management staff.[3] Although a source of controversy among reformers was the relationship between hierarchical managerialism and horizontal self-management, all reform-oriented scholars and politicians accepted that a state socialist economy suffered from the lack of efficient techniques of management and organization.[4] In order "to know more" about planning and management, experts from such diverse fields as sociology, economics or psychology developed quite an extensive apparatus of expert knowledge production during the 1960s.

However, the Warsaw Pact invasion into Czechoslovakia in August 1968 and the subsequent introduction of the consolidation regime substantially affected this attempt to promote and implement up-to-date management techniques. This field of expertize, which aimed to be among the flagships of reform communist social and economic innovations, transformed itself into an important part

---

[1] This chapter was researched and written with the support of the Czech Science Foundation (GAČR) as a part of the project GJ15-19437Y entitled "The Road to Technocratic Socialism: Concepts of Governance in Czechoslovakia (1953-1975)".
[2] "Úvod," *Moderní řízení* 1, no. 1 (1966): 1-2.
[3] For policy documents, see primarily "A resolution of the Central Committee of the CPC, concerning the main trends in improving the planned management of the national economy from January 29, 1965," in *Prameny k dějinám československé krize 1967–1970, Vol. 10, Ekonomická reforma 1965–1969*, ed. Jitka Vondrová (Prague and Brno: Ústav pro soudobé dějiny AV ČR – Doplněk, 2010), 25-35.
[4] For the controversy between proponents of managerialism and self-governance, see for example Lubomír Mlčoch, "Symposium o podniku," *Politická ekonomie* 17 (1969): 278-281, or Jaroslav Vostatek, "Čtyři typy podniku a socialistické odměňování," *Politická ekonomie* 17 (1969): 307-321.

of late socialist governance and aimed to reflect recent development of management studies in the Eastern Bloc as well as in the West while conforming to the political economy based on central planning, industrial production, authoritarian governance and specific late socialist welfare policies. This chapter explores how Czechoslovak experts discussed management and organization in the 1960s and 1970s and how they situated their field of expertize in the broader context of state socialist governance. The first part of this text explores the rise of management studies in the 1960s as a part of market-based reform policies. In the second part I will address the specific topic of social planning. As I will show below in more detail, late socialist social planning was a specific planning project aimed at expanding planning activities from the economic to the social sphere. According to the promoters of social planning, the industrial economy of "advanced socialism" had resources to further develop socialist society by means of sophisticated and detailed planning methods. The idea was that in socialism the society, including its culture and beliefs, should be planned according to fixed goals and targets. The central unit of social planning was industrial enterprise which was in charge to apply social planning to its employees, their families and surrounding towns and regions. Since the early 1970s management studies were in charge to invent and promote management techniques conforming to the welfare obligations of socialist firms. It thus mirrored the technocratic and authoritarian aspects of late socialism and simultaneously posed a serious challenge to managerial thought. Moreover, this concept of planning seemed to be tailored to the specific conditions of post-1968 Czechoslovakia when the struggle for the economic efficiency of socialist industrialism was closely interwoven with the effort to achieve social and political stability by means of welfare policies and hierarchical planning. This text analyzes two subsequent stages in the history of management studies in Czechoslovakia and covers the transition between two distinct forms of managerial thought – from the entrepreneurial discourse of the market-oriented reform towards renewed emphasis on central planning after 1968. The aim of this chapter is to discuss how this particular expert community responded to political and socio-economic challenges of the time and which roles the expertize dealing with the relationship between management and planning played in this development.

Management Studies in socialist Czechoslovakia as a subject of historiographic research

The potential for analyzing concepts elaborated by management studies scholars as a means to enable the study of governmental rationality behind particular political and economic regimes was successfully demonstrated by Luc Boltanski and Eve Chiapello[5], who studied managerial literature not as texts depicting the reality of how capitalist enterprises functioned but as works aiming to formulate normative concepts of organization and decision-making. Management studies literature is, according to them, of a primarily prescriptive nature, frequently relying on morally based arguments and thus "one of the main vehicles for the diffusion and popularization of normative models in the world of enterprise."[6] Given the pivotal role of industrial production for the functioning of modern societies, texts on management may be used as a source of knowledge about much more general ideas of economic order, organization of production and economic efficiency in the era of high modernity.

Managerial literature thus does not focus on the actual functioning of an enterprise but rather strives to describe what an ideal organization and process of decision-making should look like and what the channels to achieve such a goal are. Therefore, it is a significant source for studying the rationality of organizations and decision-making. In spite of the fact that Boltanski and Chiapello characterize thought on management as an intellectual production typical for capitalism and capitalist thinking on economy and labor, study of the texts that arose in the context of Czechoslovak management studies shows that this type of source could also be used to study how the "spirit of socialism" was transforming. The Czechoslovak management science, just like its Western counterpart, strived to create normative concepts of rational organization. The intended result was the establishment of more a sophisticated organizational culture, as well as the development of the education of managers, which was meant to focus not only on deepening their expert skills but also on cultivating their daily work habits and life-style. Management studies, termed in the Czech language of the time *teorie řízení* (theory of management), studied a wide range of topics and offered a comprehensive picture of the organizational rationality of the socialist economy. In addition, this field of expertize had a distinct critical potential. Given the very narrowly defined target group of professional recipients

---

5 Luc Boltanski and Eve Chiapello, *The New Spirit of Capitalism* (London: Verso, 2007), 57–62.
6 Ibid., 58.

this literature focused on and the strong orientation on the practical use of knowledge in managerial praxis, management studies provided a relatively critical image of the issues faced by Czechoslovak managers confronting the bleak reality of a centrally planned economy.

Any exploration of management studies in Czechoslovakia of the 1960s and 1970s should reflect the longer historical continuities of scientific management in state socialism. The idea of using contemporary scientific knowledge for the organization of work and production already resonated before World War One in the milieu of Russian social democracy and also appealed, for a long period, to Lenin and Trotsky.[7] The interest in management was apparent during the Russian civil war when the emerging Soviet state strived to tackle growing issues related to industrial production. In the course of time, an age-long controversy flared up over the relationship between scientific management and socialism, which was connected both with the issue of decision-making authority in a nationalized economy and with the power struggles buffeting the Soviet state throughout the 1920s. Issues such as the bureaucratization of the regime, establishment of the rationalization movement, the role of workers' self-management bodies, education of managerial staff, the power of managing directors or the extent to which capitalist methods of management could be adopted belonged to the central points of controversy in Soviet debates. In spite of the fact that scientific management had numerous opponents and practical application of the management methods met with considerable resistance, in the second half of the 1920s the Soviet Union had the third biggest base for research on scientific management after the USA and Germany.[8]

In the course of the 1930s, Soviet studies of scientific management were almost destroyed by Stalin's assault on bureaucracy and the so-called bourgeois specialists. The rejection of scientific management was connected to an economic policy focused on extreme increases in the volume of industrial production, a mobilizatory approach to management and a tightening of work discipline. As was the case with other Stalinist campaigns, the destruction of Soviet management studies had its roots not only in power struggles but also in the political and economic theory of Stalinist Marxism–Leninism. In particular, Mark Beissinger points out the adoration of the "school of life" with its emphasis on the acquisition of management skills not just by way of acquiring expert knowledge but through gaining practical experience on a daily basis by taking active part in

---

[7] Mark Beissinger, *Scientific Management, Socialist Discipline, and Soviet Power* (Cambridge, Mass.: Harvard University Press, 1988), 20–58.
[8] Ibid., 59.

the building of socialism. The emphasis on the immediate performance and mobilization of all available resources completely outweighed the need to introduce organizational and decision-making methods on the basis of findings by international management science.[9]

Although Stalinist industrialization could boast impressive indicators of economic growth, fascinating to a good many Western observers, its characteristic feature was also the persistent failure of central planning and its striking inefficiency.[10] The crisis of state socialist regimes in the mid-1950s thus opened the issue of change in the organization of production and the seeking of alternatives to the Stalinist approach to management. Soviet authorities began prioritizing management efficiency at the expense of simple extensive enhancement of the volume of production.[11] The rediscovery of scientific management was, however, no return to the management science of the 1920s. The field of cybernetics, which had been dismissed as a "bourgeois science" during the period of Stalinism, played a key role in this development as the fittest instrument for implementing the reforms leading to decentralization and to the consequent higher performance of the Soviet economy. By focusing on the interaction of systems and information, cybernetics not only provided a new perspective on the issue of efficient management but also a new language for discussing these issues and writing about them. Soviet authors thus emphasized the significance of "optimal planning and control" as a central motif of post-Stalinist reforms.[12]

Representatives of the so-called economic cybernetics viewed the economy as a centralized system which could be managed and controlled by means of mathematical methods, computer technology and tools provided by the management studies of the time. The "optimal planning" theory proclaimed that computers can simulate a "quasi-market" and provide all the information needed for the efficient management of the socialist economy.[13] State socialism seemed to be a political regime that enabled the full application of the cybernetic approach to the management of the economy – more than capitalism, which, on the one hand, was making great use of economic planning and of state regulations, but on the other hand also had to respect the particular interests of private

---

9 Ibid., 150.
10 Stephen Kotkin, "Modern Times: The Soviet Union and the Interwar Conjuncture," *Kritika: Explorations in Russian and Eurasian History* 2 (2001): 111–164.
11 Beissinger, *Scientific Management*, 160.
12 Slava Gerovitch, *From Newspeak to Cyberspeak: History of Soviet Cybernetics* (Cambridge, Mass.: The MIT Press, 2002), 256.
13 Ibid., 270 and 274–275.

owners.¹⁴ Cybernetics also emphasized the significance of feedback which enabled the self-management of individual system components and the achievement of economic efficiency by way of decentralization and technical progress. As such, it had significant reforming potential.¹⁵

The approach to management changed considerably at the turn of the 1960s and the 1970s when the Soviet Union and several Eastern Bloc countries such as Czechoslovakia saw a turn away from reforming efforts to the gradual establishment of consolidation regimes. The renewed emphasis on centralization and on a strictly hierarchical organization of economic and political life had a considerable impact on cybernetics and research on scientific management, too. As pointed out by Slava Gerovitch, with the end of the reforms cybernetics was transformed from the tool of reform to the "pillar of the status quo."¹⁶ The ideas of "optimal planning" and of managing the economy by means of automation and extensive introduction of computer technologies now helped to reinforce central planning even more.¹⁷ Management studies met a similar fate. Starting from the late 1960s, this expertize aimed to bring "rationalization without reform" – enabling an increasing efficiency in the socialist economy without the necessity of introducing decentralization reforms relying on the deeper autonomy of enterprises and the introduction of the market.¹⁸

---

14 Ibid., 271. For the history of the information network project designed by Soviet cyberneticians, see Benjamin Peters, *How Not to Network a Nation: The Uneasy History of the Soviet Internet* (Cambridge, Mass.: The MIT Press, 2016). For the relationship between cybernetics and Soviet mathematical economics, see Adam Leeds, "Dreams in Cybernetic Fugue: Cold War Technoscience, the Intelligentsia, and the Birth of Soviet Mathematical Economics," *Historical Studies in the Natural Sciences* 46 (2016): 633–668 and Ivan Boldyrev and Olessia Kirtchik, "The Cultures of 'Mathematical Economics' in the Postwar Soviet Union: More than a Method, Less than a Discipline," *Studies in History and Philosophy of Science, Part A* 63 (2017): 1–10. For the attempt to establish a cybernetic system of economic governance in Chile under Salvator Allende, see Eden Medina, *Cybernetic Revolutionaries: Technology and Politics in Allende's Chile* (Cambridge, Mass.: The MIT Press, 2011).
15 For the analysis of cybernetics as a part of liberalization policies in the Eastern Bloc countries, see Egle Rindzeviciute, *The Power of Systems: How Policy Sciences Opened Up the Cold War World* (Ithaca: Cornell University Press, 2016) and Peter C. Caldwell, *Dictatorship, State Planning, and Social Theory in the German Democratic Republic* (New York: Cambridge University Press, 2003).
16 Gerovitch, *From Newspeak to Cyberspeak*, 279.
17 Pekka Sutela, *Economic Thought and Economic Reform in the Soviet Union* (Cambridge, UK: Cambridge University Press, 1991), and Philip Hanson, *The Rise and Fall of Soviet Economy: An Economic History of the USSR from 1945* (London and New York: Routledge 2014).
18 Beissinger, *Scientific Management*, 182 and 185.

In search of socialist manager: Czechoslovak management studies in the 1960s

The post-Stalinist vision of the "scientization" of governance by way of technological and scientific progress was a suitable intellectual framework for the unprecedented boom in management studies in Czechoslovakia. Instead of the restoration of the interwar tradition based on Taylorism and related concepts, Czechoslovak scholars of industrial organization established their field on the knowledge borrowed from both Eastern and Western cybernetics, organizational science, and economics.[19] The CPC leadership reflected this shift in its policy strategies. The resolution of the CPC's June 1956 national conference paid a great deal of attention to the issues of organization and management of the Czechoslovak economy by way of its decentralization.[20] If "rigid centralization in management and planning played its role" in the first stage of the socialist construction, the era of advanced socialism required a different organizational culture. According to Party authorities, the economy was supposed to rely on the "perfection of planning and management" leading to the growth of labor productivity, "the maximum extent of introducing and using top technologies" and "the maximum extent of economic efficiency."[21]

Experts focused on the organization of production connected the issue of decentralization with the emphasis on decision-making flexibility and the growth of managers' expert skills. They saw a close connection between the greater efficiency of economy and the expertization of management at all levels of the economic hierarchy. Josef Štěpán, deputy minister of heavy industry, stressed that economic ministries had to be organized as a "small and flexible management apparatus" that would, within the "maximum decentralization of management," transfer a range of decision-making powers to "comprehensively constructed enterprises" and their managing directors. The condition for the fundamental reor-

---

[19] For the scientific management expertize in interwar Czechoslovakia, see Jan Janko and Emilie Těšínská, *Technokracie v českých zemích (1900–1950)* (Prague: Archiv Akademie věd České republiky, 1999); Otto Smrček, "Vědecká organizace práce a její aplikace ve strojírenství do konce druhé světové války," *Hospodářské dějiny* 13 (1985): 165–223, and Jan Janko, "Technokratické tendence v českých zemích," in *Studie z dějin techniky 25: Postátňování, profesionalizace a mecenášství ve vědě českých zemí 1860–1945*, ed. Jan Janko (Prague: Institut základů vzdělanosti UK, 1996), 25–56.
[20] *Celostátní konference Komunistické strany Československa. Zvláštní číslo Nové mysli, červen 1956* (Prague: Rudé právo – vydavatelství Ústředního výboru KSČ, 1956), 246–272.
[21] Ibid., 248.

ganization of management was to be a systematic education of all decision-makers to achieve "increased independence and increased responsibility." Only professionally skilled and sufficiently flexible managers could make use of the key components of the new approach to management, i.e. "new equipment," "advanced technology" and "correct organizational methods" enabling "more economical production."[22] Construction of a more independent, more flexible and professionally more skilled management apparatus was crucial for the implementation of the most important objective in the upcoming stage of building socialism, i.e. in exceeding capitalism in economic productivity and the living standard of the population.

The first more significant works on management were published in the late 1950s and focused on automation, cybernetics and computer technologies. Arnošt Kolman, philosopher and leading Marxist-Leninist theoretician, praised cybernetics as a science of the future which was opening new horizons to theoretical thinking on organization and systems, and was promising to achieve a vast range of application not only in the field of management but also in medicine, biology, sociology or philosophy.[23] Automation and computers roused an interest on the part of authors specialized in applying technology in industrial production. Jan Auerhan's and Miroslav Stibic's books on the automation and use of computers in administration were the first fundamental domestic works to rely on detailed knowledge of the issues in question, and also sought to achieve the objective of the practical use of new technology.[24] The same period also saw the initiation of the discussion about the use of psychology in management.[25] Authors also explored organizational culture in Czechoslovak industry including, for example, Jan Prošek, a factory manager with day-to-day manage-

---

[22] Josef Štěpán, "V řízení a organisaci uvádět v život usnesení celostátní konference KSČ," *Podniková organisace* 11 (1957): 1–3.

[23] Arnošt Kolman, *Kybernetika: O strojích vykonávajících některé duševní funkce člověka* (Prague: SNPL, 1957). For the other important Czechoslovak texts on cybernetics published in the late 1950s, see Josef Metelka, *Kybernetika – myslící stroje* (Prague: Orbis, 1957), and Š. Figar, V. Ruml, and A. Špaček, "Problémy kybernetiky," *Nová mysl* 11 (1957): 448–463.

[24] Jan Auerhan, *Automatizace a její ekonomický význam* (Prague: SNPL, 1959); Vladimír Stibic, *Od mechanisace k automatisaci administrativních prací* (Prague: Státní nakladatelství technické literatury, 1959).

[25] For the early argument for the introduction of psychology in management expertise, see "Z resoluce konference československých psychologů," *Podniková organizace* 12 (1958): 63–63 and Jan Raiskup, "Více psychologie do kádrové práce," *Podniková organizace* 12 (1958): 143–144.

rial experience, who was among those attempting to write the first business management manuals.²⁶

The 1960s saw further developments in management studies towards it becoming an independent field of expertize. Czechoslovak reform communists attempted to introduce policies enabling the elimination of pervasive malfunctions and incompetence in different layers of governance. They saw the sphere of economic planning and management as affected to an extraordinary degree by the unintended consequences of socialist construction, most importantly due to recurrent problems with coordination and the efficiency of central planning. Although reform-oriented economists like Ota Šik or Karel Kouba saw that encouraging more independently acting business enterprises and establishing a balanced relationship between plan and market as a backbone of economic reform, the task to resolve the problem of "cadres" and their functioning in the organization and control of production was an inseparable part of the reform agenda. In 1964 the Czechoslovak Central Control and Statistics Office (the so-called Central Commission of People's Control and Statistics) produced a report for the Communist Party Central Committee's Economic Commission describing Czechoslovak managers as usually undereducated and thus not properly prepared to work in a reformed economy.²⁷ This report posed the question of whether they were capable of mastering more sophisticated techniques of management and planning, and to what extent they could handle greater independence in decision-making.

As a consequence of the reformist attempts to cope with these problems, the institutional network of Czechoslovak management studies became quite developed in the second half of the 1960s and covered a wide range of activities from academic research to more practically oriented expertize focused on management in individual branches of the Czechoslovak economy, the development of computer technology, or the building of an information infrastructure to deal with the data necessary for mastering a complex economic reality. The higher learning institutions, the institutes of the Czechoslovak Academy of Sciences,

---

26 Jan Prošek, *Ze zkušeností podnikového ředitele* (Prague: SNTL, 1957). Prošek was harshly criticized in the Party journal *Život strany* (The Life of the Party) which characterized his book as an anti-Party statement and "harmful book." See "O jedné škodlivé knížce," *Život strany* 5 (1958): 299–301.

27 National Archives in Prague, Ekonomická komise ÚV KSČ 1963–1968, sv. 2, a.j. 6, bod 4, Rozbor kvalifikace vedoucích hospodářských pracovníků. For the early critique of management inefficiency, see the 1957 report for Czechoslovak Politburo called "Principles of Increasing the Industrial Management Efficiency" in National Archives in Prague, Politické byro ÚV KSČ 1954–1962, sv. 144, a.j. 190–191, bod 12, Zásady zvýšení ekonomické účinnosti řízení průmyslu.

or even the research unit at the Party School of Higher Learning at the Central Committee of the Communist Party covered issues like management and industrial organization.[28] In 1965 the Czechoslovak government established the Institute of Management, a specialized institution concerned with research, consultancy and the education of managers.[29] The founder and first director of this institution was Jaroslav Jirásek, the most prominent Czechoslovak management studies scholar, who attempted enthusiastically to disseminate the most up-to-date knowledge about management, organization and decision-making borrowed predominantly from Western literature. Aside from the publication of numerous books and booklets the institute also issued two journals which published original as well as translated materials.[30] However, the most important task of the Institute of Management was the organization of various courses and lectures for managers.[31]

In the 1960s management studies included research in the fields of cybernetics, economics, industrial sociology, psychology, the study of industrial organization as well as practically oriented consultancy activities. Theoretical research into the prerequisites for efficient management showed the significant role of cybernetics,[32] but management science primarily addressed managerial praxis in

---

28 "Československé instituce zabývající se řízením," *Moderní řízení* 1, no. 1 (1966): 89–92; "Československé instituce zabývající se řízením – pokračování," *Moderní řízení* 1, no. 2 (1966): 90–92; "Československé instituce zabývající se řízením – pokračování," *Moderní řízení* 1, no. 3 (1966): 91–92; "Československé instituce zabývající se řízením," *Moderní řízení* 1, no. 6 (1966): 90–92.

29 The Institute of Management was founded on the basis of the decree of 28 July 1965 issued by the Czechoslovak government and became operative in the autumn of that year. It consisted of an expert institution, the so-called Institute for Research and Rationalization of Management, and an education facility called the Centre for Education of Managerial Staff. See, National Archives in Prague, Institut řízení, Informační zpráva o Institutu řízení (Návrh zprávy pro sekretariát nebo předsednicvo ÚV KSČ a předsednictvo vlády ČSSR k projednání v řídícím výboru dne 14. října 1965) and Poslání, pracovní náplň a způsob práce institutu řízení (Výpis z důvodové zprávy k vládnímu usnesení č. 362 ze dne 28. července 1965)

30 The Institute of Management published two journals: *Moderní řízení* (Modern Management) and *Organizace a řízení* (Organization and management).

31 "Úvod – Patnáct let Institutu řízení," *Moderní řízení* 14, no. 11 (1980): 5–10.

32 The most important theoretical contribution was focused on the theory of information. See Pavel Pelikán, *Člověk a informace (studie o člověku a jeho způsobech zacházení se zprávami)* (Prague: Svoboda, 1967). Pelikán was a visiting scholar at the Centre Européen Universitaire in Nancy in 1964 and 1965 and was a collaborator of Jacob Marschak and Thomas Marschak. He was also a visiting fellow at the University of California in Berkeley and Carnegie-Mellon University in Pittsburgh between 1967 and 1969. The outcomes of his research were published in French as Pavel Pelikán, *Homo informationicus: réflexions sur l'homme et l'informatique* (Nancy: Centre européen universitaire, 1967).

industry. Authors such as Jaroslav Kohout, who became the most important Czechoslovak scholar in the field of industrial sociology, discussed the direct application of sociology and psychology in management as a tool of social analysis on the shop-floor, or as a technology enabling the efficient organization of employees.[33] The more technically-oriented literature covered the organization of daily operations in industrial enterprises and elaborated detailed organizational blueprints and models usable in managerial praxis.[34] Czechoslovak authors also discussed marketing, public relations, human resources management, advertisement or quality management.[35] In addition, management studies investigated personal conduct of managers from the organization of meetings and office work to life-style and work as well as personal habits.[36] The authors of these self-help manuals, most prominently Karel Pavelka, attempted to create a socialist manager as a specific professional identity characterized by particular competencies, professional values and personal qualities.

It was thus not surprising that Czechoslovak management studies discussed issues related to specific aspects of management in state socialist countries like planning, forecasting, using computers in central planning, or economic reform. However, the reception of Western knowledge, mostly from the USA, West Germany, France and the United Kingdom was extensive. The experts like Jirásek and many others attempted to actively promote these concepts and to present capitalist managerial thought as an example of well-developed expertize contributing to efficient organization and decision-making both in capitalism and socialism. They flooded Czechoslovak journals with translations from Western publications of different sorts, from theoretical texts to more popular accounts.[37] Apart from the Institute of Management, the management studies department at the Party School of Higher Learning contributed significantly to the dissemination of Western knowledge, most importantly from fields like systems analysis or game theo-

---

33 Jaroslav Kohout, *Sociologie a řízení ekonomiky* (Prague: Práce, 1967).
34 Jiří Řezníček, *Vědecká organizace řídící práce: Vybrané kapitoly* (Prague: NPL, 1965).
35 The *Moderní řízení* journal published special issues dedicated to marketing and management of quality. Issues like advertisement, design and human resources management were covered by this journal as well. For the public relations literature, see Ladislav Hájek, *Public Relations: Podnik a veřejnost* (Hradec Králové: Institut pro sociální analýzu, 1970).
36 Karel Pavelka, *Jak lépe řídit* (Prague: Svoboda, 1970); Karel Pavelka, *Jak lépe rozhodovat* (Prague: Svoboda, 1970); Karel Pavelka, *Vedoucí a kolektiv* (Prague: Svoboda, 1970); Ladislav Svatuška, *Vedoucí potřebuje informace* (Prague: Svoboda, 1971).
37 Apart from the rich publication activity of the Institute of Management journals it is primarily the Czech translations of Peter F. Drucker published in 1968 or 1970 that are worth mentioning. See Peter F. Drucker, *Podnikové řízení a hospodářské výsledky* (Prague: Svoboda, 1968); Peter F. Drucker, *Výkonný vedoucí* (Prague: Institut řízení, 1970).

ry.[38] Czechoslovak experts also had direct experience of Western research on management thanks to visits by Western scholars to Czechoslovakia or fellowships and research trips to capitalist countries.[39] An example of the latter is provided by Stanislav Vácha, an economist, novelist, and management studies scholar with personal experience of being a factory manager, who was visiting fellow at Harvard University in 1969/1970 and authored a book about the organization of industrial enterprises in the context of capitalism.[40] Like Vácha, the economist Lubomír Mlčoch also carried out extensive research on Western theories of firm. His extensive introduction to the theory of firms under capitalism was among the most important contributions to the highly topical Czechoslovak debate about the relationship between enterprise organization and economic efficiency.[41] It is possible to characterize this patient observation of Western management as a critical fascination with the ability of capitalism to achieve efficiency by the introduction of various innovations in the spheres of control, organization and decision-making.[42]

This rapid development of Czechoslovak management studies, which was connected to the rise of socialist managerialism, also mirrored a more general trend closely connected to market-oriented economic reform. Such ideas as more independent enterprises and the introduction of the market to the socialist economy meant that a new type of manager was required. The thought that the objective of economic reform would also consist of the development of entrepreneurship in the socialist economy resonated not only in the milieu of management science but also at the highest political level. In November 1968, the Czechoslovak government debated the "Act on Socialist Enterprise" and the "Act on

---

38 The Party School of Higher Learning published several edited volumes composed of translations from various fields of research related to management and organization, for example cybernetics, system analysis or game theory. See for example *Texty ke studiu teorie řízení. Řada: Modely konfliktních situací. Část 2., Teorie her a zkoumání sociálního jednání 1* (Prague: Vysoká škola politická Ústředního výboru KSČ – Katedra teorie řízení, 1967), or *Texty ke studiu teorie řízení. Řada: Aplikace kybernetiky ve společenských vědách. Část 1., Kybernetika a ekonomie* (Prague: Vysoká škola politická ÚV KSČ – Katedra teorie řízení, 1966).
39 For the visits by Western scholars to Czechoslovakia, see for example "Jak má pracovat ředitel?," *Moderní řízení* 3, no. 4 (1968): 16–18. For the transnational communication between East and West in the field of management studies, see Sandrine Kott's chapter in this volume.
40 Stanislav Vácha, *Moderní kapitalistický podnik a jeho cíl* (Prague: Svoboda, 1970).
41 Lubomír Mlčoch, *Teorie firmy* (Prague: Ekonomický ústav ČSAV, 1970).
42 This close observation of capitalism was even highlighted by attempts to search for inspiration in the Czechoslovak capitalist past, for example by the reserved appraisal of the most important example of domestic interwar Fordism, the so-called Baťa management system. See Miroslav Stříteský, *Řízení – zvláštní profese* (Prague: Svoboda, 1970), 66.

Conditions of Entrepreneurship," the goal of this legislation being to create new "economic conditions" in which enterprises would be transformed "from mere objects of administration into active entities behaving in an entrepreneurial fashion and making decisions based on their own impetuses."[43] It meant that a manager primarily had to be a socialist entrepreneur rather than a person responsible simply for the fulfillment of hierarchically imposed plans. The reform was aimed at connecting "expert and professional management with the growing democratism of the society" and achieving a situation in which "the entrepreneurial and management system exceeds the level of European entrepreneurship and managerialism."[44] The socialist entrepreneurship was a path to both individuals' and work collectives' self-fulfillment in a manner that enabled "each worker's work and life to correlate" in accordance with the motto "one should be able to live in line with the way they work."[45] Developing entrepreneurship not only required a thorough rebuilding of the organizational structure of enterprises but also an overall change in the approach to managerial work. A managing director acting as a socialist entrepreneur had to pay more attention to marketing and public relations, follow international markets and be in the picture regarding the field of the latest technological innovations. At the same time, an important part of his activities was to work with his subordinates, which was supposed to focus on their motivation, development of skills and the further education of employees in general.[46] A socialist entrepreneur was a completely different type of manager than the former managing director of a nationalized enterprise, whose primary goal was to obediently fulfill the instructions provided by central planning institutions. The 1960s economic reforms gave birth to a new socialist manager, one capable, by means of modern management science, of running a business in a manner that enabled it to succeed in the competitive environment of domestic and international markets.

---

43 See "Informativní zpráva o stavu a dalším postupu prací na právní úpravě postavení, úlohy a řízení socialistického podniku a podmínek podnikatelské činnosti, Příloha č. 2: Hlavní principy postavení a řízení socialistického podniku, 19. listopadu 1968," in Vondrová, *Prameny k dějinám československé krize 1967–1970*, Vol. 10, 353.
44 "Úvod," *Moderní řízení* 3, no. 7 (1968): 5.
45 Ibid.
46 This characteristics of "socialist entrepreneurialism" is based on V. Fencl, "Koncepce podnikání, řízení a organizace podniků," *Moderní řízení* 3, no. 7 (1968): 35–38. See also "Rozhovor o družstevním podnikání," *Moderní řízení* 4, no. 3 (1969): 7–11; Jaroslav Schulz, "Klíč k podnikání je v personální politice," *Moderní řízení* 4, no. 3 (1969): 14–16; Miloslav Benda, "Vnitropodnikové řízení a podnikatelská funkce," *Moderní řízení* 4, no. 4 (1969): 47–51; "Rozhovor o podniku, který podniká," *Moderní řízení* 4, no. 6 (1969): 7–15.

Consolidation as control of social and economic development: Management expertize after 1968

After 1968, when the Prague Spring political project collapsed, the subsequent rapid refusal of market-oriented reforms and a return to central-planning posed a serious challenge to all expert projects focused on economic governance. In order to cope with the now denounced legacy of reform communism, management studies pundits reinvented their field in accordance with politics calling for the reestablishment of centralized Party control and a Marxist-Leninist ideological monopoly. It led to attempts to formulate a new theoretical framework of management studies enabling them to emphasize the importance of this field to the more authoritarian regime.

Czechoslovak management studies managed to adapt to the new political conditions in spite of the fact that the ideological campaign accompanying the onset of the consolidation regime also found the roots of the criticized revisionism in the reception of knowledge originating from capitalist countries. It was thus necessary to defend the significance of management science for the new economic policy and also to prove that it was possible to adopt Western management techniques to make them usable under the conditions of central planning. The policy statements formulating consolidation strategies of management studies viewed the Prague Spring as a period of political chaos enabling the introduction of irresponsible and ultimately unsuccessful economic experiments. However, the crisis could not be left behind by returning to the outdated centralism of the Stalinist period.[47] The programmatic texts of "consolidated" management studies, mostly anonymous editorials published in the journal *Moderní řízení*, called for a renewal of discipline, order and authority in organizing economic life by means of a deeper interest in the theory and praxis of central planning and respecting the "leading role" of the Party. The intention was also to further develop research into the latest management techniques, ones based both on socialist and capitalist experience, but with respect to the decisive role of the plan and the Party in the socialist economy.[48]

---

[47] "Úvod," *Moderní řízení* 4, no. 10 (1969): 5–8; "Rozhovor o plánování a řízení československé ekonomiky," *Moderní řízení* 5, no. 1 (1970): 7–13.
[48] "Úvod," *Moderní řízení* 5, no. 1 (1970): 5–6; "Úvod," *Moderní řízení* 5, no. 2 (1970): 5–6; "Úvod," *Moderní řízení* 5, no. 5 (1970): 5–6.

This authoritative turn was legitimized ideologically as a return to the "Leninist approach" to management.⁴⁹ Czechoslovak experts referred to the Soviet tradition of scientific management and stressed the need to develop a specifically socialist managerialism.⁵⁰ As the Institute of Management outlined in its early 1970 statement on the new approach to management studies, it was necessary to keep cultivating Czechoslovak managers' skills "while learning both from friends and foes" but also to respect the ideological framework of Marxism–Leninism and to refuse "such circumstances of managerialism which spring from Western managers' class status when controlling the capitalist economy and from the class composition of the capitalist society."⁵¹ In accordance with an ongoing campaign against "revisionism," management studies scholars refused reform communists' ideas and introduced forecasting, management and planning methods elaborated in other state socialist countries in their field more extensively than before 1968. However, these authors did not deny the importance of Western knowledge and capitalist techniques of management and organization. They framed the idea of efficient economic organization using the primacy of central planning and hierarchical control of the economy. As a consequence, the aim of management studies was to connect certain methods borrowed from Western authors and observed in capitalist managerial praxis with advanced concepts of planning and organization tailored exclusively for socialist economies.

The most important change in the conceptualization of management after 1968, one which was also a specific product of socialist management science, was the strong reception for social planning. Since the early 1970s, Czechoslovak industrial sociologists, most prominently Jaroslav Kohout and his colleagues from the sociology and psychology department at the Higher School of Economics in Prague, promoted social planning as a tool that enabled the coordinated development of welfare to be pursued in accordance with the objectives of central economic planning. This concept of social planning differed fundamentally from projects under a similar name developed in the context of the Keynesian welfare state.⁵² It offered a new conceptualization of the relationship between in-

---

49 This emphasis on "Leninism" was extraordinarily present in the writing of authors based on the Party School of Higher Learning about necessary changes in the management of human resources. See, for example, Karel Kovář, Miloš Hendl, and Karel Fryč, "Obnova leninských zásad kádrové práce," *Moderní řízení* 6, no. 11 (1971): 5–12, *Moderní řízení* 6, no. 12 (1971): 5–11.
50 František Machát, "V. I. Lenin a řízení," *Moderní řízení* 5, no. 3 (1970): 15–20.
51 "Co znamená "manažerství" v našem pojetí?," *Moderní řízení* 5, no. 1 (1970): 31.
52 For the issue of social planning from the transnational perspective, see Valeska Huber, "Introduction: Global Histories of Social Planning," *Journal of Contemporary History* 52 (2017): 3–15.

dustrial production, management and welfare in state socialism that was distinct from a Stalinist emphasis on mobilizing a workforce based on charismatic leadership and personal sacrifice as well as from reform communists' experimentation with the market, entrepreneurship, self-government and decentralization. The idea of social planning was initially discussed at the 23rd Congress of the Communist Party of the Soviet Union in 1966, where the Leningrad delegation proposed organizing social planning in Leningrad's industrial enterprises and the Council of Ministers' Chairman Alexei Kosygin highlighted the necessity of introducing social planning in the Soviet managerial praxis.[53] From this point Soviet sociologists further developed social planning primarily as a planning exercise applied at the level of individual enterprises. In the early 1970s it started to be discussed in Czechoslovakia, for example at the conferences of industrial sociologists, as a new planning technique to "broaden the planning activities from their present technical and economic approach to the complex planning including also social changes."[54] The main topics of the 7th ISA World Congress of Sociology in Varna (1970) were prediction and social planning, which allowed for a knowledge exchange which further influenced the reception of social planning in Czechoslovakia. Apart from the reception of Soviet and other literature on the topic, Czechoslovak experts participated at international workshops and conferences and took part in the international social planning and forecasting "working group" together with scholars from Bulgaria, Hungary, Poland, GDR and USSR. This body coordinated and integrated social planning research as a joint project of scholars from socialist countries.[55] As a consequence by the mid-1970s social planning was among the most prominent research topics in Czechoslovak sociology whether reflected in the Czechoslovak Academy of Sciences or in specialized institutions like the Institute for the Research on Labor in Bratislava. The research activities varied from empirical sociological surveys of welfare policies in enterprises, for example in projects by research collectives around Jaroslav Kohout, to more theoretical accounts of the "programming of so-

---

The case study of postwar Great Britain is analyzed in Glen O'Hara, *From Dreams to Disillusionment: Economic and Social Planning in 1960s Britain* (Basingstoke: Palgrave Macmillan, 2007).
53 Běla Stíbalová, *Sociální plánování v ČSSR a SSSR* (Prague: ÚVTEI, 1976), 3 and 15.
54 Jaroslava Bauerová, Jaroslav Kolář, Jiří Růžička, Jaroslav Kohout, Eva Bidlová, and Miloslav Tomšík, *O sociálním plánování* (Prague: Práce, 1972), 3.
55 The main outcomes from three conferences organized by the "working group" were published in František Kutta, ed., *Planning and Forecasting Social Processes: Undertaken within the Framework of the Problems Committee for Multilateral Cooperation of the Academy of Sciences, and Dedicated to the 9th World Sociological Congress Uppsala, Sweden 1978* (Prague: Academia, 1978).

cial processes" promoted by the economist František Kutta. Although the main field of social planning application was an industrial enterprise, Czechoslovak sociologists also carried out experiments to plan the "social development" of selected cities and regions in order to "improve the control of socio-economic development at the territorial level" and to "contribute to more effective shaping of socialist life-style in territorial community."[56]

In the sphere of policy-making the National Planning Committee, federal government, trade unions and a special committee related to the Communist Party Central Committee supervised the establishment of social planning programs.[57] In 1972 the 7th Trade Union Congress initiated the completion of annual social plans in enterprises and in 1973 the Czechoslovak government issued a decree encouraging enterprises to implement "experimental" welfare projects. The implementation of social planning was further promoted in 1975 when the government decided that all Czechoslovak enterprises were obliged to elaborate "complex welfare programs" for the period from 1976 to 1980.[58] The enterprises were also active participants in the social planning activities. For example, in 1974 the Třinec Steel-Works hosted an international conference on the "welfare activities of socialist enterprise" which gathered sociologist, economists, psychologists as well as factory managers and trade unionists.[59] The businesses also organized their own inquiries into social planning in order to find a way of tayloring welfare programs for the specific environment of particular industrial branches or with the respect to local socio-economic conditions.[60]

What kind of rationality stood behind such a strong reception for social planning after 1968? In the 1970s Czechoslovak experts have formulated at least two lines of explanation. The first research perspective focuses on the theo-

---

56 František Kutta, ed., *Teorie a praxe sociálního plánování a programování v ČSSR* (Prague, Svoboda, 1981), 61. The Czechoslovak experiments with the application of social planning at the level of cities and regions are described in Jaroslav Novotný and Miroslav Štráchal, *Poznatky z experimentů v plánování sociálního rozvoje měst a obcí* (Ústí nad Labem: Ústav pro filozofii a sociologii – pobočka Ústí nad Labem, 1980).
57 This account of the history of social planning is based primarily on Kutta, ed., *Teorie a praxe sociálního plánování a programování v ČSSR*, 51–69, and Stíbalová, *Sociální plánování*, 43–44.
58 For the social planning instructions issued by ministries and trade unions, see "Směrnice a pokyny federálního a republikových ministerstev práce a sociálních věcí a ÚRO pro sestavení "komplexních programů péče o pracovníky" na roky 1976 až 1978," *Příloha časopisu Odborář* 28, no. 13 (1975): 1–14.
59 *Mezinárodní konference Péče socialistického závodu o člověka: Sborník přednášek* (Třinec: Třinecké železárny, 1974).
60 Emil Rigo, K niektorým otázkam plánovania sociálneho rozvoja vo Východoslovenských železarniach," *Plánované hospodářství* 26 (1973): 25–35.

ry of social planning which offered an optimistic and future-oriented narrative about the role of social planning in so-called advanced socialism. According to theoretical texts, the main object of social planning was a collective of employees, and the principal aim was to "overcome the separation between economic and social function of enterprise."[61] This meant that enterprises, which were owned by the socialist state and thus became specific state institutions, had to be involved not only in the production of particular goods but also in the organization of welfare and, more generally, the life-styles of their employees.[62] It was thus an attempt to introduce a complex planning technology connecting economic planning with welfare policies and strategies that aimed to develop and socially implement specific socialist values, cultural and consumer preferences or, more generally, a socialist way of life.[63] Social planning promoters like Kohout and Kutta recognized this approach to management as a technique that allowed for a broadening of the scope of managerial and planning activities from the organization of the labor force to the active shaping of employees' "personal structure," with the aim of achieving "harmonious development in all spheres of human life." Instead of coercion or direct control, social planning was primarily oriented towards cultivating a worker's "personal values" like self-discipline and his or her relationship to work.[64] The implementation of social planning had to be enabled by enterprises' annual social plans. According to the Soviet methodology of social planning, which was translated in to Czech in 1973, this planning exercise was concerned with the following issues: the social structure of a collective in an enterprise (mobility of employees, qualifications); working conditions in an enterprise (occupational safety), living standard of employees; the "communist education" of employees (cultivation of the work ethics, "aesthetic development of personality," leisure, working discipline, youth issues, physical development of personality, further education of employees) and the cultivation of "socio-psychological" relationships in a collective.[65]

---

61 Bauerová, O sociálním plánování, 15.
62 Ibid.
63 For total planning in the Soviet context, see Stephen J. Collier, *Post-Soviet Social: Neoliberalism, Social Modernity, Biopolitics* (Princeton and Oxford: Princeton University Press, 2011), 48–64.
64 Bauerová, O sociálním plánování, 14.
65 D. A. Kerimov, *Metodika plánování sociálního rozvoje podniku* (Prague: Práce, 1973). Soviet literature also discussed application of "social norms," i.e. normatively given targets of social development. See Vladimír Asejev and Ovsej Škaratan, *Sociální normativy a sociální plánování* (Prague: Práce, 1986).

Apart from these highly theoretical accounts of social planning, the same expert milieu also offered more realistic and significantly less optimistic arguments for the need to introduce social planning. Jaroslav Kohout formulated this pragmatic explanation in the mid-1970s in his examination of sociological surveys which were conducted in Czechoslovak factories between 1965 and 1975.[66] Kohout discussed the fluctuation of employees as a serious social and economic problem that destabilized the Czechoslovak economy. He argued that the level of economic development meant that a disposable labor force was not available in the country. Moreover, the main sources of economic growth were new technologies, efficient management and vocational training. These surveys also showed that the fluctuation of employees was influenced by the everyday running of Czechoslovak enterprises. Workers were dissatisfied with organizational malfunctions, workplace conditions and low salaries. The Czechoslovak population seemed to be less and less attracted by exhausting and not really very well-organized employment in the industrial sector which, however, was still the backbone of the socialist economy. In an economic system without a functioning labor market and with limited sources of cheap immigrant labor the authorities and experts had to find policy instruments to stabilize and control the existing structure of employment. In short, as Kohout showed quite explicitly in his work, the aim of social planning was to keep employees in industrial companies and thus secure the functioning of a centrally-planned economy. From this perspective, social planning was primarily a form of pragmatic policy intervention and a specific technique of management. Although its final objective was, at least theoretically, the development of a socialist society and the cultivation of socialist values and habits, the practical and less visionary aspect of social planning was the need to control the labor force in order to achieve a certain degree of stability in the sphere of industrial production. It was thus an attempt to stabilize a state socialist socio-economic arrangement based on the primacy of industrial production and central planning. Instead of coercive policies such as strict labor discipline, which were typical of the era of Stalinism, Kohout and others emphasized social planning as a certain kind of soft-power – an elaborated policy instrument based on detailed knowledge of social and economic reality.

The effort to apply social planning as a policy measure leading to social and economic stability without market-oriented reform (typical of reform communism of the 1960s) as well as without more direct and repressive control of the

---

[66] Jaroslav Kohout, *Sociální analýza a řízení socialistického podniku: vznik-pojetí-aplikace* (Práce: Praáce, 1976), 168–175.

labor force (typical of Stalinism) was specific to the consolidation regime of the 1970s. For example, while Stalinist recipes for the treatment of labor fluctuations included the introduction of repressive measures on the shop-floor and the mobilization of workers by aggressive propaganda campaigns, the authors active in the 1970s highlighted the importance of welfare programs in enterprises and the significance of "optimal working conditions."[67] Similarly, contemporary empirical research emphasized the need for fundamental technological and organizational innovation as a precondition for successfully mastering limited supplies of qualified labor in the Czechoslovak economy.[68] Welfare policies, which were organized and supported by individual enterprises, had to be combined with up to date managerial and organizational methods in order to secure the running of the centrally-planned economy and, more generally, the existence of the political arrangement established after 1968. It was a significant shift from the reform communists' conception of entrepreneurial management, for which the market operations of an enterprise were the highest priority. From the early 1970s socialist management had to focus not just on the control of production, most importantly on the fulfillment of hierarchically imposed production plans, but also on broader welfare objectives.

Conclusion: Late socialist management studies and the transformation of industrial modernity

The idea of connecting economic planning, management and social planning posed a certain challenge to managerial praxis. In its theoretical writings Czechoslovak management studies underwent a transition from the reform communist vision of the socialist manager as a more or less independent entrepreneurial actor in the market-oriented socialist economy to a late socialist manager characterized as an educated, competent and efficient organizer and decision-maker acting in the centralized planning system. However, from the perspective of an individual manager, the late socialist concept of management required mastering the most recent techniques of everyday management, partly borrowed from Western management theory and capitalist management praxis, and, si-

---

[67] For the writing on fluctuation in the early 1950s, see Josef Stýblo and Borek Sýkora, *Do rozhodného boje proti absenci a fluktuaci a za vysokou pracovní kázeň* (Prague: Práce, 1953). For the late socialist social planning approach, see Pavel Vašák, *Fluktuace pracovních sil* (Prague: Práce, 1976).

[68] Lenka Kalinová, *Máme nedostatek pracovních sil?* (Prague: Svoboda, 1979).

multaneously, to cultivate managerial competencies based on the knowledge of social planning. This understanding of management emphasized three essential qualities of the socialist manager: discipline in the system of central planning, creativity in the everyday organization of an enterprise, and competencies in social planning allowing the welfare functions of the socialist firm to materialize. Late socialist management was in charge of achieving an organizational efficiency comparable with capitalist forms of industrial organization while fulfilling the welfare strategies of "advanced socialism."

This conceptualization of management mirrored the centrality of industrial production for the organization of social and economic life in late socialism. According to many observers on both sides of the "Iron Curtain", it seemed that the 1960s were a decade when capitalism and state socialism regimes were heading towards a shared industrial modernity.[69] This perspective, based on the notion of "convergence," highlighted, among others, the importance of industrial production for the social and economic order under both capitalism and state socialism. However, while the economies of Western Europe and the USA underwent substantial transformations from the 1970s towards de-industrialization, financialization and flexible organization, late socialism cultivated a certain form of "frozen" industrialism – a social and economic order structured primarily around central planning and strong connections between welfare and industrial production.[70] Specific late socialist management studies and social planning expertize thus aimed at producing knowledge that would allow this late socialist industrialism to be governed efficiently and with regard to long-term perspectives of thoroughly planned social and economic development. This case also shows that the relationship between planning and management studies was complicated and primarily reflected changes in economic policy. In the 1960s, the reformers saw the application of management studies knowledge as more or less a substitution of strict central planning. It meant that with more competent, flexible and independent managers on the shop-floor, the old central planning methods seemed to be obsolete and superfluous. After 1968, when the Czechoslovak au-

---

69 Alfred G. Mayer, "Theories of Convergence," in *Change in Communist System*, ed. Chalmers Johnson (Stanford: Stanford University Press, 1970), 313–341; David C. Engerman, "To Moscow and Back: American Social Scientists and the Concept of Convergence," in *American Capitalism: Social Thought and Political Economy in the Twentieth Century*, ed. Nelson Lichtenstein (Philadelphia: University of Pennsylvania Press, 2006), 47–68.
70 For the development in Western Europe and the USA, see for example Anselm Doering-Manteuffel and Lutz Raphael, *Nach dem Boom: Perspektiven auf die Zeitgeschichte seit 1970* (Göttingen: Vandenhoeck & Ruprecht, 2010); Gretta R. Krippner, *Capitalizing on Crisis: The Political Origins of the Rise of Finance* (Cambridge, Mass.: Harvard University Press, 2012).

thorities renounced the idea of market socialism and replaced reform-oriented policies with a renewed emphasis on central planning, management studies scholars rationalized their expertize as a necessary supplement to central planning. They characterized their knowledge as advanced methods of organization capable of making a centralized and hierarchical planning system work more efficiently. It thus depended on the politics of expertize if this field was to be market-friendly or planning-friendly. In this chapter, my aim was to emphasize how management studies was not inherently reformist or conservative but produced its expertize according to the current policies of the state.

The project of connecting management and social planning, which resulted from the typically modernist conviction of the socialism's vital dependence on the growth of industrial production, never succeeded in meeting its ambitious goals. It follows that social planning lost its significance during the 1980s when the overall disintegration of late socialist social and economic order produced significant shifts in the way Czechoslovak experts discussed issues like planning and management.[71] The economic literature of the late 1980s re-discovered the economic rationality build around the market. The "market forces" seemed to be universally applicable in different social and economic realms and were increasingly described as the only organizational logic capable of resolving all the problems of a dying socialism – from economic crises to environmental degradation or social pathologies.[72] Czechoslovak management studies experts like Stanislav Vácha attempted to open the question of "socialist entrepreneurship" again. In the 1980s Vácha aimed to promote a new type of management which was based on the implementation of capitalist-style entrepreneurship in socialist conditions. In his expert as well as his popular writing Vácha focused on the then famous Slušovice agricultural cooperative – a new type of socialist enterprise which developed a specific management framework based on individual incentives, a market-like decentralized organization of the enterprise and a use of highly competitive "human resources" management. According to Vácha, the new socialist entrepreneur was an active, educated, highly motivated, profit-oriented, and flexible market actor who was fully dedicated to the

---

[71] The application of sociology in social planning policies as the so-called "sociotechnique" (*sociotechnika*) was critically discussed in the late 1980s by sociologists in Slovakia, see Vladimír Krivý, "Sociotechnika: možnosti a hranice," *Sociológia* 20 (1988): 417–425.

[72] For example, see Valtr Komárek, ed., *Vazby vědeckotechnických, ekonomických a sociálních aspektů dlouhodobého rozvoje ČSSR* (Prague: ÚVTEI, 1988), 26–27. For the most important works written in the late 1980s, see Valtr Komárek, *Prognóza a program* (Prague: Academia, 1990) and Josef Zieleniec, ed., *Československo na rozcestí: zpráva o stavu národního hospodářství a možnostech jeho nápravy* (Prague: Lidové noviny, 1990).

growth of his or her company. In his writing about Slušovice, which also included a didactic novel written as the *Bildungsroman* of a young engineer, this new type of manager was an individual more compatible with the market economy than with a centrally planned system based on the imperative of plans and directives imposed from above.[73] This introduction of market rationality in management studies opened the way to a slow but inevitable return of the private entrepreneurship paradigm in Czechoslovak expert and political discourses, which was fully complete after 1989.

While the reform politics of the second half of the 1980s brought back the idea of socialist entrepreneurship, the fall of state socialism in 1989 instigated a transformation towards capitalism. This historical change opened a range of new opportunities for experts familiar with the contemporary state of Western research on management. Thus, for the second time since 1968, Czechoslovak management science succeeded in transitioning to new political conditions and maintaining a high degree of personal and conceptual continuity. This time in the transformation from late socialist industrialism to an era characterized by extensive privatization and the construction of capitalism in post-socialist conditions.

---

[73] For the novel about agricultural cooperative, see Stanislav Vácha, *Hauři* (Prague: Práce, 1987). Vácha analyzed the Slušovice management system in Stanislav Vácha, *Jak řídí Slušovice* (Prague: Novinář, 1988).

Michael Hutter
Ecosystems Research and Policy Planning: Revisiting the Budworm Project (1972–1980) at the IIASA

> "As Karl Marx used to say, any beginning is difficult. IIASA has succeeded in overcoming its initial problems. We are in the ocean of systems analysis and we have no choice but to swim in this ocean."[1]

Introduction: The rise of Applied Systems Analysis

In 1972 the United Nations Conference on the Human Environment was held in Stockholm and received broad media coverage, while in the same year the Limits to Growth report was published under the auspices of the Club of Rome. Shortly after these events the contemporary environmental protection imperative provided a further reason for policymakers to engage in international scientific cooperation in order to address and solve a variety of complex environmental problems facing industrialized societies. With its focus on the exchange of environmental knowledge for policy making, this chapter underlines the processes that informed the International Institute for Applied Systems Analysis (hereafter IIASA) as it studied and contributed to the shaping of the environmental change paradigm. In particular this chapter will analyze ways in which new forms of knowledge were produced as an interplay between computerized modeling and environmental management in interactions between the East and the West. By following the beginnings of an early research project at IIASA, the following will expose how IIASA mediated international negotiations on the standardization of systems analysis which was understood to be a key tool for policy making and planning processes.[2]

---

1 Abel G. Aganbegyan, "Future Research Directions," in *IIASA Conference '76* (IIASA, Laxenburg, Austria: IIASA, May 1976), 208.
2 As a center for planning the future, the IIASA provided the space for incorporating and negotiating scenarios related to that future. They framed their models into technocratic solutions, which is also captured by Jenny Andersson's analysis of the OECD and the Trilateral Commission in this volume.

https://doi.org/10.1515/9783110534696-013

IIASA's research infrastructure was legally consolidated as an Austrian association (*"Verein"*) located in a former Hapsburg castle in Laxenburg near Vienna, with the support of 12 national member organizations (NMOs), represented by the national academies of science for the USA, the USSR, Hungary, Czechoslovakia, and the GDR, and by similar national research facilities in the member states of France, Canada, the FRG, Bulgaria, Japan, the UK, and Italy. During the 1970s, the scientific academies of Austria, Sweden, the Netherlands and Finland were accepted as additional contributors.[3] Recent historiographical accounts about IIASA's impact on international scientific cooperation focused on the institute's research strategy as an interface that merged methods from large-scale computerized system simulations and the natural sciences and denoted IIASA as a prime example of innovatively established practices in environmental and civil engineering.[4] Likewise, IIASA was presented as an entity that prepared models for policymaking to consolidate improvements in ecosystem planning methods.[5] By following these accounts, IIASA provided an image of an institute that worked in a coordinated way in relation to environmental knowledge, by "teasing out what was and was not physically possible [to] enable 'policymakers' to feed the world, supply it with energy, keep it watered and so on."[6] When looking into the institutional arrangements in 1972, however, research that concerned global and international subjects originated primarily from the experience of national systems analysis. Common methodologies for research priorities were not yet visible.

Systems analysis at IIASA was conceived as an interface between political decision making in industrialized societies and the application of scientific approaches. With the use of systems analysis, policy making processes included studies of social and environmental impact that measured the risks and benefits of future decisions and the future behavior of systems. Political debates have been externalized to involve scientific experts, who were invited to provide "objective" grounds and a spectrum of possible decisions. IIASA's main research ob-

---

[3] United States Congress House Committee on Science and Technology, *European Oversight Trip: Report of the Committee on Science and Technology, U.S. House of Representatives, Ninety-Fifth Congress, First Session, Serial, 95th Congress* (U.S. Government Printing Office, 1977), 11.
[4] In this respect, see Andersson and Rindzevičiūtė, *The Struggle for the Long-Term in Transnational Science and Politics: Forging the Future*; Rindzevičiūtė, *The Power of Systems: How Policy Sciences Opened Up the Cold War World*. For the influence of social sciences, see also: Pierre Gremion, *The role of the social sciences in East–West relations*, Technology in Society 23, no. 3 (2001): 427–439.
[5] See, for example, Michael Thompson, *"IIASA's Take on Policy and Governance,"* (IIASA Archives, unpublished Final Draft, located in the IIASA Library), 1.
[6] Ibid.

jective was to inquire about how technological, social, and environmental systems correlated. In this respect, systems represented an arrangement of factors in a mathematically deducted boundary, where encompassed factors and their inter-dependency were elaborated for a specific time range. Systems analyses created visualized scenarios of potential future behaviors of a system at IIASA, researchers from various scientific disciplines participated in the evaluation of each factor. The crafting of systems and its inherent properties has become paramount with the emerging calculation power of computers since the 1940s. A method that once dominated modeling in the life sciences such as cell biology, and that was later used for military purposes during the Second World War, subsequently expanded to the public policy sector in the United States, the UK, and France. Twenty years later, the IIASA incorporated the computerized systems methodology with the aim of solving environmental and globally relevant problems.

This chapter argues that knowledge exchange of systems analysis at IIASA was accompanied by considerable amounts of friction; and these differences in national research traditions and agendas reshaped the transnational systemic approach during the time of its construction. Guided by a review of IIASA publications such as research reports and research memoranda, and supported by historical accounts from primary sources from the IIASA Archives, the Rockefeller Foundation Archives and the Harvard University Archives, this chapter exposes the origins of applied systems analysis at IIASA in relation to environmental and forest policymaking. The specific analysis of the budworm project provides insights into how the IIASA organized the standardization of methodological frameworks within East-West cooperation during the first years of its research venture (1973–1976), while highlighting the challenges of IIASA's practice as an interdisciplinary research hub that was meant to specifically include social scientific approaches.[7]

---

[7] In this respect, Katja Naumann has elaborated on the coordination of social scientific approaches within an East-West arena since the 1950s in this volume. The IIASA has reshaped and institutionalized cooperation on social scientific methodologies since the 1970s.

Part 1. The influence of the budworm on IIASA's ecological systems modelling (1973–1976)

The starting point or this chapter highlights how a Canadian budworm pest project involving the use of systems analysis was transferred from Canada to IIASA. Research on the budworm and its spread through Canadian forests then constituted one of IIASA's most crucial applied projects in the 1970s that were later transformed into general environmental systems. Budworm systems analysis was conducted by a research group from Canada that was invited to join IIASA in spring 1973. The group from the University of British Columbia worked at the institute for two years. Beside the establishment of computerized systems, the main objective of the budworm research group was the exploration of a method to solve perturbations of natural systems with the use of novel computer power and the experience of previous systems analysis projects.

Budworm research crucially expanded the organization of IIASA's ecosystems models, which was interpreted by contemporary historiographical accounts as offering the first blueprint for more complex environmental research.[8] Nevertheless, the early stages of budworm research and the internationalization of IIASA's knowledge infrastructure and knowledge exchange between 1973 and 1976 (when the budworm project terminated) have so far not been accurately studied. The processes of exchange about the daily work, the different use of equipment by scientists at IIASA, or the effects of the invitation of the Canadian research group and its integration in IIASA's territory of international cooperation provide important elements for understanding the making of a common planning method. In a nutshell, the input of the Canadian team to the methodological work on applied systems analysis (ASA) illustrates the afflux of a whole variety of concepts and notions into IIASA's systems approach that still persist in today's thinking about ecological systems, and in practices that are covered under the widely received umbrella term of "resilience".[9]

---

8 See, for example, Isabell Schrickel, "Von Schmetterlingen und Atomreaktoren: Medien und Politiken der Resilienz am IIASA," *BEHEMOTH-A Journal on Civilisation* 7, no. 2 (2014): 17.
9 The term resilience was used as a starting point to inquire into how systems were able to absorb catastrophic disturbance and still maintain the primary relationships between populations within a given environmental setting. (In this respect, see C. S. Holling, "Resilience and stability of ecological systems," *Annual review of ecology and systematics* 4, no. 1 [1973]: 14–15) The term was coined by the Canadian research team, with its project leader Crawford Holling, which at the same time initiated budworm research at the IIASA. Current research that reframed Canadian

The Canadian ecosystems context in the making of Applied Systems Analysis (1965–1973)

Nowadays primarily understood as a diplomatic tool for solving international scientific and political problems,[10] ASA was developed at IIASA during an experimental research phase from 1973. At that moment, the institute recruited scientists from IIASA's NMO's who had various disciplinary backgrounds. The decision to include budworm modelers from Canada complemented IIASA's prioritization of projects that fulfilled the guidelines of East-West cooperation for advancing management methodologies.

In Canada, the political dimension of budworm population growth had significantly increased after World War II and regained importance in the 1970s. The budworm pest outbreak received extensive press coverage and sparked public debate, as it perturbed not only forest systems but also political futures. The spruce budworm increase was so intense that it was not just an economic threat to the Canadian forest industry. The drastic increase enticed reporters to title the budworm North America's "biological time bomb"[11] and compare the danger to a change from "Mongolian modesty to Shanghai-like extremes."[12] The conventional basic budworm management option was the spraying of aerial insecticide, mostly using the chemical insecticide DDT. This led at first to great successes in tackling cyclic defoliation of trees. The goal of spraying was to achieve a budworm-free environment, and the main challenges in reaching their objective of a stable budworm-free forest system were linked to technological advances in improving aerial spraying and a coherent budworm population statistics. At the same time, however, the spraying policy induced widespread, long-term negative effects for broader ecological systems, mammals, and humans alike. Spraying did not even prevent an unexpected long-term budworm increase. The budworm

---

Budworm Research can be seen in W Neil Adger, "Resilience implications of policy responses to climate change," *Wiley Interdisciplinary Reviews: Climate Change* 2, no. 5 (2011): 757–766; Thomas Tanner, "Livelihood resilience in the face of climate change," *Nature Climate Change* 5, no. 1 (2015): 23; Peter C Perdue, "Ecologies of Empire: From Qing Cosmopolitanism to Modern Nationalism," *Cross-Currents: East Asian History and Culture Review* 2, no. 2 (2013): 399.

10 For a nuanced contemporary discussion and US evaluation of East-West scientific exchange, see: Genevieve J. Knezo, "U.S. Scientists Abroad: An Examination of Major Programs for Nongovernmental Scientific Exchange, *Science, Technology, and American Diplomacy* Volume 2 (1977): 873–1035.

11 Time Magazine, "Environment: Battling the Budworm," *Time Magazine*, no. 80 (April 1975): 15.

12 A. Nikiforuk, *Empire of the Beetle: How Human Folly and a Tiny Bug Are Killing North America's Great Forests* (Greystone Books, 2011), 197.

pest and the ecological impact of the traditional management response triggered widespread public debates between 1950 and 1980, wherein the biologist Rachel Carson's 1962 environmental pamphlet "Silent Spring" was becoming its flagship.[13] Concerning the management options for budworms, she stated that "wherever there [were] great forests, modern methods of insect control threaten[ed] the fishes inhabiting the streams in the shelter of trees".[14] Carson's publications on the interdependence of ecosystem's actors are crucial to the understanding of changes in forest management in North America.[15] Her ecosystems approach dismantled a too-simplistic approach of forest planners that were sticking to conventional forms of decision making, such as the above noted remedy of intensified chemical spraying.[16] For Carson, forest managers urgently needed to re-consider the needs of fishes, mammals, and other natural predators of the budworm. After a fierce debate about the environmental impact of spraying, DDT was banned in 1967, while other chemical products continued to persist as a management option for aerial spraying.[17] Nevertheless, with or without DDT, the spraying option became extremely expensive. In the 1970s, the pulp and paper industry desired to move away from spraying as an all-encompassing solution.[18] The industry and political authorities of the regions looked for better and more (cost-) efficient alternatives. This led, for instance, to initiatives such as the well-funded budworm research programs in the Canadian research community in the Maritimes Forest Research Center (MFRC) or in the Institute of Resource Ecology (IRE) at the University of British Columbia. Both institutes launched initiatives for computerizing environmental simulation models. They placed parameters and systems into a prognostic calculation tool that would inform the researcher about the current state of a forest environment and help her to deduce knowledge of actual and predicted forest system behavior. The Canadian budworm models and the subsequent experience in forest systems analysis induced the IIASA administration to approach the Canadian group to provide them with methods and experience from their specific field (they had

---

[13] Peter C Perdue, "Ecologies of Empire: From Qing Cosmopolitanism to Modern Nationalism," *Cross-Currents: East Asian History and Culture Review* 2, no. 2 (2013): 400.
[14] Rachel Carson, *Silent spring* (Houghton Mifflin Harcourt, 2002), 136.
[15] Perdue, "Ecologies of Empire: From Qing Cosmopolitanism to Modern Nationalism": 400.
[16] Linda Nash, "Un Siècle Toxique. L'émergence de la 'santé environnementale" in *Histoire des sciences et des savoirs : Le siècle des technosciences*, Dominique Pestre and Christophe Bonneuil, vol. 3, Science ouverte référence (Paris: Seuil, 2015), 154–155.
[17] See Donella H. Meadows and Diana Wright, *Thinking in systems: A* primer (Chelsea Green Publishing, 2008), 93.
[18] Ibid.

mainly been active in New Brunswick, Canada) for exposure to more diverse real-world situations within a similar institutional and environmental setting.[19]

How a Canadian research group shaped the IIASA methodology between 1973 and 1976.

During the summer of 1973, staff members of IIASA organized several international conferences in Baden, a small village near Vienna to decide upon IIASA's methodology of systems analysis and to debate about the selection of relevant applied projects that matched concerns of its national member organizations. In preparation for these conferences, the early IIASA members, such as Myron Fiering, a civil engineer from Harvard University, or IIASA director Howard Raiffa, worried about the composition of IIASA researchers and the research planning that primarily assembled statisticians, computer experts or people with a systems-theoretic orientation and lacked natural scientists as for example biologists or chemists.[20] Therefore, the research on the budworm proved to be especially attractive, for as an issue mainly related to the spheres of ecology and biology it allowed scientists to extend and study the field of policy analysis and decision theory that gave it the appearance of a non-political endeavor – "through the focus on a classical ecosystem problem."[21] Subsequently, the first Environment and Ecology group took up its work at IIASA in October 1973, its aim being to improve the budworm systems model and the development of IIASA's ASA methodology in general. Crawford Holling from the University of British Columbia was persuaded by IIASA's director Howard Raiffa to come to IIASA and improve the tools of IIASA's applied systems analysis. Holling's group that travelled to Laxenburg was composed of Dixon Jones, an engineer and ecosystems simulation expert, William Clark, who was an ecosystems expert with a doctorate in ecological epidemic ecosystems, and programmer Zafar Rashid, a trained biochemist. Holling was formally assigned project leader of what became

---

19 W.C. Clark, D.D. Jones, and C.S. Holling, *Lessons for Ecological Policy Design: A Case Study of Ecosystem Management (RR-80–002)*, IIASA Research Report (Reprint) (IIASA, Laxenburg, Austria, 1979): 4.
20 Harvard University Archives, "Letter from Myron Fiering to Howard Raiffa (25 April 1973)" in *Papers of Myron B. Fiering (14498) Box 1 of 9, Folder Vienna [1972–1973]* (Harvard University Archives)
21 Harvard University Archives, "Clark's Summary of Budworm Workshop: Regional Ecosystem Management," in *Papers of Myron B. Fiering (14498) Box 2 of 9, Clark's Summaries* (Harvard University Archives): 1.

known as the Resources and Environment Project (REN) at IIASA, where in subsequent years he promoted the budworm methodology and its related resilience concepts.[22]

Holling and the IIASA administration were convinced that the budworm case could demonstrate an innovative methodology to measure systems and more efficiently evaluate the factors of systems that trigger the preconditions for planning and policy-managing frameworks. The input of the Canadian budworm research team implied that IIASA should work with techniques that accommodated the non-linear dynamic evolution of ecosystems, taking into account the oscillation and complexity of behaviors of even the smallest organisms that may harm the entire functioning of an environmental system and its management.[23] In respect to the interdisciplinary approach by IIASA, REN's budworm project epitomized a systems analysis with elements from natural and social sciences, and constituted a bridge between various disciplinary specialists at IIASA and also between researchers from the East and West. On many occasions, the spruce budworm model represented or fulgurated IIASA's and the national member organizations' desire to provide optimized and unified approaches of systems in order to support policymakers with a handbook for coping with issues of public and economic concern about large industrialized ecosystems, and yet focus on "preventing unemployment in the forest industry, or in making the industry more profitable."[24] The budworm served its purpose as a "demonstration case of broad interest to all countries coping with serious insect pest problems",[25] and represented one particular approach to ecosystems thinking that was integrated as a centerpiece of state-of-the-art large-scale optimization techniques.[26]

The continuation of the budworm project contributed in particular to the interdisciplinary exchange between IIASA's ecology and methodology projects and facilitated the testing and discovery of "novel methods for novel systems."[27] The IIASA recruited researchers to explore how to improve systems analysis results

---

[22] Clark, Jones, and Holling, *Lessons for Ecological Policy Design: A Case Study of Ecosystem Management (RR-80–002)*: 3.

[23] D.D. Jones, *Explorations in Parameter Space*, IIASA Working Paper (IIASA, Laxenburg, Austria, 1973), 1.

[24] Holling quoted in IIASA, *Annual Report 1975*: 9.

[25] C.S. Holling, *Program for Ecology and Environment Project*, IIASA Working Paper (IIASA, Laxenburg, Austria, 1973), 3.

[26] Ibid.

[27] C.S. Holling, "A journey of discovery" (Personal Memoir, December 2006, Final Draft), 19, last modified March 15, 2018, https://www.resalliance.org/files/Buzz_Holling_Memoir_2006_a_-journey_of_discovery_buzz_holling.pdf

for policy-makers and planners. Among them was George Dantzig, who became an eminent authority in the field of systems analysis and operations research. Dantzig was widely known for his work in statistics, operations research and mathematical programming. Since the mid 1940s he elaborated methods for the optimization of systems, that were used in the military, e. g. by illustratively calculating the most efficient and cost-effective diets for soldiers, or later, for public, industrial, and defense planning purposes.[28] He worked at IIASA between 1973 and 1974 with the goal of reducing the complexity of model worlds used in relation to the Canadian budworm. IIASA's systems analysis was intended to bring ecosystems models to realizable political decisions, so that policy-makers could understand and control the most relevant elements of a system and plan a decision by knowing its respective impact. In Dantzig's opinion, a "curse of dimensionality"[29] prevailed in large-scale ecosystems which, on the contrary, needed a more synthetic approach. As a result of Dantzig's expertise members of the ecology group could plausibly argue how the budworm project led to a simplification and optimization in methodology. REN evolved, as "[...] an astonishing group of outstanding people gave their all to something as silly as a budworm [...]."[30] This methodological simplification to an applicable model for the budworm was still praised forty-one years later. For instance Harvard Business School professor Daniel E. Bell lauded Dantzig's achievements when he endorsed the ecologists' idea for improving planning and decision making. After reducing, compressing and formalizing the most pertinent management options, they were later ranked according to the preferences of the concerned stakeholders and discussed with forest experts in subsequent workshops and training sessions.[31] The optimized methodology for management models continued to generate debates in the REN and the Methodology group respectively.

Since 1976, in the aftermath of the budworm project, it seems that IIASA's role as a clearing house of systems analysis "[...] influenced the analytic perspective for IIASA's research planning, including systems analysis of freshwater and

---

28 The fellow scientist at the IIASA Myron Fiering referred to Dantzig's "elaboration of the simplex method" that provided elements of linear programming and systems analysis that "nobody had imagined before." See in this respect M.B.Fiering, "Why is the new algorithm better than simplex method and ellipsoid method?" in *Papers of Myron B. Fiering (14498) Box 7 of 9*, (Harvard University Archives).
29 Winkler was Dantzig's PhD student back then. Besides his appointment at IIASA, he worked for the newly founded Systems Optimization Laboratory (SOL) at Stanford University.
30 G.A. Norton and C.S. Holling, *Proceedings of a Conference on Pest Management, 25–29 October 1976*, IIASA Collaborative Paper (IIASA, Laxenburg, Austria, September 1977): 87.
31 IIASA, "Howard Raiffa Session. David E. Bell: Policy, probability and preference," last modified March 15, 2018, https://www.youtube.com/watch?v=AP4KnjXajfo.

oceanic fisheries, terrestrial grazing, other insect pest, and tropical and temperate forest ecosystems."[32] Until the beginning of the 1980s, research of single insect management methodology was integrated in different sections within IIASA projects. IIASA persisted in standardizing and regulating the transfer of models, concepts or realities[33] from its own international research groups and other national or international institutes that dealt with the effects and control of ecosystems problems. The result of reduction and compression led to precisely formulated strategies of how to standardize applied systems analysis: since the evolution from the focus on the budworm, REN proposed crafting simplified ecological "modules" that could be used interchangeably within numerous ecological problems. For Holling, smaller modules would significantly facilitate and simplify policymaking processes. Holling's approach, which went so far as to establish an entire library collection of modules, mirrored IIASA's early research planning objective for 1975 to craft and communicate usable knowledge, and also to expand it to "significant economic problems throughout the whole of the north eastern part of North America, the Pacific region, the USSR, forested regions of Europe (e.g. Poland) and Japan."[34] The module library symbolized IIASA's eagerness to convey "information in forms which are understandable and controllable by the various role players in the decision process."[35] Regional problems, pest outbreaks or any other occurring perturbation of complex systems were condensed and synthesized for more general use due to their "universal functions for linking these events."[36]

The budworm turned into IIASA's demonstration tool (1978–1980)

Subsequently, the budworm experience led to a more general approach of ecosystems thinking that was illustrated by the publication of the widely known compendium "Adaptive Environmental Assessment and Management" (hereafter: AEAM) in 1978. AEAM revived Holling's module idea and provided techni-

---

32 Clark, Jones, and Holling, *Lessons for Ecological Policy Design: A Case Study of Ecosystem Management (RR-80–002)*: 3.
33 Ibid.: 6.
34 Harvard University Archives, "A Case Study of Ecosystem Management," in *Papers of Myron B. Fiering (14498) Box 1 of 9, Folder: NSF [National Science Foundation] Documents, 1975–1977]* (Harvard University Archives).
35 Holling, *Development and Use of Ecological Modules in Resource Development Simulation*: 7.
36 Ibid.: 5.

ques for a set of systems, composed by "packages of techniques [...] available for broad applicability to any problem of single species management, whether of pests of crops or of man or of populations of fish or wildlife."[37] As the main editors, Holling and Clark noted that the budworm model helped to create educational tools in management and the organization of "model gaming sessions."[38] Therefore, the budworm project gave new directions to the implementation of "nontraditional communication formats"[39] for communication with affected parties, including managers, policymakers and the public. Since then, IIASA has launched education and training programs and sequences of "participatory workshops" on a national and international level,[40] using a bottom-up approach to educate participants on the key principles of ecosystems modeling for policymaking. AEAM was used in a broader management context, whereas IIASA "mix[ed] representatives and customers" and operated as a mediator between diverging perceptions within the spectrum of different management options. AEAM was regarded as an important framework for dealing with problems using ASA, for instance in 1977, when IIASA invited representatives from the UK Ministry of the Environment to learn the techniques of AEAM.[41] The strategic dissemination of budworm systems analysis within quick and cheap group modeling sessions at the IIASA was intended to equip managers of ecosystems with a concept they could use to obtain more efficient and controllable feedback, based on addressing the adaption to future events and unexpected turbulence well in advance of their occurrence. Since its appearance in the literature of AEAM, where the budworm model served as an example in slide show presentations, it was continuously used in the context of turbulence theory in forest ecosystems in general, and thereafter, in presentations delivered to demonstrate how to manage complex systems with systems thinking; in regard to forestry with specific responses deduced from budworm-optimized decision models.[42]

---

[37] Holling, *Summary of Budworm Workshop*.
[38] Clark, Jones, and Holling, *Lessons for Ecological Policy Design: A Case Study of Ecosystem Management (RR-80–002)*: 29.
[39] Ibid.: 1.
[40] Ibid.: 45–46.
[41] IIASA Archives, "M.W. Holdgate, Annex B: Talk delivered to IIASA senior staff and participants in workshop adaptive impact assessment on 14 June 1977," in *Resources and Environ. Conferences and Workshops 1976–1977* (IIASA Archives, June 1977): 2.
[42] IIASA Archives, "Conference Agenda, 21.5.1977," in *Resources and Environ. Conferences and Workshops 1976–1977* (IIASA Archives, June 1977).

Part 2. The attempts at East-West knowledge circulation (1975–1980)

In this vein, it is crucial to keep in mind how IIASA's entire institutional structure possessed strong links with a national policy-making milieu through the participating national member organizations and the representatives and invitees from academies of sciences from each nation state. Each of the academies of sciences sent researchers or policy experts to IIASA conferences that worked at some stage with governmental agencies and ministries. The planning methods and debates about how to transfer budworm knowledge to other environmental problems – and how to orientate applied systems analysis- were occurring in debates held by IIASA members during bi-annual IIASA Council meetings, where the IIASA director was required to report on the state of IIASA research. The example of the USSR's Academy of Sciences shows the close relationship with policy making in the environment through the organization of common expert panels for each policy relevant subject.[43] The USSR was strongly supportive of obtaining methods of systems analysis for the nation's planning processes in the 1970s via IIASA, notably in the systems sciences and computer sciences departments located in the facilities of the USSR's Academy of Sciences.[44]

A common interest for Applied Systems Analysis for planning purposes in the West and East

More than the integration of the budworm model and its contextual origin for IIASA's systems analysis, it was the particular East-West infrastructure that motivated historians to capture the "performativity"[45] of scientific East-West cooperation. Studies about East-West bridge-building structures discussed the making of IIASA in the wider context of US President Lyndon Johnson's "Great Society programs,"[46] or a "global New Deal" initiative that would have extended scien-

---

[43] Eglė Rindzevičiūtė, *The Power of Systems: How Policy Sciences Opened Up the Cold War World*, 17.
[44] Ibid., 85
[45] Eglė Rindzevičiūtė, *The Power of Systems: How Policy Sciences Opened Up the Cold War World* (New York: Cornell University Press, 2016), 23.
[46] Agatha C Hughes and Thomas P Hughes, *Systems, Experts, and Computers. The Systems Approach in Management and Engineering, World War II and After* (Cambridge, Mass.: MIT Press, 2000), 7.

tific, technological, and managerial innovation towards the stabilization of international problems. IIASA was seen as acting according to US interests in maintaining global security through the securing of a common standard of science and environmental sciences in particular.[47] For commentators on IIASA, its East-West focus drew on the Johnson administration's idea that "[...] scientific collaboration would be the solution of large-scale problems common to advanced economies."[48] From this perspective, supported among others by US physicist and scientific adviser William Nierenberg, IIASA provided a joint forum for different societies to "expose their methodologies in dealing with [common] problems,"[49] mainly from the viewpoint that knowledge was transferable from one side to another. The content of systems analysis was secondary to the diplomatic advances made through IIASA, and often, Western narratives dominated the historical discourse. This Western perspective on East-West bridge-building was recently expanded with more integrative Eastern perspectives by the historian Elke Seefried. Seefried elaborated the ways in which IIASA's research and its central elements of studies of systems, structures, and feedback loops, reflected the USSR's ideological position of Marxism-Leninism, which advocated the study of causal relations of phenomena. The USSR's homegrown interest in systems analysis and its support for IIASA was at least as important as newly introduced Western systems analysis theories[50] and reinforced the trend of East-West "governmental elites [to] embrace the same scientific methods [...] during the Cold War."[51]

---

[47] In this respect see Ronald E. Doel and Kristine C. Harper, "Prometheus Unleashed," *Osiris* 21, no. 1 (2006): 83; Hughes and Hughes, *Systems, Experts, and Computers. The Systems Approach in Management and Engineering, World War II and After*, 1; David R Jardini, "Out of the blue yonder: The transfer of systems thinking from the Pentagon to the great society, 1961–1965," in *Systems, experts, and computers: the systems approach in Management and Engineering, World War II and After* (Cambridge, Mass.: MIT Press, 2000), 327; Thomas Schwartz, "Moving Beyond the Cold War: The Johnson Administration, Bridge-Building and Détente," in *Beyond the Cold War: Lyndon Johnson and the New Global Challenges of the 1960s*, F.J. Gavin and M.A. Lawrence (New York: Oxford University Press, 2014).
[48] Jay Hauben, "Across an Ideological Divide: IIASA and IIASANET," in *Computer Networks, the Internet and Netizens*" Symposium at the 22nd International Congress of History of Science (July 2005).
[49] William A Nierenberg, "NATO science programs: origins and influence," *Technology in Society* 23, no. 3 (2001): 372.
[50] Elke Seefried, Zukünfte: *Aufstieg und Krise der Zukunftsforschung 1945–1980*, vol. 106 (Oldenbourg: De Gruyter, 2015), 191–92; In this respect see also Rindzevičiūtė, *The Power of Systems: How Policy Sciences Opened Up the Cold War World*, 143.
[51] Rindzevičiūtė, *The Power of Systems: How Policy Sciences Opened Up the Cold War World*, 2.

What seems evident when following the above noted historical accounts is that for both the Eastern and the Western member organizations, the standardization of systems analysis became the binding element behind the building of East-West cooperation. The systems approach to planning correlated with the *realpolitik* of the member states' foreign offices during the Cold War. Within IIASA's East-West prism, the Canadian budworm research project was undoubtedly attractive: it involved a group that followed the perturbations and future behaviors of large-scale systems through a small intrusive element, such as the budworm. The budworm model thus provided an ideal type of how to measure and respond to perturbation, while it could also figure as a non-political prototype for computer systems models that provided a controllable, testable and dynamic approach towards future systems behavior. Moreover, as a result, analysts would provide decision-making bodies with ready-made frameworks that facilitated the exchange of methods and techniques. Was this a perfect match for science and policy-making? At least for the participating member organizations and for the IIASA staff, the budworm set standards regarding how far "[IIASA] could go in developing a coherent science of ecological management"[52] and how to arrange and extend East-West research into energy, water, ecology, urban, computer science, industry, bio-medicine, decision analysis or large-scale organizations.[53]

Difficult beginnings, organizational change and East-West knowledge exchange

The joint making of systems analysis was not without friction. Two years after the budworm research was launched at IIASA, Holling presented a brief account of its successes and pitfalls, noting that cross-cultural and international interactions had not been as effective as he had intended.[54] Holling remained critical of the USSR's participation in the analysis of ecosystems. According to him, USSR computer models in 1975 still lacked the economic, political and human behavioral indicators that were necessary to propose optimized policy design. In addition, he voiced skepticism about the strong Soviet focus on descriptive

---

52 Roger E. Levien, "Systems Analysis in an International Setting," in *Record Group 1.8/Project Files /Box 164, Folder 7878: International Institute for Applied Systems Analysis, Supplementary Material 1975–1977* (The Rockefeller Foundation Archives, 1975): 8.
53 IIASA, *Annual Report 1973*: xi.
54 IIASA Archives, "C. S. Holling, Proposed Activities Ecology/Environment at IIASA after 1975," in *DI- Resources and Environ. Core (-December 1978)* (IIASA, June 1975): 3.

"biological and optimal control laws that seem rather abstract and impractical,"[55] even though he admitted the efficiency of their compromise for ready-to-use models "in a context appropriate for their country [...]."[56] On the basis of these criticisms, the budworm modeling at first remained a merely Canadian endeavor, even though the methodology influenced IIASA's basic methodological premises.

The situation changed significantly in late 1975, when East-West cooperation was given new impetus by Roger Levien's debut as the second IIASA director. Levien had extensively studied the development of systems analysis in the Soviet Union at the RAND Corporation, where he reviewed a wide range of Russian literature on systems analysis. RAND was a US-American think tank that worked with systems analysis in order to solve planning issues for the US-military and defense operations and later expanded its research program to include modeling policy scenarios for public policy planning. Based on his experience in frameworks for systems modelling at RAND, Levien understood the prestige attributed to studies of systems and computers by the USSR from the mid-1950s on, while the same amount of enthusiasm was lacking in the United States.[57] When Levien was appointed director at IIASA, he introduced a dichotomous research matrix for IIASA's long-term planning. He did this by dividing research into global and universal issues, thus supporting the inclusion of heterogeneous research interests in applied systems analysis from both the East and West.

The focus on planning options and the focus on management problems in regional, national and international spheres newly increased the international recognition of ASA. However, Levien's matrix required a clear standard of ASA methodology that was crucial for both universal and global research areas. In this respect, the general conference on ASA that took place with participants from both East and West in 1976 focused on the standardization of methodology. During the conference, the budworm experience once more appeared as an exemplary case of ASA. In his introduction to the purposes of ASA, Levien referred to the budworm project as an ideal type that proved how the added value of methodological work of IIASA formalized into applicable management principles. He repeatedly alluded to Dantzig's "optimizer" method that condensed the highest-ranking forest policy options. Levien metaphorically compared the optimizer to a brain as it was able, as a systems machine, to understand and pri-

---

55 IIASA Archives, "Memorandum from C. S. Holling o W. Bossert, A. Bykov, W. Häfele, H. Raiffa," in *DI – Resources and Environ. Core (-December 1978)* (IIASA Archives, June 1975): 3.
56 Ibid.: p.s.
57 R. Levien and M. E. Maron, *Cybernetics and its development in the Soviet Union, RM-4156-PR* (RAND Corporation, 1964): 14

oritize the values and perceptions of affected humans in the forest system; a cybernetic device that could even compare and determine feasible compromises of policy options for long-term planning.[58]

Levien's advocacy of the budworm model's optimization gained access to an even wider audience when it reached the science section in the *New York Times* that described IIASA's East-West joint effort against budworms as a new form of counterintuitive management, where "'[o]ptimization' in terms of production, profit or some such factor [was] partially sacrificed in favor of [...] stability."[59] At the above noted international conference for ASA in 1976, Holling returned to IIASA from his Canadian home institution and delivered a speech about the successes in forest and pest management in Canada by applying IIASA's methodology. His speech was seconded with a presentation by Wesley K. Foell, who introduced IIASA's newly planned East-West centered environmental modelling projects. Foell indicated how IIASA's methodological experience from budworm modelling influenced contemporary national and cross-regional projects in Wisconsin (USA), in the *Rhône-Alpes* region (France), or in the GDR, while IIASA developed novel networks with other international research facilities with experiences in optimization and centralized planning processes.[60] For example, the *Institut für Energetik* in Leipzig. Holling and Foell's introductions both provided several theoretical frameworks for subsequent state-of-the-art case studies of IIASA's staff, large-scale regions which possessed a long tradition of social and environmental planning such as the Tennessee Valley Project (TVA) in the USA and the analysis of the Bratsk-Limsk Complex in the USSR.[61]

The conference also attracted well-known scientists from the East, including Leonid Kantorovich from the All-Union Research Institute for Systems Studies in Moscow, and Yuri Ermoliev from the Institute of Cybernetics in Kiev. Both sat in IIASA's auditorium and participated in the debate.[62] These visits were not coin-

---

58 Levien, "Systems Analysis in an International Setting": 14–15.
59 Walter Sullivan, "A New Systems Analysis Helps to Fight Budworm," *New York Times* CXXV, nos. 43,234 (1976): 36.
60 IIASA Archives, "Council Minutes, Tuesday 25 Nov, 9:20 am," in *Council, Fifth Meeting, November 24–26 1975* (IIASA Archives, June 1975): 11.
61 The Rockefeller Foundation Archives, "Program of the IIASA Conference 76'," in *Record Group 1.3, Projects areas, 103 International Organizations, IIASA Energy Supplementary Material Drafts, Box 8, Folder 50–103* (The Rockefeller Foundation Archives, 1976).
62 The Rockefeller Foundation Archives, "Strengthening the International Interdisciplinary Activities of the American Academy of Arts and Sciences: Support for the IIASA/Appendix B," in *Record Group 1.3 (FA388), Projects areas, Series 103 International Organizations, Box 1164 Folder 7874, IIASA* (The Rockefeller Foundation Archives, 1982): 10.

cidences but were preceded by complex organizational arrangements. The invitations to Eastern researchers were issued during trips by Geoff Norton from Imperial College, London, in early 1976. Norton played a key role via the British NMO in bringing researchers from the USSR to the IIASA and supported the establishment of unified knowledge among existing pest management knowledge circles. He also reported on research and the needs of countries such as Yugoslavia, Japan, and Poland, and traveled to the USSR with IIASA member Alexandr Bazykin from the USSR's Academy of Sciences, seeking East European groups to hold presentations at the IIASA 1976 conference.[63]

Among Eastern participation in the conference, Alexandr Bazykin was the leading figure in improving relations between East-West ecosystems research. Bazykin was among the first Soviet scientists who directly cooperated with Holling's environmental group at IIASA in 1975, providing mathematical improvements of Holling's systems models and Dantzig's reduced management models. Bazykin's participation established a new focus at REN, striving to measure more precisely the ecological boundaries of budworm-endangered ecosystems. Bazykin continued to work on principles that originated from mathematical (so-called bifurcation) theories that were explored in the USSR in the 1950s[64] which subsequently influenced the work of the REN group. He complemented IIASA's forest systems research with precise mathematical formulas, novel indicators of dynamic behaviors of variables in environmental systems, and with an elaborated, well-received approach to integrating these systems boundary evaluations into existing ecosystems models.[65] Bazykin represented the most important link to the cybernetic research culture from the USSR and the ecological approach at the IIASA. He had been leading the laboratory of Mathematical Problems in Biology in the USSR's Academy of Sciences Computing Center, and had already organized symposia on mathematical modelling of complex biological systems in the USSR. Due to his work in areas such as genetics, theory of

---

[63] IIASA Archives, "Memorandum from Levien- Conversation with Buzz Holling today (24 May 1976)," in *Resources and Environ. Conferences and Workshops 1976–1977* (IIASA Archives, June 1977).
[64] Application oriented bifurcation theory was explored at the USSR Academy of Sciences, among others, by A M. Molchanov, A. E. Bazykin and A.I. Khibnik. See in this respect Yuri Kuznetzov, *Elements of Applied Bifurcation Theory* (New York: Springer, 1995), preface.
[65] Alexander D Bazykin, *Nonlinear dynamics of interacting populations*, vol. 11 (World Scientific, 1998), xiv. After working on IIASA's Ecology project, Bazykin continued to work as a vice chairman of the Section of Mathematical Modeling and System Analysis within the USSR's Academy of Sciences Council on the Biosphere. The groundwork prepared at IIASA proved even more important when Bazykin became Deputy Minister in Gorbachev's government under the Minister of Natural Research Management and Environmental Protection, Nikolai Vorontsov.

evolution, ecology, and mathematical modelling of population and ecosystems, he was considered "one of the founders of that branch of science in Russia".[66]

Eastern participation at IIASA was further enhanced through a follow-up international conference in autumn 1976, where the IIASA launched the "Pest Management Network". It was a platform that facilitated debates in member organizations and integrated information for making a state-of-the-art budworm modeling and programming handbook, which distributed scientific debates and results within a so-called "IIASA Pest Management Series."[67] The annex of the conference report recorded 70 participants of the Pest Management Network, both from Eastern and Western research institutes.[68] The increasing number of workshops and international conferences from 1976 was related to Levien's plan to reinforce IIASA's influence in management knowledge and the establishment of more nuanced decision making, through "IIASA's potential as a catalytic agent and clearinghouse".[69] From 1976 and with the support of Levien's input as IIASA director, IIASA sought to increase the number of Eastern scholars, something that was visible in the employment of mathematical ecologists from the Soviet Union who participated in the generalization of applied systems analysis in the USSR's academies of sciences. [70]

From a Canadian endeavor to East-West water resources research

In 1976, IIASA expanded its budworm research and intensified East-West cooperation, in particular with the USSR, the FRG, the GDR, France, Poland and the USA.[71] The modeling principles of the budworm model were transferred to new projects. The Pacific salmon fishery and river management project included territories in Japan, the USA, and the USSR.[72] The budworm model was crucial in framing systems knowledge of how to measure, manage, and control the robust-

---

[66] Bazykin, Alexander D. *Nonlinear Dynamics of Interacting Populations*. (Vol. 11. Singapore, World Scientific, 1998), xiii.
[67] Norton and Holling, *Proceedings of a Conference on Pest Management, 25–29 October, 1976*: 1.
[68] Ibid.: 345–349.
[69] Levien, "Systems Analysis in an International Setting": 17.
[70] Ibid.
[71] C.S. Holling, *Summary of Budworm Workshop*, IIASA Working Paper (IIASA, Laxenburg, Austria: IIASA, 1974): 9.
[72] IIASA, *Annual Report 1976* (IIASA, 1977): 5.

ness of environmental systems endangered by prior human mismanagement. The desire to control and stabilize oceanic fish exploitation and the experiences in fishery management displayed parallels with the needs and worries of forest managers in Canada.[73] Between April 1976 and December 1977, IIASA organized ten international conferences and workshops on how to improve water resources research.[74] While the budworm project was analyzed in depth in order to extract its novel methodology, the applied projects with their new thematic needed new regionally experienced researchers, who were recruited for IIASA soon after the Canadian budworm project ended. The new composition of the Resources and Environment (REN) project at IIASA in 1976 demonstrates how regional forest ecosystems experts were replaced by water resources research experts from the East and the West, improving the equilibrium of researchers from both sides. After the Canadian team left Laxenburg, newly appointed researchers stayed at IIASA for shorter terms, but at least for six months. At that time, Alexandr Bazykin still assisted in the transition of the Resources and Environment Area, and continued to integrate the development of mathematical modeling in ecology and resources management. After the experimental phase, in which Dantzig co-developed Holling's computerized models, and with Holling and Dantzig's respective returns to Canada and the US, IIASA focused on maintenance of outputs and results of its decision-modeling methodology that it was understood could be easily re-used by regional experts.

The substantive achievement of the budworm experience was to de-contextualize environmental systems knowledge that first concerned forest agencies and the pulp and paper industry, and transferred the methodology to other environmental problems such as water or climatic pollution with different systems boundaries and a different social and political context. Through new thematic orientation, the approach was maintained whereby every environmental system could be categorized, systematized, and modelled. Each system could be reduced to key variables from which would originate a range of feasible scenarios for a decision maker. The transfer from forest management based on budworm perturbation to water resources management was fulfilled as a result of scientists arriving at the IIASA after 1975. They did not start working from scratch, but added their experience to pre-existing approaches. The water resources and fishery project and its participating researchers provide an insight into the interconnectedness of the IIASA within the national academies of sciences, governmental

---

73 Levien, "Systems Analysis in an International Setting": 10.
74 IIASA Archives, "Listing of Conferences," in *Resources and Environ. Conferences and Workshops 1976–1977* (IIASA Archives, June 1977).

agencies, and a broader scientific and political elite, either from the East or the West. Zdzislaw Kaczmarek, for example, was a water resource specialist from Poland and had worked as Deputy Minister to the Ministry of Science, Higher Education and Technology of the government of Poland before he became a project leader at IIASA.[75] Ilya Gouevsky, a well-known Bulgarian cybernetician took over responsibility for the planning and operating of water demand at IIASA. Roman Kulikowski, former director of the Computation Center of the Polish Academy of Sciences, joined IIASA to improve the entangled modeling of social and environmental systems[76]. Further Eastern members of the water resources group included Todor Popov, a Bulgarian macroeconomic lecturer and Director General for International Relations at the State Committee for Science, Technical Progress and Higher Education in Bulgaria. Popov also participated in IIASA's state-of-the-art encyclopedic research to collect the methodological work at IIASA.[77] Jürgen Schmidt participated at IIASA as a water quality management expert from the Institute of Water Resources in Berlin (GDR). He was the former head of the Laboratory for Water Biology and Chemistry; he elaborated methodologies for data processing in the fields of environmental protection and environmental engineering. András Szöllösi-Nagy, a Hungarian researcher, joined IIASA as an eminent water resources expert, with a focus on a joint European project for the application of systems analysis to problems in relation to the Tisza River Basin.[78]

The above listed researchers indicate IIASA's prioritization of recruiting applied regional researchers with policymaking experience that would integrate IIASA's early environmental systems thinking. Western scholars in water resource management confirm IIASA's tendency to prioritize regional experience, even in the organization of new methodological experiments. Wesley Foell from the USA became the leader of IIASA's methodology group. He started his career at Stanford, continued at MIT and later joined the EURATOM where he focused on the combination of nuclear reactor research and environmental impact of energy systems. Kirit Parikh, an Indian computer systems expert from the Indian

---

[75] After his stay at IIASA, Kaczmarek became Chief of the Polish Governmental Water Resources Program from 1976–1985.
[76] Kulikowski came with the experience from a PhD at the Moscow Electrotechnical Institute; when he left Poland, he had already been pursuing an international career as a visiting professor at Columbia University, New York, the UCLA Berkley and the University of Minnesota.
[77] See, for example, IIASA Archives, "Letter from Todor Popov to Ed Quade (5 April 1977)," in *Folder/Directorate-Survey Project (-1978)* (IIASA Archives, 1977).
[78] András Szöllösi-Nagy also was a member of the American Geophysical Union, until 2014, and was rector of the UNESCO-IHE Institute for Water Education.

Statistical Institute in Delhi, participated in modeling research with a focus on water management and energy policy.[79] The composition of Eastern and Western researchers mirrors IIASA's shift in recruitment priority to obtain a visible symmetry of Eastern and Western researchers as well as experts who would apply REN models to subjects that could be integrated in supporting member countries. Following the work conducted by Dantzig and Holling, the experimental methodological work was mostly considered completed. IIASA opted to broaden ecosystems research geographically as well as thematically, with the internationally relevant fields of water resources and energy systems research at its forefront.

Conclusion

The insights acquired through computerized modelling in budworm research not only led to the recognition (and quantification) of previous mismanagement in the tackling of the budworm pest in Canada, but through IIASA's international framework the continuing use of computerized models for decision-making in environmental management extended to more nuanced mathematical calculations and policy recommendations that were distributed internationally by researchers from the East and the West. The example of the moth-like budworm and its desires and needs saw it surpass human-induced conceptual limits. A focus on thresholds and the attempt to calculate the complexity of ecosystems after the budworm's pest outbreak became a trigger for the reinforcement of calculations of similar threshold levels, in fields and contexts that became relevant to East-West management sciences of IIASA-affiliated countries. The Canadian budworm methodology prescribed a consolidated pathway for IIASA and became a vivid example for the dissemination of ecosystems knowledge. 40 years later, when Holling drafted his autobiography in 2006,[80] he continued to highlight that the approach he and his team had followed had constituted a "kind of Kuhnian revolution."[81] The budworm models implemented a framework that inspired several IIASA member organizations to become acquainted with systems thinking and policy options deduced from the application of systems analysis. The development of formalized computer models (that Levien compared to the functioning of a "brain"), the economic calculation of environmen-

---

79 If not otherwise mentioned, all biographical data was taken from a small booklet about the IIASA staff published in 1976 by IIASA. See IIASA, *Annual Report 1976*.
80 Holling, "A journey of discovery."
81 Ibid.: Preface.

tal policy, or the design of policy strategies was developed subsequent to conventional measures such as DDT spraying being proven ineffective for coping with the reappearance of the budworm pest. The making of forest policies and the approach to management of the paper and pulp industry in Canada may have affected current approaches to systematizing environmental problems and the notion of being capable of governing and controlling ecosystems significantly.

A second conclusion reflects upon the budworm experience in respect to IIASA's management theory. The interdependent calculation and testing of forest systems and its actors, the wider ecological implication of timber production, or the changes within the paper and pulp industry due to the budworm pest in particular, posed questions about how to successfully establish coherent management principles due to the increase of new computerized calculations. The budworm case study reappeared in Howard Raiffa's lecture materials at Harvard Business School, and since the case study referred to the experience gained by a well-connected research collective that wished to include computerized technologies, international institutions and East-West diplomacy were considered necessary passage points in order to improve standards in planning and decision making. In modern management theory, there are subtle clues regarding which school of thought this form of management might be associated with. The knowledge gained at IIASA defined decision making within a framework deduced from an interdisciplinary and international division of labor; with models, workshops and international scientific and non-scientific conferences at its core. The experience constituted a shift from a planning focus on mere productivity and the making of simple machinery towards more flexible, computer-supported, and dynamic management options. These management options were considerably nuanced through the modelling of future environmental behavior and measures of the probability of its societal impact.[82] In hindsight, IIASA's approach to environmental management, its urge to computerize and simulate decision making of the complex budworm pest and the inclusion of dynamic optimization processes by Dantzig reflected a significant shift in the role of systems and their effect on planning and decision-making processes. The crafting of environmental knowledge systems was guided by a complex formula of international research of scholars, practitioners and policymakers within a "rapid movement of people

---

[82] IIASA's experience with alternative frameworks for systems management might point to novel insights in management theory, something that for the last three decades has been discussed as a shift towards a Post-Fordist conception that favored more flexible specializations of labor. In this respect, see: Michael J. Piore and Charles F. Sabel, *The second industrial divide: possibilities for prosperity* (New York: Basis Books, 1984), 263.

and resources in space, swiftly changing markets, production, and products"[83]. Holling's budworm approach was counterintuitive and provocative at the time, which underpinned a significant change in using scientific analysis as a guideline for policy making and management in the 1970s.

Finally, IIASA's activities around budworm research encouraged the continuation of exchanges in the environmental field between the East and the West. In 1985, during a symposium and planning meeting in Moscow, IIASA signed a collaboration agreement for monitoring environmental systems and strengthening international data exchange[84], just prior to the establishment of the Intergovernmental Panel on Climate Change (IPCC) in 1988. When IIASA directors Robert H. Pry and Peter de Janosi laid out IIASA's main results of 18 years of research before the US House of Representatives Subcommittee on Science and Technology in 1990, they noted that some of the most important projects at IIASA were studies of ecological management.[85] In the 1990s, IIASA's highly relevant modeling projects on inland lake environmental problems in the East and the West, including studies of Lake Balaton in Hungary, Lake Como in Italy or Lake Erie in the US and Canada,[86] pointed back to methodological origins derived from the study of the budworm pest. The budworm and the subsequent economic calculations and computerized models presented the key element for the systematization of common environmental and economic problems of industrialized countries of the East and West during the Cold War. According to the late biomathematician Carol M. Newton, the budworm project at IIASA was "indeed abstract theoretical work", but, as she claimed, it was "for the purpose of developing tools that subsequently could be applied to real complex problems"[87] that interested members

---

83 Emily Martin, "Fluid Bodies, Managed Nature," in *Remaking Realty: Nature at the Millenium*, ed. B. Braun and N. Castree (London and New York: Routledge, 1998), 76.
84 W. C. Clark and R. E. Munn, *Sustainable development of the biosphere* (Cambridge: Cambridge University Press / IIASA, 1986), v; furthermore, see Clark and Munn, *Sustainable development of the biosphere*, chapter 13.
85 See Robert Pry's contribution in United States Congress House Committee on Science and Technology, *U.S. participation in the International Institute for Applied Systems Analysis (IIASA): hearing before the Subcommittee on Natural Resources, Agriculture Research, and Environment and the Subcommittee on International Scientific Cooperation and the Subcommittee on Science, Research, and Technology of the Committee on Science, Space, and Technology, U.S. House of Representatives, One Hundred First Congress, second session, April 18, 1990*, 4 (U.S. Government Printing Office, 1990), 10.
86 Ibid.
87 C.M.Newton in Appendix G, *Statements on the IIASA*, The United States' Membership in the IIASA 1984, Russell Sage Foundation, Series 3 (Grant Files), Subgroup 2, Box 64, Folder 567.

in both the East and the West that desired to maintain, control and calculate stable environmental behavior.

Acknowledgements

I would like to thank Michaela Rossini from the IIASA Library, George E. Clark from the Harvard Library Archives, and the staff of the Rockefeller Foundation Archive Center for their generous support during my research in the archives. Many thanks also to Martina Leutoff for reviewing and correcting my idiosyncratic English.

Michel Christian
"It is not a Question of rigidly Planning Trade" UNCTAD and the Regulation of the International Trade in the 1970s

UNCTAD (United Nations Conference for Trade and Development) was founded following an international conference convened in Geneva in 1964 and subsequently every four years in a different location. In the 1970s it became a focal point for the discussion of world trade[1] in close connection with the demands for a New International Economic Order (NIEO) formulated at the UN by the developing countries with oil exporting countries as leaders. UNCTAD as well as NIEO aimed to reach a "structural adjustment" between developed and developing countries that would be more profitable to the latter.[2] However, once an essential forum where the world economy was hotly debated, UNCTAD has today lost its importance, to the point where even its past centrality has almost fallen into oblivion. In the 1980s and the 1990s, interest in UNCTAD declined dramatically, until it fell again within the scope of interest shown by historians in the 2000s, along with the NIEO.[3] Renewed interest came on the one hand from research into the origins of what came to be called "globalization" in the 1980s[4]

---

[1] Most of the studies on UNCTAD were completed in the 1970s by jurists or political science specialists, when the organization was at its zenith: see Georges Merloz, *La CNUCED. Droit International et Développement* (Bruxelles: Bruylant, 1980); Boualia Benamar, *La CNUCED et Le Nouvel Ordre économique International* (Paris: Université de droit, d'économie et de sciences sociales, 1984); Autar Krishan Koul,. *The legal framework of UNCTAD in world trade* (Leyden: A. W. Sijthoff, 1977) and Robert L. Rothstein, *Global Bargaining: UNCTAD and the Quest for a New International Economic Order*. Princeton, N.J.: Princeton University Press, 1979. See also the UN internal publication *The History of UNCTAD 1964–1984* (New York: United Nations Publication, 1985).
[2] Jagdish N. Bhagwati, *The New International Economic Order: The North-South Debate* (Cambridge, Mass.: MIT Press, 1983); Robert Cox, "Ideologies and the NIEO: Reflections on some recent litterature". *International Organization* 33, no. 2 (1979): 257-302; William Loehr and John P. Powelson, *Threat to development. pitfalls of the NIEO* (Boulder, Colo., 1983); Craig Murphy, *The Emergence of the NIEO Ideology* (Boulder, Colo.: Westview Press, 1984).
[3] For a more recent account see the special issue *Toward a History of the New International Economic Order. Humanity: An International Journal of Human Rights, Humanitarianism, and Development* 6, no. 1 (2015).
[4] Sönke Kunkel, "Contesting Globalization: The United Nations Conference on Trade and Development and the Transnationalization of Sovereignty," *International Organizations and Development, 1945–1990*, ed. Sönke Kunkel, Corinna Unger, and Mark Frey (Basingstoke: Palgrave Macmillan, 2014), 240–259; see more generally John Toye and Richard Toye. *The UN and Global

and on the other hand from a historiography critical of the current neoliberal consensus in economic thought, especially since the 2008 crisis.[5] Whether the attempt to build a new world trade order was successful is not the subject of the present chapter. Drawing mainly on internal sources of UNCTAD and especially on archival material held by its General Secretariat, it intends instead to raise the question of planning in the field of international trade, using the 1970s attempt to build new trade relations at the world level as an opportunity to observe how international trade was debated and how policies were elaborated in that field.

At first glance trade might seem unlikely to fall within the scope of planning. Resulting from the mutual consent of two parties, trading activities hardly seems to be fit to be 'planned' by anyone else other than by those parties. This first impression is reinforced by the notion of the market as it was defined by classical liberal economists. A 'market' can be considered as a space where parties exchange goods multilaterally according to prices resulting from supply and demand, thus creating its own spontaneous order that seems to exclude any form of planning. However, at the earliest in the late nineteenth century, among neo-classical economists, and at the latest in the mid twentieth century with the Keynesians, it became obvious that markets were not self-regulating institutions, and this opened the debate on the sort of action that could be taken toward markets and trade.

Drawing upon the belief that markets had to be regulated to be efficient, UNCTAD was founded as a response to the failure of the project of a World Trade Organization after the Conference of Havana in 1948 analyzed by Francine McKenzie in her chapter. It aimed at redefining world trade relations multilaterally to bring development to every country in the world, especially to the newly independent countries that appeared in the wake of Decolonization. As a result of that goal, the member countries sat in groups that were created according to their perceived level of development. However, UNCTAD also had to take into account different regional groupings as well as the Cold war divide, accommodating so-called different "economic and social systems" among its members. As a result country members did not vote individually but collectively, according to

---

Political Economy: Trade, Finance, and Development (Bloomington: Indiana University Press, 2004).

5 Johanna Bockman, "Socialist Globalization against Capitalist Neocolonialism: The Economic Ideas behind the New International Economic Order," *Humanity: An International Journal of Human Rights, Humanitarianism, and Development* 6, no. 1 (2015): 109–128.

their affiliation to "groups" that had been created to take into account development, regional as well as ideological factors (see table 1).[6]

Table 1: Groups at UNCTAD and their number of votes

	1964	1972
Group A (developing countries)	22	29
Group B (market economy developed countries)	18	21
Group C (Latin America)	19	11
Group D (socialist countries)	6	7
Total	55	68

Thanks to the diversity of ideological and economic models it had to deal with, UNCTAD offers a stimulating insight into different models of planning it strove to reconcile in order to reach its own goals as an international organization.

UNCTAD and the notion of "planning"

UNCTAD's executive organ was the Trade and Development Board, where every country member basically had a representative. When he made a statement before the Trade and Development Board in 1970, Secretary General Manuel Perez Guerrero very clearly set the terms of debate:

> It is not a question of rigidly planning trade, but rather of acting within a flexible framework, introducing dynamic incentives and disincentives which favor particular trends and avoid dangerous disruptions in terms of the International Development Strategy and, in addition, enable all countries to draw up their plans on more secure and harmonious bases.[7]

In that statement Perez Guerrero rejected any idea of planning international trade in a narrow sense but he did find it necessary to shape a frame for the market in order to steer the trade activity toward a desirable goal.

Michel Christian,"UNCTAD" in *Den Kalten Krieg vermessen. Über Reichweite und Alternativen einer binären Ordnung*, ed. Frank Reichherzer, Emmanuel Droit, Jan Hansen (forthcoming in 2018).

7 UNCTAD, TDB/A8015/Rev.1: Report of the Trade and Development Board (24 September 1969–13 October 1970), 1971, 234.

To understand what Perez-Guerrero meant, it must be recalled that UNCTAD's project rested on three principles. First, in contrast to the theory of modernization popularized by W. Rostow, UNCTAD's founders saw the many countries of the world not through their individual path but through their mutual relations. That perspective mostly reflected the ideas of the first UNCTAD Secretary-General Raul Prebisch (1964–1969), who had been an high ranking Argentinian economic official and Director of the Central Bank of Argentinia in the 1930s and the Executive Secretary of the UN Economic Commission for Latin America in the 1950s. Together with the German economist Hans Singer, he developed the "thesis of the deterioration of the relative prices of primary commodities," known as the Prebisch-Singer thesis. As a result of that "structural" perspective, UNCTAD supported a multilateral and global approach based on the idea of an economic adjustment that would apply to poor and wealthy countries alike in order to create a new, fair international division of labor.[8] That idea of a "structural adjustment," which in the 1980s would be imposed unilaterally on poor countries, had its roots in the studies of the "world economy" that saw the world as a single economic unit in which disparities of development had to be reduced progressively as had already begun in national economies.[9]

Secondly, UNCTAD by no means questioned the necessity of the market as the natural framework for international trade. This is why the terms "trade" and "development" were linked in the very name of the organization. In fact, one of the recurring demands of the developing countries, backed by the socialist countries, was the "liberalization" of the market in the field of manufactured products as well as the removal of the "protections" that existed in the developed countries, in order to foster a new international division of labor. Yet, the international market needed interventions to be stable, as had been practiced in national economies since the Great Depression, and those interventions had to be coordinated.

Thirdly, whether it be to ensure market stability or to implement a mutual adjustment between developing and developed countries, economic planning was needed. A shared view within the UNCTAD General Secretariat, such planning included international measures giving the developing and especially the "least developed" countries the material possibility – in terms of transportation, shipping or storage – to produce goods and sell them to every country in the North as well as in the South. Other non material measures had to be taken to

---

[8] Johanna Bockman, "Socialist Globalization against Capitalist Neocolonialism."
[9] Johanna Bockman, "Eastern European Economists and the Notion of Development: Socialist Economists in the UN Conference on Trade and Development," *American Journal of Sociology*, 108, no. 2 (September 2002): 310–352..

create regional monetary institutions or to favor regional economic cooperation.[10] The necessity of framing international trade was very well reflected in the explanations given by the Indian economist and newly appointed UNCTAD staff member Surendra Patel in a letter he wrote in 1967 to a friend in his homeland:[11]

> In theory this is of course quite true [that multilateral trade has advantages] – no more or less than the validity of the statement that under certain competitive conditions general equilibrium in an economy is maintained by the changing relationships between the factors of input and their prices. But as you know, real economic life rarely provides a perfect example of a general theory. Hence the significance of the changes toward planned economic development in post-war years. Nowadays, economists have come a long way in accepting that planned development is not after all impossible, or even irrational, as compared with unplanned development. The next logical step in my way of thinking is to extend this experience to the sphere of international trade. In any such extension, bilateral (or triangular, or multilateral) trade agreements would seem to serve in the field of international exchange presumably the same purpose as planning is now serving in the domestic field.

The consensus on the necessity of some planning in the field of international trade was congruent with the fact that from the 1960s to the 1980s, the UNCTAD Secretaries-Generals had prior experience in national economic planning in their home countries. That was for instance the case with Manuel Pérez-Guerrero, UNCTAD Secretary-General from 1969 to 1974, who had been Director of the Office for Coordination and Planning in Venezuela from 1959 to 1963 and Gamani Corea, UNCTAD Secretary-General from 1974 to 1984, who had been Head of the Planning Secretariat in Sri Lanka from 1952 to 1960. On the contrary, the Ghanaian Kenneth Dadzie who was UNCTAD Secretary-General from 1986 to 1994, at a time when planning ideas had declined, had led a diplomatic career as an ambassador – and not as a planner – in several African and European countries before joining UNCTAD.

In spite of their respective backgrounds as planners, the successive Secretaries-General did not use the term "planning" to deal with international trade. As showed by the minutes of the Trade and Development Board, they preferred other words like "stabilization," "framework" or "forecast." They might have avoided use of the term"planning" because they did not want to take a stand in the rivalries between the so-called "market economies" and the "centrally

---

[10] *Proceedings of the United Nations Conference on Trade and Development*, 1964, vol.2, Policy statements, 60 – 63.
[11] UNCTAD, ARR 40/1929, box 547, TD 810: Patel to Rosario, 1 June 1967.

planned economies". It is yet more convincing to suppose that, heading an international organization, they could hardly have supported economic planning directly, because international trade was too complex a level to be planned and because it would have been perceived as an infringement of the sovereignties of the member States. More generally, in the discussions at the Trade and Development Board, where every member-State had a representative, the term "planning" was mainly used in two contexts. Either it was used for the national level referring to "national plans," "economic plans," "industry planning" or "technology planning," which included the socialist countries (until the 1960s also called "centrally planned economies"), or it was used for the planning of development, as in the expression "development plans," which was often linked with the national level as in the expression "national development plans."

In this regard, there was little about the use of the term "planning" that distinguished UNCTAD from the other UN agencies. In the UN, the term appeared in the 1940s in the context of "housing and town planning" but from the 1960s on it became closely associated with the notion of "development". A "Committee for Development Planning" – also often referred to during the Trade and Development Board session – was created in 1966 as a consultative body of experts chaired by economist Jan Tinbergen, with the task of "making their experiences in development planning available to the UN for use in the formulation and execution of development plans."[12] More frequently, the term "planning" was used to describe planning instances in specific countries. Reflecting this selective use of the term, Maurice Bertrand – a long-life UN civil servant and respected member of the "Joint Inspection Unit" – noted in a comprehensive 1969 evaluation report on the UN system, that "programming methods" were "more and more efficient," yet they remained "in a well defined national scope," He emphasized that "all the known methods . . . have been put to the service of the States" and that "such programming is not possible at the level of the UN."[13] As in UNCTAD vocabulary, the term "planning" was associated with national sovereignty, which means that any form of planning in the field of international trade implied a cooperation between States in the first instance.

---

[12] Department of Economic and Social Affairs of the United Nations, *Planning and plan implementation, Publications des Nations unies* (New York: United Nations publications, 1967).
[13] "Les méthodes de programmation restent dans un cadre bien défini qui est le cadre national . . . Toutes les méthodes connues . . . ont été développées pour être mises au service des Etats. Une telle programmation n'est pas possible à l'échelle de l'ONU," UNCTAD, ARR 40/1929, box 543, JIU/REP 69/7 : *Projet de rapport sur programmation et budgets dans la famille des Nations Unies*, 20 June1969. I thank Emilie Dairon for her comment on Maurice Bertrand.

Promoting policies to reshape world trade in the 1970s

At the beginning of the 1970s, the end of the Bretton Woods fixed exchange rates regime and the oil embargo that had changed the world's power balance were taken as an opportunity by developing countries to have a declaration adopted in April 1974 by the UN General Assembly "for the Establishment of a New International Economic Order,"[14] which was followed in December by a "Charter of Economic Rights and Duties of the States."[15] Like UNCTAD, the NIEO aimed at redefining the world economic order more in favor of developing countries, without questioning the market mechanisms and without taking a position on the most desirable economic model at the national level. Identifying itself with the NIEO program, UNCTAD's General Secretariat became instrumental in promoting policies aimed at building a new framework for international trade.

Yet the General Secretariat, in UNCTAD as in other UN institutions, had no decision-making power. The main policy orientations were adopted by the Conference while their implementation depended upon the work carried out by commissions formed on an intergovernmental basis and upon the decisions of the Trade and Development Board as UNCTAD's executive organ. This is why the UNCTAD General Secretariat had to use other, softer means to have new policies adopted and implemented. On the one hand, it tried to craft a common framework that could reconcile the free market with various conceptions of planning. At the same time, he sought to build coalitions with different actors, avoiding as well as using the Cold war divide. This concern for planning as well as for East-West and North-South relations makes UNCTAD a relevant ground for observing planning models and how they circulated, coexisted or competed.

With its General Secretariat as the main driver, UNCTAD developed a wide range and a great variety of policies.[16] The core of UNCTAD activity since its foundation in 1964 had been the elaboration of new trade regulations more favorable to the developing countries. This included first and foremost commodities which made up the largest part of the developing countries' exports. There had been some international agreements on olive oil as well as on tin previous to the foundation of UNCTAD. Not only did UNCTAD help to extend those previ-

---

14 UN, A/RES/S-6/3201, see also http://www.un-documents.net/s6r3201.htm (accessed on 15 February 2017).
15 UN, A/RES/29/3281, see also http://www.un-documents.net/a29r3281.htm (accessed on 15 February 2017).
16 For a detailed presentation of UNCTAD policies, see Merloz, La CNUCED.

ous agreements but it also negotiated new ones on sugar, wheat and cocoa, adopting a so-called "commodity by commodity" approach. Initiated in 1974 and officially adopted by UNCTAD IV in Nairobi in 1976, the "Integrated Program of Commodities" broke new ground in supporting a systematic approach, promoting the establishment of a common fund and of buffer stocks to stabilize export earnings while at the same time launching a coordinated round of negotiations on 18 commodities.

Another matter of discussion in trade regulations at UNCTAD was the elaboration of a Generalized System of Preference (GSP). According to free trade principles, every country should offer others the same conditions as it offered the most favored country ("most favored nation clause"). That principle was questioned given that reciprocity and non-discrimination could only work between countries with similar levels of development. As a result, the GSP was launched at the second convening of UNCTAD in New Dehli in 1968. UNCTAD II adopted the reverse principle of the "most favored nation clause" by taking into account the structural asymmetry between developed and developing countries and by offering them systematic non-reciprocal preferences and compensating discrimination. The principle of a GSP in the field of manufacture was acknowledged by the GATT in 1971 but it was only progressively implemented, beginning with the EEC in 1971.

One of the problems the developing countries faced was their trade dependency on the developed countries' markets, often continuing previous colonial trade relations. This is why UNCTAD also supported "economic cooperation between developing countries" by helping them to create regional market organizations, such as the Andean Group in 1969. However, during the course of 1970, mainly as a result of the embargo led by oil exporting countries, economic cooperation began to be envisioned as a way to help developing countries develop themselves independently of the developed countries, which was termed "self reliance."

A last UNCTAD policy in trade regulation was to promote the trade "between countries having different economic and social systems," meaning the trade between socialist countries and developing countries. UNCDAT acknowledged the existence of state planned economies and popularized their potential advantages for the developing countries. Socialist economic planning was viewed as more predictable and thus more likely to bring stability to international markets. Trade with socialist countries took the form of trade agreements between sovereign states. They were negotiated and often also had a technical aid dimension which could be attractive to non-industrialized countries, as industrial plants made up an important part of exports from socialist countries. In a longer-term view, state-planned economies had another advantage from the perspective of a global mutual economic adjustment. Because of their central and hierarchical character, they were regarded as easier to restructure and more likely to contribute to a new international division of labor. The program adopted by the countries of the Council for Mutual Economic Aid (CMEA) in Bucharest in 1971 explicitly mentioned their efforts to integrate more trade relations in their plans, although these were external factors.

The UNCTAD General Secretariat did not limit itself to mere trade regulations. According to its global vision of trade and development, it also worked on the material and practical conditions of trade. Transport was a problem. Most of the trade was done through liners owned by companies that were based in the developed countries and decided freight rates on their own at so-called "liner conferences." UNCTAD supported the adoption of a "Code of conduct on liner conferences" as well as the creation of national fleets. The difficulties were even greater for landlocked or insular countries, for which UNCTAD elaborated a special aid program. Not only material but also immaterial infrastructure played a significant role in trade. This is why legislation on patents and licenses was also a concern from the beginning of UNCTAD, which led to the elaboration of an International Code of Conduct for Technology Transfer in the late 1970s. Likewise, the lack of national insurance and reinsurance systems in the developing countries worsened the dependence upon the developed countries. UNCTAD helped the former build their own systems.

In the 1970s, in the new context created by the affirmation of the NIEO, UNCTAD's General Secretariat not only became more assertive in the areas where it had already developed policies, but it also took the initiative in two new areas. First, it took the opportunity of the crisis surrounding the Bretton Woods system to attempt taking over the role of a forum for the setting up of a new international monetary system. In particular, UNCTAD's General Secretariat advocated for the inclusion of the developing countries in that process and for the so-called "link principle" between Special Drawing Rights and the financing of development. Second, UNCTAD's General Secretariat not only made an attempt at redefining regulations but also at bringing direct help in creating and strengthening the industrial capacities of the developing countries. It did so by researching how to use subventions and elaborate "national foreign export plans" as well as national "technology plans." Those initiatives were taken in collaboration with the United Nations Industrial Development Organization (UNIDO), which was increasingly influential in the 1970s, as illustrated by the "Program of Lima" that was adopted at its conference in 1975. This extension from the concern for regulation to the concern for industrialization was accompanied by the development of "technical aid," mainly in the form of training, a kind of activity that had originally not been envisioned by UNCTAD's founder and first Secretary General Raul Prebisch.[17] The concern for the industrialization of developing countries reflected the long-term project of building a new international division of labor, which lay at the core of UNCTAD's endeavors.

Crafting a common intellectual framework

Having those policies adopted was not an easy task. A first means of influence on member states was upstream work: thanks to its own staff and to numerous collaborations with external research institutions, UNCTAD's General Secretariat was able to demonstrate an expertize capacity that was used to craft an intellectual framework in which the promoted policies would make sense for all parties. That framework was meant to link planning with free market and was opened to a wide range of options, from Keynesian market economies to socialist planned economies.

Regulating the market of commodities

Any proposal that had successfully moved from draft to official policy in fact already had a long history as a research topic in the various divisions of the General Secretariat, well before being put on the political agenda. This is well illustrated by UNCTAD's attempt at establishing "buffer stocks," that is, internationally-owned stocks covering a wide range of commodities in order to stabilize market prices. The idea was not a new one and had already been formulated – but not adopted – at the Bretton Woods Conference in 1944.[18] The establishment of buffer stocks financed by a common fund was set as a goal at UNCTAD's fourth conference in Nairobi in 1976.[19] But the topic had been announced and dealt with at the Trade and Development Board for the first time in 1974[20] and UNCTAD's Commodity Division had been working on it at least since 1969. That year the Commodities

---

[17] As stressed by UNCTAD official Paul Berthoud, who described Prebisch in his memoirs as "rather indifferent to the involvement of UNCTAD in micro-assistance of a technical nature," see Berthoud, Paul, A Professional Life Narrative and Some Related Stories: http://www.edinter.net/paulberthoud/narrative/ (accessed 14 February 2017).

[18] Eric Helleiner, "The Development Mandate of International Institutions: Where Did It Come From?" *Studies in Comparative International Development* 44, no.6 (2009): 189–211.

[19] Conference resolution 93(IV) 30 May 1976, section 1, Preamble.

[20] UNCTAD, TDB/ A/9615/Rev.1: *Report of the Trade and Development Board (12 September 1973–13 September 1974)*, 1975, 26.

Division contributed to a study on the "Stabilization of Prices of Primary Products" initiated by the World Bank,[21] in which the proposal of buffer stocks was very clearly articulated.[22]

The same year, UNCTAD's Commodities Division was charged with the task of working out a framework to prepare the work of an intergovernmental technical group on buffer stocks. For that purpose, the division commissioned a study from Sri Lankan economist Lal Jayawardene. That study was to draw on Keynes' proposals for the establishment of buffer stocks, dating back to 1942 when he was preparing the Bretton Woods conference. Jayawardene's study was not supposed to repeat but to adapt Keynes' proposal to the current situation. In a series of critical comments written to Jayawardene, UNCTAD researcher Alfred Maizels underlined that, while Keynesian proposals of buffer stocks were of course relevant, their envisioned implementation was far too limited, Keynes's view even being called "extreme laissez-faire." In Maizels' mind, buffer stocks should in fact not only be used for short-term stabilizing purposes, but also for "long-term action to improve the trend of prices and earnings."[23] At the same time, however, Maizel thought that the study should also deal with "supply engagements" in order to respond to the concern of the developed countries that were affected by the oil embargo. The latter would then be more likely to accept the principle of buffer stocks. While providing a study to a "technical" group, the Commodities Division was in fact giving guidelines for the future discussions.

However, that process was not exclusively determined by experts. Each division of the General Secretariat was accountable to the Trade and Development Board where representatives of the member states had a word to say on the activity of the divisions, including on their research agendas. This is clearly shown by the debate over the question of the indexation of the prices of commodities that polarized the Trade and Development Board in the 1970s. The indexation was meant to counteract the "deterioration of the terms of trade" between developing and developed countries. When Secretary General Gamani Corea mentioned a study on indexation in 1974,[24] he triggered a debate on the very sub-

---

21 UNCTAD, ARR 40/1882, box 409, TD 310/3: Maizels to Macone, 7 August 1969.
22 See World Bank, *Stabilization of Prices of Primary Products. A Joint Study IMF-IBRD*. Washington: 1969, 69–73 and 93–103. The report is available on line: http://documents.worldbank.org/curated/en/903841468780623537/The-problem-of-stabilization-of-prices-of-primary-products (accessed 15 February 2017).
23 UNCTAD, TDB/ A/9615/Rev.1: *Report of the Trade and Development Board (12 September 1973–13 September 1974)*, 1975, 25–27.
24 UNCTAD, TDB/503: *The indexation of prices. Report by the Secretary-General of UNCTAD on the findings of his study*, 6 August 1974.

stance of the subject. Whereas the representatives of developing countries emphasized "the critical importance [to them] of earnings from exports of primary commodities," the representatives of the developed countries stressed the complexity of such a policy as well as its potential negative consequences for all consumer countries including the developing countries.[25] In 1975, hot debates were rekindled when the Secretary-General presented a report on the work of the Expert Group on Indexation, one representative stating that "this question raised insoluble problems and that it was practically impossible to establish a scientific index or to determine objectively the reference prices on which to base indexation."[26] The debate had practical consequences for the research project: at stake was the extended funding of a position to have the study on indexation continued.[27] Thus, the production of knowledge had a political dimension from the start.

Bringing together socialist state planning and UNCTAD's action

This political dimension of knowledge production systematically appears in the work of the Division "for the commerce between countries with different economic and social systems" – also called Division for the Trade with socialist countries or TRADSOC division. A result of a special demand from the USSR dating back to 1963, this rather small division of five to ten members consisted in the majority of citizens from socialist countries (mainly from the USSR and from Bulgaria), supplemented by citizens from developing countries or neutral European developed countries. The division had the primary goal of promoting trade between socialist and developing countries and was accordingly tasked with reporting on "trends and policies in trade between countries having different economic and social systems," with popularizing "technical assistance projects in the sphere of trade relations between socialist and developing countries" and with documenting the "problems of co-ordinating long-term agreements with de-

---

25 UNCTAD, TDB/ A/9615/Rev.1: *Report of the Trade and Development Board (12 September 1973–13 September1974)*, 1975, 30–31.
26 UNCTAD, TDB/ A/10015/Rev.1: *Report of the Trade and Development Board (10 March–2 October 1975)*, 1976, 150.
27 Ibid.

velopment plans and programs in both socialist and developing countries, including possibilities of co-operating in planning."²⁸

Building a coalition involving different and potentially conflicting views on planning was not an easy task, because of the tensions not only between the member states but also inside the various General Secretariats divisions. These kinds of tension clearly appeared during the preparation of a training seminar for the "planning of foreign export." First entrusted to the UNCTAD's New York Office, the preparation was then transferred to the Research Division in Geneva that included trade with the socialist countries in the program "to make the topic a little more concrete," as trading with planned economies appeared to be a logical way to plan foreign export.²⁹ Disagreeing with that initiative, the New York office took back the project, focusing exclusively on market matters like protection, forecast, econometric analysis or capital requirements.³⁰

More fundamentally, the TRADSOC division had to counter negative discourses or representations of socialist countries as being unable to trade efficiently with developing countries. First, it had to refute the idea that planned economies were autarchic economies. When UNCTAD was founded, there was no clear conception of the role of foreign trade in the socialist planned economies. Exports were often said to be first of all a means to gain foreign currencies necessary to pay imports that were needed for the national economy, as stated by the Soviet expert M.Gousev himself at a UN-funded training session in 1964.³¹ At exactly the same time, however, East German experts participating in the CMEA working group that had been formed for the preparation of the first UNCTAD stressed the necessity to anticipate a change in the current exports of the developing countries, from primary commodities to more manufactured or semi-manufactured goods. Although the GDR would experience some "adjustment difficulties, since [it had] important production capacities for those commodities in the country," this trend was seen as rational and the GDR should be able to find its place by delivering machines or turnkey industrial plants, thus contributing to a new division of labor.³² By the beginning of the 1970s, the latter conception had

---

28 UNCTAD, ARR 40/1929, box 546, TD 802/8: *Division for trade with socialist countries. Functions*, 1976.
29 UNCTAD, ARR 40/2344, Research: El Naggar to Pérez-Guerrero, 3 December 1969.
30 UNCTAD, ARR 40/1929, box 558, TD 977/21: Seminar on the Planning of the Foreign Trade Sector to be held in the course of 1970, 8 December 1969.
31 Department of Economic and Social Affairs, *Rapport sur le cycle d'études des Nations Unies sur les techniques de la planification*, United Nations Publications, 1964, 22–23.
32 SAPMO-BArch, DY 30/IV A 2/6.10/118: *Programm zur Gestaltung und weiteren Entwicklung des Handels der DDR mit den Entwicklungsländern*, 8 October 1963.

become central to the discourse of the TRADSOC division, drawing on the 1971 CMEA Program of Bucharest. The draft statement prepared for the intervention of the UNCTAD Secretary General at the 1971 session of the Trade and Development Board strongly recalled that the "need for rational structural changes in national economies" appeared "among the priorities in national plans." As a result, "the idea of complementing progressively economic structures of the socialist countries with those of the rest of the world [seemed] to be becoming more and more part of the planning considerations."[33]

Second, there was the "wrong concept" – as presented in a draft letter to be sent to the delegates of developing countries in 1970 – that "the import policy in the socialist countries of Eastern Europe [was] rather a result of arbitrary decisions of the central management without them giving due weight to the existing demands and preferences of final consumers." To counter this argument, the division prepared two studies on the "[d]ecision making process in respect of import in selected socialist countries (the interdependence of central management and final users)" and on the "[w]ays of introducing new products from developing countries into selected socialist countries' markets."[34]

A third and final obstacle the division had to deal with was the strong bilateral character of socialist countries' trade. CMEA integration, which was decided in the 1971 Bucharest program was supposed to favor multilateral trade, as explained by the UNCTAD Secretary-General at a session of the Trade and Development Board in 1977: "Over the recent past, the bilateral economic relations of socialist countries of Eastern Europe with developing countries are gradually supplemented by various forms of multilateral co-operation which provide for greater flexibility in their trade and economic relations."[35] He mentioned the transferable ruble that enjoyed considerable attention because it was supposed to be used by socialist countries to pay their trading partners, who in turn could use that currency to buy products in any other socialist country. The division even created an ad hoc commission composed of international experts to deal with the transferable ruble.[36] But in the same statement, the UNCTAD Secreta-

---

[33] UNCTAD, ARR 40/1929, box 546, TD 804: *Opening Statement of Item 7 of the Agenda (11th Session of the Board, 26 July 1971)*, 3.
[34] UNCTAD, ARR 40/1929, box 549, TD 820/9: *Study on marketing with socialist countries (October1968-May 1971)*.
[35] UNCTAD, ARR 40/1929, box 546, TD 804: *Report by Secretary General of UNCTAD to the 8th special session of Trade and Development Board*, 25 February 1977, 3.
[36] UNCTAD, ARR 40/1830, box 67, TDO 287/5: Intergovernmental group of experts to study a multilateral system of payment between the socialist countries of Eastern Europe and developing countries, October 1977-December 1977.

ry-General had to recognize that "bilateral links will continue to play a predominant role in the future."³⁷ In a similar statement the same year, he added that "the transition to multilateralism was a long process."³⁸

Along with those efforts to clear up any misunderstanding, the division avoided any glorification of socialist countries' type of state-planned economy as opposed to capitalism. Instead, the line of the division for trade with socialist countries consisted in highlighting again and again the objective positive effects of state-planned economies on trade with developing countries. In this way, the division performed a kind of translation from the usual Marxist-Leninist discourse to the UNCTAD's developmental discourse. As a result, some dividing issues were carefully avoided. Among them was the question of the ownership of the means of production: the very terms of "capitalism" or "capitalist countries" were not used in the TRADSOC division. But the same division regularly recalled that any country that wished to trade with the socialist countries first had to establish some kind of state organization to deal with them, assuming that states were the only relevant agents in trade matters. Another core issue at UNCTAD, the idea of development through trade, was also avoided: while showing a real interest in trade with developing countries, socialist countries were at odds with the idea of implementing national development plans primarily on the basis of export earnings. Their representatives at the Trade and Development Board, unlike the more cautious staff of the TRADSOC division, instead called for deeper political and social transformation at the national level, having in mind their own historical path.³⁹

UNCTAD as an agent in the field of economics

As shown above by their cooperation with researchers of the World Bank, UNCTAD researchers did not work alone. That was particularly true in the 1970s in the matter of commodities. UNCTAD's researchers had a relationship of trust with some of their World Bank's counterparts, contributing to a common

---

37 UNCTAD, ARR 40/1929, box 546, TD 804: *Report by Secretary General of UNCTAD to the 8th special session of Trade and Development Board*, 25 February 1977, 3.
38 UNCTAD, ARR 40/1929, box 546, TD 804: *Secretary General's report for the 8th Special Session of the Trade and Development Board*, 11 March 1977.
39 See for instance the intervention of a representative of a socialist country in 1975: UNCTAD TDB/ A/10015/Rev.1: *Report of the Trade and Development Board (10 March -2 October 1975)*, 1976, 63.

mode of thinking and calling them by their first names and vice versa.[40] World Bank official Dragoslav Avramovic, in a letter to Director of UNCTAD's Commodities Division Bernard Chidzero in 1974, referred for instance to their "stimulating discussion in Geneva" and shared with him some thoughts on the "adequacy of current stock levels" and on the possibility that the IMF make resources available for the acquisition of stocks.[41] Those relationships show that there were horizontal networks between international organizations, which were likely to play a role in the production of legitimate knowledge.

However, the majority of UNCTAD studies, as in other international organizations, was not produced internally, but via commissions to experts who were most often scholars in universities and research institutes. Those studies were then supervised by UNCTAD's own staff, as in the case of Lal Jayawardene's study on bufferstocks mentioned above. Due to UNCTAD's status as an international organization, its staff came from a great variety of countries. On the contrary, the cooperation with non-UNCTAD experts involved a majority of US American universities, like the University of Pennsylvania, Georgetown University or Cornell University, and British universities, like those of Sussex, Bristol or Manchester. In some areas like trade with socialist countries, there was also some cooperation with French institutions, like the Centre d'Economie internationale des pays socialistes in the Sorbonne, East German and Soviet institutions, not forgetting the ties with numerous foreign trade ministries in the socialist countries. Among the developing countries, UNCTAD only had strong ties in one country, India, with Bombay University and the Indian Institute of Foreign Trade in New Dehli.

Not only did UNCTAD employ economics experts from various, mainly developed countries, but it also tried to influence the research agenda in economics. In accordance with its project of building new relations in international trade, the UNCTAD General Secretariat had a strong interest in macroeconomic models. Buffer stocks for instance made sense only "on the assumption that the necessary prescience [was] shown in anticipating the trends."[42] At the beginning of the 1970s, macroeconomic modeling was flourishing, with models being elaborated on a global scale as analyzed by Jenny Andersson in her chapter. One of the most significant among them was the so-called "Link project," that was launched in 1969. It immediately caught the attention of UNCTAD's Commodities Division researchers, who described it as "a new econometric project trying to

---

[40] UNCTAD, ARR 40/1882, box 409, TD 310/3: Maizels to Macone, 7 August 1969.
[41] UNCTAD, ARR 40/1882, box 411, TD 312(1): Avramovic to Chidzero, 27 September 1974.
[42] See World Bank, *Stabilization of Prices of Primary Products*, 157–158.

link models in different countries with a model of network of trade and financial flows in order to build an econometric world model."[43] As early as December 1969 UNCTAD General Secretary wrote to the leader of the project, Lawrence Klein from the University of Pennsylvania.[44] While expressing his support for the Link project, he also suggested some changes in the orientation of the project. First, he emphasized the significance of primary commodities exports for developing countries, thus asking for a "much finer breakdown of exports than is contemplated at the present time." Second, he asked for "longer term projections," because it was "important for the long range planning of adjustments in world trade policies to have some notion of the most important changes to be expected in the structure of world trade over periods, say, ten years ahead." Yet, participants in the Link project seemed to have precisely the opposite interests. They were described by UNCTAD's researchers as a "relatively homogenous group with similar interests in short-term projections for developed countries," while "the question of international commodity trade" appeared to them to be "peripheral." Accordingly, UNCTAD's researchers saw it as their task to persuade "them to accept the complication which will inevitably result for them from introducing commodity trade into the picture."[45]

On the one hand, their efforts to influence the Link project seemed to be successful. In 1977, Secretary General Corea made an announcement to the Trade and Development Board. By then, the Link project consisted of "72 forecasting models for developing countries and 36 commodity models of export interest to developing countries."[46] UNCTAD had greatly contributed to the integration of the developing countries into the model and the same was true for the socialist countries that were first mentioned in 1971[47] and were the subject of a meeting of experts in Geneva two years later.[48] Lawrence Klein also referred positively to UNCTAD participation in his press statements.[49] In 1976, he saw the future of the

---

[43] UNCTAD, ARR 40/1882, box 409, TD 310/5: Viteri de la Huerta to Groby, El Naggar, and Maizels, 13 November 1969.
[44] UNCTAD, ARR 40/1882, box 409, TD 310/5: Guerrero to Klein, 18 December 1969.
[45] UNCTAD, ARR 40/1882, box 409, TD 310/5: Dell to Chidzero, 14 July 1970.
[46] UNCTAD, TDB A/32/15, vol.2: *Report of the Trade and Development Board (First part of the 17th session and first part of the 9th special session)*, 1978, 12.
[47] UNCTAD, ARR 40/1882, box 409, TD 310/5: Guerrero to Klein, 25 January 1971.
[48] UNCTAD, ARR 40/1882, box 409, TD 310/5: *Report by the UNCTAD secretariat on the Meeting of Experts on Projections Methods for Socialist Countries Foreign Trade, Vienna, 28 August to 4 September*, undated (1973).
[49] UNCTAD, ARR 40/1882, 409, TD 310/5: Project Link: Entering a New Phase, June 1973; Klein, Lawrence R., "Project LINK: Linking National Economic Models,", *Challenge* 19, no. 5 (1976): 25-29.

Link project as an "international development agency" that would work out a "full global simulation of economic activity."[50] On the other side, UNCTAD's staff seemed to be completely overwhelmed by the task implied by the project. As early as 1970, the director of the Commodities Division wrote to the General Secretary that working out 20 to 25 commodity models in one year would make a team of 30 necessary, instead of three individuals. In 1973, a member of the Commodities Division said he doubted whether "we shall have resources for undertaking studies the usefulness of which would be restricted to the development of the LINK model." While praising the integration of the developing and socialist countries as well as of the commodities in the Link model, Klein and his colleagues remained mainly interested in the initial question of the Link project, as shown by their personal publications.[51] Only a few of his students published works on developing countries and intermittently asked the Commodities Division for help, as economist Kanta Marwah did in 1973.[52] The results of UNCTAD's attempts to influence the research agenda had thus only been half a success.

Building coalitions

Without the support of a vast majority of member states, it was not possible for the General Secretariat to have its policies adopted. Thus, while crafting a common intellectual framework, UNCTAD's General Secretariat developed an intense diplomatic activity, maintaining relationships with various countries and organizations in the hope of forming a vast coalition. An initial task of the General Secretariat was of course to maintain unity inside the Group of 77 where very different countries coexisted. All were considered as "developing," but they were at the same time both large and small, socialist or capitalist, more developed or less developed. The unity among the Group of 77 became all the more crucial after the Organization of the Petroleum Exporting Countries (OPEC) decided on an oil embargo in 1973. With the rebalancing between developing and devel-

---

50 Klein, "Project Link: Linking National Economic Models," 29.
51 Keith Johnson,and Lawrence R. Klein, "Link Model Simulations of International Trade: An Evaluation of the Effects of Currency Realignment," *The Journal of Finance* 29, no. 2 (1974): 617-630; Lawrence R. Klein, "The Interdependence of National Economies and the Synchronization of EconomicFluctuations: Evidence from the LINK Project," *Weltwirtschaftliches Archiv* 114, no. 4 (1978): 642-708.
52 UNCTAD, ARR 40/1882, box 409, TD 310/5: *Research Work on Project Link – Progress Report*, 10 April 1973.

oped countries there was hope for an increase in economic cooperation among developing countries. Soon after the OPEC decision, the term "self-reliance" began to be used at the sessions of the Trade and Development Board[53] and was central in the "Program for Collective Self-Reliance" adopted in Arusha in 1979. It took a great deal of diplomatic efforts on the part of the General Secretariat to promote that idea of cooperation among developing countries.

However, at no point did the General Secretariat leave aside cooperation with the developed countries, without which no global agreement on world trade was to be found. But the acceptance of the new UNCTAD policies by the latter was variable and fragile, if not impossible. That was the great weakness of UNCTAD. In particular, the USA expressed an ongoing hostility towards UNCTAD's new policies in the 1970s, as did other European countries like Great Britain, France or Belgium. That did not prevent individuals from those countries expressing their support. British citizen and member of the House Commons Jeremy Bray for instance wrote several letters to the Secretary General to air his views on the planning of the markets, drawing on the so-called "control theory."[54] But on the whole, the General Secretariat experienced difficulties in finding allies among developed countries. Yet, there were at least two cases of successful diplomatic work, with the socialist countries and with the European Economic Community (EEC). These two very different and even opposed groups of countries helped to build a coalition around the newly promoted policies.

The socialist countries: dealing with the forbidden issue of East-West trade

Socialist countries had strongly supported UNCTAD from the beginning but with their own agenda.[55] Evidence from the GDR archives shows that the primary concern of the socialist countries in the phase of preparation for the first UNCTAD conference in 1964 was not the development of poorer countries, but the removal of the barriers socialist countries of Eastern Europe were facing when trading with Western Europe. Only when it became clear that UNCTAD would concentrate on development exclusively did they shift their position and support the de-

---

53 UNCTAD, TDB/ A/9615/Rev.1: *Report of the Trade and Development Board (12 September 1973–13 September 1974)*, 1975, 17.
54 UNCTAD, ARR 40/1882, box 411, TD 312(1): Bray to Corea, 15 June 1976.
55 Marie Lavigne, *Économie internationale des pays socialistes* (Paris: A. Colin, 1985); Arie Bloed, *The External Relations of the Council for Mutual Economic Assistance* (Utrecht: Martinus Nijhoff Publishers, 1988).

mands of the developing countries.⁵⁶ After the foundation of UNCTAD, the socialist countries did not give up. They obtained the creation of a division "for the trade between countries having different economic and social systems," a convoluted wording that left the door open to a possible inclusion of the East-West trade issue on the agenda. However, that issue was in fact not a priority in the work program of the division, because UNCTAD was not meant to deal specifically with trade between countries considered as "developed."

This is why the socialist countries used their representatives in the Trade and Development Board sessions to address the matter of East-West trade barriers and express their demands. Their exchanges with their West European counterparts had a quasi-ritual character, Eastern European socialist countries blaming Western European countries for de facto discrimination, while the latter simply recalled that East-West trade was already dealt with in the Economic Commission for Europe, where negotiations were in fact completely deadlocked. As the very expression of the trade discrimination they allegedly suffered, socialist countries systematically denounced the EEC. The negative effects of that so-called "economic grouping of western countries" were regularly discussed on their initiative as a specific agenda item. For socialist countries it was the occasion to focus on the trade discrimination measures the EEC was supposed to impose not only to them but also to developing countries. They used UNCTAD as a forum to try to structure the internal power balance around the East-West divide. The UNCTAD General Secretariat did not counteract that strategy because socialist countries regularly backed its proposals.

That diplomatic bargain entered a new phase at the beginning of the 1970s, with the adoption of the Bucharest Program by the member states of the CMEA in 1971⁵⁷. The General Secretariat had in fact anticipated that initiative with a 1970 study on the "expansion of trade through the promotion of complementary economic structures."⁵⁸ Welcoming that new program in his speech at the 1971 session of the Trade and Development Board, Secretary General Perez-Guerrero considered that "the idea of co-ordinating progressively the economic structures of the socialist countries with those of the rest of the world might become more

---

56 See Christian, "UNCTAD."
57 Marie Lavigne, *East-South Relations in the World Economy* (Boulder, Colo.; London: Westview Press, 1988); Robert M Cutler, "East-South Relations at UNCTAD: Global Political Economy and the CMEA," *International Organization* 37, no. 1 (1983): 121-142; Sara Lorenzini, "COMECON and the South in the years of *Détente:* A study on East-south economic relations," *European Review of History* 21 (2014): 183–199.
58 UNCTAD, TDB/125: *Expansion of trade through the promotion of complementary economic structures*, 27 November 1970.

and more part of their planning considerations" and drew attention "to the positive foreign trade impact of the new economic plans which would guide the economies of the socialist countries of Eastern Europe in the period 1971–1975."[59] As a result of that new interest, the staff of the division for the trade with the socialist countries grew from five to ten between 1968 and 1983. One of its tasks now consisted in using the sessions of the Trade and Development Board to encourage meetings between representatives of the socialist countries and interested developing countries and enter into talks, which was a first step towards the conclusion of a trade agreement.[60] UNCTAD's General Secretariat also built a new relationship with the CMEA itself, which had not enjoyed a great deal of interest so far, not even in the TRADSOC division.[61] Secretary General Corea paid the first official visit to the CMEA's headquarters in Moscow in 1975. As a result of that initial contact, the TRADSOC division soon asked CMEA for studies on industrialization and leveling of regional development gaps[62] as well as on the possibilities of interregional trade.[63]

That initiative was not without benefit for the socialist countries. Promoting trade between socialist countries and developing countries was also an opportunity to spread their specific model of state-planned economy. The attractiveness of that model in UNCTAD reached its zenith in the second half of the 1970s. In a 1976 policy paper prepared by the TRADSOC division from the perspective of UNCTAD IV in Nairobi, economic national planning and UNCTAD's goals were almost made identical: "In view of the growing role of planning in developing countries' economic management in recent years and the rich experience of the socialist countries of Eastern Europe in this sphere, multilateral effort in the field of planning could be of particular importance in the context of UNCTAD's contribution to the establishment of a new international economic order."[64] Likewise, a 1979 study by the same division not only described the positive effects of the socialist planned economies on trade with developing coun-

---

59 UNCTAD, TDB/8415/Rev.1: Report of the Trade and Development Board (14 October 1970 – 21 Septmebr 1971), 1972 UNCTAD, TDB/8415/Rev.1: *Report of the Trade and Development Board (14 October 1970 – 21 September 1971)*, 1972, 152.
60 This activity is well documented in UNCTAD, ARR 40/1929, 546, TD 804:Trade with socialist countries Trade and Development Board, 27 March 1969 – 22 November 1988.
61 See UNCTAD, ARR 40/1929, 547, TD 808/1: Trade with Socialist Countries, CMEA, September 1970-September 1987.
62 Ibid., *Note verbale to CMEA member countries and letter to CMEA Secretariat*, 21 June 1976.
63 Ibid., Davydov to Luft, 5 May 1980.
64 UNCTAD, ARR 40/1929, box546, TD 803: *Multilateral action for expanding the trade and economic relations between countries with different economic and social systems, in particular action which would contribute to the development of developing countries*, november 1975, 11.

tries, but also how those countries had progressively come to adopt some features of the socialist planned economies.[65] The will to spread the socialist model of economic planning was also congruent with the fact that every trade agreement with a socialist country involved the state as a contracting party even in a market economy, thus strengthening its role as an economic actor. When participating in a seminar with representatives of developing countries, staff members of the TRADSOC division stressed the necessity of "an appropriate mechanism at the governmental level, bringing together various organizations and enterprises of the partner countries."[66] The division for trade with socialist countries also gave a lot of attention to the "mixed commissions" that were created between the trading partners and worked as a channel to exert influence on their economic model.[67]

Another significant benefit for the socialist countries resulted from a revision of the General Secretariat's previous policy of not dealing with East-West trade. As it was not possible to address intra-European matters in UNCTAD, the General Secretariat chose an indirect strategy by making a case for the so-called "trilateral industrial co-operation." That co-operation resulted mainly from the context of the détente. It was intended to associate economic actors (business organization as well as governmental agencies) from the socialist countries and from the capitalist developed countries in a third, developing country[68]. The idea was formulated as early as 1969 in a proposal made by a representative of developing countries to have those countries participate "as sub-contractors in East-West industrial co-operation projects."[69] In fact, the idea of socialist and capitalist developed countries cooperating for the benefit of developing countries enjoyed great support among the Group of 77. In this spirit, the TRADSOC division conducted surveys of such cooperative ventures, analyzed them, and formulated recommendations to promote the practice. Accordingly, the division held a seminar

---

[65] UNCTAD, TD 243 Supp.4: *Co-operation in planning between socialist countries of Eastern Europe and developing countries: the experience of the USSR. Report by the UNCTAD Secretariat*, 28 February 1979, 10 – 11.
[66] UNCTAD, ARR 40/1929, box 547, TD 806/3: *UNCTAD's activities in trade between the socialist countries of Eastern Europe and the developing countries*, 10 September 1979, 3.
[67] UNCTAD, TDB/452: *The role of mixed intergovernemental commissions in trade relations among countries having different economic and social systems*, 21 December 1973
[68] Patrick Gutman and Francis Arkwright, "La coopération industrielle tripartite entre pays à systèmes économiques et sociaux Différents, de l'Ouest, de l'Est et Du Sud," *Politique étrangère* 40, no. 6 (1976): 621– 655.
[69] UNCTAD, TDB/A/7616: *Report of the Trade and Development Board (24 September–23 September 1969)*, 1970, 162.

on the subject in December 1975.⁷⁰ Division director Mikhail Davydov went on to participate in a conference organized by the GDR Academy of Sciences in Dresden in March 1976⁷¹ that was attended by academics from the United States, the USSR, Poland, and Great Britain. The division also published two studies on that topic in 1979 and 1984.⁷² Yet, while officially supporting cooperation for the benefit of the developing countries, socialist countries had their own interest in participating. Due to the technological asymmetry between East and West, they would actually benefit from the transfer of technology that was intended for developing countries. This is why trilateral industrial cooperation appeared to be the magic formula that would satisfy everyone.

EEC: the good boy of UNCTAD?

In July 1971, the member states of the EEC became the first developed countries to implement their "system of preferences" towards developing countries. It formed the first part of the General System of Preferences, designed by UNCTAD to favor the exports of manufactures from developing countries. Other European countries would only follow in 1973, like Hungary and Sweden, while the USA would wait until 1976. By 1971, the establishment of a common external tariff was a recognized advantage of the EEC. But that achievement of the EEC system of preferences was also the result of close work between the EEC and UNCTAD. In preparing the future system, the Commission worked closely with the UNCTAD Manufacture Division. As early as 1966, the Assistant Director of the Manufacture Division, Harry Stordel, mentioned an "informal contact" he wished to strengthen with Di Martino, from the EEC External Relations General Directorate. Calling him his "dear friend," Di Martino sent material about tariff matters to Stordel the same year. In 1968, Stordel in turn sent documents to Di Martino, stressing that he should "treat them as having been given to [him] on an informal basis" and that he should "ensure that they are not at any stage quoted as an official source."⁷³ One month later, the Director of the Manufacture Division,

---

70 UNCTAD, TDB 599: Report *on the Seminar of Industrial Specialization through Various Forms of Multilateral Co-operation, held in the Palais des Nations, December 2–5 1975*, 23 February 1976.
71 UNCTAD, ARR 40/1929, box TD 830: *UNCTAD and tripartite industrial co-operation*, 25 March 1976.
72 UNCTAD, TDB 243/Supp.5: *Tripartite industrial co-operation and co-operation in third countries*, 20 April 1979 and UNCTAD, TDB 1000: *Recent developments in East-West co-operation in third countries and in tripartite co-operation*, 6 June 1984.
73 UNCTAD, ARR 40/1842, TDO 440, box 164: Stordel to Di Martino, 16 June 1968.

Rangaswami Krishnamurti, forwarded a study on the rule of origin to the EEC Director-General for External Relations Axel Herbst,[74] who acknowledged receipt, saying he was "greatly impressed" by that work.[75] The same year, Krishnamurti went to Brussels and after his return to Geneva, wrote to Herbst: "My discussions in Brussels on the subject of tariff preferences were most helpful and provided me with the opportunity to establish the necessary contacts with the officials in the various departments in the Commission."[76]

In addition to that working relationship, UNCTAD Deputy Secretary General Stein Rossen also had ties with the European Parliament, as shown by the letter he wrote to its President in 1970 in thanks for the support the Parliament gave to the General System of Preferences.[77] Likewise, the Secretary General of UNCTAD himself, accompanied by the main division's directors, paid several official visits to Brussels, where he met the successive Presidents of the European Commission – Jean Rey in March 1969,[78] Franco Malfatti in May 1971[79] and Sicco Mansholt in November 1972.[80] The relationship with Mansholt, which was especially friendly, seemed to rely on common ideals and when he left the European Commission, Perez-Guerrero wrote to him personally: "We in UNCTAD have felt always that you were one of us in this fight for justice in the international economic relations which at present are so much lacking of it."[81]

For the European Commission, the commitment to the General System of Preferences was not merely a way of helping the developing countries. Since the achievement of the customs union in 1968, it in principle had the ability to set the external common tariff, and working on a system of preferences was an opportunity for the EEC to assert its new competence in foreign trade simply by implementing it. However, that involvement was also causing problems because, like other UN organizations, UNCTAD was based first of all on sovereign nations, and international organizations like the EEC were not supposed to have more than an observer status. Yet, in the meetings on manufacture and commodities, the EEC representatives claimed an exclusive right and power in the name of the member states, which led the Director of the Manufacture Division Krish-

---

[74] Ibid., Krishnamurti to Herbst, 20 June 1968.
[75] Ibid., Herbst to Krishnamurti, 3 July 1968.
[76] Ibid., Krishnamurti to Herbst, 21 November 1968.
[77] Ibid., Stein-Rossen to Walter, 26 October 1970.
[78] Ibid., Perez-Guerrero to Prebisch, 7 March 1969.
[79] Ibid., Perez-Guererro to Parmentier, 18 March 1971.
[80] Ibid., Martin to Guerrero, 26 October 1972.
[81] Ibid., Perez-Guerrero to Mansholt, 5 January 1973

namurti to ask for internal legal advice.[82] UNCTAD's lawyers' opinion was to allow only a limited participation of the EEC.[83] But UNCTAD's officials who worked with EEC representatives expressed a different opinion: in the Manufacture Division, Stordel supported EEC's participation as such, as was already the case in the GATT;[84] in the Commodities Division, Assistant Director Unsworth suggested the EEC be given a status "somewhat more different from that of a mere observer."[85] Secretary General Perez-Guerrero again asked UNCTAD's Legal Counsel about the status of the EEC "as observer or as participating fully," stressing the difference between the committees' meetings on manufacture or commodities and the sessions of the Trade and Development Board, where only states could sit. The Legal Counsel acknowledged it and suggested a status as participant without the right to vote, seating them next to representatives of EEC member states. But it also invited the EEC to "recognize that it would not be in its interests to process for a more formal status, to the point of arousing opposition from members of the body concerned," probably bearing in mind socialist countries' hostility towards the EEC.[86]

To link the EEC to UNCTAD's project of building a new economic order was an achievement that resulted largely from the personal ties and good working relationships formed at the lower level. Beside that achievement, there was however a matter of permanent concern in UNCTAD: the EEC led its own trade and development policy towards African and Asian countries that had been under colonial rule by the European countries[87]. Until the Treaty of Rome was signed in 1957, France had negotiated very hard to ensure its colonies the same trade privileges in the EEC as the metropolitan territory. Those privileges were then granted in 1963 and renewed in 1969 for the newly independent states that sign-

---

82 Ibid., Krishnamurti to Coidan, 26 February 1969.
83 Ibid., Okunribido to Coidan, 11 March 1969.
84 Ibid., Stordel to Krishnamurti, 20 March 1969.
85 Ibid., Unsworth to Perez-Guererro, 14 March 1969, 4
86 Ibid., Stavropoulos to Perez-Guerrero, 10 March 1970.
87 Siegfried Schoene, "UNCTAD III: das Problem der besonderen Beziehungen zwischen der Europäischen Gemeinschaft und Afrika," *Africa Spectrum* 7, no. 1 (1972): 27-43; Vahsen, Urban. *Eurafrikanische Entwicklungskooperation: Die Assoziierungspolitik der EWG gegenüber dem subsaharischen Afrika in den 1960er Jahren*. Stuttgart: Steiner, 2010; James Mayall, "The shadow of the Empire: the EU and the former colonial world," in *International relations and the European Union*, ed. Christopher Hill and Michael Smith (Oxford: Oxford University Press, 2011); see also Giuliano Garavini, *After Empires: European Integration, Decolonization, and the Challenge from the Global South 1957–1986* (Oxford: Oxford University Press, 2012).

ed the Yaoundé Agreement.[88] The Lomé Convention of 1975 not only extended trade preferences to new, former British colonial countries, forming the African, Caribbean and Pacific Group of States (ACP), but it also introduced some new stabilization mechanisms. The most important among them was the STABEX (Système de Stabilisation des Recettes d'Exportation), a kind of regional common stabilization fund that was strikingly similar to the buffer stocks dealt with at UNCTAD.[89] On the one hand, the Lomé Convention seemed to be in line with UNCTAD's project and even to be ahead of it. On the other hand, such a regional trade organization ran counter the very principles of UNCTAD by maintaining and strengthening ties with the former metropolitan countries and preventing the new independent developing countries from trading with their neighboring countries, thus hampering economic cooperation between the developing countries.

The EEC's policy of "association" was internally criticized in UNCTAD itself. This is for instance how the Deputy Secretary of the Trade and Development Board, Moses Adebanjo, understood "association":

> There is a strong international pressure for the removal of barriers to trade and for gaining freer access to world markets especially for products exported by the developing countries. Association is incompatible with the the objectives of UNCTAD as it creates artificial economic relationships between the metropolitan states and the associated countries and also restricts through the ingenious contrivance of reverse preferences the developing countries' choice of suppliers.[90]

This suspicion of the EEC policy of association was also reflected in the fact that the Joint Assembly of EEC and ACP countries established by the Lomé Convention was not recognized before 1990, when Secretary General Dadzie wrote an official Letter to its then president Leo Tindemans.[91] During the sessions of the Trade and Development Board, the association policy was regularly under attack from the socialist countries as well as from some developing countries. In 1973, as the Convention was discussed, one representative stated for instance that association "constituted a threat to the principle of non-discrimination and

---

88 Martin Rempe, *Entwicklung im Konflikt: die EWG und der Senegal 1957–1975* (Cologne: Böhlau Verlag, 2012).
89 Lili Reyels, *Die Entstehung Des Ersten Vertrags von Lomé Im Deutsch-Französischen Spannungsfeld 1973–1975* (Baden-Baden: Nomos Verlag, 2008).
90 UNCTAD, ARR 40/1842, TDO 440, box 164: Adebanjo to Parmentier, 31 January 1970.
91 Ibid., Dadzie to Tindemans, 5 January 1990.

faced the developing countries with a new form of discriminatory policy."[92] Another asserted that "compensation for commodities imported from 'associable' countries were intended to destroy the unity of developing countries."[93] An EEC spokesman tried to recall that the EEC "had paid special attention to the interests and the preoccupations of developing countries."[94] He especially presented the Lomé Convention as an extension of the General System of Preferences to the field of commodities.[95] In 1975, as the Convention had been signed, he went a step further by calling it "an example of the way in which common problems could be tackled."[96] It must be stressed that not all developing countries were hostile to that policy, as shown by the statement of by a representative from one of the beneficiary countries, stating that the Lomé Convention was "a useful example of the type of treatment that must be accorded to all developing countries."[97] The fact that the developing countries did not share the same views on the one hand and desired to save the good results obtained with the General System of Preferences on the other hand, might explain why the General Secretariat did not make a case against the Lomé Convention.

Conclusion: the decline of UNCTAD

In the 1970s, UNCTAD's strength rested not only on the political consensus among the developing countries in the Group of 77, but also on its ability to involve developed countries from the West as well as from the East. UNCTAD's General Secretariat managed to do that by crafting a common intellectual framework in which Keynesian views on market regulation could coexist with state planning, while making diplomatic trade-offs with groupings of countries like the socialist countries or international organizations like the EEC.

However, most of the policies promoted by UNCTAD were implemented very slowly, if at all, because they were confronted by a strong reluctance from developed countries. That reluctance culminated in Ronald Reagan's refusal to go into

---

92 UNCTAD, TDB/ A/9015/Rev.1: *Report of the Trade and Development Board (26 October 1972 – 11 September 1973)*,1974, 22.
93 Ibid., 19.
94 Ibid., 23.
95 UNCTAD, TDB/ A/9615/Rev.1: *Report of the Trade and Development Board (12 September 1973 – 13 September 1974)*, 1975, 7.
96 UNCTAD, TDB/ A/10015/Rev.1: *Report of the Trade and Development Board (10 March 1975 – 2 October 1975)*, 1976, 138.
97 Ibid., 132.

further into discussions at the Conference of Cancun in 1981, thus putting an end to the NIEO process. In a lucid report he wrote to the new Secretary General, Kenneth Dadzie, in 1986, Commodities Division's Director Ashiabor gave a negative assessment of the previous ten years since the NIEO program had been adopted.[98] At the same time, differentiation had been increasing among the developing countries, with the South Asian countries booming, the South American countries suffering from a deep financial crisis and the majority of the "least developed" countries remaining in Africa. The basis of consensus was crumbling among the developing countries, while developed countries were not as ready as before to collaborate.

At the level of UNCTAD's divisions, it is possible to document the deterioration of the coalitions built in the 1970s. For instance, the EEC's status in Commodities or Manufacture Committee was again questioned in a 1982 letter from the General Secretariat's Legal Council[99] and no solution was found in the following years. At committee sessions, EEC member states were not allowed to group themselves under a common 'EEC' sign. The interdivision tensions about the socialist countries also rose: the "consultative machinery" that had been created to facilitate trade contacts between the developing and the socialist countries was now criticized by the Manufacture Division, whose proposal it was to integrate it into the Special Committee for the General System of Preferences.[100] Staff members of the TRADSOC division were increasingly confronted with the view that the socialist countries had protectionist practices too, and they struggled in response to present a "correct picture" of those countries.[101] Such criticism gave the impression that the TRADSOC was losing ground: in 1986, division director Evgeni Krasnov expressed his feeling to the Secretary General that his division was excluded from preparations for the forthcoming UNCTAD.[102]

The very intellectual framework that had made it possible to conceive such coalitions was under severe strain. The assumption that laid the basis for the NIEO was national sovereignty, which was congruent with the legitimacy of

---

98 UNCTAD, ARR 40/1882, 411, TD 312: International Policy on Commodities. Some Preliminary Ideas, 19 March 1986.
99 UNCTAD, ARR 40/1842, TDO 440, box 164: Scott to Suy, 18 February 1982.
100 UNCTAD, ARR 40/1929, box 546, TD 802/5: Consultative machinery of UNCTAD dealing with problems in trade and economic relations among countries having different economic and social systems, 24 February 1978.
101 UNCTAD, ARR 40/1929, box 546, TD 802/5: TDB/981 (Part 1): Protectionism and structural adjustment in the world economy. Part 1: analysis of major issues and policy, 2 March 1984.
102 UNCTAD, ARR 40/1929, box 546, TD 804: Krasnov to Dadzie, 17 January 1986.

state intervention and planning in the economic field. But in the 1980s, as a result of the rise of neoliberal economic conceptions. Many countries shifted their policies accordingly, not only in Europe and North America, but also among developing countries, like India, South Korea or Vietnam. By redefining the role of the state, the neoliberal ideology also broke the framework that combined Keynesian regulation and socialist state planning as two forms of economic planning in a continuum. In that sense, the failure of the NIEO and UNCTAD was first of all a failure of the state as a political model.

It is true that during the 1980s, UNCTAD's Secretariat General promoted a range of policies that relied on state intervention: among others, it supported the idea of state trading and of "countertrade"[103] and helped to found the Association for State Trading Organization (ASTRO) in 1984, meant as an expression of "self-reliance,"[104] by organizing a training seminar to promote it in 1980.[105] However, the initial project of planned world trade resulting from a multilateral dialogue between equal nations had in fact shrunk to a handful of countries practicing countertrade due to their lack of currency and levels of indebtedness. This was very far from the initial project of the New International Economic Order, which aimed to "correct inequalities and redress existing injustices, make it possible to eliminate the widening gap between the developed and the developing countries and ensure steadily accelerating economic and social development and peace and justice."[106] Founded in 1994, the World Trade Organization (WTO) represented a new attempt at establishing a new world trade order, yet it was based on free trade principles that were completely contrary to NIEO's and UNCTAD's principles and contributed to the marginalization of those organizations. The WTO experienced few successes and many contestations. With the ongoing crisis of multilateralism from the failure of the Doha Round to the present situation, a new fair world trade order is still ahead of us.

---

[103] UNCTAD, ARR 40/1929, box 589, TDE 171/3: State trading (January 1984-May 1991).
[104] See UNCTAD, ARR 40/1929, box 589, TDE 171/3: *Association of State Trading Organizations of Developing Countries (ASTRO)*, 29 March 1985, as well as ibid., TDE 171/3(1): Cooperation among State trading enterprises of developing countries (January 1980–December 1986).
[105] Ibid., TDE 171/3(7): *Seminar on the promotion of Trade by Stade tarding organizations (STOs)*, 28 August 1980.
[106] UN A/RES/S-6/3201, see also http://www.un-documents.net/s6r3201.htm (accessed 14 February 2017).

Jenny Andersson
Planning the Future of World Markets: the OECD's Interfuturs Project

In 1975, the Organisation for Economic Co-operation and Development (OECD) launched a research project entitled *Interfutures. Research project into the development of the advanced industrial societies in harmony with the developing world*.[1] The purpose of the project, initiated by the Japanese government and funded partly by the Toyota foundation, was to investigate alternative patterns of development for the Western economies in a new and interconnected world. What was referred to, in the project, as the advanced industrialized societies were increasingly addressing what Interfutures described as "structural challenges." Interfutures was appointed at the same time as a group led by the American economist William McCracken. The McCracken report introduced the idea of structural challenges in Western economies, with the purpose of bringing home the argument that the long period of growth and welfare statism was over.[2] While the McCracken group dealt with the prospect of post-OPEC economic policies specifically, Interfutures was charged with reflecting on the need for a new long term strategy for the West, a strategy that could surpass the habitual horizon of conjectural planning and deal with the new phenomenon of uncertainty in a changing world economy. The problem of increasing uncertainty in the world environment would be met by setting out a "long term vision of the major problems to which society will be confronted."[3]

'Structural issues,' 'interdependence,' and 'uncertainties' were among the many 1970s neologisms that informed the Interfuturs group but that also positioned Interfuturs in a new field of emergent planning methods and forms of expertize from the mid-1970s on. The literature describes the 1970s as marking a watershed moment and break from the long postwar period: a shock of the global due to the arrival, center stage, of the developing world as actors in their own right; a structural *nach dem Boom* marked by the end of stable industrial growth;

---

[1] OECD archives, *Interfutures*, 1975–1979. The research leading to these results has received funding from the European Research Council through ERC Grant 283706.
[2] Paul McCracken, Guido Carli, Herbert Giersch, Attila Karaosmanoglu, Ryutaro Komiya, Assar Lindbeck, Robert Marjolin and Robin Matthews, *Towards Full Employment and Price Stability: A Report to the OECD by a Group of Independent Experts* (Paris: The Organisation for Economic Co-operation and Development, 1977).
[3] Interfutures, "Proposed meeting of senior policy officials, draft of the background paper," 5 February, FUT (78) 3.

a crisis of predictability that shook patterns of national cohesion and social stability; or, as Matthias Schmelzer has most recently suggested, an ideological crisis of growthmanship – the governmental regime par excellence of the postwar period. [4] Interfutures was a key reflection on all of these issues, and of the way that they raised a profound challenge to the historical category of the Western world in an emergent world order that no longer reflected the stability of the Bretton Woods era. As such, the Interfutures project stands as a key record of a 1970s reflection on an open-ended process of globalization that challenged Western notions of hegemony and control. This chapter places the Interfutures group in the context of other groups of research, planning and policy concern that emerged in the 1970s and that were, in different ways, reflections on radical interdependence, such as indeed the McCracken group, the American Trilateral Commission or the Club of Rome. These groups were central Western sites of circulation and definition of the meaning of globality, in the sense of the correct interpretation of the challenges to a postwar world order dominated by the industrial visions of the nineteenth century and by a stable power balance between East and West. In the context of a wider global struggle over the meaning of interdependence, a struggle in which the developing or so-called Third world had for the first time its own arguments, Interfutures demonstrates how these spaces became the sites of a structured Western response to notions of globalization that seemed to run counter to the socioeconomic interests of the Western world. This refers in particular to the radical visions of globalization that emerged from, on the one hand, environmentalism, and, on the other, Third worldism and the so-called New International Economic Order. In line with an emerging historiography, this chapter argues that the Interfutures group carried early versions of neoliberal arguments organized around a dominant notion of the world market, and that its main purpose was to set out a distinctly Western, liberal, and defensive strategy of globalization. This strategy had as its purpose the management of the challenge of interdependence over the long term, so that Western interests could be assured in the future.

---

4 Matthew Connelly, "Future Shock: The End of the World as They Knew It," in *Shock of the Global*, ed, Niall Ferguson, Charles S. Maier, Erez Manela, Daniel J Sargent (Cambridge, Mass.: Harvard University Press, 2010), 337–351, 339; Daniel Rodgers, *Age of Fracture* (Cambridge, Mass.: Harvard University Press, 2011); Matthias Schmelzer, *The Hegemony of Growth: The OECD and the Making of the Economic Growth Paradigm* (Cambridge: Cambridge University Press, 2016); Anselm Doering-Manteuffel and Raphael Lutz, *Nach dem Boom: Perspektiven auf die Zeitgeschichte seit 1970* (Bonn: Vandenhoeck & Ruprecht, 2012); Matthias Schmelzer, "The crisis before the crisis: the 'problems of modern society'and the OECD, 1968–74," *European Review of History: Revue européenne d'histoire* 19, no. 6, (2012): 999–1020.

By pointing to the link between such originally defensive reactions to a set of radical world discourses, and an emergent neoliberal Western world view, the argument allows us to add nuance to the prevailing understanding of the geneaology of neoliberalism in global politics since the 1970s. What we call in shorthand neoliberalism was never a clear cut paradigm but should be understood as a gradual outcome of a battle between a set of much larger discourses on the world's future in the 1970s.[5] The OECD, an organization that was first created in the context of the Marshall Plan in 1948, emerged in the context of the oil crises in the early 1970s as the "steward of globalisation," the overseer of a process of global interconnectedness that seemed to threaten the interests of the Western world and that required, therefore, new tools of planning, management and control.[6] Several studies have pinpointed the role of the OECD as a site for the circulation of early neoliberal ideas. These ideas, carried by the high level expert reports circulated by the OECD in the 1970s were different in nature than the first generation of neoliberal thinking that had emerged from the "neoliberal thought collective" of Hayek's Mount Pelerin Society in the 1950s.[7] They were allegedly non-ideological and did not take place on the level of doctrine or political theory. Rather, they were inscribed in pragmatic and technocratic arguments concerning planning and policy tools and showcased as forms of problem solving for welfare capitalist economies. Around such arguments, liberal, neoliberal, as well as progressive economists and planners could gather.[8]

Meanwhile, the ideas presented by the Interfutures group stood in close connection to other notions of interdependence. The McCracken report, which included some of the world's most famous economists, became a landmark report not only for its diagnosis of problems hitherto understood as conjectural and structural, and thus having endemic causes within Western industrial economies, but also for the remedies that it proposed: liberalization of labour markets and social systems, a new set of social compromises based on lower expecta-

---

[5] Johanna Bockman, "Socialist Globalization against Capitalist Neocolonialism: The Economic Ideas behind the New International Economic Order," *Humanity: An International Journal of Human Rights, Humanitarianism, and Development* 6, no. 1 (2015): 109–128.
[6] Mathieu Leimgruber, "Stewards of globalisation." Unpublished paper.
[7] Dieter Plehwe and Philip Mirowski, *The Road from Mount Pelerin: The Making of a Neoliberal Thought Collective* (Cambridge, Mass.: Harvard University Press, 2010).
[8] Vincent Gayon. "L'OCDE au travail. Contribution à une sociologie historique de la 'coopération économique internationale' sur le chômage et l'emploi (1970–2010)" (PhD. Diss, Université Paris I-Panthéon Sorbonne, 2010) ; Francois Denord, *Neoliberalisme version française. Histoire d'une idéologie politique* (Paris: Demopolis, 2007); Laurent Warlouzet, *Governing Europe in a Globalizing World. Neoliberalism and its Alternatives following the 1973 crisis* (London: Routledge, 2018).

tions on growth and redistribution, less state intervention and more market mechanisms, and more openness toward global markets.[9] As Vincent Gayon has shown, the publication of the McCracken report settled a central dispute as both Keynesian and monetarist economists agreed on what was essentially a turn to monetarism in the organization's ensuing economic expertize.[10] Rawi Abdelal has shown how the OECD in a similar manner became the privileged arena for the creation of a liberalized framework for the financial markets, and that this framework, designed to foster a global expansion of capital markets, was in fact pushed through by former socialists such as the French premier Jacques Delors, with the idea that liberalization would provide a new market rationality and stability.[11] This turn within the OECD to seemingly apolitical forms of expertize is important because it permits us to add nuance to the historiography of neoliberalism as a project of ideological vanguards, the influence of which was for the most part still very marginal in the 1970s. What it instead brings out is how specific notions of expertize in themselves became the solution for settling an intensely contested process of globalization.

It is pertinent to place the notion of the future in this context. Interfutures is of interest to this volume because of its interest in new future-oriented planning technologies through which it thought world relationships might be made manageable over the 'long term,' in other words, over a new horizon of time stretching beyond the conventional horizon of planning systems. In addition, as presented by Interfutures, such tools, which included the much marketed scenario tool, were thought to have a new and global spatial scope, through which they could embrace problems of complexity, interdependence and uncertainty in a world system. A central element of the Interfutures project was indeed that it proposed shifting the gaze of planning from conjectural macro economic planning, toward the setting of long-term strategic goals and objectives. This included an emphasis on shaping shared images of the process of globalization and the diffusion onto the world level of positive images of the world market.

---

9 Paul McCracken Guido Carli, Herbert Giersch, Attila Karaosmanoglu, Ryutaro Komiya, Assar Lindbeck, Robert Marjolin, Robin Matthews, . *Towards Full Employment and Price Stability: A Report to the OECD by a Group of Independent Experts* (Paris: The Organisation for Economic Co-operation and Development, 1977). See Charles S. Maier, "'Malaise': The Crisis of Capitalism in the 1970s," in *Shock of the Global*, 25–48. Robert Brenner, *The Economics of Global Turbulence: The Advanced Capitalist Economies from Long Boom to Long Downturn, 1945–2000* (London: Verso, 2006).
10 Gayon, *L'OCDE au travail*.
11 Ravi Abdelal, *Capital Rules : The Construction of Global Finance* (Cambridge Mass.: Harvard University Press, 2007).

Interfutures marked a turn here in international organizations as tools, such as scenarios, forecasts and indicators, in which coping with uncertainty and unpredictability by setting out images, expectations and scenarios of development was key.

The problem of interdependence

Interdependence was a Western term, used to describe a phenomenon of planetary disorder, a shake-up of global power relations and a threat to the category of the industrial world. As such, the term interdependence also served to reiterate Western interests in this potentially messy process. Interdependence as a term had antecedents in earlier postwar reflections on the impact of an emergent *tiers monde* that introduced an element of chaos into world relationships. In 1953, the French demographer Alfred Sauvy, famous for having coined the term 'Third World,' wrote that this new world was defined precisely by its rejection of Western images of the future, and its ambition to create images of its own. Sauvy did so in a context that is not without importance for us here, as a member of the circle of French planners who developed the so-called *prospective* method as a form of long term planning.[12] The *prospective* method would resurface as the method of choice of the Interfutures project, in direct proximity to scenarios taken from American forecasting. The emphasis on interdependence as a process that needed guidance in order to shift from a potentially conflict-ridden state of affairs, into a question of 'harmonious' relationships, was a response to other 1970s discourses on the world economy, which, inspired by dependency and world system theory, emphasized global structures as reflections of profound imbalances between a developed and a developing world, or even as a projection of the Marxist class struggle at the global level. Interdependence could, as Interfutures would suggest, be managed by the active creation of new and "harmonious relations" between the West and the Third World, if methods for such management were found. It was precisely through an emphasis on methods that Interfutures set out the elements of what were to become the dominant Western interpretation of globalization, and arguably, it was precisely as the methods of steering new world relationships appeared that forms of future research found their relevance on the global level.

---

12 Alfred Sauvy, *Le Tiers Monde* (Paris: Presse Universitaires de France, 1956).
　　Jenny Andersson, *The Future of the World: Futurists, Futurology and the Struggle for the Post Cold War Imagination* (Oxford: Oxford University Press, forthcoming 2018).

Interfutures sat at the same time as the American Trilateral Commission, appointed to resuture an American worldview broken by the problem of multipolarity. "Managing interdependence," as formulated both in the Trilateral commission and the Interfutures program, was a euphemism for finding the political technologies and planning tools with which a new confrontational world situation could be pushed toward forms of strategic cooperation.[13] Another shared denominator between the Interfutures group and the Trilateral Commission was the theme of 'ungovernability,' a definition proposed by the Trilateral Commisson to denote problems of rigidity in Western welfare states and social systems.[14] Both Interfutures and the Trilateral Commission performed a central analytical move as they joined together, in the notion of interdependence, problems of uncertainty in the outside world environment with the idea of uncertainty within Western societies. The latter were understood as having been unleashed by forms of social crisis with roots in Western systems of governance. By joining these two elements of crisis together, both Interfutures and the Trilateral Commission also came to the conclusion that the capacities of the West to meet a transformed world order in which the Third World now had a bargaining position hinged on its ability to draw developing countries into an expanding world market. In addition, Western competitiveness needed to be restored through the reform of labor markets and welfare states.[15] In this sense, 'interdependence' was more than a description of a new phenomenon of globality, it was term charged with a heavy historical legacy of Western hegemony and a diagnosis of a situation in which the colonial relationships inherited from the nineteenth century were giving way to a new symmetry in power relations. In this world situation, the meaning of First, Second and Third World was no longer clear.

The Interfutures program defined interdependence as a threefold problem: First, the oil crisis was the final indication that the long period of stability around industrial society was over. Faltering growth rates and new forms of social conflict eroded the basis of Fordist societies. Moreover, the volatility that

---

[13] Stephen Gill, *American Hegemony and the Trilateral Commission* (Cambridge, Mass.: Harvard University Press, 2009). Phillip Golub, "From the new international order to the G20," *Third World Quarterly*, 34, no. 6 (2013): 1000–1015.

[14] Trilateral Commission, *Towards a Renovated International System* (Washington, 1977). Interfutures, Documents concerning the Interfutures program 1977–1980 MAS 80.9, ED 80–11, OECD archives, Paris. Interfuturs, *Facing the Future* (Paris: The Organisation for Economic Co-operation and Development, 1977), 179.

[15] "Resume of the Interfutures conceptual framework regarding the Advanced Industrial Societies Rigidities." OECD archives.

growth rates and price levels had encountered in the 1960s and the first half of the 1970s seemed to mark the end of conjectural market patterns, and introduced a concern with fluctuations in commodity markets that defied predictability and governability. Second, the liberal capitalist economies were increasingly competing with the socialist planned economies over resources, technological development and investment. A relatively stable Cold War relationship was thus changing as both worlds were entering the post-industrial era and encountered similar problems of value and labor change, the skills revolution, and new struggles for energy and raw materials. Third, this process of possible convergence (convergence theory boomed in the decade prior to the Interfutures group) was disturbed through the confrontation with the Third World, which forced both Western societies and the economies of the Eastern bloc to seek new competitive alliances. In the years leading up to OPEC, the Third World had shown that it was no longer content to be the object of development policies, and was increasingly claiming a fair share of world development. This included access to markets for advanced industrial goods, an increased share of world industrial labor, and controls over prices of its raw materials in what to Interfutures was nothing less than a full shake-up of the postwar world order.[16] In summary, world hierarchies were in flux. Interfutures gave expression to this flux as the group proposed a new categorization of the world into the 'Advanced Industrial Economies,' AIS, which included the socialist countries, on the one hand, and on the other, the LDCs of the developing world. Meanwhile, the Interfutures report, published in 1979, foresaw important processes of fracture also disintegrating these new geopolitical categories. The Western world was, in the light of problems such as price fluctuations, wage drift, expanding public sectors, and stop and go policies, at the risk of no longer representing a coherent and unified system of organized market economies. Some countries (France, the UK) ressembled developing nations in their reliance on a growing state apparatus and failing macro economic policies. The incoherence in the use of macro economic planning was a threat to a united AIS position that might have been able to meet Third Worldism with a single Western strategy. The core problem with the second category, the developing countries, was of course its new and menacing role as a collective agent in an inverted bargaining game. But Interfutures pointed out that the hope for new and harmonious relations between the Third World and the OECD countries lay in the fact that Third Worldism was not stable and was al-

---

16 Glenda Sluga, "The transformation of international institutions: Global shock as cultural shock," in *Shock of the Global*, ed. Niall Fergusson, Charles S. Maier, Erez Manela, Daniel J Sargent (Cambridge, Mass.: Harvard University Press, 2010), 223–237.

ready breaking up between oil exporters and importers. A number of countries – Iran, India, Brezil, South Africa, Mexico, and Algeria – were contenders for industrialism, while other Third World countries – such as Bangladesh – were basically only the sites of location for Western industries. Japan (the third node of the Trilateral Commission) occupied an intermediary place with its hyper industrialization and increasing reliance on raw materials. Highly energy sensitive, Japan was challenging Europe for oil. With its Western system of governance after 1945 and the direct links between its planning elites and Western networks, Japan was an extension of the Western world in Asia. Interdependence was thus a fundamentally fractious process which posed not one but many problems of coordination, but also the opportunity for strategic alliances if common interests over the long-term could be found. Interfutures' problem was how to reassert the AIS' interests over the long-term by possibly making strategic concessions to the most advanced LDCs for the purpose of protecting long term hegemony.[17]

The vision of global challenges put forward by the notion of interdependence was thus one that reflected a highly Western biased conception of changes to world order, and a limited take on globality. The Interfutures group also used the term to refer to a different set of issues that by the mid 1970s were labelled 'world problems' or 'common problems,' and that went beyond problems of coordination between categories and depicted planning problems that could not be dealt with within the frame of the nation state and national planning systems such as those developed during the postwar period. In radical globality discourses, so-called 'world problems' were understood as problems that necessitated common solutions, in other words forms of planning and decision-making surpassing the national, the bipolar or even the transnational level and that could only efficiently take place on a new level of world, for instance in the form of world government, world regulation or indeed world plans. This latter notion – the idea that the entire world system could be planned – was as we will see an idea that flourished along with the many different models of the world economy that marked the first half of the 1970s. In most of these models, problems in the world economy were perceived as shared, or indeed common. The Club of Rome, in many ways a twin project to that of Interfutures but guilty in the eyes of the OECD of the problematic *Limits to Growth*-report in 1972, spoke of problems in the world system using the term *world problematique*, denoting encompassing problems that concerned the world as a whole.

It is important to note, in this regard, that Interfutures dealt to only a small extent with such notions of common or world problems, and spoke instead of

---

[17] Interfutures, chapter drafts (in particular VI, XI, XIX), OECD archives.

'problems of development.' This was a highly conscious choice. The euphemism 'problems of development' hid the fundamental tension between discourses affirming globality by arguing that the interests of the whole world required change on the level of the world system, and discourses that either emphasized 'common futures' by pinpointing trans-border problems such as environment or armament, or reaffirmed, like Interfutures, the stakes of the Western world and new strategic alliances with the South.[18] Interfutures did not set out to address development as a common world problem of over vs. under development in a systemic whole, as did radical planners such as the Dutch Jan Tinbergen or the Armenian born American systems analyst Hazan Ozbekhan in connection to NIEO debates at the same time (see below). Rather, it addressed development as a set of fractures that challenged the dominance of the industrialized world in a new struggle over an international division of industrial labor. The first of these fractures was the acute crisis in relationships between AIS and LDCs already described. The second fracture was the conflict between resource extraction and nature, highlighted by the Club of Rome-report and directly in conflict with the OECD's prevailing notion of development as economic growth. [19] The third fracture was more subtle but the most important, as a large part of Interfutures would also cater to the issue of reactions to development in terms of 'changing socio-cultural values' and instability within Western nations. The problem of interdependence, in other words, was not a problem of addressing problems common to the world in the interest of all, but rather, a problem of reigning in an emergent new world order so that fundamental categories of the developing and developed world could be restored. By articulating and framing problems of interdependence as problems that could be solved if the interest of each was reasserted, the OECD reiterated the liberal capitalist West as a category under threat of losing its world dominance, but with a historically legitimate interest in maintaining its hegemonic position.

Planning the world: origins of futurology

Interfutures' mission was in fact a two fold one, as its work not only consisted in the strategic analysis of a new world situation marked by interdependence, but

---

[18] Jenny Andersson and Sibylle Duhautois, "The future of Mankind " in *The Politics of Globality Since 1945: Assembling the Planet*, ed. Casper Sylvest and Rens van Munster (New York: Routledge, 2015), 106–125.
[19] Schmelzer, *The Hegemony of Growth*.

also in examining which new methods of planning could permit overseeing and managing this new situation. Interfutures was thus devoted from the onset to the question of methods, and to the particular technologies that could transform a global situation of conflict and struggle for resources into one of "harmonious development."[20] The program proposed using forms of long-term or long range planning, including scenarios, *prospective* and modelling, as its particular method.

Futurological tools proliferated in planning circles in the period from the mid 1960s to the mid 1970s. While historians have dealt with the transnational networks of planners in the interwar and postwar era, much less historical research has been devoted to the circulation of concepts and tools of planning informed by ideas of complexity, interdependence, risk and having as their focus the long term from the 1970s on.[21] Meanwhile, as argued here, this second mode in planning implied a notable expansion of planning rationalities, both with reference to the 'long term' as temporal horizon, and to the global scale. Future research, for instance the scenario method experimented with by Interfutures, originated in technological forecasting and Cold War strategy. Both focused on the idea of the 'long range,' a category produced by nuclear strategy and ballistic research. From the mid 1960s on, forms of forecasting began to be considered as ways of planning change in non-technological systems, including social organizations and the political system.[22] In the Eastern bloc, the proclamation of the Scientific and Technological Revolution emphasized scientific management, and rehabilitated forecasting as a key planning technology (it had already been used as part of Lenin's NEP in the interwar period). A decision by the central Party committee for the use of forecasting as part of scientific management in 1967, led to the explosion of sectoral and governmental forecasting activities in socialist economies, and in 1967 and 1968 there were several transnational meet-

---

20 Interfutures, "Mission statement. Description of the research project". OECD archives.
21 Patricia Clavin, "Defining transnationalism," *Contemporary European History* 14 (2005): 421–439. David Engerman and Corinna Unger, "Introduction: Towards a Global History of Modernization," *Diplomatic History* 33, no. 3 (2009): 375–385. David Engerman, Nils Gilman, Mark H. Haefele, Michael E. Latham *Staging Growth: Modernization, Development, and the Global Cold War* (Boston: University of Massachusetts Press, 2003).
22 On the transfer of planning tools from the military to the civilian apparatus, see Jennifer Light, *From Warfare to welfare* (Baltimore: John Hopkins Press, 2002); David Jardini, *Out of the Blue Yonder: The RAND Corporation's Diversification into Social Welfare Research* (Baltimore: Carnegie Mellon University, 1996); Sharon Ghamari Tabrizi, *The Intutitive Science of Herman Kahn* (Cambridge, Mass.: Harvard University Press, 2005).

ings of socialist forecasters.²³ On the other side of the Atlantic, a national Science and Technology policy which included a much more active role for federal government and a turn to new planning tools such as cost benefit analysis and forecasting began under the Kennedy and subsequently the Johnson administrations.²⁴ From 1972 on, the debate over future research as a new planning tool also inspired the creation of ad hoc commissions to national planning systems in Europe – the Netherlands, Sweden, France, West Germany, UK – and Japan. These commissions were national spaces but they also functioned as international hubs for the circulation of methods, writing, and forms of expertize. The methods of forecasting, systems analysis, global modelling and scenario analysis laid the basis for new communities of planners, oftentime consultants, who moved between national planning commissions and transnational sites such as the Club of Rome, IIASA, or Interfutures.²⁵

Like its more insubordinate twin, the Club of Rome, Interfutures stemmed from a central gathering of planners organized by the OECD in Bellagio in 1969. The Bellagio conference, the theme of which was "Long range forecasting and planning" was called by the OECD's Science Policy Unit around the theme of 'problems of modern societies.' ²⁶ As Matthias Schmelzer has shown, problems of modern societies was a euphemism for the concern within parts of the OECD with the critique of growth by the late 1960s and the discovery of both the environmental and social costs of economic development. The OECD's Science Policy Unit was created by Alexander King, the initiator, with Aurelio Peccei, of the Club of Rome, as part of a turn away from the strict postwar focus on growth within the organization. King used the Science Policy Directorate in order to criticize the standing of the idea of industrial development, convinced as he was that the prerequisites for industrial development were exhausted and that growth based on resource extraction had reached maturity in the Western world.²⁷ He thought that the Western world had to develop a more nuanced ap-

---

23 See Viteszlav Sommer, "Forecasting the Post-Socialist Future: Prognostika in Late Socialist Czechoslovakia, 1970 – 1989," in *The Struggle for the Long Term in Transnational Science and Politics*, ed. Jenny Andersson and Egle Rindzeviciute (New York: Routledge, 2015), 144 – 168. Lukasz Becht, "From euphoria to frustration. Institutionalising a system of prognostic research in the people's republic of Poland, 1971–1976," forthcoming and with the permission of the author.
24 Light, *From Warfare to Welfare*, 160 on.
25 Egle Rindzeviciute, *Power of System* (Ithaca: Cornell University Press, 2017).
26 Matthias Schmelzer, "Born in the corridors of the OECD: The forgotten origins of the Club of Rome, transnational networks, and the 1970s in global history," *Journal of Global History* 12 (2017): 26 – 48.
27 Schmelzer, "The crisis before the crisis."

proach to problems of industrial development if capitalism was to survive. This included harnessing the forces of science in better ways and picking up the competition over productivity with the socialist world and the US, as well as developing methods of planning that drew on the so-called policy sciences, the scientific approach to planning that had emerged as part of systems analysis or Operations Research in the 1950s and 1960s. The Bellagio Declaration expressed the OECD's wish to concentrate Western nations' efforts in planning, and stressed the need that Western nations develop forms of long-term forecasting that could help them manage the long-term effects of development in and on their social structures, deal with possible value conflict, and establish priorities for policies.[28]

The Bellagio meeting gathered many of the forecasters and consultants who had been active in spreading the tools of future research. One of these was the German-born engineer Eric Jantsch. Jantsch wrote a much read report on planning and technological forecasting in 1967. It presented the idea that technological change could be actively governed and planned for the benefit of welfare societies and that the unintended consequences and cybernetic feedback loops of new technologies could be forecasted, so that the system of economic and technological change was in actual fact a malleable, controllable entity. It introduced the idea of the *long range*, to a European public of planners. The report also proposed that human values and value reactions to industrial and technological processes were among the things that could be planned and foreseen as systemic feedback functions. This was no small point in the aftermath of 1968 and turbulent years in European societies marked both by anti-nuclear protests and labor market unrest.[29] Jantsch edited the 1969 volume from the Bellagio conference, and in 1972 published *Long range policy and planning* which circulated widely amongst European, American and Japanese planners (and was also translated into Russian and prefaced by Dzhermen Gvishiani).[30] Another participant at Bellagio was the former RAND strategist and software engineer Hasan Ozbekhan. Ozbekhan designed the first model for the Club of Rome, meant to address a 'global predicament' by stressing interdependence in a world system. [31] At Bel-

---

28 Eric Jantsch, *Perspectives on Planning: Papers from the Bellagio Conference* (Paris: The Organisation for Economic Co-operation and Development, 1969).
29 Eric Jantsch, *Technological Forecasting in Perspective* (Paris: The Organisation for Economic Co-operation and Development, 1967).
30 Jantsch, *Perspectives on Planning*.
31 Hasan Ozbekhan, *The Predicament of Mankind: A Quest for Structured Responses to Growing World-wide Complexities and Uncertainties. Original Proposal to the Club of Rome* (New York: Club of Rome, 1970).

lagio, Ozbekhan presented his 'general theory of planning,' which argued that the world could be considered to be a holistic system, and that this system could be planned in order to work towards an overarching value, such as for instance human development or environmental balance. The 'critical problems' of the world could be solved, if the world future was not treated as a problem of prediction, but as a normative problem of setting out an image of what an ideal world future would be like. To Ozbekhan's mind, this had to be about the envisioning of ideal states such as a world without hunger, and an end to the dichotomy of over and under development.[32] Ozbekhan is an example of the radical use of systems theory in forging radical visions of a better and more rational world by the late 1960s and 1970s. But Ozbekhan's model for the Club of Rome, which explicitly incorporated the variable of Western value change as a precondition for a new world equilibrium, was never used and the *Limits to Growth* report published in 1972 was based instead on Jay Forrester's World 2 model, initially designed to monitor the flow of goods in commercial warehouses in Boston harbor.[33] The Interfutures report made use of some of Ozbekhan's ideas but translated the idea of a world system with an ideal future objective into a completely different concern with the future interests of the industrialized nations and the necessity of maintaining the 'market image.'

From systems analysis to world consultancy: Jacques Lesourne and the MITRA group

It is clear from this argument that Interfutures did not represent future research as such, nor an engagement with the more radical attempts to use future research as a way of engaging with globality that existed at the same time. Rather, Interfutures represented a very specific Western take on the world's future. This take needs to be understood in the context of the rationale of the OECD and its mandate to oversee the process of globalization, but in addition, it was a view directly influenced by the conditions of material production within the Interfutures group, by the scenario method used, and specifically, by the use of consultancy. As argued, future research represented a widening of the repertoires of planning, and the extension of the scope of planning rationalities both in

---

[32] Hasan Ozbekhan, *A General Theory of Planning* (Santa Barbara: Systems Development Corporation, 1969).
[33] Elodie Vieille Blanchard, *Les limites à la croissance dans un monde global: modélisations, prospectives, réfutations* (PhD Diss., Paris, EHESS, 2011).

space and time. To this it might be added that future research also involved new forms of circulation, in particular of management techniques, between the public and the corporate spheres. Future research had origins both in military planning, and in the planning entities of large multinational, predominantly American, corporations such as IBM, Kodak, Bell laboratories, Lockheed, Kaiser Aluminum, or the Swiss Battelle Industries. As such, it had direct links to the idea that market mechanisms in various ways could be used as a method of steering and as a complement to plans, but that market activities also required a precision of operational objectives, goals, and processes. In the Eastern bloc, future research was part of a new reform communist toolkit which included management science and systematic forecasting.[34] In the West, future research contributed to a growing industry in indicators of long-term developments in technology and prices, but it also reflected a market metaphor in that it drew on emerging forms of consultancy. Transnational organizations after 1945 put in place new forms of mobility of expertize, as experts moved from national to international planning entities and back again. The growth of the multinational corporation, in the Cold War era, fostered a new kind of mobile expert which was that of the consultant in matters of strategy and decision, who facilitated the interface between corporations and public decision-making bodies on both the national and transnational levels. The OECD's modus operandus with expert groups privileged the use of consultancy, as in many ways the UN-system and the European Community did. Consultants could be academics, on leave for shorter missions, but they could also be professional expert-strategists whose origins were not in academia but in contract-seeking agencies with a mediating role between corporations and national or transnational organizations. As a form of expertize, consultancy enabled new forms of circulation between national and transnational spaces, and forecasting, scenarios, models and forecasts were all technologies that were, from the mid 1960s on, carried by consultancy. Consultancy also created a specific mode for the translation between planning technologies taken from public sectors and decision tools taken from the corporate world. Interfutures mobilized a number of consultants, including the French planner Bernard Cazes, the British sociologist Andrew Shonfield, and the American sociologist Daniel Bell, all of whom were prominent within the field of future research and forecasting (both Shonfeld and Bell wrote central books on forecasting and planning in post-industrial society). It was directed by yet anoth-

---

[34] See Kott and Sommer in this volume.

er consultant, the French systems analyst and *prospectiviste* Jacques Lesourne.³⁵ The method used by Interfutures, the scenario method and *prospective* analysis, was a product of consultancy and the circulation of expertize between decision-making in corporations and forms of public planning. The scenario method had been invented by the nuclear strategist Herman Kahn, first at RAND and then at the neoconservative Washington thinktank, the Hudson Institute. From there, the scenario method was transferred to simulations of domestic developments in the American context (in particular in the field of value tensions and race relations). Kahn also sold a package known as 'Corporate Scenarios' to leading corporations, and in the early 1970s, the French systems analyst Pierre Wack brought the scenario method from the Hudson Institute to Royal Shell, as a means with which to oversee uncertainty in oil markets and reserves.³⁶ The scenario method, which aimed to actively invent or script possible futures, was closely related to another method which influenced the field of future research from the mid 1960s on, French so-called *prospective*. *Prospective* was brought into the Interfutures group through Jacques Lesourne and was essentially a form of decision science that developed in the large French public companies, in particular the SNCF but also the private Saint Gobain. It was to a large extent a consultancy activity that began in the so-called Clubs that grouped together business leaders and politicians, and *prospective* was a key element in the introduction of economic forecasting, business cycle theories, and labor management in France.³⁷ As such *prospective* is highly indicative of what Francois Denord has described as French neoliberalism, a strange alliance between French planners, engineers, and leaders of public and national industries.³⁸ *Prospective* was integrated into the French *Commissariat au Plan* in the mid 1960s. After 1968, its focus became that of considering the impacts of revolutionary value change on French society.³⁹ Both scenarios and *prospective*, in other words, where methods with an ap-

---

35 Jacques Lesourne specialized in labor market issues and also became the editor of *Le Monde*. Biographical note, Interfuturs archives, and Jacques Lesourne, *Les mille sentiers de l'avenir*, (Paris, 1981). Jacques Lesourne, "L'exercice Interfuturs, réflexions méthodologiques," *Futuribles*- no. 26: 20 – 38. Walter Michalski, "The OECD Interfuturs project revisited twenty years later," in *Decision, prospective, auto-organisation. Essais en l'honneur de Jacques Lesourne*, ed. Walter Michalski (Paris, 2000), 318 – 331.
36 Timothy Mitchell, *Carbon Democracy* (Cambridge, Mass.: Harvard University Press, 2013). John R. Williams, "World futures," *Critical Inquiry* 42 (2016): 473 – 546.
37 Jenny Andersson and Pauline Prat, "Gouverner le 'long terme' La production des futurs buraucratique en France," *Gouvernement et action publique*, 3 (2015): 9 – 29.
38 Denord, *Néoliberalisme*.
39 Groupe 1985, *La France face au choc du futur* (Paris: Commissariat General au Plan, 1972).

parent focus on the social, on monitoring values and forms of uncertainty resulting from value change and potential unrest.

Lesourne was well familiar with *prospective*. He was an engineer and management consultant, who as the author of a number of books on business management and planning had introduced key elements of econometrics and business cycle theory in France. In 1958, Lesourne created a consultancy firm SEMA (*Société d'économie et de mathématiques appliqués*) which worked in *prospective* analysis, econometrics and information management.. At the time that he was recruited to Interfutures, Lesourne was centrally placed in the futurological field as assistant director to the International Institute for Applied Systems Analysis, IIASA, and president of the French *Futuribles* association.[40] But in the 1950s Lesourne had also ventured into global consultancy through SEMA's international branch, METRA, which worked on exporting systems analysis and management consultancy to key countries in the south, in particular Morocco, and which had as its particular market niche the aim of helping French multinationals maintain relationships with the former colonies after decolonisation. As demonstrated by Christian in this volume, France, Britain and Belgium reacted against the volatility in commodity markets by the early 1970s by strengthening their ties with former colonies and setting in place systems for price negotiations on primary materials. At the same time, the former colonies, and particularly those on the path of industrial development, became interesting markets for European technological solutions in communication and finance. SEMA-METRA continued to work on strategic advice for French investment banks and companies in North Africa, the Middle East and Iran.[41] In 1975, SEMA became METRA Iran, specialized in providing systems analytical tools for the management of Iranian oil production. Anglo-Persian Oil had been nationalized by the Mossadegh regime in 1951. In 1977, SEMA-METRA produced a report for UNIDO analyzing actor strategies of the Third World and the "future consequences of achieving the Lima objectives" (the Lima objectives were voted in 1975, see below). The re-

---

[40] IIASA was a central site for the development of global modelling from 1972 on in particular in energy and world resources. Egle Rindzeviciute, "Purification and Hybridisation of Soviet Cybernetics: The Politics of Scientific Governance in an Authoritarian Regime," *Archiv für Sozialgeschichte*, 50 (2010): 289–309.

[41] Manfred Pohl, *Handbook on the History of European Banks* (New York: Edward Elgar, 1994), 249. From 1962 on Sema Metra published a periodical on investments and branch structures in Middle Eastern and African economies, *Cahiers Sema*. See "Le développement international du groupe METRA," in *PCM, Révue publiée par l'association professionnelle des ingénieurs des Ponts et Chaussees et des Mines, Les entreprises françaises a l'étranger* 68, no. 10 (1971): 93–99.

port drew on the prospective method that Lesourne was at the same time experimenting for *Interfutures*.[42]

Overcoming limits: reshaping international order

The Interfutures group, and in particular Lesourne, used scenarios as the method for constructing a vision of interdependence that protected key Western interests, and with which it could also reject alternative visions of a new world order and in particular those coming from the *Limits to Growth* report, published a year before OPEC sent oil prices searing, and the RIO-report, written by Jan Tinbergen for UNITAR. RIO codified the theme of a New International Economic Order (NIEO).

Limits to Growth was based on computer models produced by a team of computer analysts and systems programrs under the direction of Dennis and Donatella Meadows at MIT. *Limits* sent a shock wave through the industrialized world with its projection of an "overshoot and collapse" scenario.[43] The report was publically marketed and spread in ways that were strategically oriented at catching public attention, its models and scenarios also intended to work as triggers of the global imagination and to raise attention about an ensuing environmental collapse. As Matthias Schmelzer has shown, the publication of *Limits* created profound tensions within the OECD.[44] The Club of Rome, a group of industrialists and planners under King and Aurelio Peccei (another world consultant, having worked for the Olivetti foundation in Abyssinia) was the creation of the OECD Science Policy Unit as part of its search for a broader idea of planning, capable of embracing common problems and negative feedback loops. But the final message of the report, projecting a future determined by the tension between population and finite available resources and prophesying the end to capitalist development was a little hard to swallow for an organization devoted to protecting the economic development of the Western world. Interfutures was, as Schmelzer shows, a central component in the OECD's attempt to save a fragilized growth paradigm from the mid 1970s onward, by accepting the idea that environmental problems needed to be managed, but by reiterating the importance of growth to lasting social stability in the Western world and by a new insistence on the role of market mechanisms. Interfutures was appointed at the same 1975 Ministerial

---

42 "Industrial development in the Third world. Actor's strategies" (SEMA, METRA International, 1977).
43 Vieille Blanchard, *Limites a la croissance*.
44 Schmelzer, "Born in the corridors of the OECD."

meeting that launched the McCracken group and its theme of structural adjustment. The meeting "put an end to previous debates about the problems of modern society by reaffirming without any qualifications the pursuit of growth as the key responsibility of governments." The ministerial meeting in 1975 included a new emphasis on market mechanisms, as planning and welfare statism were now understood as incapable of overcoming the endemic problem of stagflation.[45] The formulation 'in harmony' in the description of the Interfutures project was a core rejection of the idea of physical boundaries to growth: it referred not only to a reconciliation of interests with the ambitions of development of strategic countries in the Third World, but also to the idea that the physical limits to development as posited by *Limits* could be overcome with less than life altering changes in industrial strategies. In fact there were deemed to be no physical limits to growth. The Interfutures group acknowledged that Mankind was entering a critical stage in its relationship to the ecosphere. But it rejected (as did the McCracken group) the idea that there were physical limits to growth: "The question of physical limits *is not of the form frequently proposed.*" Limits to industrial development were not found in natural resources, but identified instead in a range of others factors and in particular political phenomena such as the protectionist stances motivated by forms of Third Worldism and nationalism, or, importantly, the range of 'socio cultural factors' standing in the way of industrial growth in the advanced capitalist economies.[46] By socio cultural factors was meant the kind of 'psychological' protests against nuclear energy and environmental effects of industrialization that the Western world had witnessed since the late 1960s. Addressing problems of growth meant addressing these sociocultural factors. This included reigning in social struggles so that competitiveness could be restored and cycles of wage expectations broken.[47]

It is unfortunate that the existing literature has not made the links between the environmentalist message of the Club of Rome, the rise of Third Worldism and NIEO, and the ensuing ideas of interdependence in the Western world. These three debates were not isolated, but part of a great conflict over the world's future that makes little sense considered in isolated pieces. Indeed the relevance of Interfutures only stands out if we consider it as a set of counterargu-

---

45 OECD Ministerial meeting 1975, "The imperatives of growth and cooperation," 28 May 1975, quoted in Schmelzer, 317.
46 Interfuturs, FUT (77)S, 9 May 1977. "Midway through Interfutures. A first assessment of world problems. Intermediary results of the Interfutures research project phase A and B," Interfutures Main issue paper 79, 7. OECD archives.
47 Ibid,; Manpower unit, Documents concerning the Interfutures program 1977–1980, MAS (80) 9ED(80)11. OECD archives.

ments to much more radical visions in a wider debate on the world future. The *Limits to growth*-report spawned a global controversy about the uses of modelling, which was technical on the surface but in fact concerned the very idea of world order.[48] The neo-Malthusian framework of *Limits* opened the door for a radicalization of the development debate: if the resources controlling world development were finite within fixed planetary boundaries, then the struggle over the rights of exploitation of these resources was acute.[49] This problem transposed, in a way, the nineteenth-century problem of the class struggle to the level of the world, which Interfutures recognized in its own analysis of a postwar global division of labor.

The Interfutures report has to be understood here as a key building stone in the monumental rejection of the *Limits to Growth* report after 1975, and in the gradual transformation of the apocalyptic arguments of *Limits* into an emphasis on management and sustainable development. These rejections came from different camps. The idea that there were physical limits to growth was inacceptable not only to prevailing Western notions of capitalism, but also to socialist ones. On the initiative of the Romanian president Nicolae Ceaușescu, an alliance of Romanian and African socialist forecasters challenged *Limits* by arguing that post-industrialism and the Scientific Technological Revolution made the resource dependency taken for granted in the model irrelevant by replacing natural resources with intellectual ones. A world of learning and creativity had no limits. The *Limits* report was, they argued, a product of a limited Western capitalist imagination and a "bourgeois futurology."[50] Other models accepted the idea of planetary limits but challenged the way that models partitioned the right to development between the developing and the developed world. The most important intervention here was the so-called Bariloche-Report, written by the Latin American Fondacion Bariloche and deeply influenced by dependency theory. The Bariloche-report argued that *Limits* was an erroneous representation of events, as world catastrophe was not an impending scenario but already at hand with two thirds of global populations living in poverty. Rejecting the idea of a static equilibrium point in the system, the Bariloche-report proposed using modelling in order to answer the question of how a dynamic system could be made to meet what the model referred to as the 'basic needs' of human populations. Covering global needs in the model required a total reorganization of the world economy and international order, in fact a new system that moved beyond both capitalism

---

[48] Andersson, *The Future of the World*, forthcoming.
[49] See Elke Seefried, *Zukunfte. Aufstieg und Krise der Zukunftsforschung* (Munich: de Gruyter, 2016).
[50] Majdi Elmandjra and Mircai Malitsa, *No Limits to Learning* (Bucharest: Club of Rome, 1974).

and socialism and allowed estimates of human needs to determine the rate of production within environmentally sustainable limits.[51] This would be the message of RIO, written by the Nobel Prize Laureate and World Bank economist Jan Tinbergen for UNITAR.[52] In 1973, the so-called Group of 77 of the non-aligned countries met in Algiers to follow up on the Third World forum held during the 1972 conference for the environment in Stockholm. The Third World was concerned that the problem of the environment would take attention away from problems of development.[53] The Algiers conference launched the New International Economic Order. NIEO was voted by the UN General assembly in 1974. The following year, the Lima conference of UNIDO set the goal for the developing countries to obtain a 25 percent share of world manufacturing.[54] NIEO led to interpretations in the Western world of the UN as the arena of a new and militant form of Third Worldism that threatened to overthrow the existing economic order.[55] The core concern of the NIEO was the right to self reliance, to a choice of one's own economic and social model which to most meant a version of socialism, and a share in what was projected as a new global division of industrial labor (see Christian in this volume). NIEO economists attacked an international division of labor destined to reproduce a global proletariat. They also rejected so-called cascading, by which the developing world could not access the high value added part of production dependent on some of its key minerals.[56] Some miner-

---

[51] See Sam Cole, Jay Gershuny, and Ian Miles, "Scenarios of world development," *Futures* 10, no. 1 (1978): 3–20.

[52] Jan Tinbergen, *Reshaping the International Economic Order: Aa report to the Club of Rome* (New York: Club of Rome, 1976).

[53] Mahbub Al Huq, *The Poverty Curtain: Choices for the Third World* (New York: Columbia University Press, 1976).

[54] UNITAR, *A New International Economic Order: Selected Documents 1945–1975* (New York: United Nations Institute for Training and Research, 1976). See also UNESCO, *International Social Science Journal* 4, 1976, devoted to the NIEO; Mark T. Berger, "After the Third world? History, destiny and the fate of Third worldism," *Third World Quarterly* 25, no. 1 (2012): 9–39; Arif Dirlik, "Spectres of the Third world: global modernity and the end of the three worlds," *Third World Quarterly*, 25, no. 1 (2012): 131–145; Nils Gilman, "The new international economic order: A reintroduction," *Humanity: An International Journal of Human Rights, Humanitarianism, and Development* 6, no. 1 (2015): 1–16; Sibylle Duhautois, "Un destin commun? Etudes sur le futur et formation d'une conscience globale 1945–1989," (PhD Diss., Centre d'histoire de Sciences Po, 2017), chapter 4.

[55] UN Charter of the economic rights and duties of states, and Declaration of the principles of international law concerning friendly relations and cooperation among states in accordance with the charter of the United Nations, 1974. GA resolution 3201, 1974.

[56] Samir Amin, "Self reliance and the New International Economic Order," *Monthly Review* 29, no. 3 (1977): 1–21; see Christian in this volume.

als – aluminium, bauxite, iron – were singled out in particular as targets of cascading (these were also at the center of attention in the Interfutures report). In 1974, following the NIEO and the incorporation of principles such as 'unjust enrichment' in the UN Declaration on International Law, Jamaica shocked world markets by nationalizing bauxite. European countries reacted through the so-called Lome convention, giving former African, Caribbean and Pacific colonies privileged access to European markets in the hope of preventing collective protectionist stances.[57]

The RIO report followed the conceptions of the world as a systemic whole put forward by planners such as Tinbergen or Ozbekhan, and rejected the distinction between developed and developing world in favor of a perspective on the world as a whole. This was reflected in the production of the report which brought in two experts for each chapter, one from the developed and the other from the developing world. The report argued for the need for an entirely new international architecture aimed at promoting peace and development and providing for basic human needs. This included giving Third World countries control of their own resources, pooling the world's material wealth including capital and technology, and developing an overarching notion of the common heritage of Mankind. RIO also gave OPEC an increased role in new global financial institutions and foresaw equal representation of all nations in something called the World Treasury. UNCTAD would be transformed into a World Development and Trade Organisation dominated by the Third World, and complemented by a World Bank and a World Technological Development Authority which would aim to close the technological gap by lowering the prices for Third would countries' access to knowhow.[58]

Historians and development scholars have shown how the NIEO gradually failed, after 1976, as a Third Worldist attempt to collectively challenge the rules of the postwar economic order. Faced with Western resistance and in particular by American monetary extortions by the late 1970s, the attempts at mobilization demonstrated by OPEC broke down. Third Worldism in the UN system prompted the US in particular to create an alternative structure of international organization in the G7.[59] Interfuture was as much a part of this rejection of NIEO as it was part of the mounting rejection of the Limits report, and the value of the

---

[57] Golub, "From the new international order to the G20": 1005.
[58] In 1974 the World Bank was given a new target to work for the eradication of basic needs. Corinna Unger, *International Organizations and Development, 1945–1990* (Amsterdam: Springer, 2016).
[59] See in particular the special issue in *Humanity*, *Humanity: An International Journal of Human Rights, Humanitarianism, and Development* 6, no. 1 (2015).

Interfuture group's work lay in the way that it presented a different image of the world's future, in which the core elements of a global division of labor between commodity producing nations and industrial actors was preserved. The final report, published in 1976 as *Facing the Future*, was a mirror image of RIO's description of a fundamentally transformed world economic order, and the report also directly regrouped the themes introduced by the NIEO (which developed from a set of statements in 1973 and 1974 to a set of actual negotiations between the developing countries and the Western world): commodity prices, in particular minerals and oil, technology and technology transfer, the monetary order of the Bretton Woods system including debt and currency prices, and the international division of labor between commodity producing and industrialized countries.[60] In Interfutures' own narrative of a new economic world order, only the Western world maintained an advantage as the main manufacturer of industrial products, and what the report referred to as new and 'harmonious' relationships with the Third World depended not on a reconfiguration of this system but on integrating the industrializing nations of the third world – India, Algeria, Iran – into a 'shared' vision of a growing world market. Such an emphasis on a growing world market can be put in the perspective of the *Limits*-report, which of course foresaw a firm limit to capitalist accumulation. Interfutures also dismissed RIO's conception of shared world interests – arguing that RIO did not take into consideration the needs of the Northern countries and that its conception of the world was therefore biased. The idea of a World Plan was understood as an unacceptably bureaucratic (socialist) conception that neglected market mechanisms. Market mechanisms, Interfutures proposed, would instead need to be given a larger space in Western economies in the coming decades.[61] This rejection of planning often returned in the Interfutures report, which was concerned with how market mechanisms could be protected for the long term, and with how they could be used in order to solve possible conflicts between short and long-term issues in policy planning. As Christian shows in this volume, in the years 1971–1976, forecasting became a key tool of UNCTAD in order to plan the development of commodity prices; from the mid 1970s, the socialist countries also attempted to consolidate relationships with the Third World by forecasting trade relationships and prices; and from the mid 1970s the EEC also engaged in forecasting as a way of stabilizing commodity prices. These forms of forecast were different in kind than the idea of a World Plan that informed RIO, but they were also different from the argument that would be put forward by Interfutures and that fa-

---

60 Interfutures, "Searching for a new order of the world economy," draft. OECD archives.
61 Interfutures, Newsletter, summary of the RIO report, July 1977. OECD archives.

vored the use of scenarios as a way of creating 'shared' and 'harmonious' images of the world economic future.

Scenarios: a method for managing world relationships

The actual scenarios proposed by Interfutures followed directly on the recommendations of the McCracken group. The main issues paper produced by Lesourne in 1978 focused on two scenarios, one in which there was growth in the Western world that went through a process of rapid structural adaptation, and one in which this world encountered an enduring stagflation scenario followed by an escalation of social conflicts. A conflict-ridden Western world would not be able to put up a united front toward the Third World.[62] It was however not only the message of these scenarios, but also the use of the scenarios as method for shaping forms of opinion and decision-making that was important in Lesourne's work for Interfutures. While *Limits* and *RIO* were circulated widely, intended for global publics, the scenarios created by Interfutures were written by expert consultants, and also included the creation of a specialized public of targeted decision-makers and experts of the world community. Interfutures worked with a motley crew of consultants strategically recruited to inform the group of developments in the developing nations,[63] but also to spread the message of the Interfutures report of the necessity of a long-term harmonious strategy to decision-makers in these nations. In other words, consultancy was a form of expertize chosen not only in terms of its input, but also to form the basis of a form of circulation which was part of the notion of shaping a positive image of the future. The importance of actively shaping this positive image led to the choice of scenarios as method, and to the rejection of computer modelling, which was accused of leading to deterministic representations of static trends. Interfutures (in fact Jacques Lesourne) argued that scenarios contained a dynamic and normative element. Through this dynamic element, they could be used to actively influence social relationships within Western societies as well as between the advanced industrialised world and the developing nations. To Lesourne, scenarios were, like systems analysis, a way of managing Third world re-

---

62 Main issues paper for the meeting of senior officials, Paris, 2 February 1979.
63 I have not been able to find a complete list of these in the remaining archives.

lations.⁶⁴ *Prospective*, he argued, was a method that allowed for the evolution of dynamic situations and focused on actors and governments as actively creating strategies of cooperation or conflict that shaped the future of the 'system.'⁶⁵ A normative vision of the future could be chosen, and communicated through prospective analysis and scenarios to decision-makers in this system.

The methodological pertinence of prospective analysis and scenarios had also been indicated by the conclusions of the McCracken group, in which it was suggested that a shift from the conjectural developments that had hitherto been the focus of economic planning to structural and long-term issues that could not as such be planned had to be accompanied by a new concern with the analysis of fundamental 'trends and developments.'⁶⁶ The McCracken group came to the conclusion that the instabilities in Western economies due to price fluctuations had rendered the macro economic models that had been used through the postwar period of Keynesian management inefficient. The idea of the Interfutures project was therefore to move beyond conventional modelling and economic planning to examine 'numerous trends' and in particular those driving up inflationary prices. This provided scenarios with yet another purpose, because preeminent among the trends driving up prices were, as argued both by McCracken and Interfutures, value revolutions and 'unsatisfied aspirations' in the developing world as well as within the West.⁶⁷ Fluctuations in commodity prices, raw materials and currencies were understood as based on irrational sentiments and psychological reactions in the developing world, adding to social tensions in the West by pushing prices up and in their effect on protectionist modes by governments, organizations and interest groups in Western societies.⁶⁸ Among the major obstacles targeted by the McCracken group were thus competing social claims and expectations, as well as a lack of preferences for economic growth in terms of the critique of growth that Western societies had witnessed since the late 1960s.⁶⁹ Echoing contemporary developments in eco-

---

64 Jacques Lesourne, "L'exercice Interfuturs, réflexions méthodologiques," *Futuribles*, no. 26: 20–38.
65 Interfuturs, chapter II, draft, world models. OECD archives. *Facing the future. Mastering the probable and managing the unpredictable* (Paris: The Organisation for Economic Co-operation and Development), 4–5.
66 Letter to Paul McCracken from Emile van Lennep, 15 April 1976. Summary of discussions at the 4th meeting of the steering committee 20–21 October 1977, FUT M (77)3. OECD archives.
67 *Facing the Future*, 7.
68 Draft to the McCracken report by Assar Lindbeck. Undated, OECD archives, McCracken folders.
69 Memorandum, second meeting of the McCracken group, 22–23 January 1976. OECD archives, McCracken folders.

nomic theory toward the idea of rational expectations, rising prices were defined as "a psychological problem which depends on expectations." This was, to the McCracken group as well as to Interfutures, a deeply problematic situation that forced the need for governments to deal with such rigidities by opening up to more flexible relationships with the developing world.[70] Managing such value problems, defined as the real challenges to growth, hinged on a new element in planning: the capacity to set a positive image of the future that would help ease conflict and induce cooperation. "The more the OECD governments can lead the public to share a constructive vision of the future, the greater will be the ability of these governments to implement sets of consistent long term policies."[71] Decision-making needed a 'positive' message that brought home the message that possible physical limits in natural resources over the long term could be overcome by political, social, and institutional adaptation. The "method should include economic, social and political elements and provide the basis for the scenarios."[72] Through scenarios, psychological aspects of structural challenges could thus be dealt with.

The final report of the Interfutures project proposed five different possible scenarios for the OECD world until 2000, based on the different factors (derived from the NIEO structure) that had been considered.[73] But the main issues paper produced by the group to a high level meeting of senior officials at Chateau de la Muette in Paris in 1978 only focused on two central scenarios. The first was a new growth scenario, in which the rigidities of Western nations were handled through a rapid adaptation of values and a 'conscious drive' towards new patterns of output and consumption. Scenario two was that of enduring stagflation, with a dual fragmentation of advanced societies, and prevailing conflicts about the distribution of national income that also rendered the Western world incapable of putting up a united front toward the Third World.[74] In order to push the situation from scenario two to scenario one, Interfutures emphasized the role of governments in "attacking the psychological basis of present problems" and "replacing the prevailing negative attitude toward the future by a positive one." Education and other forms of public opinion should be used as ways to shape long-term preferences that avoided competing social claims, and also explained to Western

---

70 Interfutures, Meeting of senior policy officials, draft of the background paper, 5 February 1978, Fut (78)3. OECD archives.
71 *Facing the future*, 195.
72 Ibid.
73 Interfutures, chapter draft, ixx, "Scenarios of world development". OECD archives.
74 "Main issues paper for the meeting of senior officials," Paris, 2 February 1979 FUT (78)7. OECD archives.

populations that the interdependent relationship with the Third World set limits on consumption and redistribution. Scenarios, it was suggested, was a key method for enlightening both national policy makers and their electorates about structural challenges and the need to address them through a coherent long-term strategy. This idea of scenarios as a new form of planning that not only set objectives of development, but created positive images of development, also came from the McCracken report, which ascribed a new role to governments in terms of constructing positive images of the future that might wear down negative feelings and influence "creative and energetic people grasping opportunities." Such positive images would increase the "social willingness to accept the continuing adjustment of economic structures."[75] "Instead of the real danger of introducing rigidities in dealing with crisis, AIS have potentially enormous capabilities of influencing their futures if they develop forward looking activities and sustained efforts to influence the future in positive ways."[76] While the McCracken report had the interior workings of the Western nations in focus; Interfutures applied the same logic to relationships with the developing world. By creating positive images of the benefits of a long-term integration in world markets through cooperation with the AIS, the protectionist stances of OPEC could be averted, and the Third World divided into those nations remaining in a basic needs approach, and those who might through industrialization become eventual members of the AIS.[77] As full members of an expanding global market, the latter could be expected to take an increased responsibility for the functioning of this, as well as for carrying the 'burdens of development.' It was therefore essential to create positive images of development that could be shared by populations in the West and strategic parts of the Third World alike and "consolidate areas of common interest."[78] The scenarios were a communicative tool for this, as was the use of consultants and strategic communication meetings set up by Interfutures with policy makers both in the West and in the developing world, through which the scenarios could be spread.

The emphasis on 'sociocultural factors' came from the original Japanese proposal to create the Interfutures project.[79] The Japanese delegation, led by Saburo Okita, head of the Japanese Overseas Fund, was concerned with the value reac-

---

[75] Ibid; McCracken report, "The origins of the present problems."
[76] Interfutures, "Mid Term meeting, Summary of Conclusions." OECD archives.
[77] See Rudiger Graf, "Making Use of the Oil Weapon. Western Industrial Countries and Arab PetroPolitics in 1973–1974, *Diplomatic History*, 36, 1 (2012): 185–208.
[78] Chapter 3 draft "The evolution of international relations"; Summary of conclusions of the 4th meeting of the steering committee, 20–21 October 1977. OECD archives.
[79] Letter by the Japanese government to the Secretary General, 9 May 1975. OECD archives.

tions to the high postwar growth rates that could be observed in the Western world. They drew the conclusion that Japan, with its extreme levels of industrialization in the postwar decades and anticipations of a leap into a post-industrial economy, ran a high risk of similar developments. Saburo Okita had a background in futures research as the former chair of the Japanese futurological society (several members of the Japanese OECD delegation had emerged from the futurological society, including Yoshihiro Kogune and Yoneji Masuda). The futurological society was directly associated to the Japanese Office of Technological Planning and a central overseer of Japan's industrialization process, and it also seems to have had a link to the Institute for Information Society, which planned the transition into post-industrialism.[80] As a correspondent of, in particular, Daniel Bell and Betrand Cazes, Okita was very familiar with futurological tools. The specific focus on socio-cultural factors as something that could be systematically analyzed and anticipated and thus planned was outsourced within the Interfutures group to a particular project draft written by the Toyota foundation and referred to as the 'Japanese project.'[81] The Toyota proposal was tightly focused on the relationship between quick economic and technological change, and value reactions, which were linked to the problems of stagflation in the Western world, through changes in demand and a new governmental impossibility of satisfying expectations. The proposal identified a failure to realize a welfare society as the source of a new structural contradiction between economic and technological development, on the one hand, and human satisfaction, on the other. The aim of the Toyota proposal was thus the 'systematic identification of the main factors of socio cultural background to be introduced into the analysis of future consumption and production patterns' and the integration of changing motivations of individuals and groups. The final report to Toyota was entitled "Changing value patterns and their impact on economic structure" and listed excesses of the welfare state and new, conflicting social demands as 'structural challenges' and 'ridigities' in Western market societies that could be anticipated and managed through scenarios.[82] These themes of the Toyota proj-

---

[80] Interfutures, "Note by the secretariat. New elements and their policy implication in AIS." 16 May 1978. OECD archives.
[81] Folder 212779, letter from Oshima to Lees, 24 December 1975, and Memorandum, 12 December 1979, signed Oshima."Proposed financial contribution from a private foundation to the Interfutures project, note by the General secretary," 24 May 1977, C (77) 89. OECD press release, 28 January 1976. OECD archives.
[82] "Proposed financial contribution from a private foundation to the Interfutures project. Note by the secretary general," 24 May 1977, Annex A, "Changing value patterns and their impact on the economic structure, a report to the Toyota foundation," 8 January 1979.

ect had also gained in significance within the Interfutures project as a whole, as a summary of discussions in 1977 decided to focus more on values as the main problem of the 'manageability' of AIS economies.[83]

Conclusion

The Interfutures program, lost in the dust of the less than transparent OECD archives, was a strategic reflection on how to close a future window opened by the emergence of a set of alternative discourses on globalization. It was a key carrier of the proto-neoliberal worldview – emphasizing the need for structural adjustments of welfare statist structures in the West, an image of a growing world market as a shared strategic interest of the Western and the developing worlds, the existence of sociocultural reactions and values as the main obstacles for growth – that by the mid 1970s was taking over within the organization. A few years later the OECD became an active diffuser of such ideas into the global environment.

The idea of the long term played a key role in these proto neoliberal discourses. As shown here, Interfutures stemmed from a desire within the OCED to find a new method of world management, which allowed for an active influence on world relationships and also permitted the organization to fend off at least two of the organization's disastrious images of the world's future, presented in *Limits* and the RIO report. Scenarios were such a method, and offered both the possibility to put forward partisan responses to alternative images of globalization. As such they represented a hope for a new governmental mechanism that could shift from the national to the global focus and allow OECD nations to act as global players.

This chapter has pointed to another key aspect of this Western resistance, namely, the way that the reaction to the alternative visions of globalization pushed by the Third World led to responses in the West. These contained two elements: the willingness to accept certain countries in the Third World within an extended category of Advanced Industrial Societies, and the conclusion that meeting the challenges from these in a new international division of labor would require significant changes in the social structures of Western economies. In this narrative, the link created both by Interfutures and the Trilateral Commission between forms of upheaval in the world environment and forms of social crisis within Western societies is crucial. Restoring competitiveness de-

---

[83] "Summary of discussions," 13–14 October 1977. OECD archives.

manded, both in Western countries and in the surrounding world, re-establishing positive images of development and in particular, of a creative and flexible world market. It might be argued that the role of tools such as scenarios and long-term forecasts was exactly to stabilize expectations around this world market, and entrench them in national governments and publics.

Works Cited

Abdelal, Ravi. Capital Rules: The Construction of Global Finance. Cambridge Mass.: Harvard University Press, 2007.
Adizes, Ichak and Elisabeth Mann Borgese. *Self-Management: New Dimensions to Democracy.* Santa Barbara and Oxford: Clio Press, 1975.
Adizes, Ichak. *Industrial Democracy: Yugoslav Style.* New York: Free Press, 1971.
Adler-Karlsson, Gunnar. *Western Economic Warfare 1947–1967. A Case Study in Foreign Economic Policy.* Stockholm: Almqvist & Wiksell, 1968.
Aglietta, Michel and Raymond Courbis. Un outil pour le Plan: le modèle FIFI. *Économie et statistique* 1, no. 1 (1969): 45–65.
Agrawal, S. P. and J. C. Aggarwal, *UNESCO and Social Sciences: Retrospect and Prospect.* New Delhi: Concept, 1988.
Ahrens, Ralf. Spezialisierungsinteresse und Integrationsaversion im Rat für Gegenseitige Wirtschaftshilfe: Der DDR-Wekrzeugmaschinenbau in den 1970er Jahren. *Jahrbuch für Wirtschaftsgeschichte* 2 (2008): 73–92.
Al Huq, Mahbub. *The Poverty Curtain: Choices for the Third World.* New York: Columbia University Press, 1976.
Alchon, Guy. Mary van Kleeck and scientific management" in *A Mental Revolution. Scientific Management since Taylor* ed Daniel Nelson. Columbus: Columbus State University Press, 1992) 102–130.
Aldous, Richard. *Reagan and Thatcher.* London: Hutchinson, 2012.
Alekseevič, Vladímir. Vinogradov's memoirs: *Moj XX vek. Vosponimaniia.* Moscow: Izdatel'skij dom kalan, 2003.
Alexander, Jon, Adam Podgorecki, Rob Shields, *Social Engineering.* Beaconsfield, Quebec: Carleton University Press, 1996.
Alymov, Sergei. 'This is profitable for all': Agrarian Economists and the Soviet Plan-Market Debate in the post-Stalinist period. *Jahrbücher fur Geschichte Osteuropa,* forthcoming.
Amendola, Giorgio. *Antonio Gramsci nella vita culturale e politica italiana.* Napoli: Guida Editori, 1978.
Amin, Samir. Self reliance and the New International Economic Order. *Monthly Review* 29, no. 3 (1977): 1–21.
Amrith, Sunil and Patricia Clavin. Feeding the World: Connecting Europe and Asia, 1930–1945. *Past & Present* 218, no. 8 (2013): 29-50.
Andersson, Jenny and Eglė Rindzevičiūtė, *The Struggle for the Long-Term in Transnational Science and Politics: Forging the Future.* London/New York: Routledge, 2015.
Andersson, Jenny and Pauline Prat. Gouverner le 'long terme' La production des futurs buraucratique en France. *Gouvernement et action publique,* 3 (2015): 9–29.
Andersson, Jenny and Sibylle Duhautois. The future of Mankind. In *The Politics of Globality Since 1945: Assembling the Planet,* (eds.) Casper Sylvest and Rens van Munster. New York: Routledge, 2015. 106–125.
Andersson, Jenny. *The Future of the World: Futurists, Futurology and the Struggle for the Post Cold War Imagination.* Oxford: Oxford University Press, forthcoming 2018.

Andrew, Christopher. Intelligence in the Cold War. In *The Cambridge History of the Cold War*, vol II, (eds.) Melvyn P. Leffler and Odd Arne Westad. Cambridge: Cambridge University Press, 2010.

Androsova, Tatiana. Economic interest in Soviet post-war policy in Finland. In *Reassessing Cold War Europe*, (eds.) Sari Autio-Sarasmo and Katalin Miklóssy. Abingdon: Routledge, 2011.

Angeletti, Thomas. Faire la réalité ou s'y défaire. La modélisation et les déplacements de la politique économique au tournant des années 1970. *Politix* 95 (2011/3): 47–72.

Angell, Norman. *The Great Illusion: a study of the relation of military power to national advantage*. London: Heinemann, 1912.

Angresano, James. *The Political Economy of Gunnar Myrdal: An Institutional Basis for the Transformation Problem*. Cheltenham, UK and Lyme, NH: Edward Elgar, 1997.

Appelqvist, Örjan. Gunnar Myrdal i svensk politik 1943–1947: En svensk Roosevelt och hans vantolkade nederlag. [Gunnar Myrdal in Swedish Politics 1943–1947: A Swedish Roosevelt and his misinterpreted defeat] *NORDEUROPAforum* 9, no. 1 (1999): 33–51.

———. Civil Servant or Politician? Dag Hammarskjöld's Role in Swedish Government Policy in the Forties. *Sveriges Riksbank Economic Review*, no. 3 (2005): 83.

———. Rediscovering Uncertainty: Early Attempts at a Pan-European Post-War Recovery. *Cold War History* 8, no. 3 (2008): 341.

Aron, Raymond. *Sociologie des sociétés industrielles. Esquisse d'une théorie des régimes politiques*. Paris: Centre de documentation universitaire, 1961.

Asejev, Vladimir and Ovsej Škaratan. *Sociální normativy a sociální plánování*. Prague: Práce, 1986.

Assanti, Cecilia, Luigi Meneghini and Rudi Kyovski, *La Partecipazione dei lavoratori alla disciplina dei rapporti di lavoro in Italia e Jugoslavia*. Trieste: ISDEE, 1976.

Audier, Serge. *Néo-libéralisme(s). Une archéologie intellectuelle*. Paris: Grasset, 2012.

Auerhan, Jan. *Automatizace a její ekonomický význam*. Prague: SNPL, 1959.

Autio-Sarasmo, Sari and Katalin Miklóssy. *Reassessing Cold War Europe*. NY: Routledge, 2011.

———. The Cold War from New Perspective. In *Reassessing Cold War Europe*, (eds.) Sari Autio-Sarasmo and Katalin Miklóssy. Abingdon: Routledge, 2011. 1–15.

Autio-Sarasmo, Sari. Soviet Economic Modernisation and Transferring the Technologies from the West. In *Modernisation in Russia since 1900*, (eds.) Markku Kangaspuro and Jeremy Smith. Helsinki: Finnish Literary Society [Studia Fennica Historica], 2006. 104–123.

———. Knowledge through the Iron Curtain: Soviet Scientific-Technical Cooperation with Finland and West Germany. In *Reassessing Cold War Europe*, (eds.) Sari Autio-Sarasmo and Katalin Miklóssy. Abingdon: Routledge 2011.

———. Khrushchev and the challenge of technological progress. In *Khrushchev in the Kremlin. Policy and Government in the Soviet Union, 1953–1964*, (eds.) Jeremy Smith and Melanie Ilic. Abingdon: Routledge, 2011.133–143.

———. Technological Modernisation in the Soviet Union and Post-Soviet Russia: Practices and Continuities. *Europe-Asia Studies* 68, no.1 (2016): 79–96.

Azam, Nicolas. *Le PCF confronté à "l'Europe." Une étude socio-historique des prises de position et des recompositions partisanes*. Paris: Dalloz, 2017.

Badenoch, Alexander and Andreas Fickers, *Materializing Europe Transnational Infrastructures and the Project of Europe*. Basingstoke: Palgrave Macmillan, 2010.

Balfour, Campbell. *Participation in Industry*. London: Croom Helm, 1973.

Barber, William. *Gunnar Myrdal: An Intellectual Biography, Great Thinkers in Economics.* Basingstoke: Pelgrave Macmillan, 2008.
Barbieri, Katherine and Gerald Schneider. Globalization and Peace: Assessing New Directions in the Study of Trade & Conflict. *Journal of Peace Research* 36, no. 4 (1999): 389.
Bauerová, Jaroslava, Jaroslav Kolář, Jiří Růžička, Jaroslav Kohout, Eva Bidlová, and Miloslav Tomšík, *O sociálním plánování*. Prague: Práce, 1972.
Beissinger, Mark. *Scientific Management, Socialist Discipline, and Soviet Power.* Cambridge, Mass.: Harvard University Press, 1988.
Bell, Peter D. The Ford Foundation as a Transnational Actor. *International Organization* 25, no. 3 (1971): 465–478
Bellefroide, Diane de. The Commission pour l'Etude des Problèmes d'Après-Guerre (CEPAG), 1941–1944. In *Europe in Exile: European Exile Communities in Britain, 1940–45*, (eds.) Martin Conway and José Gotovitch. New York and Oxford: Berghan Books, 2001. 130.
Benamar, Boualia. *La CNUCED et Le Nouvel Ordre économique International.* Paris: Université de droit, d'économie et de sciences sociales, 1984.
Benda, Miloslav. Vnitropodnikové řízení a podnikatelská funkce. *Moderní řízení* 4, no. 4 (1969): 47–51.
Berg, Maxine. East-West Dialogues: Economic Historians, the Cold War, and Détente. *Journal of Modern History* 87 (2015): 36–71.
Berger, Mark T. After the Third world? History, destiny and the fate of Third worldism. *Third World Quarterly* 25, no. 1 (2012): 9–39.
Berliner, Joseph. *Soviet Industry from Stalin to Gorbachev. Essays on management and innovations.* Aldershot: Edward Elgar, 1988.
Berman, Edward H. *The Ideology of Philanthropy: The Influence of the Carnegie, Ford, and Rockefeller Foundations on American Foreign Policy.* Albany: State University of New York Press, 1983.
Berthoud, Paul, A Professional Life Narrative and Some Related Stories: http://www.edinter.net/paulberthoud/narrative/ (accessed 14 February 2017).
Berting, Jan, Felix Geyer, Ray Jurkovich, *Problems in International Comparative Research in the Social Sciences.* Oxford: Pergamon Press, 1979.
Bertsch, Gary. Technology Transfers and Technology Controls: a Synthesis of the Western-Soviet Relationship. In *Technical Progress and Soviet Economic Development*, (eds.) Ronald Amann and Julian Cooper. Oxford: Oxford University Press, 1986.
Beth, Helmut. Im Dialog mit Milan Machovec. In *Mistr dialogu Milan Machovec. Sborník k nedožitým osmdesátinám českého filosofa*, (eds.) Kamila Jindrová, Pavel Tachecí, and Pavel Žďárský. Prague: Akropolis, 2006. 184–199.
Bettelheim, Charles. *Choix et efficience des investissements.* Paris: Mouton & Co, 1963.
Bézès, Philippe. *Réinventer l'État. Les réformes de l'administration française (1962–2008).* Paris: Presses universitaires de France, 2009.
Bhagwati, Jagdish N. *The New International Economic Order: The North-South Debate.* Cambridge, Mass.: MIT Press, 1983)
Bianchini, Stefano. *La Diversità socialista in Jugoslavia. Modernizzazione autogestione e sviluppo democratico dal 1965 a oggi.* Trieste: Editoriale Stampa Triestina, 1984.
Blanchard, Elodie Vieille. *Les limites à la croissance dans un monde global: modélisations, prospectives, réfutations.* PhD Diss., Paris, EHESS, 2011.

Bloed, Arie. *The External Relations of the Council for Mutual Economic Assistance.* Utrecht: Martinus Nijhoff Publishers, 1988.
Blum, Alain and Martine Mespoulet, *L'Anarchie bureaucratique. Statistique et pouvoir sous Staline.* Paris: La Découverte, 2003.
Blumberg, Phillip I. Selected Materials on Corporate Social Responsibility. *The Business Lawyer* 27 (1972): 1275–1299.
Bockman, Johanna and Gil Eyal. Eastern Europe as a Laboratory for Economic Knowledge: The Transnational Roots of Neoliberalism. *The American Journal of Sociology* 108, no. 2 (2002): 317–323.
Bockman, Johanna. Eastern European Economists and the Notion of Development: Socialist Economists in the UN Conference on Trade and Development. *American Journal of Sociology,* 108, no. 2 (September 2002): 310–352.
–––. *Markets in the Name of Socialism: The Left Wing Origins of Neoliberalism.* Stanford: Stanford University Press, 2011.
–––. Socialist Globalization against Capitalist Neocolonialism: The Economic Ideas behind the New International Economic Order. *Humanity: An International Journal of Human Rights, Humanitarianism, and Development* 6, no. 1 (2015): 109–128.
Body, Zsombor. Enthralled by Size: Business History or the History of Technocracy in the Study of a Hungarian Socialist Factory. *The Hungarian Historical Review* 4, no. 4 (2015): 964–989.
Boel, Bent. *The European Productivity Agency and Transatlantic Relations, 1953–1961.* Copenhagen: Museum Tusculanum Press/University of Copenhagen, 2003.
Boettke, Peter. *Socialism and the Market: The Socialist Calculation Debate Revisited,* vol. 5. London: Routledge, 2000.
Boldyrev, Ivan and Olessia Kirtchik. The Cultures of 'Mathematical Economics' in the Postwar Soviet Union: More than a Method, Less than a Discipline. *Studies in History and Philosophy of Science, Part A* 63 (2017): 1–10.
Boltanski, Luc and Eve Chiapello. *The New Spirit of Capitalism.* London; New York: Verso, 2005.
Boltanski, Luc. America, America...: Le Plan Marshall et l'importation du 'management.' *Actes de la recherche en sciences sociales* 38, no. 1 (1981): 19–41.
Boncourt, Thibaud. *A History of the International Political Science Association.* Quebec: Association internationale de science politique, 2009.
Bornstein, Morris. *Plan and Market: Economic Reform in Eastern Europe.* New Haven: Yale University Press, 1973.
–––. *Economic Planning, East and West.* Cambridge: Ballinger PubCo, 1975.
Bornstein, Stephen and Keitha S. Fine. Worker Control in France: Recent Political Developments. In *Worker Self-Management in Industry: The West European Experience,* (ed.) G. David Garson, 152–191. New York: Praeger Publishers, 1977.
Borowy, Iris. *Coming to terms with world health: the League of Nations Health Organisation, 1921–1946.* Frankfurt am Main/New York: Peter Lang, 2009.
Boulland, Paul and Isabelle Gouarné. Communismes et circulations transnationales. *Critique internationale* 66 (January-March 2015).
Bourdieu, Pierre. Décrire et prescrire. Les conditions de possibilité et les limites de l'efficacité politique (1980). In *Langage et pouvoir symbolique.* Paris: Seuil, 2001. 186–198.

Brabant, Jozef Van. *Economic Integration in Eastern Europe. A Handbook.* New York, London, Toronto: Harvester Wheatsheaf, 1989.
Bray, Jeremy and Nicholas Falk. Towards a worker managed economy. *Fabian Tract* 430 (1974): 1–30.
Brech, Edward. *Lyndall Urwick, Management Pioneer: A Biography.* Oxford: Oxford University Press, 2010.
Brenner, Robert. *The Economics of Global Turbulence: The Advanced Capitalist Economies from Long Boom to Long Downturn, 1945–2000.* London: Verso, 2006.
Broekmeyer, Marius J. *Yugoslav Workers' Self-Management. Proceedings of a symposium held in Amsterdam, 7–9 January, 1970.* Dordrecht: D. Reidel Publishing Company, 1970.
Brückweh, Kerstin, Dirk Schumann, Richard F. Wetzell, and Benjamin Ziemann. *Engineering Society.* Basingstoke: Palgrave, 2012.
Brus, Wlodzimierz. Rapports entre politique et économie en régime socialiste. *L'Homme et la société* 6 (1967): 70
———. *Problèmes généraux du fonctionnement de l'économie socialiste.* Paris: Maspéro, 1968.
———. *Histoire économique de l'Europe de l'Est (1945–1985).* Paris: La Découverte, 1986.
Bucarelli, Massimo. Roma e Belgrado tra Guerra Fredda e Distensione. In *La politica estera italiana negli anni della Grande Distensione (1968–1975),* (ed.) Pier Giorgio Celozzi Baldelli. Rome: Aracne, 2009. 144–157.
Bystrova, Irina B. *Sovetskij voenno-promyshlennij kompleks: problemy stanovlenija i razvitija 1930–1980 gody* [The Soviet military-industrial complex: problems of structuration and development 1930–1980]. RAN: Institut Rossijskoi Istorii Moskva, 2006.
Cain, Frank. *Economic Statecraft During the Cold War: European Responses to the US Trade Embargo.* New York: Routledge, 2007.
Caldwell, Peter C. Productivity, Value and Plan: Fritz Behrens and the Economics of Revisionism in the German Democratic Republic. *History of Political Economy* 32, no. 1 (2000): 103–137.
———. *Dictatorship, State Planning, and Social Theory in the German Democratic Republic.* New York: Cambridge University Press, 2003.
Catanus, Anna-Maria. Official and Unofficial Futures of the Communism System Romanian Futures Studies between Control and Dissidence. In *The Struggle for the Long-Term in Transnational Science and Politics Forging the Future,* (eds.) Jenny Andersson and Eglė Rindzevičiūtė. New York: Routledge, 2015. 170–192.
Cayet, Thomas. Travailler à la marge: le Bureau International du Travail et l'organisation scientifique du travail (1923–1933). *Le Mouvement Social,* 228 (1 Sept., 2009): 39-56.
———. *Rationaliser le travail, organiser la production: le bureau international du travail et la modernisation économique durant l'entre-deux-guerres.* Rennes: Presses universitaires de Rennes, 2010.
Cella, Gian Primo. *Divisione del Lavoro e Iniziativa Operaia.* Bari: De Donato, 1972.
Celostátní konference Komunistické strany Československa. Zvláštní číslo Nové mysli, červen 1956. Prague: Rudé právo – vydavatelství Ústředního výboru KSČ, 1956.
Charles Bettleheim Papers, EHESS Archives (École des Hautes études en sciences sociales).
Chassé, Daniel Speich. Towards a Global History of the Marshall Plan. European Post-War Reconstruction and the Rise of Development Economic Expertise. In *Industrial Policy in*

Europe after 1945. Wealth, Power and Economic Development in the Cold War, (eds.) Christian Grabas and Alexander Nützenadel. New York: Palgrave Macmillan, 2014. 189.

Chauvey, Daniel. *Autogestion*. Paris: Editions de Seuil, 1970.

Chavance, Bernard. La théorie de l'économie socialiste dans les pays de l'Est entre 1917 et 1989. In *Nouvelle histoire de la pensée économique*, vol. 2, (ed.) Alain Béraud and Gilbert Faccarello. Paris: La Découverte, 1993. 235–262.

———. *Les réformes économiques à l'Est, de 1950 à 1990*. Paris: Nathan, 2000.

Chazal, Jacques. La participation des travailleurs aux décisions dans l'entreprise en France. *Revue syndicale suisse: organe de l'Union syndicale suisse* 66 (1974): 326–333.

Chmatko, Natalia. Les usages des sciences économiques en Russie entre les années 1960 et 1990. *Histoire Économie et Société* 4 (2002): 583–603.

Chossudovsky, Evgeny and Jean Siotis. Organized All-European Co-Operation: The Role of Existing Institutions. In *Beyond Détente: Prospects for East-West Co-Operation and Security in Europe*, (ed.) Nils Andrén and Karl E. Birnbaum. Leiden: A.W. Sijthoff, 1976. 161.

Christian, Michel, Sandrine Kott and Ondřej Matějka. International Organisation in the Cold War: The Circulation of Experts beyond the East-West Divide. *Acta Universitatis Carolinae Studia Territorialia* 17 (2017): 35–60;

Christian, Michel. UNCTAD. In *Den Kalten Krieg vermessen. Über Reichweite und Alternativen einer binären Ordnung*, (ed.) Frank Reichherzer, Emmanuel Droit, Jan Hansen (forthcoming in 2018).

Clavin, Patricia. Defining transnationalism. *Contemporary European History* 14 (2005): 421–439.

———. *Securing the World Economy: the Reinvention of the League of Nations, 1920–1946*. Oxford: Oxford University Press, 2013.

Cohen, Antonin. Du corporatisme au keynésianisme. Continuités pratiques et ruptures symboliques dans le sillage de François Perroux. *Revue française de science politique* 56 (2006/4): 555–592.

Cohen, Yves. *Le siècle des chefs: une histoire transnationale du commandement et de l'autorité (1890–1940)*. Paris: Éditions Amsterdam, 2013.

Cole, Sam, Jay Gershuny and Ian Miles. Scenarios of world development. *Futures* 10, no. 1 (1978): 3–20.

Collier, Stephen J. *Post-Soviet Social: Neoliberalism, Social Modernity, Biopolitics*. Princeton and Oxford: Princeton University Press, 2011.

Comisso, Ellen Turkish. *Workers' Control under Plan and Market: Implications of Yugoslav Self-Management*. New Haven and London: Yale University Press, 1979.

Connelly, Matthew. Future Shock: The End of the World as They Knew It. In *Shock of the Global*, (eds.), Niall Ferguson, Charles S. Maier, Erez Manela, Daniel J Sargent. Cambridge, Mass.: Harvard University Press, 2010. 337–351.

Coppolaro, Lucia. *The Making of a World Trading Power: The European Economic Community (EEC) in the GATT Kennedy Round Negotiations (1963–67)*. Farnham: Ashgate, 2013.

Coquery, Natacha and Matthieu de Oliveira, *L'échec a-t-il des vertus économiques*. Paris: Comité pour l'histoire économique et financière de la France, 2015.

Corbett, Anne. *Universities and the Europe of Knowledge: Ideas, Institutions and Policy Entrepreneurship in European Union Higher Education Policy, 1955–2005*. London: Palgrave Macmillan, 2005.

Couperus, Stefan and Harm Kaal. In Search of the Social: Languages of Neighborhood and Community in Urban Planning in Europe and Beyond, 1920–1960. *Journal of Urban History* 42 (2016): 978–91.

Couperus, Stefan, Liesbeth van de Grift and Vincent Lagendijk. Experimental Spaces – Planning in High Modernity. *Journal of Modern European History* 13 (2015): special issue, no. 4.

Cox, Robert. Ideologies and the NIEO: Reflections on some recent litterature. *International Organization* 33, no. 2 (1979): 257–302.

Cox, Robert. La participation des travailleurs à la gestion des entreprises. Etat et avancement du projet. I – Un champ d'enquete fertile. *Bullettin de l'Institut international d'études sociales* 2 (February 1967).

Crémieux-Brilhac, Jean-Louis. *Georges Boris. Trente ans d'influence. Blum, De Gaulle, Mendès France*. Paris: Gallimard, 2010.

Crombois, Jean F. *Camille Gutt and Postwar International Finance*. London: Pickering & Chatto, 2011.

Crump, Laurien and Simon Godard. Reassessing Communist International Organisations: A comparative Analysis of COMECON and the Warsaw Pact in relation to their Cold War Competitors. *Contemporary European History* 27, no. 1 (2018): 85–109.

Crump, Laurien. *The Warsaw Pact Reconsidered. International Relations in Eastern Europe, 1955–1969*. London: Routledge, 2015.

Cutler, Robert M. East-South Relations at UNCTAD: Global Political Economy and the CMEA. *International Organization* 37, no. 1 (1983): 121–142.

Dahl, Robert A. *After the Revolution: Authority in a Good Society*. New Haven: Yale University Press, 1970.

–––. Power to the Workers. *The New York Review of Books* 15 (1970): 20–24.

Damachi, Ukandi G., Hans Seibel and Jeroen Scheerder. *Self-Mangement in Yugoslavia and the Developing World*. London and Basingstoke: MacMillan, 1982.

Dangerfield, Martin. Sozialistische Ökonomische Integration. Der Rat für gegenseitige Wirtschaftshilfe (RGW). In *Ökonomie im Kalten Krieg, Studien zum Kalten Krieg, Band 4*, (eds.) Bernd Greiner, Christian Müller, and Claudia Weber. Hamburg: Hamburger Edition, 2010.

Danis, Jean-Jacques and Reiner Hoffman. From the Vredeling Directive to the European Works Council Directive – some historical remarks. *Transfer: European Review of Labour and Research* 1 (1995): 180–187.

De Gaulle, prophète de la Cinquième République (1946–1962). Paris: Presses de Science Po, 1998.

de Souza Farias, Rogério. Mr GATT: Eric Wyndham White and the Quest for Trade Liberalization. *World Trade Review* 12, no. 3 (2013): 463–85.

Degimbe, Jean. *La politique sociale européenne du Traité de Rome au Traité d'Amsterdam*. Brussels: Institut Syndicale Européen, 1999.

Denord, Fabien and Xavier Zunigo. . . 'Révolutionnairement vôtre'. Économie marxiste, militantisme intellectuel et expertise politique chez Charles Bettelheim . *Actes de la recherche en sciences sociales* 158 (June 2005): 8–29.

Denord, François. *Néo-libéralisme version française. Histoire d'une idéologie politique*. Paris: Demopolis, 2007.

Department of Economic and Social Affairs of the United Nations, *Rapport sur le cycle d'études des Nations Unies sur les techniques de la planification*. New York : United Nations Publications, 1964.

———.

———. *Planning and plan implementation, Publications des Nations unies*. New York: United Nations Publications, 1967.

Desrosières, Alain. La commission et l'équation: une comparaison des plans français et néerlandais entre 1945 et 1980. *Genèses* 34 (March 1999): 28–52.

———. *La Politique des nombres. Histoire de la raison statistique*. Paris: La Découverte, 1993); *Gouverner par les nombres. L'argument statistique*. Paris: Presses de l'École des Mines, 2008, 2 vols.

Detraz, Albert, Alfred Krumnov and Edmond Maire, *La CFDT et l'autogestion*. Paris: Les Editions du Cerf, 1974.

Deutsch, Steven. A Researcher's Guide to Worker Participation, Labor and Economic and Industrial Democracy. *Economic and Industrial Democracy* 26 (2005): 645–656.

Dezalay, Yves. Les courtiers de l'international. Héritiers cosmopolites, mercenaires de l'impérialisme et missionnaires de l'universel. *Actes de la Recherche en sciences sociales* 151–152, no. 1 (2004): 4–35.

Dezès, Marie-Geneviève. L'utopie réalisée: Les Modèles étrangers mythiques des autogestionnaires français. In *Autogestion: La dernière utopie*, (ed.) Frank Georgi. Paris, Publications de la Sorbonne, 2003. 30–54.

Dirlik, Arif. Spectres of the Third world: global modernity and the end of the three worlds. *Third World Quarterly*, 25, no. 1 (2012): 131–145.

Djelic, Marie-Laure. *Exporting the American Model: The Post-War Transformation of European Business*. Oxford: Oxford University Press, 1998.

Doering-Manteuffel, Anselm and Lutz Raphael, *Nach dem Boom: Perspektiven auf die Zeitgeschichte seit 1970*. Göttingen: Vandenhoeck & Ruprecht, 2010.

Drucker, Peter F. *Podnikové řízení a hospodářské výsledky*. Prague: Svoboda, 1968.

———. *Výkonný vedoucí*. Prague: Institut řízení, 1970.

Drulovic, Milojko. *L'autogestion à l'épreuve*. Paris: Fayard 1973); Cyrus Ardalan. Workers' Self-Management and Planning: The Yugoslav Case. *World Development* 8 (1980): 623–638.

Duhautois, Sibylle. Un destin commun? Etudes sur le futur et formation d'une conscience globale 1945–1989. PhD Diss. Centre d'histoire de Sciences Po, 2017.

Dulong, Delphine. *Moderniser la politique. Aux origines de la V République*. Paris: L'Harmattan, 1997.

ECCRDSS, *La délinquance juvénile en Europe. Actes du Colloque de Varsovie, octobre 1964*. Université libre de Bruxelles: Brussels, 1968.

Eckes, Alfred E. *Revisiting U.S. Trade Policy: Decisions in Perspective*. Athens: Ohio University Press, 2000. 22.

Eckstein, Alexander. *Comparison of Economic Systems: Theoretical and Methodological Approaches*. Berkeley: University of California Press, 1973.

Ekbladh, David. *The Great American Mission: Modernization and the Construction of an American World Order*. Princeton: Princeton University Press, 2010.

Eliæson, Sven. Gunnar Myrdal: A Theorist of Modernity. Acta Sociologica 43, no. 4 (2000): 331–341.

Ellman, Michael J. *Socialist Planning*. New York: Cambridge University Press, 2014.
Elmandjra, Majdi and Mircai Malitsa. *No Limits to Learning*. Bucharest: Club of Rome, 1974.
Elzinga, Aant. Unesco and the Politics of International Cooperation in the Realm of Science. in *Les Sciences Coloniales: Figures et Institutions*, (ed.) Patrick Petitjean. Paris: Orstom, 1996. 163–202.
Engerman, David and Corinna Unger. Introduction: Towards a Global History of Modernization. *Diplomatic History* 33, no. 3 (2009): 375–385.
Engerman, David C. To Moscow and Back: American Social Scientists and the Concept of Convergence. In *American Capitalism. Social Thought and Political Economy in the Twentieth Century*, (ed.) Nelson Lichtenstein. Philadelphia: University of Pennsylvania Press, 2006. 47–68.
———. *Know Your Enemy. The Rise and Fall of America's Soviet Experts*. Oxford/New York: Oxford University Press, 2009.
———. The rise and fall of central planning. In *The Cambridge History of the Second World War. Volume 3, Total War: Economy, Society and Culture*, (eds.) Michael Geyer and Adam Tooze. Cambridge: Cambridge University Press, 2015. 575–576.
Engerman, David, Nils Gilman, Mark H. Haefele and Michael E. Latham. *Staging Growth: Modernization, Development, and the Global Cold War*. Boston: University of Massachusetts Press, 2003.
Escobar, Arturo. Planning. In *The Development Dictionary. A Guide to Knowledge as Power*, Wolfgang Sachs (ed.), 132–145. London and New York: Zed Books, 2007.
Estrin, Saul and Milica Uvalić. From Illyria towards Capitalism: Did Labour-Management Theory Teach Us Anything about Yugoslavia and Transition in its Successor States? *Comparative Economic Studies* 50 (2008): 663–696.
Estrin, Saul. *Self-management: Economic theory and Yugoslav practice*. London: Cambridge University Press, 1983.
Etzemüller, Thomas. (ed.) *Die Ordnung Der Moderne: Social Engineering Im 20. Jahrhundert*. Bielefeld: transcript, 2009.
———. *Die Romantik der Rationalität. Alva & Gunnar Myrdal. Social Engineering in Schweden*. Bielefeld: transcript, 2010.
Etzemüller, Thomas. Social Engineering als Verhaltenslehre des kühlen Kopfes. Eine einleitende Skizze. In *Die Ordnung der Moderne. Social Engineering im 20. Jahrhundert*, (ed.) Thomas Etzemüller. Bielefeld: Transcript, 2009. 11–39.
Eyal, Gil and Johanna Bockman. Eastern Europe as a Laboratory for Economic Knowledge: The Transnational Roots of Neoliberalism. *American Journal of Sociology* 108, No. 2 (September 2002): 310–352.
Eyal, Gil, Iván Szelényi, Eleanor R Townsley, *Making Capitalism without Capitalists: Class Formation and Elite Struggles in Post-Communist Central Europe*. London; New York: Verso, 1998.
Eyal, Gil. *The Origins of Postcommunist Elites: From Prague Spring to the Breakup of Czechoslovakia*. Minneapolis: University of Minnesota Press, 2003.
Fagen, Melvin M. The Work of the Committee on the Development of Trade, 1949–1957. In *The Economic Commission for Europe. A General Appraisal*, (ed.) UNECE. Geneva: United Nations, 1957. VII–1.
———. Gunnar Myrdal and the Shaping of the United Nations Economic Commission for Europe. *Coexistence* 25 (1988): 427–435.

Favaretto, Gilda Manganaro. *Il federalismo personalista di Alexandre Marc (1904 – 2000)*. Milano: FrancoAngeli, 2006.
Favaretto, Tito. Autonomia e potere nella Repubblica Federativa Jugoslava. *Democrazia Integrale* 6 (1965): 4 – 24 and 7 (1965): 3 – 21.
Feldheim, Pierre. introduction to *International Cooperation in the Social Sciences. 25 Years of Vienna Experience,* (eds.) František Charvát, Willem Stamation, Christiane Villain-Gandossi. Vienna: European Co-ordination Centre for Research and Documentation in Social Sciences, 1988. 9 – 16.
Fencl, V. Koncepce podnikání, řízení a organizace podniků. *Moderní řízení* 3, no. 7 (1968): 35 – 38.
Figar, Š., V. Ruml, and A. Špaček. Problémy kybernetiky. *Nová mysl* 11 (1957): 448 – 463.
Fink, Carole, Philipp Gassert and Detlef Junker, *1968: the world transformed*. Cambridge: Cambridge University Press, 1998.
Fisher, David T. Worker participation in West German industry. *Monthly Labor Review* 101 (1978): 59 – 63.
Fitzpatrick, Sheila. *The Russian Revolution*, 2nd edition. Oxford: Oxford University Press, 1994.
Førland, Egil. *Cold Economic Warfare: CoCom and the Forging of Strategic Export Controls, 1948 – 1954*. Dordrecht: Republic of Letters, 2009.
Fourcade, Marion. The Construction of a Global Profession: The Transnationalization of Economics. *American Journal of Sociology* 112, no. 1 (July 2006): 145 – 194.
– – –. *Economists and Societies: Discipline and Profession in the United States, Britain & France, 1890s to 1990s*. New Jersey: Princeton University Press, 2009.
Fourquet, François. *Les Comptes de la puissance. Histoire de la comptabilité nationale et du plan*. Paris: Encres, 1980.
Frenkel, Michal. The Americanization of the Antimanagerialist Alternative in Israel: How Foreign Experts Retheorized and Disarmed Workers' Participation in Management, 1950 – 1970. *International Studies of Management & Organization* 38, no. 4 (2008): 17-37.
Frey, Mark and Sönke Kunkel. Writing the History of Development: A Review of the Recent Literature. *Contemporary European History* 20 (2011): 215 – 232.
Fromm, Erich. *Socialist Humanism: An International Symposium*. New York: Doubleday, 1965.
Gaïti, Brigitte. Les modernisateurs dans l'administration d'après-guerre. L'écriture d'une histoire héroïque. *Revue française d'administration publique* 102 (2002/2): 295 – 306.
Galbraith, John K. *The New Industrial State*. Boston: Houghton Mifflin, 1967.
Gałęski, Bogusław, Wacław Makarczyk, Lili M. Szwengrub, *Cross-national European Research Project on the Diffusion of Technical Innovations in Agriculture*. Vienna: International Social Science Council, 1969.
Garaudy, Roger. Kafka et le Printemps de Prague. *Lettres françaises* 981 (1963): 1.
– – –. *From Anathema to Dialogue: The Challenge of Marxist-Christian Cooperation*. London: Collins, 1967.
Garavini, Giuliano. *After Empires: European Integration, Decolonisation, and the Challenge from the Global South 1957 – 1986*. Oxford: Oxford University Press, 2012.
Garson, G. David. Models of Worker Self-Management: The West European Experience. in *Worker Self-Management in Industry: The West European Experience*, (ed.) G. David Garson. New York: Praeger Publishers, 1977.

Gaudier, Maryse. The International Institute for Labour Studies: its research function, activities and publications, 1960–2001. www.ilo.org/wcmsp5/groups/public/—dgreports/—inst/documents/genericdocument/wcms_194523.pdf (accessed 31 January 2017).

Gayon, Vincent. "L'OCDE au travail. Contribution à une sociologie historique de la 'coopération économique internationale' sur le chômage et l'emploi (1970–2010). PhD. Diss, Université Paris I-Panthéon Sorbonne, 2010.

Gemelli, Giuliana. *From imitation to Competitive Cooperation. Ford Foundation and Management Education in Western Europe (1950's-1970's)*. Florence: EUI, working papers, I and II, 1997.

Genscher, Hans-Dietrich. *Rebuilding a House Divided*. New York: Broadway Books, 1997.

Georgi, Frank. A la recherché de l'autogestion. Les gauches françaises et le "modèle yougoslave (1948–1981)" https://lms.hypotheses.org/288 (accessed January 2018).

Gerovitch, Slava. *From Newspeak to Cyberspeak: History of Soviet Cybernetics*. Cambridge, Mass.: The MIT Press, 2002.

Giles, Norman. *Management by objectives*. Bucharest/Paris: International Labour Office, 1970) 70B09/472.

Gill, Stephen. *American Hegemony and the Trilateral Commission*. Cambridge, Mass.: Harvard University Press, 2009.

Gillabert, Matthieu and Tiphaine Robert. *Zuflucht suchen. Phasen des Exils aus Osteuropa im Kalten Krieg / Chercher refuge. Les phases d'exil d'Europe centrale pendant la Guerre froide*. Basel: Schwabe, 2017.

Gilman, Nils. The new international economic order: A reintroduction. *Humanity: An International Journal of Human Rights, Humanitarianism, and Development* 6, no. 1 (2015): 1–16.

Girock, Hans-Joachim. *Partner von morgen?* Stuttgart: Kreuz-Verlag, 1968.

Giugni, Cfr. Gino. *Diritto sindacale*. Bari, Cacucci editore, 1986.

Godard, Simon. Une seule façon d'être communiste? L'internationalisme dans les parcours biographiques au Conseil d'aide économique mutuelle. *Critique internationale* 66, no. 1 (2015): 69–83.

———. Le Conseil d'aide économique mutuelle et la construction d'une diplomatie économique parallèle dans l'Europe socialiste. 1962–1989. In *Réinventer la diplomatie. Sociabilités, réseaux et pratiques diplomatiques en Europe depuis 1919*, (eds.) Vincent Genin, Mattieu Osmont, and Thomas Raineau. Brussels: Peter Lang, 2016. 171–187.

Golub, Phillip. From the new international order to the G20. *Third World Quarterly*, 34, no. 6 (2013): 1000–1015.

Górny, Maciej. *Die Wahrheit ist auf unserer Seite: Nation, Marxismus und Geschichte im Ostblock*. Cologne: Böhlau 2011.

Gourvish, Terry and Nick Tiratsoo. *Missionaries and Managers: American Influences on European Management Education, 1945–60*. Manchester: Manchester University Press, 1998.

Graham, Loren. *Science in Russia and the Soviet Union. A short history*. Cambridge: Cambridge University Press, 1993.

Greenaway, Frank. *Science International. A History of the International Council of Scientific Unions*. Cambridge: Cambridge University Press, 1996.

Gregory, P. and R. Stuart, *Soviet and Post-Soviet Economic Structure and Performance*, 5th edition. New York: Harper-Collins, 1994.

Gregory, Paul and Mark Harrison. Allocation under Dictatorship: Research in Stalin's Archives. *Journal of Economic Literature* 43, no. 3 (2005): 721–761.

Gregory, Paul. *The Political Economy of Stalinism*. New York: Cambridge University Press, 2004.

Gridan, Irina. Du communisme national au national-communisme. Réactions à la soviétisation dans la Roumanie des années 1960. *Vingtième Siècle. Revue d'histoire* 109 (2011): 113–127.

Griffin, Tom. The Relationship of the United Nations Economic Commission for Europe (UN/ECE, Geneva) to the Organization for Economic Cooperation and Development (OECD, Paris) and the Statistical Office of the European Communities (Eurostat, Luxembourg). *Statistical Journal of the United Nations ECE* 13, no. 1 (1996).

Grosbois, Thierry. *Origine et espoirs de la planification française*. Paris: Dunod, 1968.

———. *Programmer l'espérance*. Paris: Stock, 1976.

———. La Belgique et le Benelux: de l'universalisme au régionalisme. In *La Belgique, les petits États et la construction européenne*, (eds.) Michel Dumoulin, Geneviève Duchenne, and Arthe Van Laer. Bern: Peter Lang, 2004.

Gruson, Claude. *Propos d'un opposant obstiné au libéralisme mondial*. Paris: Éditions MSH, 2001.

Guerriero, Wilson R. The struggle for management education in Britain: The Urwick Committee and the Office Management Association. *Management and Organizational History* 6, no. 4 (2011): 367–389.

Gunn, Christopher Eaton. *Workers' Self-Management in the United States*. Ithaca and London: Cornell University Press, 1984.

Gutman, Patrick and Francis Arkwright. La coopération industrielle tripartite entre pays à systèmes économiques et sociaux Différents, de l'Ouest, de l'Est et Du Sud. *Politique étrangère* 40, no. 6 (1976): 621–655.

Haga, Lars. Imaginer la démocratie populaire: l'Institut de l'économie mondiale et la carte mentale soviétique de l'Europe de l'Est (1944–1948). *Vingtième Siècle. Revue d'histoire* 109 (2011): 13–30.

Häikiö, Martti. *Fuusio. Yhdistymisen kautta suomalaiseksi monialayritykseksi 1865–1982* [History of the enterprise Nokia 1865–1982, part 1]. Helsinki: Edita, 2001.

———. *Sturm und Drang. Suurkaupoilla eurooppalaiseksi elektroniikkayritykseksi 1983–1991. Nokia Oyj:n historia*. osa 2 [History of enterprise Nokia 1983–1991, part 2]. Edita: Helsinki, 2001.

Hájek, Jiří. *Paměti*. Prague: Ústav mezinárodních vztahů, 1997.

Hájek, Ladislav. *Public Relations: Podnik a veřejnost*. Hradec Králové: Institut pro sociální analýzu, 1970.

Hanson, Philip. *Trade and Technology in Soviet-Western Relations*. London: Macmillan, 1981.

———. *The Rise and Fall of the Soviet Economy: An Economic History of the USSR from 1945*. London: Longman, 2003.

———. The Soviet Union's acquisition of Western technology after Stalin; Some thoughts on people and connections. In *Reassessing Cold War Europe*, (eds.) Sari Autio-Sarasmo and Katalin Miklóssy. Abingdon: Routledge, 2011. 28–30.

Hare, P. G. and P. T. Wanless. Polish and Hungarian Economic Reforms – A Comparison. *Soviet Studies* 33, no. 4 (1981): 491–517.

Hart, Michael. *Also Present at the Creation: Dana Wilgress and the United Nations Conference on Trade and Employment at Havana.* Ottawa: Centre for Trade Policy and Law, 1995.

Hauchecorne, Mathieu. L'État des économistes au 'miroir transatlantique.' Circulations et hybridation de l'économie publique française et états-unienne. In *Comparaisons franco-américaines*, (ed.) Daniel Sabbagh and Maud Simonet. Rennes: Presses Universitaires de Rennes, 2016.

Helleiner, Eric. The Development Mandate of International Institutions: Where Did It Come From? *Studies in Comparative International Development* 44, no.6 (2009): 189–211.

–––. *Forgotten Foundations of Bretton Woods: International Development and the Making of the Postwar Order.* Ithaca: Cornell University Press, 2014.

Herbert, Ulrich. Europe in High Modernity: Reflections on a Theory of the Twentieth Century. *Journal of Modern European History* 5 (2007): 5–21.

Hervig, Roggemann. *Das Modell der Arbeiterselbstverwaltung in Jugoslawien.* Frankfurt am Main: Europaische Verlagsanstalt, 1970.

Hjerppe, Riitta. Teollisuus. In *Suomen taloushistoria. Teollistuva Suomi.* Osa 2 [Economic history of Finland. Industrializing Finland, Part 2], (eds.) Jorma Ahvenainen, Erkki Pihkala, Viljo Rasila. Helsinki: Kustannusosakeyhtiö Tammi 1982.

Hobsbawm, Eric. *Age of Extremes: The Short Twentieth Century: 1914–1991.* London: Abacus, 1995.

Hoffman, E. P. and R. F. Laird. *'The scientific-technological revolution' and Soviet foreign policy.* Oxford: Pergamon Press, 1982.

Horvat, Branko. Yugoslav Economic Policy in the Post-War Period: Problems, Ideas, Institutional Developments. *The American Economic Review* 61 (1971): 71–169.

Hromádka, Josef Lukl. *Komunismus a křesťanství: o nápravu věcí lidských.* Hradec Králové: Evangelické dílo, 1946.

–––. *Gospel for Atheists.* Geneva: WCC–Youth Department, 1965.

Hrzal, Ladislav and Jakub Netopilík. *Ideologický boj ve vývoji české filozofie.* Prague: Svoboda, 1983.

Huber, Valeska. Introduction: Global Histories of Social Planning. *Journal of Contemporary History* 52 (2017): 3–15.

Hunnius, Gerry, G. David Garson and John Case, *Workers' control: A Reader on Labor and Social Change.* New York: Vintage Books, 1973.

Hyman, Robert. The historical evolution of British industrial relations. In *Industrial Relations, Theory and Practice*, (ed.) P. Edwards. Oxford: Blackwell, 2003.

Ikenberry, G. John. A World Economy Restored: Expert Consensus and the Anglo-American Post-War Settlement. *International Organization* 46, no. 1 (Winter 1992): 307–308, 315–316, 318.

Interfutures. *Facing the future. Mastering the probable, managing the unpredictable.* Paris: OECD, 1977.

International Labour Office. *Workers' Management in Yugoslavia.* Geneva: International Labour Office, 1962.

–––. *The ILO and Asia.* Geneva: International Labour Office, 1962.

———. *The effectiveness of ILO management development and productivity projects, Report and conclusions*, Management Development Series, 3. Geneva: International Labour Office, 1965.
———. *Work study*. Geneva: International Labour Office, 1969.
Iriye, Akira. Historizicing the Cold War. In *The Oxford Handbook of the Cold War*, (eds.) Immermann, Richard H, and Petra Goedde. Oxford: Oxford University Press, 2013. 15–32.
Irwin, Douglas A., Petros C. Mavroidis and Alan O. Sykes. *The Genesis of the GATT*. Cambridge: Cambridge University Press, 2008.
Jackson, Ian. *The Economic Cold War. America, Britain and East–West Trade, 1948–1963*. London: Palgrave, 2001.
Jackson, John H. *World Trade and The Law of GATT*. Indianapolis: Bobbs-Merrill, 1969.
Jajesniak-Quast, Dagmara. 'Hidden Integration.' RGW-Wirtschaftsexperten in europäischen Netzwerken. *Jahrbuch für Wirtschaftsgeschichte* 1 (2014): 179–195.
Jakovina, Tvrtko. *Treća Strana Hladnog Rata*. Zaprešić: Fraktura, 2014.
Janko, Jan and Emilie Těšínská, *Technokracie v českých zemích (1900–1950)*. Prague: Archiv Akademie věd České republiky, 1999.
Janko, Jan. Technokratické tendence v českých zemích. In *Studie z dějin techniky 25: Postátňování, profesionalizace a mecenášství ve vědě českých zemí 1860–1945*, (ed.) Jan Janko. Prague: Institut základů vzdělanosti UK, 1996. 25–56.
Jantsch, Eric. *Technological Forecasting in Perspective*. Paris: The Organisation for Economic Co-operation and Development, 1967.
———. *Perspectives on Planning: Papers from the Bellagio Conference*. Paris: The Organisation for Economic Co-operation and Development, 1969.
Jardini, David. *Out of the Blue Yonder: The RAND Corporation's Diversification into Social Welfare Research*. Baltimore: Carnegie Mellon University, 1996.
Jasny, Naum. *Soviet Economists of the twenties. Names to be remembered*. Cambridge: Cambridge University Press, 1972.
Jensen-Eriksen, Niklas. CoCom and Neutrality: Western Export Control policies, Finland and the Cold War, 1949–58. In *Reassessing Cold War Europe*, (eds.) Sari Autio-Sarasmo and Katalin Miklóssy. Abingdon: Routledge, 2011. 49–65.
Jindřichová-Kadlecová, Erika. *Úloha křesťanství v historii třídních bojů*. PhD diss. Charles University, Prague, 1949.
Johnson, A. Ross *The Transformation of Communist Ideology: The Yugoslav Case. 1945–1953*. Cambridge, Mass. & London: The MIT Press, 1972.
Johnson, Keith and Lawrence R. Klein. Link Model Simulations of International Trade: An Evaluation of the Effects of Currency Realignment. *The Journal of Finance* 29, no. 2 (1974): 617–630.
Jones, Derek C. "Worker Participation in Management in Britain: Evaluation, Current Developments, and Prospects." In *Worker Self-Management in Industry: The West European Experience*, (ed.) G. David Garson New York: Praeger Publishers, 1977.
Josephson, Paul R. *New Atlantis Revisited. Akademgorodok, the Siberian City of Science*. Princeton: Princeton University Press, 1997.
Judt, Tony. *Postwar: A History of Europe Since 1945*. London: Vintage, 2010.

Kaataja, Sampsa. Expert Groups Closing the Divide: Estonian-Finnish Computing Cooperation Since the 1960s. In *Beyond the Divide. Entangled Histories of Cold War Europe*, (eds.) Simo Mikkonen and Pia Koivunen. Oxford: Berghahn books 2015. 103.

Kadlecová, Erika. Ateismus bojovný a trpělivý. *Nová mysl* 10 (1962): 1254–1262.

———. *Sociologický výzkum religiozity Severomoravského kraje*. Prague: Academia, 1967.

———. Socialismus a náboženství. *Rudé právo* (28 May 1968).

Kaiser, Wolfram and Johan Schot. Writing the Rules for Europe. Experts, Cartels and International Organisations. Basingstoke / New York: Palgrave Macmillan, 2014.

Kaje, M and O. Niitamo. Scientific and Technical Cooperation Between a Small Capitalist Country and big Socialist Country. In *Finnish-Soviet Economic Relations*, (ed.) K. Möttölä, O. N. Bykov and I.S. Korolev. London: Macmillan Press, 1983. 143–144.

Kalinová, Lenka. *Máme nedostatek pracovních sil?* Prague: Svoboda, 1979.

Kansikas, Suvi. Room to manœuvre? National interests and coalition-building in the CMEA, 1969–1974. In *Reassessing Cold War Europe*, (eds.) Sari Autio-Sarasmo and Katalin Miklossy. London: Routledge, 2011. 193–209.

———. Acknowledging Economic Realities: The CMEA Policiy Change vis-a-vis the European Community, 1970–1973. *European Review of History* 21, no. 2 (2014): 311–328.

———. *Socialist countries face the European Community. Soviet-bloc Controversies over East-West Trade*. Fankfurt am Main: Peter Lang, 2014.

Kaplan, Karel. *Kronika komunistického Československa. Doba tání 1953–1956*. Brno: Barrister & Principal, 2005.

Kaplan, Karel. *Stát a církev v Československu 1948–1953*. Brno: Doplněk, 1993.

Kardelj, Edvard. *Pravci razvoja političkog sistema socijalističkog samoupravljanja*. Beograd: Komunist, 1978.

Kaser, Michael. *The Economic History of Eastern Europe. 1919–1975*, volume III. Oxford: Clarendon Press, 1986.

Kaufman, Bruce E. *The Global Evolution of Industrial Relations: Events, Ideas and the IIRA*. Geneva: International Labour Office, 2004).

Kerblay, Basile. Entretiens sur la planification avec des économistes soviétiques. *Cahiers du monde russe et soviétique* 1, no. 1 (1959): 174–179.

Kerimov, D. A. *Metodika plánování sociálního rozvoje podniku*. Prague: Práce, 1973.

Khachaturov, Tigran Sergeevich. *Methods of Long-Term Planning and Forecasting: Proceedings of a Conference Held by the International Economic Association at Moscow*. London: Macmillan, 1976.

Kilian, Werner. *Die Hallstein-Doktrin. Der diplomatische Krieg zwischen der BRD und der DDR 1955–1973*. Berlin: Duncker & Humblot, 2001.

Kinsky, Ferdinand and Franz Knipping. *Le fédéralisme personnaliste aux sources de l'Europe de demain, hommage à Alexandre Marc*. Baden Baden: Nomos, 1996.

Kipping, Matthias. The U.S. Influence on the Evolution of Management Consultancies in Britain, France, and Germany Since 1945. *Business and Economic History* 25, no. 1 (1996): 112–123.

Kirby, Dianne. *Religion and the Cold War*. Houndmills: Palgrave, 2013.

Kis, Théofil I. État des travaux sur la problématique de la convergence: théories et hypothèses. *Études internationales* 2, no. 3 (1971): 443–487.

Kiss, Tibor and George Hajdu. International Cooperation in Planning within COMECON. *Eastern European Economics* 14, no. 4 (1976): 12.

Klein, Lawrence R. The Interdependence of National Economies and the Synchronization of Economic Fluctuations: Evidence from the LINK Project. *Weltwirtschaftliches Archiv* 114, no. 4 (1978): 642-708.

Kochetkova, Elena. A history of failed innovation: continuous cooking and the Soviet pulp industry, 1940s-1960s. *History and Technology* 31, no. 2 (2015), 108–132.

———. The Soviet Forestry Industry in the 1950s and 1960s: A Project of Modernization and Technology Transfer from Finland. *Publications of the Faculty of Social Sciences* 52 (2017).

Kohlrausch, Martin, Katrin Steffen and Stefan Wiederkehr, (eds.). *Expert Cultures in Central Eastern Europe. The Internationalization of Knowledge and the Transformation of Nation States since World War I.* Osnabrück: Fibre Verlag, 2010.

Kohout, Jaroslav. *Sociologie a řízení ekonomiky.* Prague: Práce, 1967.

———. *Sociální analýza a řízení socialistického podniku: vznik-pojetí-aplikace.* Prague: Práce, 1976.

Kolman, Arnošt. *Kybernetika: O strojích vykonávajících některé duševní funkce člověka.* Prague: SNPL, 1957.

Kolvenbach, Walter. *Partecipazione e governo dell'impresa. I modelli europei.* Rome: Edizioni Lavoro, 1984.

Komárek, Valtr. *Vazby vědeckotechnických, ekonomických a sociálních aspektů dlouhodobého rozvoje ČSSR.* Prague: ÚVTEI, 1988.

———. *Prognóza a program.* Prague: Academia, 1990.

Korbonski, Andrzej. The politics of economic reforms in Eastern Europe: The last thirty Years. *Soviet Studies*, 41, no. 1 (1989): 1–19.

Kosanović, Milan. Brandt and Tito: Between Ostpolitik and Nonalignment. In *Ostpolitik, 1969–1974: European and Global Responses*, (ed.) Carole Fink and Bernd Schaefer. Cambridge: Cambridge University Press, 2009. 232–242.

Kostelecký, Václav. *The United Nations Economic Commission for Europe: The Beginning of a History.* Gothenburg: Graphic Systems, 1989.

Kotkin, Stephen. Modern Times: The Soviet Union and the Interwar Conjuncture. *Kritika: Explorations in Russian and Eurasian History* 2 (2001): 111–164.

Kott, Sandrine and Justine Faure. Le bloc de l'Est en question. *Vingtième siècle* 109, no. 2 (2011).

Kott, Sandrine. Par-delà la guerre froide: Les organisations internationales et les circulations Est-Ouest (1947–1973). *Vingtième Siècle. Revue d'histoire*, 109 (1 Jan., 2011): 143–154.

———. Cold War Internationalism. In *Internationalisms: A Twentieth-Century History*, (eds.) Glenda Sluga and Patricia Clavin. Cambridge: Cambridge University Press, 2016. 340–362.

Koul, Autar Krishan. *The legal framework of UNCTAD in world trade.* Leyden: A. W. Sijthoff, 1977.

Kourilsky, Chantal, Armando Montanari and G. Vyskovsky, *Vienna Centre Report of Activity 1979–80.* Vienna: ECCRDSS, 1980.

Kovář, Karel, Miloš Hendl, and Karel Fryč. Obnova leninských zásad kádrové práce. *Moderní řízení* 6, no. 11–12 (1971): 5–12.

Krause, Scott H. and Daniel Stinsky. For Europe, Democracy and Peace: Social Democratic Blueprints for Postwar Europe in Willy Brandt and Gunnar Myrdal's Correspondence.

Themenportal Europäische Geschichte (2015), www.europa.clio-online.de/essay/id/artikel-3799.
Krause, Scott H. Neue Westpolitik: The Clandestine Campaign to Westernize the SPD in Cold War Berlin, 1948–1958. *Central European History* 48 (2015): 79–99.
Krippner, Gretta R. *Capitalizing on Crisis: The Political Origins of the Rise of Finance.* Cambridge, Mass.: Harvard University Press, 2012.
Krivý, Vladimír. Sociotechnika: možnosti a hranice. *Sociológia* 20 (1988): 417–425.
Kudláč, Antonín K. K. *Příběh(y) Volné myšlenky.* Prague: Nakladatelství Lidové noviny, 2005.
Kuisel, Richard F. *Capitalism and State in Modern France: Renovation and Economic Management in the 20. Century.* Cambridge: Cambridge University Press, 1983.
Kuisma, Markku. *Kylmä sota, kuuma öljy. Neste, Suomi ja kaksi Eurooppaa* [Cold War, hot oil. Enterprise Neste, Finland and the divided Europe]. Helsinki: Werner Söderström Ltd, 1997.
Kula, Marcin. *Mimo wszystko bliżej Paryża niż Moskwy. Książka o Francji, PRL i o nas, historykach* [Closer to Paris than to Moscow. About France, the Polish People's Republic and about us, historians]. Warsaw: Wydawnictwa Uniwersytetu Warszawskiego 2010.
Kunkel, Sönke. Contesting Globalization: The United Nations Conference on Trade and Development and the Transnationalization of Sovereignty. *International Organizations and Development, 1945–1990*, (eds.) Sönke Kunkel, Corinna Unger, and Mark Frey. Basingstoke: Palgrave Macmillan, 2014. 240–259.
Kunter, Katharina and Annegreth Schilling. *Globalisierung der Kirchen: der Ökumenische Rat der Kirchen und die Entdeckung der Dritten Welt in den 1960er und 1970er Jahren.* Göttingen: Vandenhoeck & Ruprecht, 2014.
Kutta, František. *Planning and Forecasting Social Processes: Undertaken within the Framework of the Problems Committee for Multilateral Cooperation of the Academy of Sciences, and Dedicated to the 9th World Sociological Congress Uppsala, Sweden 1978.* Prague: Academia, 1978.
———. *Teorie a praxe sociálního plánování a programování v ČSSR.* Prague, Svoboda, 1980.
Laak, Dirk van. Planung. Geschichte und Gegenwart des Vorgriffs auf die Zukunft [Planning. The past and presence of advancing the future]. *Geschichte und Gesellschaft* 34, no. 3 (1 July, 2008): 305-326.
Lagendijk, Vincent. *Electrifying Europe: The Power of Europe in the Construction of Electricity Networks.* Amsterdam: Aksant, 2008.
———. The Structure of Power: The UNECE and East-West Electricity Connections, 1947–1975. *Comparativ* 24, no. 1 (2014): 55.
Lanaro, Silvio. *Storia dell'Italia repubblicana. L'economia, la politica, la cultura, la società dal dopoguerra agli anni '90.* Venezia: Marsilio, 1992. 364–386
Landa, Ivan and Jan Mervart, *Proměny marxisticko-křesťanského dialogu v Československu.* Prague: Filosofia, 2017.
Laurila, Juhani. *Finnish-Soviet Clearing Trade and Payment System: History and Lessons.* Helsinki: Bank of Finland Studies A: 94, 1995.
Lavigne, Marie. The Soviet Union inside COMECON. *Soviet Studies* XXXV/2 (1983): 135–153.
———. *Économie internationale des pays socialistes.* Paris: A. Colin, 1985.
———. *East-South Relations in the World Economy.* Boulder, Colo. ; London: Westview Press, 1988.

Le Texier, Thibault. *Le maniement des hommes: essai sur la rationalité managériale*. Paris: la Découverte, 2016.
Lebaron, Frédéric. *La Croyance économique. Les économistes entre science et politique*. Paris: Seuil, 2000).
Leeds, Adam. Dreams in Cybernetic Fugue: Cold War Technoscience, the Intelligentsia, and the Birth of Soviet Mathematical Economics. *Historical Studies in the Natural Sciences* 46 (2016): 633–668.
Lees, Lorraine M. *Keeping Tito Afloat: The United States, Yugoslavia and the Cold War*. University Park, PA: Penn State University Press, 1997.
Leimgruber, Mathieu. Stewards of globalisation. Unpublished paper.
Lemoine, Françoise. *Le COMECON*. Paris: PUF, 1982. 103.
Lengyel, Peter. *International Social Science: The UNESCO Experience*. New Brunswick: Transaction Books, 1986.
Lesourne, Jacques. L'exercice Interfuturs, réflexions méthodologiques. *Futuribles*, 26, (1976): 20–38.
———. *Les mille sentiers de l'avenir*. Paris: Seghors, 1981.
Light, Jennifer. *From Warfare to welfare*. Baltimore: John Hopkins Press, 2002.
Lindbeck, Assar. Dag Hammarskjöld as Economist and Government Official. *Sveriges Riksbank Economic Review*, no. 3 (2005): 9–10.
Linkiewicz, Olga. Scientific Ideals and Political Engagement: Polish Ethnology and the 'Ethnic Question' Between the Wars. *Acta Poloniae Historica* 114 (2016): 5–27.
Lipkin, Mikhaïl. The Soviet Union, CMEA and the Question of First EEC Enlargement. Paper presented at the XIV International Economic History Congress, Helsinki, 2006.
Lochman, Jan Milíč. Dialog překračuje meze. *Literární listy* 14 (1968): 13.
———. *Church in a Marxist Society: A Czechoslovak View*. Evanston: Harper & Row, 1970. 192; Roger Garaudy, *L'alternative*. Paris: Éditions R. Laffont, 1972.
Loehr, William and John P. Powelson. *Threat to development. pitfalls of the NIEO*. Boulder, Colo., Westview, 1983.
Lomellini, Valentine and Antonio Varsori. *Dal Sessantotto al crollo del Muro: i movimenti di protesta in Europa a cavallo tra i due blocchi*. Milano: FrancoAngeli, 2014.
Lorenzini, Sara. COMECON and the South in the years of *Détente:* A study on East-south economic relations. *European Review of History* 21 (2014): 183–199.
Lutz, Raphael. Embedding the Human and Social Sciences in Western Societies, 1880–1980: Reflections on Trends and Methods of Current Research. In *Engineering Society: The Role of the Human and Social Sciences in Modern Societies, 1880–1980*, Kerstin Brückweh, Dirk Schumann, Richard F. Wetzell and Benjamin Ziemann (eds.), 41–58. Basingstoke: Palgrave, 2012.
Machát, František. V. I. Lenin a řízení. *Moderní řízení* 5, no. 3 (1970): 15–20.
Machovec, Milan. *O smyslu lidského života*. Prague: Orbis, 1957.
———. O metodách ateistické výchovy. *Filosofický časopis* 5 (1959): 678–694.
———. *O tak zvané 'dialektické' teologii současného protestantismu*. Prague: ČSAV, 1962.
———. Je naše vědeckoateistická výchova správně orientována? *Filosofický časopis* 3 (1964): 354–361.
———. *Smysl lidského života: studie k filosofii člověka*. Prague: Nakladatelství politické literatury, 1965.
———. Dialog v procesu humanizace člověka. *Osvětová práce* 15 (1965): 10–11.

———. Die Zukunft als Drohung und Chance. *Der Kreis, Sonderreihe*, 5 (1966): 31.
Mai, Gunther. Osthandel und Westintegration 1947–1957. Europa, die USA und die Entstehung einer hegemonialen Partnerschaft. In *Vom Marshallplan zur EWG. Die Eingliederung der Bundesrepublik Deutschland in die westliche Welt*, (ed.) Ludolf Herbst, Werner Bührer, and Hanno Sowade. Munich: R. Oldenbourg Verlag, 1990. 204.
Maier, Charles. Malaise. The crisis of capitalism in the 1970s. In *Shock of the Global* (eds.) Niall Ferguson et al., 25–48. Cambridge MA: Harvard University Press, 2010.
Maire, Edomond. *Demain l'autogestion*. Paris: Seghers, 1976.
Major, Patrick and Rana Mitter. *Across the Blocs: Cold War Cultural and Social History*. London: Frank Cass, 2004.
Maksimova, M. Economic Relations between the Socialist and the Capitalist Countries. In *Finnish-Soviet Economic Relations*, (ed.) K. Möttölä, O.N. Bykov and I.S. Korolev. London: Macmillan Press, 1983. 23.
Malinvaud, Edmond. Introduction: Some Notes on Assessments about Economic Systems. In *Planning, Shortage, and Transformation. Essays in Honor of János Kornai*, (eds.) Eric Maskin and András Simonovits. Cambridge, Mass.: MIT Press, 2000. 1–14.
Maraschi, Ettore. Democrazia industriale e organizzazione del lavoro. *L'Impresa* 5 (1977): 491–496.
Marc, Alexandre. Faillite de l'autogestion? *Europe en Formation*, no. 141, 1971.
Marczewski, Jean. Planification et convergence des systèmes. *Revue de l'Est* 2/4 (1971): 5–19.
Margairaz, Michel. *L'État, les finances et l'économie (1932–1952). Histoire d'une conversion*. Paris: Comité d'histoire économique et financière de la France, 1991, 2 vol.
———. La faute à 68? Le Plan et les institutions de la régulation économique et financière: une libéralisation contrariée ou différée? In *Mai 68 entre libération et libéralisation. La grande bifurcation*, (ed.) Michel Margairaz and Danielle Tartakowsky. Rennes, PUR, 2010. 41–62.
Margolis, Julius and Henri Guitton. *Public economics: an analysis of public production and consumption and their relations to the private sectors. Proceedings of a conference*. New York: MacMillan/St Martin's Press, 1969.
Marshall, T. H. *International Organizations in the Social Sciences*, revised edition. Paris: UNESCO, 1965.
Mastanduno, Michael. *Economic containment: CoCom and the politics of East-West trade*. Ithaca, N.Y: Cornell University Press, 1992.
Matala, Saara. The Business of Foreign Affairs. Unrealized visions of joint business, technology and politics in Finnish-Soviet shipbuilding at the end of the Cold War. *Proceedings of the 41th ICOHTEC Symposium 2014 Technology in times of transition*, (eds.) Helerea, E., Cionca, M, Ivănoiu, M. Brasov: Transylvania University of Brasov, 2014. 65–70.
———. Flashy flagships of Cold War cooperation – The Finnish-Soviet nuclear icebreaker project. *Technology & Culture* (forthcoming 2018).
Matějka, Ondřej. La religion est devenue l'affaire privée des citoyens. La construction du socialisme et les milieux religieux dans les Pays tchèques. *Histoire@Politique* 7 (2009).
———. Between the Academy and Power: Czech Marxist Sociology of Religion (1954–1970). In *Sociology and Ethnography in East-Central and South-East Europe. Scientific*

Self-Description in States Socialist Countries, (eds.) Ulf Brunnbauer, Claudia Kraft and Martin Schulze Wessel. Munich: Oldenbourg, 2011. 107–133.

―――. We are the Generation that Will Construct Socialism: The Czech 68ers Between Manifest Destiny and Mark of Cain. In *Talkin' 'Bout my Generation. Conflicts of Generation Building and Europe's 1968*, (ed.) Anna von der Goltz. Göttingen: Wallstein Verlag, 2011. 118–139.

―――. 'Správný komunista má také býti správným křesťanem, jako byli křesťané první.' Vztah českobratrských evangelíků ke Komunistické straně Československa 1921–1970. In *Český a slovenský komunismus (1921–2011)*, (eds.) Jan Kalous and Jiří Kocian. Prague: Ústav pro studium totalitních režimů, 2012. 284–296.

―――. A generation? A school? A fraternity? An army? Understanding the Roots of Josef Lukl Hromádka's Influence in the Czech Protestant Milieu 1920–1948. *Communio Viatorum. A Theological Journal* 3 (2012): 307–320.

Mattera, Paolo. *Storia del PSI 1892–1994*. Rome: Carocci, 2010.

Mayall, James. The shadow of the Empire: the EU and the former colonial world. In *International relations and the European Union*, (ed.) Christopher Hill and Michael Smith. Oxford: Oxford University Press, 2011.

Mayer, Alfred G. Theories of Convergence. In *Change in Communist System*, (ed.) Chalmers Johnson. Stanford: Stanford University Press, 1970. 313–341.

Mazower, Mark. *Dark Continent: Europe's Twentieth Century*. New York: Vintage, 2000.

McCracken, Paul, Guido Carli, Herbert Giersch, Attila Karaosmanoglu, Ryutaro Komiya, Assar Lindbeck, Robert Marjolin, Robin Matthews, *Towards Full Employment and Price Stability: A Report to the OECD by a Group of Independent Experts*. Paris: The Organisation for Economic Co-operation and Development, 1977.

McKenzie, Francine. *Redefining the Bonds of Commonwealth, 1939–1948: The Politics of Preference*. Basingstoke: Palgrave Macmillan 2002. 40.

―――. The GATT-EEC Collision: The Challenge of Regional Trade Blocs to the General Agreement on Tariffs and Trade, 1950–1967. *The International History Review*, 32, no. 2 (2010): 229–252.

―――. Free Trade and Freedom to Trade: The Development Challenge to GATT. In *International Organizations and Development, 1945–1990*, (eds.) Marc Frey, Sönke Konkel, and Corinna R. Unger. Basingstoke: Palgrave Macmillan, 2014. 150–170.

McKinnon, Andrew. Reading 'Opium of the People': Expression, Protest and the Dialectics of Religion. *Critical Sociology* 1–2 (2005): 15–38.

McLellan, David. Christian-Marxist Dialogue. *New Blackfriars* 577 (1968): 462–467.

Mechi, Lorenzo. Du BIT à la politique sociale européenne: les origines d'un modèle. *Le Mouvement Social* 3 (2013): 17–30.

Medina, Eden. *Cybernetic Revolutionaries: Technology and Politics in Allende's Chile*. Cambridge, Mass.: MIT Press, 2011.

Merloz, Georges. *La CNUCED. Droit International et Développement*. Brussels: Bruylant, 1980.

Mespoulet, Martine. La 'renaissance' de la sociologie en URSS (1958–1972). Une voie étroite entre matérialisme historique et 'recherches sociologiques concrètes.' *Revue d'histoire des sciences humaines* 16 (2007): 57–86.

Metelka, Josef. *Kybernetika – myslící stroje*. Prague: Orbis, 1957.

Mezinárodní konference Péče socialistického závodu o člověka: Sborník přednášek. Třinec: Třinecké železárny, 1974.

Michalski, Walter. The OECD Interfuturs project revisited twenty years later. In *Decision, prospective, auto-organisation. Essais en l'honneur de Jacques Lesourne*, (ed.) Walter Michalski. Paris: Seghors, 2000. 318–331.

Milenković, Deborah D. *Plan and Market in Yugoslav Economic Thought*. New Haven: Yale University Press, 1971.

Mioche, Philippe. La planification comme 'réforme de structure.' L'action de Pierre Mendès France de 1943 à 1945. *Histoire, économie et société* 1, no. 3 (1982): 471–488.

———. *Le Plan Monnet, genèse et élaboration, 1941–1947*. Paris: Publ. de la Sorbonne, 1987.

Miřejovský, Lubomír. *Dopisy z XX. století*. Prague: Nuga, 2004.

Mirovski, Philip and Dieter Plehwe. *The Road From Mont-Pèlerin. The Making of the Neoliberal Thought Collective*. Cambridge, Mass.: Harvard University Press, 2009.

Misgeld, Klaus. *Die 'Internationale Gruppe Demokratischer Sozialisten' in Stockholm, 1942–1945: Zur sozialistischen Friedensdiskussion während des Zweiten Weltkrieges*. Uppsala: Almquist & Wicksell, 1976.

———. Politik för Österrike. Bruno Kreisky och Sverige. [Politics for Austria. Bruno Kreisky and Sweden] *Arbetarhistoria* 125, no. 1 (2008): 8–18.

Mitchell, Timothy. *Carbon Democracy*. Cambridge, Mass.: Harvard University Press, 2013.

Mlčoch, Lubomír. Symposium o podniku. *Politická ekonomie* 17 (1969): 278–281.

———. *Teorie firmy*. Prague: Ekonomický ústav ČSAV, 1970.

Mlynář, Zdeněk. *Nightfrost in Prague: The End of Humane Socialism*. New York: Karz Publishers, 1980.

Mojzes, Paul. *Christian-Marxist Dialogue in Eastern Europe*. Minneapolis: Augsburg Publishing House, 1980.

Montanari, Armando. Social sciences and comparative research in Europe: Cross-national and multi-disciplinary projects for urban development. The role of geography. *Revue belge de géographie* 1–2 (2012), http://belgeo.revues.org/6085 (accessed 19 June 2017).

Montias, John Michael. Background and origins of the Rumanian dispute with COMECON. *Soviet Studies* XVI, no. 2 (1964): 125–151.

Morey, Maribel. A Reconsideration of an American Dilemma. *Reviews in American History* 40, no. 4 (2012): 686–92.

Mošna, Zdeněk. The New Economic System and Management Development in Czechoslovakia. *International Labour Review* 3 (1967): 61–81.

Murphy, Craig. *The Emergence of the NIEO Ideology*. Boulder, Colo.: Westview Press, 1984.

———. *The United Nations Development Programme: A Better Way?* Cambridge: Cambridge University Press, 2006.

Myrdal, Alva and Gunnar Myrdal, *Kris i befolkningsfrågan*. Stockholm: Bonniers, 1934.

Myrdal, Gunnar, Richard Sterner and Arnold Marshall Rose. *An American Dilemma: The Negro Problem and Modern Democracy*. New York; London: Harper and brothers publ., 1944.

———. Psychological Impediments to Effective International Cooperation. *The Journal of Social Issues* 8, no. 6 (1952): 5–31.

Myrdal, Gunnar. Socialpolitikens dilemma. [The dilemma of social policy] *Spektrum* 3 (1932).

———. *Varning för fredsoptimismen*. Stockholm: Bonnier, 1944.

———. Speciella organ på det ekonomiska och sociala området. In *Fred och säkerhet efter andra världskriget. Ett svenskt diskussionsinlägg*, [Specialized agencies in the economic and social field] (ed.) Utrikespolitiska Institutet. Uppsala: Almquist & Wicksells, 1945. 162–181.

———. Two Notes on ERP and East-West Trade, December 1949. UNOG Archives ARR 14/1360, Box 71.
———. The Trend toward Economic Planning. *The Manchester School of Economic and Social Studies* 19 (1951): 40.
———. The Research Work of the Secretariat of the Economic Commission for Europe. In *25 Economic Essays in English, German and Scandinavian Languages in Honour of Erik Lindahl*, (ed.) Ekonomisk tidskrift. Stockholm: Ekonomisk Tidskrift, 1956.
———. Twenty Years of the United Nations Economic Commission for Europe. *International Organization* 22 (1968): 617–628.
Napolitano, Giorgio. *Intervista sul PCI*. Rome-Bari: Laterza, 1976. 51–73.
Naumann, Katja. Avenues and Confines of Globalizing the Past: UNESCO's International Commission for a "Scientific and Cultural History of Mankind" (1952–1969). In *Networking the International System: Global Histories of International Organizations*, (ed.) Madeleine Herren. Heidelberg: Springer, 2014. 187–200.
Nelson, Michael. The Vredeling Directive: The EEC's Failed Attempt to Regulate Multinational Enterprises and Organize Collective Bargaining. *New York Journal of International Law and Politics* 20 (1988): 967–992.
Nešpor, Zdeněk R. *Ne/náboženské naděje intelektuálů: vývoj české sociologie náboženství v mezinárodním a interdisciplinárním kontextu*. Prague: Scriptorium, 2008.
Neumann, Cédric. *De la mécanographie à l'informatique. Le relations entre catégorisation des techniques, groupes professionnels et transformations des savoirs managériaux*, Thèse. Paris: ParisX, 2013. 172–244.
Niessen, Manfred and Jules Peschar. *International Comparative Research Problems of Theory, Methodology and Organisation in Eastern and Western Europe*. Oxford: Pergamon, 1982.
Niessen, Manfred, Jules Peschar, Chantal Kourilsky, *International Comparative Research: Social Structures and Public Institutions in Eastern and Western Europe*. Oxford: Pregamon Press, 1984.
Nilsson, Göran B. Den sociala ingenjörskonstens problematik. En orättfärdigt dissektion av den unge Gunnar Myrdal. In *Den svenska modellen*, (eds.) Per Thullberg and Kjell Östberg. Lund: Studentlitteratur, 1998. 167.
Nove, Alec. *An Economic History of the USSR, 1917–1991*. London: Penguin, 1992.
Novotný, Antonín. *Zpráva o činnosti ústředního výboru KSČ XI. sjezdu a současné hlavní úkoly*. Prague: Ústřední výbor KSČ. 1958.
Novotný, Jaroslav and Miroslav Štráchal. *Poznatky z experimentů v plánování sociálního rozvoje měst a obcí*. Ústí nad Labem: Ústav pro filozofii a sociologii – pobočka Ústí nad Labem, 1980.
Nyárádi, Nicholas. *My Ringside Seat in Moscow*. New York: Crowell, 1952.
Nytrová, Olga and Milan Balabán. Rozhovor s profesorem Milanem Machovcem. Jak tomu bylo s vaším křesťanstvím a marxismem? *Křesťanská revue* 7 (2000): 176.
O'Hara, Glen. *From Dreams to Disillusionment: Economic and Social Planning in 1960s Britain*. Basingstoke: Palgrave Macmillan, 2007.
Obadić, Ivan. A troubled relationship: Yugoslavia and the European Economic Community in détente. *European Review of History* 21 (2014): 329–348.
Ohlin, Bertil. Some Notes on the Stockholm Theory of Savings and Investment. *Economic Journal* 47 (1937).

Opočenský, Milan. Velice jsem po tobě teskliv. In *Mistr dialogu Milan Machovec. Sborník k nedožitým osmdesátinám českého filosofa*, (eds.) Kamila Jindrová, Pavel Tacheci, and Pavel Žďárský. Prague: Akropolis, 2006. 215.

Ornauer, Helmut and Johan Galtung, *Images of the World in the Year 2000: A Comparative Ten Nation Study*. Atlantic Highlands: Humanities Press, 1976);

Ozbekhan, Hasan. *A General Theory of Planning*. Santa Barbara: Systems Development Corporation, 1969.

–––. *The Predicament of Mankind: A Quest for Structured Responses to Growing World-wide Complexities and Uncertainties. Original Proposal to the Club of Rome*. New York: Club of Rome, 1970.

Page, Benjamin B. Dialogues. In *Mistr dialogu Milan Machovec. Sborník k nedožitým osmdesátinám českého filosofa*, (eds.) Kamila Jindrová, Pavel Tacheci, and Pavel Žďárský. Prague: Akropolis, 2006. 148–150.

Paju, Petri and Thomas Haigh. IBM rebuilds Europe. The curious case of the transnational typewriter. *Enterprise & Society* 2 (2015): 265–300.

Paju, Petri. Monikansallinen yritys ja siteet länteen. IBM Suomessa ja Länsi-Euroopassa 1940-luvun lopulla ja 1950-luvulla. [A multinational corporation and ties to the West: IBM in Finland and in Western Europe during the post-war years and the 1950s] *Historiallinen aikakauskirja* 113, no. 3 (2015): 251–269.

Paoli, Simone. *Il sogno di Erasmo. La questione educativa nel processo di integrazione europea*. Milano: FrancoAngeli, 2010. 70–125.

Parsons, Talcott. *Structure and Process in Modern Societies*. Glencoe: Free Press, 1960.

Pasić, Najdan, Stanislav Grozdanić and Milorad Radević, *Workers' management in Yugoslavia: Recent developments and trends*. Geneva: International Labour Office, 1982.

Patel, Kiran K. and Johan Schot. Twisted Paths to European Integration: Comparing Agriculture and Transport Policies in a Transnational Perspective. *Contemporary European History* 20, no. 4 (2011): 383–403.

Patel, Kiran K. and Sven Reichardt. The Dark Sides of Transnationalism: Social Engineering and Nazism, 1930s–1940s. *Journal of Contemporary History*, 51 (2016): 3–21

Patel, Kiran K. *The New Deal: A Global History*. Princeton: Princeton University Press, 2016.

Pavelka, Karel. *Jak lépe řídit*. Prague: Svoboda, 1970.

–––. *Jak lépe rozhodovat*. Prague: Svoboda, 1970.

–––. *Vedoucí a kolektiv*. Prague: Svoboda, 1970.

Pelikán, Pavel. *Člověk a informace (studie o člověku a jeho způsobech zacházení se zprávami)*. Prague: Svoboda, 1967.

–––. *Homo informationicus: réflexions sur l'homme et l'informatique*. Nancy: Centre européen universitaire, 1967.

Pemberton, Joanne. The Middle Way: The Discourse of Planning in Britain, Australia and at the League of Nations in the Interwar Years. *Australian Journal of Politics and History* 52, no. 1 (2006): 49, 51, 58.

Perović, Jeronim. The Tito-Stalin Split: A Reassessment in Light of New Evidence. *Journal of Cold War Studies* 9 (2007): 32–63.

Pestre, Dominique. La recherche opérationnelle pendant la dernière guerre et ses suites, la pensée des systèmes. *Revue scientifique et technique de la défense* 54 (2001). 63–69.

———. Repenser les variantes du complexe militaire – industriel – universitaire. In *Les Sciences pour la guerre, 1940–1960*, (eds.) Dominique Pestre and Amy Dahan. Paris: Presses de l'EHESS, 2004. 195–221.

———. Understanding and assessing complex systems to wage total war. OR and the Prime Minister Statistical Branch in the United Kingdom, 1939–1942. In *Engaged. Science in Practice from Renaissance to the Present*, (eds.) Mario Biagioli and Jessika Riskin. London: Palgrave, 2012. 83–102

Péteri, György. (ed.) Across and Beyond the East West Devide. *Slavonica* 10, no. 2 (November 2004).

Péteri, György. Sites of Convergence: The USSR and Communist Eastern Europe at International Fairs Abroad and Home. *Journal of Contemporary History* 47 (2012): 3–12.

Peters, Benjamin. *How Not to Network a Nation: The Uneasy History of the Soviet Internet*. Cambridge, Mass.: MIT Press, 2016.

Petrella, Ricchardo and Adam Schaff. *Une expérience de coopération européenne dans les sciences sociales: Dix ans d'activités du Centre de Vienne, 1963–1973*. Vienna: Centre européen de coordination de recherche et de documentation en sciences sociales, 1973.

Petrini, Francesco. The common vocational training policy in the EEC from 1961 to 1972. *Vocational Training* 32 (2004): 45–54.

———. Demanding Democracy in the Workplace: The European Trade Union Confederation and the Struggle to Regulate Multinationals. In *Societal Actors in European Integration. Polity-Building and Policy-making 1958–1992*, (ed.) Wolfram Kaiser and Jan-Henrik Meyer. London: Palgrave Macmillan, 2013. 151–172.

Petter, Amdam Rolv and Gunnar Yittri. The European Productivity Agency, The Norwegian Productivity Institute and Management Education. In *Missionaries and Managers: American Influences on European Management Education, 1945–60*, (eds.), Terry Gourvish and Nick Tiratsoo. Manchester: Manchester University Press, 1998) 121–140.

Pipkorn, Jorn. Employee Participation in the European Company. Paper for the International Conference on Trends in Industrial and Labour Relations, Montreal, Canada, 26 May 1976.

Platt, Jennifer. *Fifty Years of the International Social Science Council*. Paris: International Social Science Council, 2002.

Plehwe, Dieter and Philip Mirowski. *The Road from Mount Pelerin: The Making of a Neoliberal Thought Collective*. Cambridge, Mass.: Harvard University Press, 2010.

Polanyi, Karl. *Great Transformation: The Political and Economic Origins of Our Time*. Boston: Beacon Press, 2001.

Polh, Manfred. *Handbook on the History of European Banks*. New York: Edward Elgar, 1994.

Pons, Silvio. *Berlinguer e la fine del comunismo*. Torino: Einaudi, 2006.

Popa, Ioana. La circulation transnationale du livre: un instrument de la guerre froide culturelle. *Histoire@Politique* 15 (2011): 25–41.

Prošek, Jan. *Ze zkušeností podnikového ředitele*. Prague: SNTL, 1957.

Raiskup, Jan. Více psychologie do kádrové práce. *Podniková organizace* 12 (1958): 143–144.

Ramet, Sabrina P. *The Three Yugoslavias: state-building and legitimation, 1918–2005*. Bloomington, IN: Indiana University Press, 2006.

Ramondt, Joop. Workers' self-management and its constraints: The Yugoslav experience. *British Journal of Industrial Relations* 1 (1979): 83–94.

Rausch, Helke. Akademische Vernetzung als politische Intervention in Europa. Internationalismus-Strategien US-amerikanischer Stiftungen in den 1920er Jahren. *Jahrbuch für Universitätsgeschichte* 18 (2015): 165–188.
Reinecke, Christiane and Thomas Mergel, *Das Soziale ordnen: Sozialwissenschaften und gesellschaftliche Ungleichheit im 20. Jahrhundert.* Frankfurt am Main: Campus, 2012.
Reinisch, Jessica. Internationalism in Relief: The Birth (and Death) of UNRRA. Past and Present Supplement 6 (2011): 258–89.
Rempe, Martin. *Entwicklung im Konflikt: die EWG und der Senegal 1957–1975.* Cologne: Böhlau Verlag, 2012.
Rey, Marie-Pierre. *La Tentation du rapprochement. France et URSS à l'heure de la détente (1964–1974).* Paris: Publications de la Sorbonne, 1991.
–––. L'Europe occidentale dans la politique extérieure soviétique de Brejnev à Gorbatchev, évolution ou revolution? *Relations internationales* 147, no. 3 (2011): 73–84.
Reyels, Lili. *Die Entstehung Des Ersten Vertrags von Lomé Im Deutsch-Französischen Spannungsfeld 1973–1975.* Baden–Baden: Nomos Verlag, 2008.
Řezníček, Jiří. *Vědecká organizace řídící práce: Vybrané kapitoly.* Prague: NPL, 1965.
Rigo, Emil. K niektorým otázkam plánovania sociálneho rozvoja vo Východoslovenských železarniach. *Plánované hospodářství* 26 (1973): 25–35.
Rindzevičiūtė, Eglė. Purification and Hybridisation of Soviet Cybernetics: The Politics of Scientific Governance in an Authoritarian Regime. *Archiv für Sozialgeschichte*, 50 (2010): 289–309.
–––. A Struggle for the Soviet Future: The Birth of Scientific Forecasting in the Soviet Union. *Slavic Review* 75 no. 1 (2016): 52–76.
–––. *The Power of Systems: How Policy Sciences Opened Up the Cold War World.* Ithaca: Cornell University Press, 2016.
Rise, Svein. Karl Rahner. In *Key Theological Thinkers: From Modern to Postmodern*, (eds.) Staale Johannes Kristainsen and Svein Rise. London: Routledge, 2013. 225–238.
Riska-Campbell, Leena. *Bridging East and West: The Establishment of the International Institute for Applied Systems Analysis (IIASA) in the United States Foreign Policy of Bridge Building, 1964–1972.* Uppsala: Finnish Society of Science and Letters, 2011.
Rist, Gilbert. *Le développement: histoire d'une croyance occidentale.* Paris: Presses de la Fondation nationale des sciences politiques, 2007.
Ritschel, Daniel. *The Politics of Planning: The Debate on Economic Planning in Britain in the 1930s.* Oxford: Clarendon Press, 1997.
Robinson, E. A. G. *Backward Areas in Advanced countries: Proceedings of a Conference held the International Economics Association at Varenna.* London: Melbourne MacMillan, 1969.
Rodgers, Daniel. *Age of Fracture.* Cambridge, Mass.: Harvard University Press, 2011.
Rogers, Everett M. *Diffusion of Innovations*, Third Edition. New York: The Free Press of Glencoe, 1983.
Rojek, Chris and David Wilson. Workers' self-management in the world system: The Yugoslav case. *Organization Studies* 8 (1987): 297–308.
Rokkan, Stein and Kazimierz Szczerba-Likiernik. Introduction. In *Comparative Research across Cultures and Nations*, (ed.) Rokkan Stein. Paris: Hague Mouton. 1–13.
Rokkan, Stein. *A Quarter Century of International Social Sciences: Papers and Reports on Developments, 1952–1977.* New Delhi: Concept Publishing, 1979.

———. Cross-Cultural, Cross-Societal and Cross-National Research. *Historical Social Research* 18 (1993): 6–54,

Romano, Angela. Untying Cold War Knots: The EEC and Eastern Europe in the long 1970s. *Cold War History* 14, no. 2 (2014): 153–173.

Romanov, A. Suomen ja Neuvostoliiton välisen tieteellis-teknisen yhteistyön tuloksia. In *Suomen ja Neuvostoliiton välinen tieteellis-tekninen yhteistoiminta 30 vuotta* [The results of the Finnish Soviet scientific-technical cooperation in Soviet-Finnish STC 30 years]. Helsinki,1985.

Romero, Frederico and Angela Romano (eds.) European Socialist Regimes Facing Globalisation and European Co-operation: Dilemmas and Responses. *European Review of History* 21 (2014), special issue.

Romijn, Peter, Giles Scott-Smith, and Joes Segal, (eds.). *Divided Dreamworlds? The Cultural Cold War in East and West.* Amsterdam: Amsterdam University Press, 2012.

Rosanvallon, Pierre. *L'Age de l'autogestion.* Paris, Le Seuil, 1976.

Ross, Dorothy. Changing Contours of the Social Science Disciplines. In *Cambridge History of Science*, vol. 7: *The Modern Social Sciences*, (eds.) Theodore M. Porter and Dorothy Ross. Cambridge: Cambridge University Press, 2003.

Rostow, Walt W. The Economic Commission for Europe. *International Organization* 3, no. 2 (1949): 254–68.

Rothstein, Robert L. *Global Bargaining: UNCTAD and the Quest for a New International Economic Order.* Princeton, N.J.: Princeton University Press, 1979.

Rousso, Henry. *La Planification en crises.* Paris: Éditions CNRS, 1987.

Ruggie, John G. International regimes, transactions, and change: embedded liberalism in the postwar economic order. In *International Regimes*, (ed.) S. Krasner. Ithaca: Cornell University Press, 1983. 195–232.

Rupprecht, Tobias. Die sowjetische Gesellschaft in der Welt des Kalten Krieges: Neue Forschungsperspektiven auf eine vermeintlich hermetisch abgeschottete Gesellschaft . *Jahrbücher für die Geschichte Osteuropas* 3 (2010): 381–99.

Rusinow, Dennison. *The Yugoslav Experiment, 1948–1974.* London: C. Hurst for the Royal Institute of International Affairs, 1977.

Rutland, Peter. *The Myth of the Plan.* London: Hutchinson, 1985.

Ruzicic-Kessler, Karlo. Italy and Yugoslavia: from distrust to friendship in Cold War Europe. *Journal of Modern Italian Studies* 19 (2014): 641–664.

Sanchez-Sibony, Oscar. Depression Stalinism. The Great Break Reconsidered. *Kritika* 15, no. 1 (2014): 23–49.

———. *Red Globalization. The Political Economy of the Soviet Cold War from Stalin to Khrushchev.* Cambridge: Cambridge University Press, 2014.

Sapir, Jacques. L'économie soviétique: origine, développement, fonctionnement. In *Retour sur l'URSS. Économie, société, histoire*, (ed.) Jacques Sapir. Paris: L'Harmattan, 1997. 99–144.

Sarasmo, Antti. The Kirov Fishing *kolkhoz*. A Socialist Success Story. In *Competition in Socialist society*, (eds.) Katalin Miklóssy and Melanie Ilic. Abingdon: Routledge, 2014.

Sauvy, Alfred. *Le Tiers Monde.* Paris: Presse Universitaires de France, 1956.

Schaff, Adam. The Foundations of the Vienna Centre: Their Development and Prospects. In *International Cooperation in the Social Sciences. 25 Years of Vienna Experience* (eds.)

František Charvát, Willem Stamation, Christiane Villain-Gandossi. Vienna: ECCRDSS, 1988. 17–33.
Schipper, Frank. All Roads Lead to Europe: The E-Road Network 1950–1970. In T2M Conference, working document. Paris: Transnational Infrastructures of Europe, 2006.
–––. *Driving Europe: Building Europe on Roads in the Twentieth Century*. Amsterdam: Amsterdam University Press, 2008.
Schmelzer, Matthias. The crisis before the crisis: the 'problems of modern society'and the OECD, 1968–74. *European Review of History: Revue europeenne d'histoire* 19, no. 6 (2012): 999–1020.
–––. *The Hegemony of Growth: The OECD and the Making of the Economic Growth Paradigm*. Cambridge: Cambridge University Press, 2016.
–––. Born in the corridors of the OECD: The forgotten origins of the Club of Rome, transnational networks, and the 1970s in global history. *Journal of Global History* 12 (2017): 26–48.
Schmid, Sonja D. Nuclear Colonization?: Soviet Technopolitics in the Second World. In *Entangled Geographies. Empire and Technopolitics in the Global Cold War*, (ed.) Gabrielle Hecht. Cambridge: MIT Press, 2011. 125–154.
Schoene, Siegfried. UNCTAD III: das Problem der besonderen Beziehungen zwischen der Europäischen Gemeinschaft und Afrika. *Africa Spectrum* 7, no. 1 (1972): 27–43.
Schregle, Johannes. Labour Relations in Western Europe: Some Topic Issues. *International Labour Review* 109 (1974): 1–22.
Schulz, Jaroslav. Klíč k podnikání je v personální politice. *Moderní řízení* 4, no. 3 (1969): 14–16.
Schulze Wessel, Martin. *Revolution und religiöser Dissens: der römisch-katholische und russisch-orthodoxe Klerus als Träger religiösen Wandels in den böhmischen Ländern und in Russland 1848–1922*. München: Oldenbourg, 2011.
Schwartz, G. L. 'Why Planning?' London: A Signpost Special 1944. 3. World War II Subject Collection, Box 26, Hoover Institution.
Secrétariat général de l'ONU, *Planification en vue du développement économique*. New York: Nations Unies, 1963.
Seefried, Elke. Politics and Time from the 1960s to the 1980s. *The Journal of Modern European History* 13 (2015), special issue 3.
–––. *Zukunfte. Aufstieg und Krise der Zukunftsforschung*. Munich: de Gruyter, 2016.
Selucky, R. The impact of the economic reforms on the foreign economic relations of the socialist countries. *Soviet and Eastern European Foreign Trade* 4, no. 3 (1968): 72–86.
Seppänen, Jouko, *Tieteellis-tekninen informaatio Neuvostoliitossa* [Scientific-technical information in the Soviet Union]. Helsinki: Suomen ja Neuvostoliiton tieteellis-teknisen yhteistoimintakomitean julkaisusarja 2, 1978.
Sigurdson, Ola. *Den lyckliga filofosin: Etik och politik hos Hägerström, Tingsten, makarna Myrdal och Hedenius*. Stockholm: Brutus Östlings bokförlag 2000.
Šiklová, Jiřina. Dialogický seminář na Filozofické fakultě UK v šedesátých letech. In *Mistr dialogu Milan Machovec. Sborník k nedožitým osmdesátinám českého filosofa*, (ed.) Kamila Jindrová, Pavel Tachecí, and Pavel Žďárský. Prague: Akropolis, 2006.
Simonov, N. S. *VPK SSSR: Tempy ekonomicheskovo rosta, struktura, organizatsija proizvodstvo, upravlenie* [Tempo of economic growth, structure, organisation of production and management]. Izdanie 2,. Universitet Dmitria Pozharskovo, Moskva 2015.

Sloin, Andrew and Oscar Sanchez-Sibony. . Economy and Power in the Soviet Union, 1917–1939. *Kritika* 15, no. 1 (2014): 22.
Sluga, Glenda. The transformation of international institutions: Global shock as cultural shock. In *Shock of the Global*, (eds.) Niall Fergusson, Charles S. Maier, Erez Manela, Daniel J Sargent. Cambridge, Mass.: Harvard University Press, 2010. 223–237.
Smolik, Josef and Richard Shaull, *Consommateurs ou revolutionnaires*. Association du Foyer John Knox: Genève, 1967.
Smrček, Otto. Vědecká organizace práce a její aplikace ve strojírenství do konce druhé světové války. *Hospodářské dějiny* 13 (1985): 165–223.
Sommer, Viteszlav. Forecasting the Post-Socialist Future: Prognostika in Late Socialist Czechoslovakia, 1970–1989. In *The Struggle for the Long Term in Transnational Science and Politics*, (eds.) Jenny Andersson and Egle Rindzeviciute. New York: Routledge, 2015. 144–168.
Soutou, Georges-Henri. Teorie sulla convergenza nella Francia degli anni Sessanta e Settanta. *Ventunesimo Secolo* 9 (2006): 49–77.
Speich-Chassé, Daniel. Technical Internationalism and Economic Development at the Founding Moment of the UN System. In *International Organizations and Development, 1945–1990*, Marc Frey, Sönke Kunkel, and Corina Unger (eds.), 23–45. Basingstoke: Palgrave Macmillan, 2014.
Spenlauher, Vincent. *L'évaluation des politiques publiques, avatar de la planification*. Grenoble: Thèse de l'Université Pierre-Mendès France, 1998.
– – –. Intelligence gouvernementale et sciences sociales. *Politix* 48 (1999): 95–128.
Spufford, Francis. *Red Plenty*. London: Faber and Faber, 2010.
Stach, Stephan. The Institute for Nationality Research (1921–1939): A Think Tank for Minority Politics in Poland? In *Religion in the Mirror of Law: Eastern European Perspectives from the Early Modern Period to 1939*, (ed.) Yvonne Kleinmann. Frankfurt am Main: Klosterman, 2015. 149–179.
Stamatiou, Willem. International Cooperation in the Social Science: The Vienna Centre. *International Social Science Journal* 118 (1988): 597–603.
Stanziani, Alessandro. *L'économie en révolution. Le cas russe, 1870–1930*. Paris: Albin Michel, 1998.
Steiner, André. . The Council of Mutual Economic Assistance – An Example of Failed Economic Integration? *Geschichte und Gesellschaft* 39 (2013): 240–258.
Steiner, Helmut. Das Akademie-Institut für Wirtschaftswissenschaften im Widerstreit wissenschaftlicher, ideologischer und politischer Auseinandersetzungen. *Sitzungsberichte der Leibniz-Sozietät* 36, no. 1 (2000): 89–109.
Štěpán, Josef. V řízení a organisaci uvádět v život usnesení celostání konference KSČ. *Podniková organisace* 11 (1957): 1–3.
Stíbalová, Běla. *Sociální plánování v ČSSR a SSSR*. Prague: ÚVTEI, 1976.
Stibic, Vladimír. *Od mechanisace k automatisaci administrativních prací*. Prague: Státní nakladatelství technické literatury, 1959.
Stinsky, Daniel. Western European or All-European Cooperation? The OEEC, the European Recovery Program, and the United Nations Economic Commission for Europe (ECE), 1947–1961. In *Warden of the West? The OECD and the Global Political Economy, 1948 to Present*, (eds.) Mathieu Leimgruber and Matthias Schmelzer, Transnational History Series. New York: Palgrave Macmillan, forthcoming.

Stone, Randall. *Satellites and commissars: Strategy and Conflict in the Politics of Soviet-Bloc Trade*. Princeton: Princeton University Press, 1996.
Stříteský, Miroslav. *Řízení – zvláštní profese*. Prague: Svoboda, 1970.
Stýblo, Josef and Borek Sýkora. *Do rozhodného boje proti absenci a fluktuaci a za vysokou pracovní kázeň*. Prague: Práce, 1953.
Suri, Jeremi. Conflict and Co-Operation in the Cold War: New Directions in Contemporary Historical Research. *Journal of Contemporary History* 46 (2011): 5–9.
Sutela, Pekka. *Economic Thought and Economic Reform in the Soviet Union*. Cambridge, UK: Cambridge University Press, 1991.
–––. *Trading with the Soviet Union. The Finnish Experience 1944–1991*. Helsinki: Kikimora Publications Series B 39, 2014.
Svatuška, Ladislav. *Vedoucí potřebuje informace*. Prague: Svoboda, 1971.
Svedjedal, Johan. *Spektrum 1931–1935: Den svenska drömmen. Tidskrift och förlag i 1930-talets kultur*. Stockholm: Wahlström & Widstrand, 2011.
Svennilson, Ingvar. *Growth and Stagnation in the European Economy*. Geneva: United Nations, 1954.
Sviták, Ivan. *Devět životů: konkrétní dialektika*. Prague: SAKKO, 1992.
Swindler, Leonard. *The Age of Global Dialogue*. Eugene: Pickwick Publications, 2016.
Szalai, Alexander and Riccardo Petrella, in collaboration with S. Rokkan and E.K. Scheuch, *Cross-National Comparative Survey Research: Theory and Practice*. Oxford: Pergamon Press, 1977. 231–278.
Tabrizi, Sharon Ghamari. *The Intuitive Science of Herman Kahn*. Cambridge, Mass.: Harvard University Press, 2005.
Terray, Aude. *Des Francs-tireurs aux experts. L'organisation de la prévision économique au ministère des Finances, 1948–1968*. Paris: Comité pour l'Histoire économique et financière de la France, 2002.
Thant, U. *Planning for Economic Development: report of the secretary-general transmitting the study of a group of experts*. New York: United Nations, 1963–1965, 3 volumes.
The History of UNCTAD 1964–1984. New York: United Nations Publication, 1985.
Thomas, Brinley. *Monetary Policy and Crises: A Study of Swedish Experience*. London: Routledge, 1936. xviii.
Tinbergen, Jan. *Central Planning*. New Haven: Yale University Press, 1964.
–––. *La planification*. Paris: Hachette, 1967. 220–235
–––. *Reshaping the International Economic Order: A report to the Club of Rome*. New York: Club of Rome, 1976.
Tournès, Ludovic. *Sciences de l'homme et politique: les fondations philanthropiques américaines en France au XXe siècle*. Paris: Classiques Garnier, 2011.
Toye, John and Richard Toye. *The UN and Global Political Economy: Trade, Finance, and Development*. Bloomington: Indiana University Press, 2004.
Toye, Richard. Developing Multilateralism: the Havana Charter and the Fight for the International Trade Organisation, 1947–1948. *The International History Review*, 25, no. 2 (2003): 303.
–––. *The Labour Party and the Planned Economy 1931–1951*. Rochester: Boydell, 2003.
Trentin, Bruno. L' autogoverno nella fabbrica e nella società. *Mondoperaio* 32 (1979): 109–114.
Trilateral Commission, *Towards a Renovated International System*. Washington, 1977.

Unger, Corinna R. Histories of Development and Modernization: Findings, Reflections, Future Research. *H-Soz-Kult* (2010). http://hsozkult.geschichte.hu-berlin.de/forum/2010-12-001 (accessed 9 February 2018).
———. *International Organizations and Development, 1945–1990*. Amsterdam: Springer, 2016.
UNITAR, *A New International Economic Order: Selected Documents 1945–1975*. New York: United Nations Institute for Training and Research, 1976.
Unkovski-Korica, Vladimir. Workers' Councils in the Service of the Market: New Archival Evidence on the Origins of Self-Management in Yugoslavia, 1948–1950. *Europe-Asia Studies* 66 (2014): 108–134.
———. Self-management, development and debt: the rise and fall of the 'Yugoslav experiment.' In *Welcome to the Desert of Post-Socialism: Radical Politics After Yugoslavia*, (eds.) Igor Štiks and Srećko Horvat. London: Verso, 2015. 21–45.
———. *The Economic Struggle for Power in Tito's Yugoslavia: From World War II to Non-Alignment*. New York: I.B. Tauris, 2016.
Uschakow, Alexander. *Integration im RGW. Dokumente*. Baden-Baden: Nomos, 1983. 1018–1036.
Uvalić, Milica and Vojmir Franicević. Introduction: Branko Horvat – Beyond the Mainstream. In *Equality, Participation, Transition: Essays in Honour of Branko Horvat*, eds. Vojmir Franicević and Milica Uvalić. Basingstoke: Palgrave Macmillan, 2010.
Vácha, Stanislav. *Moderní kapitalistický podnik a jeho cíl*. Prague: Svoboda, 1970.
———. *Hauři*. Prague: Práce, 1987.
———. *Jak řídí Slušovice*. Prague: Novinář, 1988.
Vahsen, Urban. *Eurafrikanische Entwicklungskooperation: Die Assoziierungspolitik der EWG gegenüber dem subsaharischen Afrika in den 1960er Jahren*. Stuttgart: Steiner, 2010
Vanek, Jan. *The Economics of Workers' Management: A Yugoslav Case Study*. London: Allen and Unwin, 1972.
Vanek, Jaroslav. *The General Theory of Labor-Managed Market Economies*. Ithaca, London: Cornell University Press, 1970.
———. *The Participatory economy: an evolutionary hypothesis and a strategy for development*. Ithaca and London: Cornell University Press, 1971.
Varsori, Antonio. Alle origini di un modello europeo: la Comunità europea e la nascita di una politica sociale (1969–1974). *Ventunesimo Secolo* 9 (2006): 17–47.
———. La formazione professionale e l'educazione nella costruzione europea e il Cedefop. In *Sfide del mercato e identità europea. Le politiche di educazione e formazione professionale nell'Europa comunitaria*, (ed.) Antonio Varsori. Milano: FrancoAngeli, 2006. 173–212.
Vašák, Pavel. *Fluktuace pracovních sil*. Prague: Práce, 1976.
Vostatek, Jaroslav. Čtyři typy podniku a socialistické odměňování. *Politická ekonomie* 17 (1969): 307–321.
Wadensjö, Eskil. The Committee on Unemployment and the Stockholm School. In *The Stockholm School of Economics Revisited*, (ed.) Lars Jonung. Cambridge, MA: Cambridge University Press, 1991.
Wagner, Peter and Hellmut Wollmann. Social Scientists in Policy Research and Consulting: Some Cross-National Comparisons. *International Social Science Journal* 4 (1986): 601–617.

Wagner, Peter. Social Science and Social Planning during the Twentieth Century. In *Cambridge History of Science: The Modern Social Sciences*, vol. 7, (eds.) Theodore M. Porter and Dorothy Ross. Cambridge: Cambridge University Press, 2003. 591–607.

Warlouzet, Laurent. *Governing Europe in a Globalizing World. Neoliberalism and its Alternatives following the 1973 crisis.* London: Routledge, 2018.

Weiss, Jeremy. E. H. Carr, Norman Angell, and Reassessing the Realist-Utopian Debate. *The International History Review* 35, no. 5 (2013): 1160–1161.

Weit, Margaret and Theda Skocpol. The State Structures and the Possibilities for 'Keynesian' Responses to the Great Depression in Sweden, Britain, and the United States. In *Bringing the State Back* (ed.) Peter B. Evans, Dietrich Rueschemeyer, and Theda Skocpol. Cambridge: Cambridge University Press, 1985. 107–108.

Wheatcroft, Mildred. *The Revolution in British Management Education.* London: Pitman, 1970.

Wightman, David. East-West Cooperation and the United Nations Economic Commission for Europe. International Organization 11, no. 1 (1957): 2.

Williams, John R. World futures. *Critical Inquiry* 42 (2016): 473–546.

Wilson, Duncan. Self Management in Yugoslavia. *International Affairs* 54 (1978): 253–263.

Wilson, John F and Andrew Thomson, *The Making of Modern Management: British Management in Historical Perspective.* Oxford: Oxford University Press, 2006.

Winclawski, Wlodzimierz. Józef Chalasińky: A Classic of Polish Sociology. *Eastern European Countryside* 13 (2007): 169–178.

Zaccaria, Benedetto. *The EEC's Yugoslav Policy in Cold War Europe, 1968–1980.* London: Palgrave Macmillan, 2016.

Žďárský, Pavel. Milan Machovec a jeho filosofická antropologie v 60. letech 20. století. PhD Diss., Charles University in Prague, 2011.

Zeiler, Thomas W. *Free Trade Free World.* Chapel Hill: University of North Carolina Press, 1999.

Zieleniec, Josef. *Československo na rozcestí: zpráva o stavu národního hospodářství a možnostech jeho nápravy.* Prague: Lidové noviny, 1990.

Zubok, Vladislav. The Soviet Union and European Integration from Stalin to Gorbachev. *Journal of European Integration History* 2, no. 1 (1996): 85–98

Zweynert, Joachim and Ivan Boldyrev. Conflicting patterns of thought in the Russian debate on modernisation and innovation 2008–2013. *Europe-Asia Studies* 69, No. 6 (2017), 921–939.

www.ingramcontent.com/pod-product-compliance
Lightning Source LLC
Chambersburg PA
CBHW031418230426
43668CB00007B/348